An Analysis of the Prophet's Life

The Messenger of God
MUHAMMAD

M. Fethullah Gülen

New Jersey
2005

Copyright © 2005 by The Light, Inc. & Işık Yayınları

Revised edition in one volume 2005

Second impression

First edition in English published in two volumes as
Prophet Muhammad: Aspects of His Life 2000

Originally published in Turkish as
Sonsuz Nur: İnsanlığın İftihar Tablosu by Nil Yayınları 1993

08 07 06 05   2 3 4 5

Published by The Light, Inc.
26 Worlds Fair Dr. Suite C
Somerset, New Jersey, 08873, USA

www.thelightpublishing.com

Translated from Turkish by Ali Ünal

For other titles by Gülen http://en.fgulen.com

Library of Congress Cataloging-in-Publication Data for the previous edition

Gülen, M. Fethullah,
    [Sonsuz Nur. English.]
    Prophet Muhammad: Aspects of His Life / M. Fethullah Gülen.
    p. cm.
    Includes index.
    ISBN 1-932099-83-2
    1. Muhammad, Prophet, d. 632--Biography.   I. Title.
BP75 .G8213 2000
297.6'3--dc21
00-010842

Printed by
Çağlayan A.Ş., Izmir - Turkey
May 2005

[handwritten inscription] Lawrence Forman
Rabbi Emeritus,
Ohef Sholom Temple,
Norfolk, Virginia

An Analysis of the Prophet's Life

The Messenger of God

MUHAMMAD

TABLE OF CONTENTS

ABOUT THE AUTHOR

B orn in Erzurum, in eastern Turkey, in 1941, M. Fethullah Gülen is an Islamic scholar and thinker, and a prolific writer and poet. He was trained in the religious sciences by several celebrated Muslim scholars and spiritual masters. Gülen also studied the principles and theories of modern social and physical sciences. Based on his exceptional skills in learning and focused self-study, he soon surpassed his peers. In 1959, after attaining excellent examination results, he was awarded a state preacher's license (in Edirne), and was promoted to a post in Izmir, Turkey's third largest province, in 1966. It was here that Gülen started to crystallize his theme and expand his audience base. In his sermons and speeches he emphasized the pressing social issues of the times: his particular aim was to urge the younger generation to harmonize intellectual enlightenment with wise spirituality and a caring, humane activism.

Gülen did not restrict himself to teaching in the inner cities. He traveled around the provinces in Anatolia and lectured not only in mosques, but also at town meetings and corner coffee houses. This enabled him to reach a more representative cross-section of the population and to attract the attention of the academic community, especially the student body. The subject matter of his speeches, whether formal or informal, was not restricted explicitly to religious questions; he also talked about education, science, Darwinism, about the economy and social justice. It was the depth and quality of his speeches on such a wide range of topics that most impressed the academic community, and won their attention and respect.

Gülen retired from formal teaching duties in 1981, having inspired a whole generation of young students. His efforts, dating from the 1960s, especially in educational reform, have made him one of the best-known and respected figures in Turkey. From 1988 to 1991, he gave a series of sermons as preacher emeritus in some of the most famous mosques in major population centers, while continuing to deliver his message in the form of popular conferences, not only in Turkey, but also in Western Europe.

MAIN IDEAS

In his speeches and writings Gülen envisions a twenty-first century in which we shall witness the birth of a spiritual dynamic that will revitalize long-dormant moral values; an age of tolerance, understanding, and international cooperation that will ultimately lead, through intercultural dialogue and a sharing of values, to a single, inclusive civilization. In the field of education, he has spearheaded the establishment of many charitable organizations to work for the welfare of the community, both within and without Turkey. He has inspired the use of mass media, notably television, to inform the public, of matters of pressing concern to them, individually and collectively.

Gülen believes the road to justice for all is dependent on the provision of an adequate and appropriate universal education. Only then will there be sufficient understanding and tolerance to secure respect for the rights of others. To this end, he has, over the years, encouraged the social elite and community leaders, powerful industrialists as well as small businessmen, to support quality education. With donations from these sources, educational trusts have been able to establish many schools, both in Turkey and abroad.

Gülen has stated that in the modern world the only way to get others to accept your ideas is by persuasion. He describes those who resort to force as being intellectually bankrupt; people will always demand freedom of choice in the way they run their affairs and in their expression of their spiritual and religious values. Democracy, Gülen argues, in spite of its many shortcomings, is now the only viable political system, and people should strive to modernize and consolidate democratic institutions in order to build a society where individual rights and freedoms are respected and protected, where equal opportunity for all is more than a dream.

INTERFAITH AND INTERCULTURAL ACTIVITIES

Since his retirement, Gülen has concentrated his efforts on establishing a dialogue among the factions representing different ideologies, cultures, religions and nations. In 1999, his paper "The Necessity of Interfaith Dialogue" was presented to the Parliament of World's Religions in Cape Town, December 1-8. He maintains that "dialogue is a must" and that people, regardless of nation or political borders, have far more in common than they realize.

Given all of this, Gülen considers it both worthwhile and necessary for a sincere dialogue to be established in order to increase mutual understanding. To this end, he has helped to establish the Journalists and Writers Foundation (1994), whose activities to promote dialogue and tolerance among all strata of the society have been warmly welcomed by people from almost all walks of life. Again to this end, Gülen visits and receives leading figures, not only from among the Turkish population, but from all over the world. Pope John Paul II at the Vatican, the late John O'Connor, Archbishop of New York, Leon Levy, former president of The Anti-Defamation League are among many leading representatives of world religions with whom Gülen has met to discuss dialogue and take initiatives in this respect. In Turkey, the Vatican's Ambassador to Turkey, the Patriarch of the Turkish Orthodox Church, the Patriarch of the Turkish Armenian community, the Chief Rabbi of the Turkish Jewish community and many other leading figures in Turkey have frequently met with him, portraying an example of how sincere dialogue can be established between people of faith.

In his meeting with Pope John Paul II at the Vatican (1998), Gülen presented a proposal to take firm steps to stop the conflict in the Middle East via collaborative work on this soil, a place where all three religions originated. In his proposal, he also underlined the fact that science and religion are in fact two different aspects that emanate from the same truth: "Humankind from time to time has denied religion in the name of science and denied science in the name of religion, arguing that the two present conflicting views. All knowledge belongs to God and religion is from God. How then can the two be in conflict? To this end, our joint efforts directed at inter-religious dialogue can do much to improve understanding and tolerance among people."

Gülen released a press declaration renouncing the September 11th terrorist attacks on the USA, which he regarded as a great blow to world peace that unfairly tarnished the credit of believers: ". . . terror can never be used in the name of Islam or for the sake of any Islamic ends. A terrorist cannot be a Muslim and a Muslim cannot be a terrorist. A Muslim can only be the representative and symbol of peace, welfare, and prosperity."

Gülen's efforts for worldwide peace have been echoed at conferences and symposiums. "The Peaceful Heroes Symposium" (April 11-13, 2003) at the University of Texas, Austin, produced a list of peacemakers over 5,000 years of human history. Gülen was mentioned among contemporary heroes of peace, in a list which includes names such as Jesus, Buddha, Mohandas Gandhi, Martin Luther King, Jr., and Mother Teresa.

Gülen contributes to a number of journals and magazines. He writes the editorial page for several magazines. He writes the lead article for *The Fountain*, *Yeni Ümit*, *Sızıntı*, and *Yağmur*, leading popular and spiritual thought magazines in Turkey. He has written more than forty books, hundreds of articles, and recorded thousands of audio and videocassettes. He has delivered innumerable speeches on many social and religious issues. Some of his books—many of which have been best-sellers in Turkey —have been made available in English translations, such as, Prophet Muhammad: Aspects of His Life, Questions and Answers about Faith, Pearls of Wisdom, Prophet Muhammad as Commander, Essentials of the Islamic Faith, Towards the Lost Paradise, Key Concepts in the Practice of Sufism. A number have also been translated into German, Russian, Albanian, Japanese, Indonesian, Chinese and Spanish.

The educational trusts inspired by Gülen have established countless non-profit voluntary organizations—foundations and associations—in Turkey and abroad which support many scholarships.

Though a well-known public figure, Gülen has always shied away from involvement in formal politics. Gülen's admirers include leading journalists, academics, TV personalities, politicians, and Turkish and foreign state authorities. They see in him a true innovator and unique social reformer who practices what he preaches. They see him as a peace activist, an intellectual, a religious scholar, a mentor, author and poet, a great thinker and spiritual guide who has devoted his life to seeking the solutions for society's ills and spiritual needs. They see the movement he helped to nurture as a movement dedicated to education, but an education of the heart and soul as well as of the mind, aimed at reviving and invigorating the whole being to achieve competence and providing goods and services useful to others.

A GENERAL INTRODUCTION

I would like to introduce the reader to the exemplary life of the blessed Prophet Muhammad[1] and his distinguished, exalted personality. The "water of life" for the salvation of humanity should be made known to everyone.

Prophet Muhammad is the pride of humanity. For the past 14 centuries, many thinkers, philosophers, scientists, and scholars, each a radiant star in our intellectual world, have stood behind him in respect and admiration, and taken pride in belonging to his community.

It is enough to appreciate and understand his greatness that even after so many antagonism (toward religion), we still hear the words "I bear witness that Muhammad is the Messenger of God" from minarets five times a day. We rejoice while his name is being proclaimed from minarets, as do the dead and other spiritual beings. Despite concerted efforts to corrupt our young people and lead them astray, they continue to hasten to him, although they cannot perceive the full reality of Muhammad.

Time has not caused us to forget the truth about him. He is so fresh in my mind that if I mention his holy name, it is as if I am about to meet him. Once, while on pilgrimage to his radiant city, Madina, I felt that he was about to appear and welcome us. As time progresses, some thoughts become obsolete, but he remains as fresh as a rosebud in our hearts. And so whenever we hear his name mentioned from the minaret, we immediately abandon our work and, accepting his invitation, hasten to mosque.

If we had been allowed to describe him as others have been described, if we had used the social and educational institutions, then perhaps our young people would be following his way. Despite our shortcomings, many pick up their "glasses" and run to fill them from this "pure spring." In every part of the world, including the United States, England, France, and Germany, an Islamic revival is occurring. Muslims are sowing these lands with the seeds of a happy future. Islam is everywhere healthy and flourishing as it did during the Era of Happiness—the time of Muhammad.

The same is true of predominantly Muslim lands. Those Muslims whose devotion to Islam was largely unconscious and devoid of deep perception or research have given way to a new generation who are consciously following Muhammad in the light of science and advances in knowledge. Those who were previously exploiting schools and universities on behalf of unbelief are now running to him. Even such well-known people as Maurice Bucaille and Roger Garaudy have seen the falsehood of their systems and are hastening to him.[2]

MUHAMMAD AS THE MOST BELOVED OF HEARTS

I wonder whether we have fully recognized the most beloved of hearts. Even I, who have been performing five daily prayers since the age of 5 and striving to be a servant at his door, wonder if I can recognize him. Have we been able to enthuse love into the hearts of our recent generations by describing the ultimate source of all love and enthusiasm?

If only humanity had known Muhammad, they would have fallen in love with him as Majnun fell in love with Layla.[3] Whenever his name is mentioned, they would tremble with joy in anticipation of entering the ethos that surrounds him and those following his way wholeheartedly.

We can love only those whom we know and only to the extent of our knowledge. Our enemies have tried to make us forget him, to ensure that his name is no longer mentioned. Since he is supported by God, all obstacles have been torn down, and the younger generation submits to him as joyfully as one dying of thirst does upon finding water. His mighty tenderness and compassion will embrace every "thirsty" person who comes to him.

You must have noticed that when you come to the Friday prayers, the congregation consists mainly of young people. Have you ever asked why, despite the prevalence of misguidance and rebellion, young people come to mosques and sit despite cold and other difficulties? There is only one attraction: Muhammad. Whether we can grasp it or not, souls and hearts rush to him as moths to a candle. Even those "winter flies" who have not been so fortunate will soon turn to him. Scientists and great thinkers will study him. Those who are currently enemies will soon be bosom friends, and will take refuge in his warm welcome. In his time, even his enemies admired him.

He once related a dream: "They weighed me against ten people of my community, and I outweighed them. Then they weighed me against a hundred and then a thousand, and I outweighed them all."[4] He also related: "I was weighed against my whole community, and I outweighed it."[5] He outweighs all people of intellect, piety and spirituality, and faith and knowledge, for all other beings were created because of him. It is reported that God said to him: "But for you, I would not have created the spheres."[6]

MUHAMMAD DESCRIBES THE MEANING OF CREATION

The universe is a book. If Muhammad had not been created, this book would not have been understood. To create an incomprehensible book is a waste of time and effort. As God is beyond such things, He created Muhammad to describe the meaning of creation to humanity. God would be his teacher, and the Earth and firmaments would be subjected to him. He would answer all the eternal questions: "Who and where am I?" "Why have I been created?" "What is my ultimate destination?" and "Who is my guide during this journey?"

Muhammad provides creation with meaning and answers such questions. If he had been fully recognized, he would have been truly loved. Although we only know him a little, we still love him.

Let me narrate an incident that occurred during a visit to Muhammad's holy city. The atmosphere was overpowering.

Something occurred to me: I pray to God every morning, saying seven times: "O my God, save me from Hellfire and make me enter Paradise among the company of the godly people." There can be no believer who does not wish to enter Paradise. However, in this environment I asked myself: "If they were to invite you to Paradise through any of its seven gates, which would you prefer entering into the *rawdah* (the area in the mosque next to the Prophet's tomb) or entering Paradise?" Believe me, I swear by God that I said to myself: "This place is more appealing to me. I have had the chance to rub my face against the soil of my master, at whose door I prefer to be a chained slave rather than anything else in the world. I do not want to miss this chance."

I believe this is the desire of every believer. When I was blessed with this great opportunity, I was with a member of the Turkish Parliament, Mr. Arif Hikmet. He told me he had promised himself that he would roll in the soil like a donkey when he stepped across the border and entered the land of Madina. This great man kept his promise. When I remember this incident, I cannot prevent my eyes from watering.

MUHAMMAD'S MESSAGE EMBRACES HUMANITY AND JINN

Since Prophet Muhammad came with a sacred Law that will never be abrogated, a Message that embraces humanity and jinn, and has hundreds of miracles excelling those of all other Prophets, he is the head of all Prophets. Therefore, he has the core of all their miracles and their unanimous confirmation. In other words, all other Prophets' agreement on the same faith and the testimony of their miracles support Muhammad's honesty and truthfulness. He is, at the same time, the master and leader of all saints and scholars of purity and profound knowledge who have attained perfection through his teaching and guidance, and through the light of his sacred Law.

In addition, he has the core of their wonders, their unanimous affirmation, and the strength of their verified conclusions. Since the way they have followed to reach the truth was the one opened and left open by him, all of their wonders and conclusions established through meticulous research and intuition, as well as their consensus on the same faith, support his Prophethood and truthfulness. This is why his coming was promised by all the Prophets before him. God made a covenant with them that they would believe in him and support him.

> God took a covenant with the Prophets: "I have given you of Book and Wisdom; then there shall come to you a Messenger confirming what is with you—you shall believe in him and help him." He said: "Will you affirm this, and take My load on you in this matter?" They answered: "We affirm it." He said: "Bear witness, and I shall be with you among the witnesses." (3:81)

All of the Prophets led their lives in perfect loyalty to their promise. When Prophet Muhammad was about to make his *mi'raj* (Ascension to the Heavens), he led the prayers before the souls of all the other Prophets.[7] All of them, including Abraham, Moses, Noah, and Jesus, displayed their desire to become his *muezzin* (the one who calls to prayer).

In the Bible, Jesus repeatedly gave his disciples the glad tidings of Muhammad's coming. According to John (see 14:16, 26, 30; 16:7), he said:

> It is better for you that I go away, because if I do not go, the helper will not come. I have much more to tell you, but for now it would be too much for you to bear. When, however, the spirit of the Truth, the lord of the world, who reveals the truth about God comes, he will lead you to the truth.

I wonder if we realize how unique he was as the head of family. Do we know how he brought up his children or grandchildren, each of whom would have been a great leader in any succeeding century? He dealt with his wives so successfully that there was no serious disagreement among them. He is beyond all comparison as father, husband, or human being.

He had such sublime virtues in his blessed being, such exalted qualities in his Messengership, and such precious merits in the religion and sacred Law that he preached, that even his bitterest

enemies could find no fault with him. Since he combines function, religion, and the most praiseworthy virtues in his personality, he is certainly the embodiment, master, and representative of
all perfections and high, laudable virtues found in creation.

This perfect a commander challenged the world with only a
few followers. He repelled all who opposed his teachings and
was never defeated, although he had no mortal teachers and never attended a military academy. He was so informed about science that he told his followers about almost all the major events
that would occur until the Last Day. It was as if he were watching television or reading from an unseen tablet.[8]

Some time ago, a friend brought me a video cassette in
which Keith Moore, a Canadian pediatrician who had realized
how the Qur'an describes the development of the human
embryo in the womb, declared his conversion to Islam. On the
same tape, a Japanese psychologist who had discovered that
Islam explains many problems that baffle modern scientists, was
trying to get his tongue around the Arabic words to make the
same declaration.

Who taught all these scientific facts to Muhammad? Certainly
he did not speak on his own. Whatever he spoke was a Revelation
revealed to him by his teacher, the One Who knows everything,
Who is All-Knowing and All-Aware. As science advances, humanity will come to discover a new aspect of his personality and will
regret not having known him earlier.

His Companions knew him and loved him more than they
loved themselves. They were prepared to sacrifice their lives to protect him. For example, he dispatched a group of teachers to the
Hudayl tribe at their request. The Hudayli unbelievers betrayed
their teachers and killed most of them. Zayd ibn Dasina and
Hubayb were handed over to the Quraysh, then enemies of the
Muslims.

When they were about to be executed, someone asked
Hubayb: "Don't you wish that Muhammad were in your place
so that you could be with your family in Madina?" Hubayb was
startled, and replied: "I would rather be cut into pieces than

wish Muhammad were in my place. I don't want even a thorn to hurt his blessed foot in exchange for my being returned to my family." Hubayb prayed that God would convey his wish of peace and greetings to His Messenger, and inform him that he had remained loyal to him until he died. Meanwhile, the Prophet informed his Companions of Hubayb's martyrdom and returned his greetings.[9]

Sumayra, from the Dinar tribe, hurried to the battlefield when she learned that the Muslims had experienced a reverse in Uhud. They showed her her father's corpse, and those of her husband and sons, but she ignored all of them. She just kept asking what had happened to the Prophet. When somebody guided her to him, she threw herself to the ground at a short distance from his feet and exclaimed: "All misfortunes mean next to nothing to me, provided that you are alive, O Messenger of God!"[10]

He was so loved that his Companions would have given their lives if it meant that he could live forever. But, of course, he was mortal like other created beings. The appointed hour drew near, and he had to say farewell to his friends of 23 years. Mu'adh ibn Jabal had been shuttling between Madina and Yemen carrying the Prophet's Message. On the day he was about to leave, the Messenger of God told him: "Mu'adh, leave now for Yemen. When you come back, you will probably visit my mosque and my tomb." These words were enough to bring Mu'adh to the point of emotional collapse.[11]

FOLLOWING PROPHET MUHAMMAD

The problems of our time will be solved by following the way of Muhammad. This has been acknowledged by unbiased Western and Eastern intellectuals. As Bernard Shaw once admitted, humanity can solve its accumulated problems by turning to Prophet Muhammad, who solved the most complicated problems as easily as one drinks coffee.

Humanity is waiting for the return of the Muhammadan spirit, for the Message of Muhammad. When they turn to him to solve their problems, they will be saved from exploitation, freed from misery, and attain true peace and happiness. This second revival has already begun, despite the aversion of unbelievers:

> They desire to extinguish the light of God with their mouths; but God will perfect His light, even though unbelievers are averse. He has sent His Messenger with the guidance and the religion of truth, that He may uplift it above every religion, even though the polytheists are averse. (61:8-9)

God will uplift His religion, and people will run to Prophet Muhammad. In him, they will find peace and happiness. Humanity finally will learn to live in security through him, and it will seem as if they are already living in Paradise despite still being in this temporary world. This will take place despite the presence in every country of unbelievers, wrongdoers, hypocrites, and those who ignore him. The lord of the Prophets, whose name we proclaim from our minarets five times a day, sooner or later will enter the hearts of all human beings. And since Prophet Muhammad was a man of peace, humanity will attain happiness through the Message he brought: Islam.

CHAPTER 1

The Prophet Sent as a Mercy

THE PROPHET SENT AS A MERCY

THE DARK PERIOD OF IGNORANCE

Every period of history characterized by associating partners with God, whether by worshipping idols, deifying individuals, or attributing creativity to nature and material causes, is wholly dark. When belief in God's Unity is removed from people's hearts, their minds and souls darken, standards change, and things and the world are judged from false points of view. The Qur'an defines this moral, spiritual, social, and even economic and scientific state as ignorance (jahiliyya):

> Or like darkness on a deep sea obscure, covered by a wave, above which is a wave, above which is a cloud. Layers of darkness one upon the other. When he holds out his hand, well-nigh he cannot see it. And he for whom God has assigned no light, for him there is no light (24:40).

I do not like describing falsehood. Besides, it is wrong to do so where truth may be described. In the words of God: *What is there, after truth, but misguidance?* (10:32). However, to clarify the subject, I will say a few words about the pre-Islamic era, known as the Age of Ignorance.

Prophet Muhammad appeared at a time when people had lost their knowledge of the true religion and had reverted to worshipping idols of stones, earth, bread, and even cheese. As stated in the Qur'an:

> They were serving, apart from God, what hurts them not, neither profits them, and they say: "These are our intercessors with God." (10:18)

They were so degraded in thought and morals that, as reported by Abu Dharr al-Ghifari, they would cut their idols into pieces and eat them. The only excuse offered was that they were following in the steps of their forefathers:

> When it is said to them: "Follow what God has sent down," they say: "No. We follow that wherein we found our fathers." (2:170)

They also buried their daughters alive:

> When any of them is given the good tidings of a girl, his face is darkened and he chokes inwardly, as he hides himself from the people because of the evil of the good tidings that have been given to him, whether he shall preserve her in humiliation, or trample her into the dust. (16:58-59)

Women were despised, not only in pre-Islamic Arabia but also in the Roman and Sassanid lands. The Qur'an openly declares that men will be questioned concerning this: *When the female (infant) buried alive is questioned—for what crime was she killed?* (81:8-9).

After Muhammad had declared his Prophethood, a Companion told him what he had done with his daughter:

> O Messenger of God, I had a daughter. One day I told her mother to dress her, for I was taking her to her uncle. My poor wife knew what this meant, but could do nothing but obey and weep. She dressed the girl, who was very happy that she was going to see her uncle. I took her near a well, and told her to look down into it. While she was looking into the well, I kicked her into it. While she was rolling down, she was shouting: "Daddy, Daddy!"

As he was recounting this, the Prophet sobbed as if he had lost one of his nearest kinsfolk.[1]

Hearts had become hard. Every day a pit was dug in the desert for an innocent girl to be buried. Human beings were more brutal and cruel than hyenas. The powerful crushed the weak. Brutality was taken for humanity, cruelty received approval, the bloodthirsty were exalted, bloodshed was considered a virtue, and adultery and fornication were more common than legal marriage. The family structure had been destroyed.

This dark period was followed by Islam. In addition to eradicating all other evils, God declared in the Qur'an: *Do not slay your children because of the fear of poverty: We provide for you and for them* (6:151).

THE PROPHET'S LIFE BEFORE HIS PROPHETHOOD

Prophet Muhammad was brought up in God's sight and care. His father 'Abd Allah died before he was born, which meant that he had to put all his trust in God and submit completely to Him. He visited his father's tomb in Madina years later, cried his heart out, and on his return said: "I wept for my father and entreated God to forgive him."

With the death of his father, God deprived him of all human support and directed him to the realization that there is no deity but God, Who has no partners.

His grandfather and uncle protected him to some extent, but he came to perceive that his real guardian was God. Behind every phenomenon and every cause and effect, he could discern the hand of the Single Creator of the universe and of causes. The Oneness of God would be manifested to him in the light of Divine Unity. That is, he would be tested in this world of wisdom, where material causes and means have a part in every attainment, and so would have to use necessary material causes and means and take all necessary measures to attain anything. He would have to depend wholly on his Lord and ask Him for any help, thereby demonstrating that only God creates the result and gives success.

As a result of his father's death, he came to be called the "Matchless Orphan Pearl." In reference to this, God addressed him years later:

> Your Lord shall give you, and you shall be satisfied. Did He not
> find you an orphan and shelter you?... Did He not find you

needy and suffice you? As for the orphan, do not oppress him,
and as for the beggar, scold him not. (93:5-6, 8-10)

The Matchless Orphan Pearl also lost his mother, Amina, at
an early age. When she died in Abwa at age 25 or 26 on her way
back from visiting her husband's tomb in Madina, Muhammad
was only 6 years old. Thus, he learned the pain of having no
father or mother. Indeed, he would learn and suffer everything,
for he was sent to teach everything to humanity and to be an
example in every respect.

His grandfather 'Abd al-Muttalib, a respected Makkan elder, undertook his protection. For this reason, God saved 'Abd al-
Muttalib from misfortune. He embraced his beloved grandson,
and always offered him the seat of honor in his house.

He felt that Muhammad would grow up to save humanity.
Muhammad was so noble and well-mannered that his grandfather anticipated his Prophethood. He was not the first of his
forefathers to do so, however: Ka'b ibn Luayy, who some consider a Prophet, predicted that the Last Messenger would be
raised from his own progeny. He mentioned him by name:

> Suddenly Prophet Muhammad will appear;
> He will give tidings, and is truthful in his tidings.

'Abd al-Muttalib, whom even the great army of Abraha
could not bring to tears, wept bitterly when he took to his
deathbed. When his son Abu Talib asked what was wrong, he
replied: "I'm weeping because I'll no longer be able to embrace
Muhammad," and added: "I'm afraid something might happen
to my Matchless Pearl. I entrust him to you."

Abu Talib assumed Muhammad's protection and, in return,
his son 'Ali would be blessed with being the father of
Muhammad's progeny. After Prophethood, the Messenger of
God said to 'Ali: "Every other Prophet's progeny descended
from himself, but my progeny will descend from you." 'Ali
would be the father and the greatest saint until the Last Day,
as the representative of the Prophet's sainthood. This is Abu
Talib's reward for helping Muhammad.

Abu Talib protected Muhammad with great care. Ibn Ishaq, among other historians and biographers, relate that he took his nephew to Syria in a trade caravan when he was 10 or 12 years old. They stopped near Damascus and left him, as he was the youngest, to watch the caravan. From his nearby monastery, the Christian monk Bahira was observing the caravan. He was expecting the arrival of the Last Prophet, and so always studied people. He noticed that a cloud followed the caravan, stopping and starting when it did so, so that one of its members would be shaded.[2] He thought: "This is a special characteristic of Prophets. The expected Prophet must be in that caravan."

When the caravan stopped near his monastery, Bahira invited its members over for a meal. Noticing the cloud still hovering over the caravan, he asked Abu Talib if someone had been left behind. Abu Talib answered that they had left a young boy to watch over their things. The monk asked them to fetch him. When Muhammad came, Bahira took Abu Talib to one side and asked him about his relationship with the boy. "He is my son," Abu Talib answered, but Bahira disputed this, saying: "He can't be your son. According to our books, his father must have died before his birth." Then he added: "Let me give you this advice. Take this boy back immediately. The Jews are envious. If they recognize him, they'll harm him." Abu Talib made an excuse to the other caravan members and returned to Makka with his nephew.[3]

Prophet Muhammad made a second journey when he was 25 years old, with the trade caravan of Khadija, a respected widow he would later marry. On the journey, he encountered Bahira once more. The monk was very pleased with this second meeting, and told him: "You will be a Prophet, the Last Prophet. I wish that God would allow me to live to see you raised as a Prophet. I would follow you, carry your shoes and protect you against your enemies!"

A major event of Muhammad's early life was the *fijar* (sacrilegious) war that occurred during his later teens. This was the fourth war that violated the sanctity of the sacred months (Dhu al-Qa'dah, Dhu al-Hijjah, Muharram, and Rajab) and the sacred territory of Makka. Its immediate cause was two men's jealousy and animosity. One belonged to the Banu Kinanah (a confederate of the Quraysh tribe) and the other to the Qays–'Aylan (an important clan of the Hawazin tribe). The future Prophet, who would end all injustice and lawlessness, helped his uncle Zubayr ibn 'Abd al-Muttalib, who represented Banu Hashim in the war, gather the arrows shot by the enemy.

Another important event was his presence at the meeting that resulted in the *hilf al-fudul* (the alliance of the virtuous). This league against injustice was sponsored mainly by the Banu Hashim and the Banu al-Muttalib tribes. It was formed to ensure that foreign merchants would no longer be deprived of their rights, as happened when the Qurayshi 'As ibn Wa'il usurped a Yemeni merchant's goods. The Yemeni appealed to the Qurayshi leaders for help, but they ignored him.

When the Banu Hashim, Muhammad's clan, heard of this, they decided to form the *hilf al-fudul* and force the return of the merchant's money. They also took an oath that whenever someone in Makka, whether citizen or stranger, suffered an injustice, they would offer their support until justice was done. Muhammad was so impressed with its noble objectives that he would say long after: "I attended the conclusion of an agreement at 'Abd Allah ibn Jud'an's house. I would not exchange it for the best material gain. If someone appeals to it in Islam, I would respond."

Muhammad's childhood and youth were a prelude to his Prophethood. Besides his other exalted and laudable characteristics, everyone agreed upon his truthfulness and trustworthiness. He never lied, cheated, broke his word, or participated in pagan rituals. He was called "the Truthful, Trustworthy Man" even by his bitterest enemies. People would say:

> If you have to travel and need someone to look after your wife, entrust her to Muhammad without hesitation, for he will not even glance at her face. If you want to entrust your wealth for safeguarding, entrust it to this trustworthy, honest man, for he will never touch it. If you look for someone who never tells a

lie and never breaks his word, go directly to Muhammad,
because whatever he says is true.

Those who knew him from his childhood immediately
believed in his Prophethood: Abu Bakr, 'Uthman, Talha, Zubayr,
Abu Dharr, and Yasir, among others. When 'Ammar told his
father that he believed, the latter responded: "If Muhammad says
that God is One, it is true. He never lies."

In the early days of his Prophethood, Prophet Muhammad
once summoned the Qurayshis to the foot of Abu Qubays hill.
He asked them: "Would you believe me if I told you an enemy
host was waiting behind this hill to attack you?" Everyone
answered that they would, even his uncle Abu Lahab, who
would become his bitterest enemy.[4]

When humanity was in dire need of someone to destroy
unbelief and breathe new life into the world, God raised
Muhammad to stop all forms of wickedness. In the words of
Ahmad Shawky:

> *The sun of guidance was born,*
> *and the entire universe was illumined.*
> *A smile appeared on the lips of time,*
> *and his praises were sung.*

When he appeared on the horizon of Madina years later, the
pure, innocent children of that illumined city would sing:

> *The "full moon" rose upon us from the hills of Wada',*
> *So it is incumbent upon us to thank God so long as*
> *Those who pray and entreat Him continue to do so.*[5]

THE AWAITED PROPHET

The Torah and the Psalms

A Companion once asked God's Messenger to talk about himself. He said: "I am the one for whose coming Abraham prayed
and of whom Jesus gave glad tidings."[6] This alludes to the following Qur'anic verses:

(Abraham prayed): "Our Lord, raise up in their midst a Messenger from among them who shall recite unto them Your signs, and teach them the Book and Wisdom, and purify them. Verily you are the All-Mighty, the All-Wise." (2:129)

When Jesus, son of Mary, said: "O children of Israel! I am indeed a Messenger of God to you, confirming that which was [revealed] before me in the Torah, and bringing good tidings of a Messenger who shall come after me, whose name is Ahmad [the Praised One]." (61:6)

The Messenger of God was expected. All preceding Prophets spoke of and predicted his coming. The Qur'an (3:81) specifically states that God made a covenant with the Prophets that they would believe in and help the Messenger who would come after them and confirm the Message that they brought.[7]

The current versions of the Torah, the Gospel, and the Psalms still contain verses alluding to Prophet Muhammad, and even to his Companions. The late Husayn Jisri found 114 such allusions and quoted them in his Risalat al-Hamidiya. We cite a few examples here, beginning with: *The Lord came from Sinai and dawned over them from Seir; He shone forth from Mount Paran* (Deuteronomy 33:2).

This refers to the Prophethood of Moses, Jesus, and Muhammad, respectively. Sinai is where Prophet Moses spoke to God and received the Torah. Seir, a place in Palestine, is where Prophet Jesus received Divine Revelation. Paran is where God manifested Himself to humanity for the last time through His Revelation to Prophet Muhammad.

Paran is a mountain range in Makka. It is mentioned in the Torah (Genesis 21:19-21) as the desert area where Hagar was left by her husband Abraham to live with her son Ishmael. The Zamzam well also is located there. As stated in the Qur'an (14:35-37), Abraham left Hagar and Ishmael in the valley of Makka, which was then an uninhabited place between the mountain ranges of Paran.

It is because of such explicit predictions in the Torah that the Jews were expecting the Last Prophet and knew that he would appear in Makka.

The verse of Deuteronomy, according to the Arabic version published in London (1944), continues: *He came with myriads of holy ones; in his right hand was an axe of fire with two edges.* This refers to the promised Prophet, who would have many Companions of the highest degree of sainthood and would be allowed—even ordered—to fight his enemies.

The following verses also promise his coming:

> The Lord said to me [Moses]: "What they say is good. I will raise up for them a Prophet like you among their brothers; I will put My words in his mouth, and he will tell them everything I command him. If anyone does not listen to My words that the Prophet speaks in My name, I will Myself call him to account." (Deuteronomy 18:17-19)

It is clear from these verses that a *Prophet like you among their brothers* means a Prophet from Ishmael's line, for Ishmael is the brother of Isaac, the forefather of the Children of Israel. The only Prophet who came after Moses and resembled him in many ways (e.g., bringing a new law and waging war against his enemies) is Prophet Muhammad. The Qur'an points to this: *We have sent to you a Messenger as a witness over you, even as we sent to Pharaoh a Messenger* (73:15).

'Abd Allah ibn 'Amr, an ascetic warned by the Prophet not to neglect sleeping with his wife and to fast only on alternate days, is reported to have said: "It was common knowledge to the communities of previous religions that God would send a Prophet to humanity as a bearer of good tidings and a warner. I personally read in the Torah these verses about him:

> We have sent you, O Prophet, to humanity as a bearer of good tidings and a warner, and as a support and refuge for the common folk. You are My servant and Messenger. I have called you Mutawakkil [the one who puts his trust in God]. He is not one rude, repelling and angry, and shouting in the streets. He does not repel evil with evil; instead, he excuses and forgives. God will not make him die before He guides through him the deviating nation to the right path by declaring there is no deity but God."[8]

This report was confirmed by 'Abd Allah ibn Salam and Ka'b al-Akhbar, the most learned scholars of the Jewish community at the time of the Prophet. They later converted to Islam.

We also read about Muhammad in the Psalms of David:

> He will rule from sea to sea and from the river to the ends of the Earth. The desert tribes will bow before him, and his enemies will lick the dust. The kings of Tarsish and of distant shores will bring tribute to him; the kings of Sheba and Seba will present gifts to him. All kings will bow down to him and all nations will serve him, for he will deliver the needy who cry out, the afflicted who have no one to help. He will take pity on the weak and the needy, and save the needy from death. He will rescue them from oppression and violence, for precious is their blood in his sight. Long may he live! May gold from Sheba be given to him. May people ever pray for him and bless him all day long. Let corn abound throughout the land; on the tops of the hills may it sway. May his name endure for ever; may it continue as long as the sun. All nations will be blessed through him, and they will call him blessed. (Psalms 72:8-17)

The Gospels

More emphatically and frequently than any other Prophet, Jesus gave good tidings of Muhammad. In the Gospel of John, Jesus promises his arrival using several names:

> But I tell you the truth: It is for your good that I am going away. Unless I go away, the Paraklit will not come to you; but if I go, I will send him to you. When he comes, he will convict the world of guilt in regard to sin and righteousness and judgment. (John, 16:7-8)

Here, Prophet Muhammad is referred to as the Paraklit. This Greek word means "the Distinguisher between Truth and Falsehood" and "one who is much praised." Christian interpreters have given it various meanings, such as Counselor (New International Version by International Bible Society, placed and distributed by *Gideon's International*), Helper (*American Bible Society*), or Comforter (*The Company of the Holy Bible*), and claim that it refers to the Holy Spirit. But they have never been able to establish whether the Holy Spirit came down after Jesus and did what Jesus said it would do.

If the Holy Spirit is Archangel Gabriel, he came many times to Prophet Muhammad to bring Divine Revelations. Further, Jesus mentioned and predicted the Paraklit with other names but the same function, as seen below:

> When Paraklit comes—the Spirit of truth—who comes from the Father, he will testify about me. (John 15:26)

> I have much more to say to you, more than you can now bear. But when he, the Spirit of truth, comes, he will guide you into all truth. He will not speak on his own; he will speak only what he hears, and he will tell you what is yet to come. He will bring glory to me by taking what is mine and making it known to you. (John 16:12-14)

> I will not speak with you much longer, for the Prince of this world is coming. And I posses nothing of him. (John 14:30)

Who has come after Jesus other than Prophet Muhammad, as the Comforter who has comforted human beings against their fear of death, worries of the future, and spiritual ailments? As the Helper, who has helped humanity attain real peace and happiness in both worlds? As the Prince of the world, who has ruled almost half the world for fourteen centuries and has become the beloved of billions? As the Spirit of truth, who has testified to Jesus, brought glory to him by declaring his Prophethood against the Jews' denial and the Christians' deification, and restoring his religion to its pristine purity through the Book revealed to him?

What shortcomings do some Christians attribute to Prophet Muhammad, in contrast to Jesus and other Prophets, that, while many among them believed in him within a few decades of his death, they persist in denying him?

Mawlana Jalal al-Din al-Rumi, a great Sufi saint, expresses in the following stanza the good tidings of Prophet Muhammad found in the Gospel:

> In the Gospel Mustafa is mentioned with his attributes. In him
> is the mystery of all the Prophets; he is the bringer of happi-
> ness. The Gospel mentions him with his external form and fea-
> tures, and also with his personal virtues and Prophetic qualities.

The Old and New Testaments, despite the questionable
authenticity of their current versions, still contain references to
Prophet Muhammad. We have quoted some of these. If, one day,
the original copies or the least altered copies of the Torah and the
Gospel are discovered, they will contain explicit references to the
last Messenger. This may be deduced from the Traditions that say
Christianity will be purified of its borrowed elements.

Many Others Awaited the Prophet

Owing to the numerous predictions of his coming, everyone was
waiting for Prophet Muhammad. In that dark era of human history, humanity was waiting for one who would destroy unbelief
and breathe new life into the world. Judaism and Christianity,
being God-revealed religions in origin, had no more to offer.
Those who had studied the old books without prejudice, especially the monk Bahira, were waiting for him to come.

Many Makkans also were waiting, one of the foremost being
Zayd ibn 'Amr, 'Umar ibn al-Khattab's uncle. He had rejected
idolatry, led a pure life, and used to address people as follows:
"There's no good in the idols you worship. I know of a religion
that will soon be taught and spread. It will be proclaimed no later than a few years from now, but I don't know whether I'll live
long enough to witness it."

According to 'Amr ibn Rabi'a, Zayd gave a detailed description of the expected Prophet:

> I am expecting a Prophet who is about to come. He will appear
> among Ishmael's descendants and 'Abd al-Muttalib's grand-
> sons. He is of middle height, neither too tall nor too short. His
> hair is neither curly nor straight. His name is Ahmad. His
> birthplace is Makka. His people will force him to leave Makka,
> and he will emigrate to Yathrib (Madina), where his religion
> will spread. I have traveled from place to place searching for

Abraham's religion. However, all the Jewish and Christian scholars I spoke to advised me to wait for him. He is the Last Prophet; no Prophet will come after him. I may not live long enough to see him, but I have believed in him.

At the end of his introduction, Zayd told 'Amr ibn Rabi'a: "If you live long enough to see him, greet him for me." Years passed before Prophet Muhammad declared his Prophethood. 'Amr ibn Rabi'a, having declared his faith to the Prophet, explained what Zayd had told him and conveyed his greetings. Muhammad returned his greetings and added: "I saw Zayd in Paradise, trailing his robes."[9]

Among those seeking the truth was Waraqa ibn Nawfal, a Christian scholar and paternal cousin of Khadija, wife of Muhammad. When the first Revelation came, Khadija told Waraqa what had happened. Waraqa replied: "Muhammad is a truthful man. What he saw is that which occurs at the beginning of Prophethood. The being who came to him is Gabriel, who also came to Moses and Jesus. Muhammad will be a Prophet. If I live long enough to witness his declaration of Prophethood, I will believe in him and support him."[10]

One of those seeking the Last Prophet was the Jew 'Abd Allah ibn Salam. The Jews had such confidence in him that they called him "the lord, son of a lord." His greatness equaled that of even the greatest Companions, such as Abu Bakr and 'Umar, and God would consider his testimony to the Qur'an equal to the testimony of a people:

> Say: "Have you considered? If it be from God, and you do not believe in it, and a witness from among the Children of Israel bears witness to its like, and believes, and you wax proud, God guides not the people of the evildoers." (46:10)

This great Companion describes how he found the Prophet:

> When God's Messenger emigrated to Madina, I went to see him, as did everyone else. He was sitting amidst a group of people when I went in, and saying: "Give food to others and greet them." His speech was so sweet and his face so charming

that I said to myself: "I swear by God that one with such a face cannot lie." Without delay I declared my belief in him.[11]

The Jews and Christians of that time recognized God's Messenger. As stated in the Qur'an, They recognize him as they recognize their sons (2:146). After his conversion, 'Umar asked 'Abd Allah ibn Salam if he had recognized God's Messenger. "I recognized him," Ibn Salam answered, and added: "I may doubt my children, my wife might have deceived me, but I have no doubt about God's Messenger being the Last Prophet."[12]

Although the Jews and Christians recognized him, most envied him and, out of prejudice and envy, did not believe:

> When there came to them a Book from God confirming what was with them—and they aforetime prayed for victory over the unbelievers—when there came to them what they recognized, they disbelieved in it; and the curse of God is on the unbelievers. (2:89)

After his conversion, 'Abd Allah ibn Salam said to God's Messenger: "O Messenger of God, hide me in a corner and then summon all the Jewish scholars in Madina to ask about me and my father. Their assessment will certainly be positive. Then let me come out to declare my conversion." God's Messenger accepted this suggestion.

When the Jewish scholars gathered, God's Messenger asked them what they thought of Ibn Salam and his father. All of them answered: "They are among our noblest and most learned people." Upon this, God's Messenger asked again: "How would you react if he affirms me?" They responded: "It is impossible that he will affirm you!" Ibn Salam then came out and declared his conversion, whereupon the Jewish scholars immediately changed their attitude and retorted: "Ibn Salam is the most wicked among us, and the son of the most wicked."[13]

Prophet Muhammad was one who had been sought for centuries. Salman al-Farisi was one of those seekers. Originally a Magian (a fire worshipper), he had left his native Persia due to his burning desire to find the eternal truth. Before embracing Islam, he worked for several Christian monks, the last of whom advised Salman on his deathbed:

> Son, there is nobody left to whom I can commend you. But according to what we read in our books, the Last Prophet is about to appear. He will come with the pure creed of Abraham and will appear in the place to which Abraham migrated. Nevertheless, he will emigrate to another place and settle there. There are explicit signs of his Prophethood. For example, he will not eat of charity but will accept gifts, and the seal of Prophethood will be between his shoulders.

Now, let Salman narrate the rest of his story:

> I joined a caravan heading for the place mentioned by the late monk. When we arrived at Wadi al-Qura', they sold me to a Jew as a slave. When I saw gardens of date palms, I thought the Prophet would emigrate to this place. While I was working there, another Jew from the Banu Qurayza bought me and took me to Madina. I began working in his date-palm garden. There was no news yet of God's Messenger. However, one day I was harvesting dates when a cousin of my Jewish owner came up hurriedly. He said in great anger: "Damn it! The people are flocking to Quba. A man from Makka, who claims Prophethood, has come. They think he's a real Prophet."

> I began to tremble with excitement. I climbed down from the tree and asked: "What are you talking about?" My owner saw my excitement and slapped my face with the back of his hand, saying: "It doesn't concern you, mind your own business!"

> On the same day, as the sun set, I went to him in Quba and gave him as alms the food I had brought with me. God's Messenger did not touch it, but said to those around him: "Help yourself to this." I told myself: "This is the first sign." On another occasion I gave him something as a gift. He accepted it and ate it with his Companions. "This is the second sign," I told myself.

> Once, I attended the funeral for a deceased Companion. I came close to God's Messenger in the cemetery. After greeting him, I stood behind him in the hope of seeing the Seal of Prophethood. His shoulders were bare, and the seal was just as the monk had

> described it. I couldn't help kissing it in tears, after which I told
> him my story. He was very pleased and wanted his Companions
> to hear my story.[14]

People who sincerely sought him found him. Whoever
seeks him will find him, whereas those who remain obstinate
and ruled by their evil-commanding selves will drown in unbelief and hypocrisy. Mughira ibn Shu'ba narrates:

> One day I was with Abu Jahl in Makka. God's Messenger came
> over and invited us to accept Islam. Abu Jahl rebuked him, say-
> ing: "If you are doing this so that we will testify before God in
> the other world that you performed your mission of
> Prophethood, we will do it. Leave us then, O man, to our-
> selves!" When God's Messenger left us, I asked Abu Jahl if he
> admitted Muhammad's Prophethood. He said that he did, and
> then added: "I know he is truly a Prophet. Nevertheless, we
> compete with the Hashimites in everything. They have been
> boasting of providing food and water to the pilgrims. Now if
> they begin to boast of having a Prophet, I won't be able to
> endure it at all."[15]

This is typical of the thoughts cherished by the Abu Jahls of
the past and the present. Intelligent people who are not preju-
diced and whose willpower is not paralyzed cannot help but
believe in Islam and God's Messenger. In this respect, God says
to His holy Messenger: *We know well that their talk grieves you; in
truth they deny not you, but it is the signs of God that the evildoers
condemn* (6:33).

How could they accuse him of lying, for he was known by
everybody as al-Amin (the truthful one)? The testimony of one
of his bitterest enemies, 'Utba ibn Abi Rabi'a, proves that even
his enemies admitted his truthfulness.

The Qurayshi leaders met to discuss how to prevent the spread
of Islam. They sent 'Utba in the hope that he could persuade the
Messenger to stop. He asked: "Who is better, O Muhammad, you
or your father?" God's Messenger did not answer, probably because
silence is the best answer to such an absurd question. 'Utba continued: "If your father was better than you, he cannot have been fol-

lowing the religion you are now preaching. If, by contrast, you are better than your father, then I am ready to listen to what you have to say."

God's Messenger inquired: "Is that all you intend to say?" 'Utba said that it was, and fell silent. Then, God's Messenger knelt and began reciting from *Surat al-Fussilat*. By the time he reached: *But if they turn away, then "I warn you of a thunderbolt [as fell in times past upon the tribes] of 'Ad and Thamud"* (41:13), 'Utba was trembling as if caught by fever. He had to put his hand on the lips of God's Messenger and said: "Please stop, for the sake of the God in whom you believe!" 'Utba returned home bewildered.

The Qurayshi leaders were waiting for him anxiously. Fearing that 'Utba might have accepted Islam, Abu Jahl knocked at his door and, when admitted, angered 'Utba by saying: "I heard Muhammad treated you very generously and feted you, and in return you believed in him. This is what the people are saying." Angrily, 'Utba replied:

> You know I don't need to be feted by him. I am richer than all of you. But his words shook me. They weren't poetry, nor did they resemble those of a soothsayer. I don't know how I should respond. He's a truthful person. While I was listening to his recitation, I feared that what happened to 'Ad and Thamud might happen to us.[16]

They had been expecting a Prophet for a long time. Everybody knew al-Amin's character, and no one had ever heard him lie. They were charmed by his personality and the Qur'an's eloquence, but yet could not overcome their pride and arrogance, or the envy and rivalry, and proclaim their belief. Nor could they bring their habits and lifestyle into accord with his Message. Is this not true of all those who, knowing the truth, persist in unbelief?

CHAPTER 2

Why Prophets are Sent

WHY PROPHETS ARE SENT

TO ILLUMINATE HUMANITY'S WAY

Today, our greatest problem is that many do not recognize Prophet Muhammad, and that others neglect or refuse to follow his way. God sent Muhammad, as He sent all previous Prophets, to illuminate our way:

> God was gracious to the believers when He raised up among them a Messenger from themselves who recites to them the verses (of His Book) and shows them His signs [in their selves and in the universe], purifies them [of their sins and deviations], and instructs them in the Book and the Wisdom. They were evidently in manifest misguidance before. (3:164)

God sent Messengers to guide people to the truth and so they could be purified of sin. Those who were enlightened by the Messengers found the way to the Divine Presence and attained the highest rank of humanity. In the words of Ibrahim Haqqi: "God declared that He could not be contained by the Heavens and Earth. He can be known and reached only through hearts." This is why Messengers led humanity to the knowledge of God.

Those who follow this guidance are touched by Him in their innermost selves, whether it is called heart, soul, or conscience, for only that can grasp God in His entirety. Minds cannot comprehend Him, and philosophy cannot reach Him. Therefore, the Prophets purified souls so they could be mirrors in which God might manifest Himself. Prophet Muhammad left us the Qur'an and Sunna to show us how to live in a way that fulfills the purpose for which the Prophets were sent.

Here, it is necessary to emphasize three points. First, Prophets were not ordinary men; rather, they were chosen men through whom God manifested Himself. God chose them and paid great attention to their upbringing so that they always would seek to gain His approval. Like his predecessors, Prophet Muhammad always pursued God's approval and good pleasure. His last words were: "To Rafiq al-A'la (the Highest Abode)." His wife 'A'isha gives the following account of his last moments:

> I was with him during his last moments. Whenever he became ill, he would ask me to pray for him and, expecting my prayer to be accepted through the blessing of his auspicious hand, I held his hand and prayed. During his last illness, I wanted to do the same and pray, when he suddenly withdrew his hand and said: "To Rafiq al-A'la."[1]

Second, the world is never left devoid of successors who devote their lives to preaching and teaching the truth. They should seek what the Prophets sought, preach what the Prophets preached, and strictly follow the Prophets in enjoining and spreading good and discouraging and forbidding evil.

Third, death is not total annihilation, but rather a changing of worlds without completely breaking away from this one. Prophets' deaths are special. In the case of martyrs, whose spiritual degree is lower than a Prophet's, the Qur'an says: *Say not of those slain in God's way: "They are dead," they are alive but you understand not* (2:154). So we cannot say that Prophets are dead. Thus Prophet Muhammad did not die as we understand this word; he only changed places and passed into another dimension or degree of life.

Those who can penetrate other dimensions with their inner faculties experience different dimensions of time and space, see different creatures, and look into things and events from different viewpoints. We consider things and events according to the stream in which we are.

Those who rise high enough to see all dimensions of this stream have the scope of their sight enlarged as they ascend higher. Thus their capacity and judgment when considering matters is more comprehensive. Such people might be sitting with us and, at the same time, in the presence of God's Messenger. While praying with us, some may be leading the same prayer in the Hereafter before the angels. There is a particular class of saints called *abdal* (substitutes). When one dies, he or she is replaced immediately with a new one who can see the Prophet whenever they wish. Jalal al-Din al-Suyuti, a sixteenth-century scholar, once said: "I have seen God's Messenger 28 times while awake."

TO GUIDE PEOPLE TO THE SERVICE OF GOD

God declared in the Qur'an: *I have not created jinn and humanity except to serve me* (51:56).

We were not created only to eat, drink, and reproduce; these are natural facts of our life and natural needs. Our main purpose is to recognize and serve God. All Prophets were sent to show us how to do this: *We never sent a Messenger before you except that We revealed to him: "There is no god but I, so serve Me"* (21:25), and:

> We sent forth among every nation a Messenger, saying: "Serve God, and eschew taghut [idols and tyrants, Satan and his followers]." Then some of them God guided and some were justly disposed to misguidance. (16:36)

God sent Prophets to guide us to His service. Their missions were the same. However, whereas the earlier Prophets were sent to their own people and for a set period, Prophet Muhammad was sent as a mercy to humanity and jinn, and for all time.

According to an authentic narration, Ibn Mas'ud reports the Prophet's preaching to the jinn:

> Once God's Messenger and I went somewhere. He drew a circle around me and told me not to leave it until he returned. He left, and after a while some tumult broke out on the other side. I wondered whether something had happened to him, but as he had told me to stay put until he returned, I did so. Some time later, he returned and I asked him about the uproar. He replied: "The jinn have believed and taken the oath of allegiance to me. When some of them insisted on unbelief, fighting broke out.

The uproar you heard was the fighting. This implies that my life is about to end."[2]

God's Messenger used this last sentence to indicate that he had been sent to open the way to the guidance of humanity and jinn. Once this had been done, there would be no reason for him to live, for he would have nothing more to do. This also implies that believers should never neglect their essential duties here, and should pray, as instructed by God's Messenger: "O God, make me die if death is good for me; or else, make me live long as long as living is good for me!"[3]

TO TEACH PEOPLE GOD'S LAWS

Another purpose for sending Prophets is to reveal Divine Commandments (i.e., the five daily prayers, fasting Ramadan, paying zakat, and not indulging in any illicit sexual relations, alcohol, and gambling). This function is called Messenger-ship. According to the Qur'an: *They deliver the Messages of God and fear Him, and do not fear anyone except God* (33:39). In addition, God told Muhammad:

> O Messenger, deliver that which has been sent down to you from your Lord; for if you do not, you will have not performed His Messengership. God protects you against people; verily God will not guide the people of unbelief. (5:67)

The Messenger was sent to enlighten humanity about all dimensions of human life. Any neglect in delivering God's Message would amount to leaving humanity in darkness. For this reason, he continually sought unadulterated minds and hearts to which he could impart God's Message.

God's Messenger might have talked to people like Abu Bakr and 'Umar only a few times before they embraced Islam. But when it came to people like Abu Jahl, it was a different story. Each time he met them, he would say: "Proclaim there is no god but God and be saved." He would visit places where people gathered and make the same call. Occasional fairs were held in Makka and such nearby places as 'Arafat, Mina, Muzdalifah, and

'Aqabah. He would go to them every year, looking for receptive people.

When the Makkan polytheists' indifference was replaced with derision and mocking, and then with increasingly unbearable persecution, torture, and boycott, God's Messenger took Zayd ibn Haritha with him and went to Ta'if. But the people of this city also treated him harshly. The children lined up on either side of the road and threw stones at him. As he was wearing no armor, by the time he had left the town and found a tree under which to rest, he was bleeding profusely. He held up his hands and supplicated:

> O God, unto You I complain of my frailty, lack of resources and significance before those people. O Most Merciful of the merciful, You are the Lord of the oppressed and are my Lord. To whom do You abandon me? To that stranger who looks askance and grimaces at me? Or to that enemy to whom You have given mastery over me? If Your indignation is not directed at me, I have no worry. But Your grace is much greater for me to wish for. I seek refuge in the light of Your Countenance, which illumines all darkness and by which the affairs of this life and the Hereafter have been rightly ordered, lest Your wrath alight upon me, or Your indignation descend upon me. I expect Your forgiveness until You are pleased. There is no resource or power but in You.

After saying this, he noticed that a tray had been placed before him. Addas, a Christian slave from Nineveh, had seen God's Messenger being stoned and tormented from the vineyard in which he was working. Putting some grapes on a tray, he had brought them to him. God's Messenger said "In the name of God" and began to eat. This surprised Addas, for it was the first time he had heard this phrase among the polytheists. So he asked God's Messenger who he was and why he had come to Ta'if. Upon hearing the answer, "I am Muhammad, from Makka, the Last Prophet," he said with tears in his eyes, Addas remarked: "God has made me find you," and embraced Islam.[4]

Prophet Muhammad was entirely focused on his mission. As a result, the circle of light broadened day by day, and the party of unbelief became more and more frustrated: *They desire to extinguish with their mouths God's light; and God refuses but to perfect His light, though the unbelievers are averse* (9:32). When no more could be done in Makka, he emigrated to Madina and continued his mission there. Here he faced a different problem: established communities of hostile Jews and, eventually, a fifth column of Hypocrites who would ally themselves with his enemies.

In the twenty-third year of his mission, he began to feel that his life was almost finished. He had performed the minor pilgrimage ('umrah) a few times, but never the major pilgrimage (hajj). He was able to do this during this final year. Ascending 'Arafat on the back of his camel, he preached what has become known as the Farewell Sermon. In it, he stressed that feuds and interest-based transactions were forbidden and that women have certain rights, and talked about family ties as well as tribal and national relationships.

A huge, tearful congregation listened to him. While speaking, he frequently asked them if he had communicated God's Message. With each positive reply, he raised his index finger toward Heaven and said: "O God, be witness!"[5] In deep consciousness of Divine service, he might have thought: "God sent me to perform the duty of Messengership. Just as these people bore witness that I fulfilled this duty, I hope I may be regarded as having truly done it." He was prepared to meet God in perfect satisfaction.

TO BE EXAMPLES

Prophets were sent to serve as examples who must be followed consciously. After mentioning the Prophets in Surat al-An'am, God told His last Messenger: *Those are they whom God has guided, so follow their guidance* (6:90). In particular, we are told to follow Muhammad's example: *You have a good example in God's Messenger for whoever hopes for God and the Last Day, and remembers God oft* (33:21).

God's Messenger is our leader. Just as we pray as he prayed, we must strive to live as he lived. Those who followed him during the first Islamic century were real representatives of the true Islamic life. God's Messenger says of them:

> Muslim armies will arrive, after me, at the gates of cities. They will be asked: "Did any of you see the Prophet?" The answer will be affirmative, and the gates will be opened for them. Those who succeed them also will perform jihad and be asked: "Did any of you see those who saw the Prophet?" They will reply in the affirmative, and the cities will be conquered by them. As for the third generation, its members will be asked: "Did any of you see those who saw the followers of the Prophet's Companions?" When this question is answered in the affirmative, their conquest will be successful.[6]

In another narration by Bukhari and Muslim, God's Messenger says: "The best of you are those who live in my period, then those who succeed them, and then those who follow them."[7]

Those three generations strictly followed the Prophet and, accordingly, were granted great victories throughout the world. Jesus had predicted them: "The banners of the holy ones are in their hands."[8] They are the Companions of Muhammad and those who follow his way in every century.

In a Tradition, although with a weak chain of transmission, God's Messenger declares: "The pious scholars of my nation resemble the Prophets of the Children of Israel."[9] 'Umar submitted himself to God so sincerely that, as a servant of God, he was far more effective than had been expected. During his caliphate, Iran, Iraq, and Egypt were conquered. Muslim armies marched throughout a vast area, led by such great commanders as Abu 'Ubayda ibn al-Jarrah, Shurahbil ibn Hasana, Sa'd ibn Abi Waqqas, 'Amr ibn al-'As, and Yazid ibn Abi Sufyan.

Jerusalem was conquered during his caliphate. When the Muslims' supreme commander asked its priests to submit the keys of the city, they answered: "We cannot see among you the man to whom we are to submit the keys." They had read in their religious books a description of who was qualified to receive the keys.

So the priests and Muslim commanders waited while 'Umar and his servant were riding a camel, by turns, toward Jerusalem.

Although 'Umar ruled over vast lands, he did not own a camel. He borrowed one from the state treasury and set out with his servant. When they approached the river Jordan, his waiting commanders on the other side were excited, praying: "O God, let 'Umar be the one riding when they reach the river, for these Romans are fond of pomp and display. They may not esteem us if they see the caliph pulling a camel ridden by a servant." But God had destined the latter scenario. When 'Umar approached, the priests noticed, among other things, several patches on his robe. This was the man described in their books, and so they gave him the keys of Jerusalem.

'Umar never deviated from the path of God's Messenger. While on his deathbed, after being fatally stabbed by a Magian slave, he refused food and water because he was too weak. However, he always prayed when it was time to do so, even if it caused his wounds to bleed. He would say: "Those who don't pray have nothing to do with Islam."[10] An exemplary follower of God's Messenger, his own example would be followed by succeeding generations.

TO ESTABLISH BALANCE

At a time when some people lived in monasteries and others drowned in luxury, Prophet Muhammad came with the Qur'anic instruction: *Seek the Last Abode amidst that which God has given you, and do not forget your portion of the present world* (28:77).

All Prophets came to establish balance between the material and spiritual life, reason and soul, this world and the next, and indulgence and abstinence. While we should declare all that God has bestowed on us to show our gratitude and due praise for Him (*And as for your Lord's blessing and bounty, declare it* [93:11]), we must not forget that we will have to account for every good we enjoy (*Then you shall be questioned that day concerning every good you enjoy* [102:8]).

The Prophet inculcated this principle so deeply in his Companions' hearts that it could be seen in every aspect of their lives. For example, once when breaking fast during Ramadan,

Abu Bakr, the first caliph, was offered a glass of cold water. He had just taken a sip when he suddenly burst into tears and stopped drinking. When asked why, he replied: "Once I was with God's Messenger. He acted as if he were pushing something with his hand and saying to it: 'Keep away from me!' I asked him what he was doing, and he replied: 'The world appeared to me in an ideal form, with all its pomp and luxury. I pushed it away, saying: "Leave me. You can't seduce me." It withdrew and said: "I can't conquer you, but I swear by God I'll captivate those who come after you."' After narrating this Tradition, Abu Bakr concluded: "Just now, I thought that the world tempted me with a glass of cold water, and I wept."[11]

Abu Bakr and most Companions lived a balanced life, despite the fact that they had every chance to live in comfort.

TO BE GOD'S WITNESSES

Prophets also were sent so that people cannot plead ignorance in the Hereafter. Regarding this, the Qur'an says: *Messengers bearing good tidings and warning, so that humanity might have no argument against God* (4:165).

Humanity, who has followed many so-called guides or leaders only to be led astray, has received true guidance through the Prophets. These servants of God were created for a special mission. Already Prophets in their mothers' wombs, their births were extraordinary. Their lives resembled a beautiful symphony, perfectly harmonious and balanced. Their words were like sweet melodies that penetrated souls.

All of existence, animate or inanimate, hearkened to them. Trees and rocks would greet Prophet Muhammad, and he would answer them. In his well-known *Qasidat al-Bur'a*, Busiri says: "Trees answered his call, prostrating." When he called them, trees came to him. Both living beings and inanimate objects acquired meaning through his advent, existence became a "cosmos" out of "chaos," and each thing became a tongue glorifying God with praise: *There is not a thing that does not glorify Him with praise, but you do not understand their glorification* (17:44).

The extraordinary harmony in the universe displays God's Existence and Unity. Nothing is created in vain and without purpose: *Does humanity think it will be left aimless?* (75:36).

If the Prophets had not been sent, we might have had an argument against being punished in the Hereafter. But, as the Qur'an states: *We never punish until We have sent a Messenger* (17:15), God must send Prophets so that people can distinguish good from evil. Thus, people cannot plead ignorance when they must defend their actions on the Day of Judgment.

CHAPTER 3

Characteristics of Prophets

CHARACTERISTICS OF PROPHETS

TOTAL DEPENDENCE ON REVELATION
AND SUBMISSION TO GOD

Although every Prophet was intelligent and endowed with a comprehensive understanding and a pure soul, these play no role in God's choice of a Prophet. Most Prophets, including Muhammad, were unlettered and therefore taught by God. Prophet Muhammad, despite his illiteracy, had knowledge of the past and the future, and insight into every branch of knowledge. He did not attend any school or have any human teachers, yet even his enemies admitted (and still do) that he displayed perfect justice in family affairs, perfect competency in state administration, and perfect command of armies.

Prophets were specially brought up by God. To cite an example, the Last Prophet recalled: "I intended twice in my childhood to attend a wedding ceremony. On both occasions, I was overpowered by sleep half-way [and thus was protected against any sin I would later prohibit]"[1]; and "While repairing the Ka'ba, prior to my Prophethood, I was carrying stones. As everyone did, I wrapped my garment's lower part over my shoulder to avoid injury. Part of my thigh was left uncovered. All of a sudden, the angel I had seen several times in my childhood appeared to me in all his majesty. I fell down and fainted. That was the first and last time I uncovered any part of my body that God ordered to be covered."[2]

Prophets were protected by God against all sins, for they were created for a special purpose. They were protected from going astray, for even a minor deviation could result in humanity's almost complete deviation.

Prophethood is distinguished by Divine Revelation:

> And thus have We revealed to you a spirit of Our command.
> You did not know what the Scripture was, nor what the faith.
> But We have made it a light whereby We guide whom We will
> of Our servants. And you, surely you guide unto a straight
> path. (42:52)

As a result, Prophets never spoke on their own accord: *Nor
does he speak of (his own) desire. It is naught but a Revelation revealed*
(53:3-4).

Prophet Muhammad, particularly when asked about the
essentials of belief, would wait for Revelation. Sometimes the
polytheists asked him to alter the Qur'an. But as it is a Divine
Scripture whose wording and meaning belong completely to
God, he would reply, as instructed by God: Say: *"It is not for me
to alter it of my own accord. I follow nothing, except what is revealed
to me"* (10:15).

Prophets submitted themselves wholly to God, and fulfilled
their mission solely because God commanded them to. They never compromised or deviated from their way in order to achieve
success. When confronted with threats or seductive offers, they
replied with words similar to those of the Prophet: "If you were
even to put the sun in my right hand, and the moon in the left, I
will never give up preaching my cause." He knew that the Qur'an
is the Word of God, and so bore all hardship and opposition.[3]

TRUSTWORTHINESS AND ASKING NO WAGE

Prophets were completely trustworthy and asked no wage for
their services. This very important characteristic is mentioned
five times in Surat al-Shu'ara'. All Prophets said the same thing:
"I am for you a trustworthy Messenger, so serve you God, and
obey you me. I ask of you no wage for this; my wage falls only
upon the Lord of the Worlds" (26:107-9, 125-27, 143-45, 162-
64, 178-80).

Among his own people, Prophet Muhammad was famous for
his trustworthiness even before his proclamation of Prophethood.

He was known as *al-Amin* (the Trustworthy). Like his predecessors, he asked no wage for calling to God.

Prophets never thought of material gain, spiritual reward, or even Paradise—they strove only for God's good pleasure and to see humanity guided to the truth. Prophet Muhammad was the foremost in this respect. As he devoted his life to humanity's welfare in this world, he will do so in the Place of Gathering. While everybody else will care only about themselves, he will prostrate before God, pray for the Muslims' salvation, and intercede with God on behalf of others.[4]

Those who intend to spread the perennial values of Islam should follow these practices. Any message based on an impure intention, regardless of eloquence, will have no effect on people. This point is frequently emphasized in the Qur'an: *Follow such as ask no wage of you, that are right-guided* (36:21).

Imam Busiri expresses the altruism, sincerity, and patience of God's Messenger in vivid language: "Mountains desired to run on his either side in heaps of gold, but he refused." The Messenger once said: "A day comes when I am hungry so as to endure it with patience; on another day I am full to praise my Lord, acquiring thus the reward of both patience and praising."

'A'isha reported that sometimes was no food was cooked for four successive days in their house.[5] Abu Hurayra also reports: "Once I went into the Prophet's room. He was praying while seated and groaning. I asked him if he was ill. He replied that he was too hungry to stand. I began to sob bitterly, but he stopped me, saying: "Don't cry, for one who endures hunger here will be safe from God's torment in the next."[6]

One day he told Gabriel: "It has been several days since someone has lit a fire to cook food in the house of Muham-mad's family An angel appeared and asked: "O Messenger of God, God greets you and asks if you would like to be a Prophet–king or a Prophet–slave?" He turned to Gabriel, who recommended humility. The Prophet raised his voice and replied: "I wish to be a Prophet–slave, who entreats God in hunger one day and thanks Him in satisfaction the next."[7]

God's Messenger used to eat with slaves and servants. Once a woman saw him eating and remarked: "He's eating as if he were a slave." God's Messenger responded: "Could there be a better slave than me? I am a slave of God."[8]

God's Messenger is, by virtue of being a slave of God, our master and that of creation, as eloquently stated by Galip Dede:

> *An exalted king, the King of the Messengers, O my Master.*
> *You are an endless source of help for the helpless, O my Master.*
> *God honored you by swearing by your life in the Qur'an, O my Master.*
> *In the Divine Presence, you are the greatest, O my Master.*
> *You are the beloved, lauded and praised one of God, O my Master.*
> *Our "eternal" king you are, sent to us by God, O my Master.*

COMPLETE SINCERITY

Another indispensable characteristic is sincerity, which in this context means "purity of intention, to do everything solely for the sake of God." We are told to worship God sincerely: *They were commanded only to serve God, making the religion His sincerely, people of pure faith, and to perform the prayer, and pay the alms* (98:5). God also mentions sincerity as the foremost attribute of the Prophets: *And mention in the Book Moses; he was made sincere, and he was a Messenger, a Prophet* (19:51).

We worship God only because we are His servants and He has told us to do so. Obeying Him allows us to secure His approval and be rewarded in the Hereafter. Said Nursi, the great twentieth-century Turkish thinker, said: "Do what you do only for God's sake, start for God's sake, work for God's sake, and act within the sphere of God's good approval."[9]

God's Last Prophet worshipped God so sincerely that people could say: "No one can remain as humble as he was at the beginning of his career or quest after attaining its height. Muhammad was an exception to this." He is so great and sublime that we still stand out of respect for him, although he used to warn his Companions: "When I come upon you, don't stand up as the Persians do (for their elders)."[10]

Although his Companions had complete respect for him, he considered himself a poor slave of God. On the day he conquered Makka, he was the same as when he humbly had begun his mission. At the outset of his mission, he would sit and eat with the poor and slaves. As he entered Makka in triumph, he rode a mule in such deep submission and humility before God that his forehead touched its pack-saddle. He was prostrating before God and taking refuge in Him from being a tyrannical, haughty conqueror.

God's Messenger had one intention: to please God and worship Him sincerely. He worshipped Him at a level of perfect goodness and sincerity, as he himself stated in a famous Tradition: "Perfect goodness or virtue is to worship God as if you were seeing Him, and while you see Him not, yet truly He sees you."[11]

CALLING PEOPLE WISELY AND WITH KINDNESS

Another attribute of Prophets is calling people to the way of God with wisdom and fair exhortation. They never resorted to demagogy and dialectics, but acted and spoke with wisdom. God ordered His Last and Greatest Messenger: *Call to the way of your Lord with wisdom and fair exhortation, and reason with them in the best way* (16:125).

People are more than just minds or hearts. We are complex beings with many faculties, including the mind, intellect, heart, and soul. All of our faculties, even the innermost ones, require satisfaction. The Prophets addressed all of them.

Those taught by the Prophets acquired certainty, and their view of things differed from those with limited external sight and devoid of insight and spiritual vision. Their conviction of religious truths was unshakable, and they were continually fed with Divine Revelation. They combined speech with action, knowledge with practice, and action with contemplation. 'Ali ibn Abi Talib, among others, would say: "If the veil of the Unseen were lifted up, my certainty would not increase."[12] There was no further degree of certainty left for them to attain.

The education given by the Prophets to their disciples, or the function of the Prophets, is described precisely:

We have sent among you, of yourselves, a Messenger, to recite
Our signs to you and to purify you, and to teach you the Book
and Wisdom, and to teach you what you know not. (2:151)

CALLING HUMANITY TO GOD'S UNITY

The cornerstone of the Prophetic mission was to preach Divine
Unity. All Prophets concentrated on this basic principle: *O my
people, serve God: You have no god other than He* (11:84).

God has sent at least one Prophet to every people. The fact
that all of them, regardless of time or place, agree on one basic
principle shows that they did not speak or act on their own;
rather, they did no more than teach the Message received from
God. Philosophers and thinkers, no matter how great they may
be, disagree among themselves because they depend on their
own intellect and findings. Frequently, the same philosophical
or sociological school contains different opinions.

Such a development was unknown among the Prophets,
further evidence that they were taught by a Single, Eternal
Teacher—God—and not guided by defective human reasoning.
Such a unity of belief is also a strong evidence of Divine Unity,
the fundamental principle of their mission, as declared by
Muhammad: "The most meritorious of the words spoken by me
and the Prophets before me is: 'There is no god but God, He is
One, having no partners.'"[13]

CHAPTER 4

The Essentials of Prophethood

THE ESSENTIALS OF PROPHETHOOD

According to Muslim theologians, the essentials of Prophethood are truthfulness, trustworthiness, communicating of God's messages, intelligence, infallibility, and freedom from all bodily and mental defects. These are found in every Prophet.

TRUTHFULNESS

Truthfulness is the cornerstone of Prophethood. No lies or deceit, whether explicit or implicit, were ever heard from them. The Qur'an declares: *Mention Abraham in the Book: Surely he was a most truthful Prophet* (19:41); *Mention Ishmael in the Book; surely, he was a man of his word, and he was a Messenger, a Prophet* (19:54); and *Mention Enoch (Idris) in the Book; surely he was a most truthful Prophet. We elevated him to an exalted place* (19:56-57). We also read in the Qur'an that a fellow prisoner addressed Prophet Joseph: *Joseph, O most truthful one* (12:46).

The Prophets had to be endowed with truthfulness, for God wants everybody to be truthful and extols the truthful: *O you who believe, fear God and be with the company of the truthful!* (9:119), and: *The believers are those who believed in God and His Messenger without ever feeling doubt thereafter, and strove with their souls and possessions in the way of God; those are the ones who are the truthful* (49:15).

The Qur'an praises believers who, without faltering, carry out their promises:

> Among the believers are the valiants who have kept their promise which they gave to God: Some of them carried out their word [and were martyred] and the others are expecting (their turn); they have never thought of going back on their word. (33:23)

This verse extols the heroes of Uhud, a decisive turning point in Islamic history. After the Qurayshi unbelievers were defeated at Badr, they had spent a whole year preparing for a deadly retaliatory blow at the Muslims. Meeting at the foot of Mount Uhud, a few miles from Madina, the Muslims at first were victorious and the Quraysh began to flee. At this crucial point, the archers whom God's Messenger had positioned at 'Aynayn pass left their positions, against the Prophet's command, and pursued the enemy. Khalid ibn Walid, commander of the enemy's cavalry, took this opportunity to surround the Muslims from behind. As a result, the Muslims experienced a reverse. Such leading figures as Hamza, Mus'ab ibn 'Umayr, 'Abd Allah ibn Jahsh, and Anas ibn Nadr were martyred. Even the Prophet was wounded.

Let us note here that during the battle, God's Messenger, the Prophet of forgiveness and mercy who was sent as a mercy for creation, raised his hands toward God and, while bleeding profusely, asked for the enemy to be forgiven: "O God, forgive my people, for they do not know."[1]

Anas ibn Nadr was the uncle of Anas ibn Malik, the servant of God's Messenger. Although he had sworn allegiance with God's Messenger in 'Aqabah before he emigrated to Madina, for some reason he did not fight at Badr. He regretted this so much that he told God's Messenger: "O Messenger of God, if God allows us to confront them once more, they will see what sufferings I will inflict on them!" He fought fearlessly at Uhud, especially when the Muslims suffered a reverse. Just before being martyred, he told Mu'adh ibn Jabal with a smile: "By God, I sense the scent of Paradise behind Uhud."

The Qur'an exalts in the above verse (33:23) those martyrs who fulfilled their promise to God through His Messenger, as well as others expecting martyrdom, to show that they were true to their words. They are not the only ones extolled here; rather, all who fulfill their words and keep their promises are mentioned here.

God's Messenger was known as a truthful person even before Islam. The Makkans, even the unbelievers, called him *al-Amin* (the Trustworthy One, the Truthful). Even his enemies did not accuse him of lying after he proclaimed his Prophethood. Abu Sufyan, for example, confessed to the Emperor of Byzantium that he never lied.

Struck by Abu Sufyan's answers, at that time the bitterest enemy of Islam, the Emperor acknowledged Muhammad's position: "It is inconceivable for one who has never told a lie during his whole life to invent lies against God."[2] He was right. Why would a believer who had never told a lie, even in jest, suddenly begin to lie, especially against God, when he is 40 years old and getting closer to the grave?

The Makkans agreed unanimously that God's Messenger was a truthful person. Once before his conversion, Yasir asked his son 'Ammar where he was going. 'Ammar said that he was going to Muhammad. Being fully satisfied of his son's safety while with Muhammad, he replied: "Muhammad is a trustworthy person. The Makkans recognize him so. If he claims Prophethood he must be telling the truth, for no one has ever heard him tell a lie."

God's Messenger always encouraged truthfulness, as can be seen in his words as recorded in the following Traditions:

- Promise me six things and I will promise you Paradise: Speak the truth, keep your promises, fulfill your trusts, remain (sexually) chaste, don't look at what is unlawful, and avoid what is forbidden.[3]
- Abandon what arouses your suspicions and follow what is certain. Truthfulness gives satisfaction; lying causes suspicion.[4]
- Seek truthfulness even if it might bring you to ruin.[5]
- Always be truthful, for truthfulness leads to righteousness and righteousness leads to Paradise. If you are always truthful and seek truthfulness, God records you as such. Never lie, for lying leads to shamefulness and shamefulness leads to Hell. If you insist on lying and seek deceit, God records you as such.[6]

Due to his truthfulness, God's Messenger rose to such a high rank that his nearness to God is expressed metaphorically in the

Qur'an as follows: *Then he approached and came nearer, till he was [distant] two bow-lengths, or even nearer* (53:8-9).

Truthfulness always brings salvation, even if it causes one's death. We die through truthfulness only once, whereas each lie is a different kind of death. One of the most striking examples of this is the case of Ka'b ibn Malik, a famous Ansari poet who swore allegiance to God's Messenger at 'Aqabah. Although he took part in almost all the battles, he missed the campaign of Tabuk without a justifiable excuse.

The Tabuk campaign was very difficult. It took place in midsummer and, what is more, against the Roman Empire. Although God's Messenger always kept the destination of such campaigns secret, this time he disclosed it and wanted every believer to participate. Ka'b completed his preparations but, at the last minute, uncharacteristic negligence kept him from joining the army.

When God's Messenger returned from the campaign, he asked those who had not fought why they had stayed at home. The Hypocrites lied and made excuses, but Ka'b, being unable to lie, told the truth. God's Messenger told him to leave. Thereafter, Ka'b and two other believers who had done the same thing were boycotted. On the order of God's Messenger, no Muslim met with them or spoke to them. They repented publicly, begging God for forgiveness, for 50 days. After this, it was revealed that:

> As for those three, the acceptance of their repentance was delayed until, for them, the Earth, vast as it is, was straitened and their own souls were straitened to them, and they perceived that there is no fleeing from God and no refuge but with Him. Then He accepted their repentance so that they could recover their former state. Verily, God is the One who accepts repentance, Most Merciful. (9:118)

After this revelation, Ka'b ibn Malik told the Messenger, upon him be peace and blessings: "I promise to speak the truth as long as I live."[7]

Truthfulness is the pivot of Prophethood. It could not be otherwise, for if a Prophet were to lie, everything connected with the Divine religion would be upset. All it takes is one lie to call a mission into question. Thus God declares:

> If he [Muhammad] had invented false sayings concerning Us, We would surely have grasped him firmly, and then cut off the artery of his heart, and none of you could have withheld Us from doing this. (69:44-47)

The Prophet never lied or broke his promise, either prior to or during his Prophethood. A Companion remembered:

> Before his Prophethood, we made an appointment to meet somewhere. It was, however, 3 days after the appointed time when I remembered it. When I hastened to the appointed place, I found the future Prophet waiting for me. He was neither angry nor offended. His only reaction was to say: "O young man, you have given me some trouble. I have been waiting here for you for 3 days."[8]

Some of His Predictions

Ordinary people can establish their truthfulness by their detractor's inability to provide any proof to the contrary. In the case of a Prophet who has brought a universal Divine system, people expect more. They want explanations and rules for everything: theology, law, sociology, human psychology, economics, history, and so on. Moreover, a Prophet must be proven truthful in all of them.

The explanations of God's Messenger concerning theology (Divine Essence, Attributes, and Names) are such that philosophers, religious scholars, and saints cannot compete with him. Instead, they study his explanations and try to perceive the truths behind them. In addition to these, he dealt with the most subtle matters of Destiny and human free will so ably and convincingly that if his knowledge is ignored, we cannot obtain a true understanding of such matters.

What he said about past nations and previous Prophets has been confirmed by historical research and followers of previous Scriptures. Although unlettered, never enjoying the benefit of being able to read or being taught by another person, he established the most rational, practical, and just system known to history. Islamic civilization, which based itself on this system, enabled a large portion of humanity to experience true happiness for centuries. Indeed, the universal system of life revealed to him continues to offer a unique alternative for our future in general. The happy world of the future will be built upon its principles.

Out of hundreds of his predictions, the vast majority of which already have come true, I would like to present a selection to show his truthfulness in this matter.

'Umar reports that one day the Prophet ascended the pulpit after the dawn prayer and spoke about almost everything from the creation of the world to the Last Day. He mentioned certain past events and what will befall humanity until that Day. These predictions demonstrate that his teacher was God, the All-Knowing, and that he related only what was revealed to him. Before giving specific examples, we must clarify a few points concerning knowledge of the Unseen.

Knowledge of the Unseen

The concept of the Unseen pertains to what is suprasensory and metaphysical, or even metacosmic. In this sense, the past, the future, and everything beyond ordinary human senses are included in the concept of the Unseen, provided that certain concrete indications have not been manifested. In a narrower sense, the Unseen pertains only to the future. It is this second sense that is used in the following section, as I intend to concentrate on his predictions.

The knowledge of the Unseen is, first of all, with God. As we read in the Qur'an:

> With Him are the keys of the Unseen, none knows them but
> He. He knows whatever is in the ground and the sea. Not a
> leaf falls but He knows it. There is not a grain in the darkness
> of the ground nor anything wet, fresh, or dry but is in a
> Manifest Record. (6:59)

Say, [O Muhammad]: "I do not tell you that with me are the treasures of God, nor that I know the Unseen, nor do I tell you that I am an angel. I but follow what is revealed to me." Say: "Are the blind and the one who sees equal? Will you not then reflect?" (6:50)

Say: "I have no power over any benefit or harm to myself except as God wills. If I had the knowledge of the Unseen, I should increase good for myself and no evil should have touched me. I am only a warner and a bringer of glad tidings unto people who believe." (7:188)

Does this mean that no one can obtain even a small part of this knowledge? To answer this question, we should consider the following points:

- Whatever we have (e.g., health, knowledge, and power) essentially belongs to God and is, accordingly, from God. We have no power except that which He has given us, and no knowledge except that which He has taught us or enabled us to learn. We see and hear because He makes this possible. This being so, the verses do not exclude people absolutely from acquiring some of this knowledge, but only if He allows this.

- The concept of the Unseen relates to the future and the past. The Qur'an presents the stories of past nations as stories of the Unseen. Historical research informs us of the past.

- Many people can, by God's Will, glimpse part of the future in dreams or other ways that are beyond the scope of this book.

- The Qur'an, like the universe and humanity, is an organic entity, for each verse is interrelated with the others. Thus the first and foremost interpreter of the Qur'an is the Qur'an itself. This means that a complete and true understanding of a verse depends on understanding all other relevant verses. It is a creedal principle and explicitly declared that knowledge of the Unseen, like power, seeing, and hearing, belongs to God. However, He reveals some of this knowledge to a Messenger whom He has chosen:

[God alone is] the knower of the Unseen and He does not disclose His Unseen to anyone, except a Messenger whom He has chosen. (72:26-27)

God revealed many secrets to His Messenger, who then related to his people those that they needed to know. The number his predictions reported in authentic books of Tradition exceed 300, and fall into three categories: his own time, events after his death, and miraculous explanations that can be understood only in conjunction with scientific developments.

Predictions: His Own Time

- As reported by authentic books of Tradition, including Sahih al-Bukhari, one day God's Messenger mounted the pulpit, preached, and then told the congregation to ask him whatever they wished to. They did so. Finally, a young man named 'Abd Allah stood up and asked who his father was. Since illicit intercourse was widespread in pre-Islamic times, this young man was attributed to someone other than Hudafa al-Sahmi, whom he called father. God's Messenger told him his father was Hudafa al-Sahmi. Freed from groundless accusations, 'Abd Allah was relieved and thereafter was called 'Abd Allah ibn Hudafa al-Sahmi.

    People continued to ask questions until, eventually, 'Umar, noticing the anger of God's Messenger,[9] stood up and said: "We are pleased with God as our Lord, with Islam as our religion, and with Muhammad as our Messenger." This eased the Prophet and he came down from the pulpit.[10] This event took place before all the Companions, and no one was reported to contradict what he said.

- 'Umar reports in a narration recorded in Sahih al-Muslim: Before the Battle of Badr started, God's Messenger walked around the battlefield and pointed to some locations, saying: "Abu Jahl will be killed here, 'Utba here, Shayba here,

Walid here, and so on." By God, after the battle we found their corpses in those exact places.[11]

- Ahmad ibn Hanbal reports: One day, God's Messenger was sitting in the mosque with his Companions. He told them: "In a few minutes, a man with a shining face will come. He is one of the best people of Yemen, and has on his forehead an angel's handprint." After a short while the man came and, kneeling before God's Messenger proclaimed his conversion. He was Jarir ibn 'Abd Allah al-Bajali.[12]

- In his Dala'il al-Nubuwwah, Bayhaqi narrates: Abu Sufyan accepted Islam during the conquest of Makka, but belief had not yet been established firmly in his heart. While God's Messenger was circumambulating the Ka'ba, it occurred to him: "I wonder what would happen if I formed a new army to confront this man once more." No sooner had he thought this than God's Messenger approached him and said: "If you do, God will defeat you again."[13] This strengthened Abu Sufyan's belief, and he begged God's forgiveness. He finally understood that the Messenger was taught by God, the All-Knowing.

- As related in the reliable books of Tradition, 'Umayr ibn Wahb, known as a "diabolic man" before his conversion, conspired with Safwan ibn Umayya to assassinate God's Messenger. He went to Madina for this purpose and pretended to be a Muslim. He was taken to the mosque. However, since the Companions had no trust in him, they formed a protective circle around God's Messenger. The Messenger asked 'Umayr why he had come to Madina. All of 'Umayr's lies could not convince God's Messenger, who finally told him: "As you are not telling the truth, I will tell it. You conspired with Safwan to kill me in return for 100 camels." Shocked by the truth of this answer, 'Umayr held the Prophet's hands tightly in awe and amazement and became a Muslim. He became so deeply committed to Islam that he came to be called "a most ascetic devotee of Islam."[14]

Predictions: The Near Future

The reliable books of Tradition contain approximately 300 such predictions, among them the following:

- Bukhari and Muslim report from Usama that: One day I was with God's Messenger on the roof of a tall building in Madina. Looking around, he said: "I see seditious events and internal conflicts pouring down like raindrops among your houses."[15]

  'Umar was very afraid that disorder and sedition might appear in the Muslim community. One day during his caliphate, he asked Hudhayfa ibn al-Yaman, to whom God's Messenger had disclosed many secret things, including future events and who the Hypocrites were, about them. Hudhayfa responded: "They have nothing to do with you, 'Umar. There is a gate between you and them." 'Umar asked if the gate would be opened or broken down. When Hudhayfa replied it would be broken down, a shocked 'Umar exclaimed: "Then this gate will never be closed again!" 'Umar was the gate between the Muslim community and sedition.[16] After he was stabbed by a treacherous Persian slave, Muslim unity received a fatal blow. Since that day, the Muslim world has suffered discord and sedition.

- Bukhari and Abu Dawud quote Habbab ibn Arat, who said: "During the days of trouble and torture in Makka, I went to God's Messenger while he was sitting in the shade of the Ka'ba. I was still a slave then, and the Makkans tortured me severely. Unable to endure it any longer, I asked him to pray to God for help and salvation. But he faced me and said:

  > By God, previous communities endured much more than this. Some people were forced to lie in ditches and then sawed in half. This did not make them forsake their faith. They were skinned alive, but never became weak against the enemy. God will perfect this religion, but you are impatient. A day will come when a woman

will travel alone by herself from San'a to Hadramawt fearing nothing but wild beasts. However, you show impatience.

Habbab concluded: "By God, what God's Messenger predicted that day has all come true. I have personally witnessed it all."[17]

- During his last illness, God's Messenger called his daughter Fatima to his bedside. He whispered something to her, and she burst into tears. He called her again and whispered something else to her. This time she displayed great joy. 'A'isha saw this and asked Fatima about it. At first, Fatima said: "This is a secret belonging to God's Messenger." But after the Prophet's death, Fatima told her: "The first time he said he would die of that illness, which made me weep bitterly. Then he told that I would be his first family member to join him after his death, and this made me very happy."[18] The Prophet died of that illness, and Fatima joined him in death 6 months later.[19]

- As related in most of the six authentic books of Tradition, one day on the pulpit God's Messenger took his grandson Hasan into his arms and declared: "This son of mine is a noble one. It is hoped that God will reconcile through him two large hosts of Muslims."[20] Hasan was indeed a noble person. About 35 years after this prediction, he renounced the caliphate in favor of Mu'awiya, thus demonstrating the truthfulness of his noble grandfather.

- One day the Messenger put his hand on 'Abd Allah ibn Busr's head and said: "This boy will live 100 years, and those warts on his face will disappear."[21] 'Abd Allah lived for 100 years and died without warts on his face.

- As recorded in almost all books of Tradition and the Prophet's biography, the Muslims dug a ditch around Madina during the Battle of Trench. The Prophet shared in this work and, to reinforce his Companions morale, occasionally prayed for them: "O God, the true life is the life of the Hereafter, so forgive the Helpers and the

Emigrants."[22] His Companions would reply enthusiastically: "O God, had it not been for Your help and grace, we could not have found the Straight Path, paid alms, or prayed. And so, send down upon us serenity, and make our steps firm if we encounter the enemy!"[23]

While digging, a huge rock was uncovered. The Companions could not remove it, and so called God's Messenger. He came with a lever and pickaxe, and set out to smash it. Each blow produced a spark and, through God's inspiration, he predicted a future conquest, saying: "I have been given the keys of Byzantium; I have been given the keys of Persia; I have been given the keys of Yemen,"[24] and so on. Within 20 years, Persia and many parts of Byzantium belonged to the Muslims, thanks to the brilliant military leadership of Khalid ibn Walid and Sa'd ibn Abi Waqqas. Byzantium was conquered later by the Ottoman ruler Sultan Mehmed the Conqueror.

• 'Adiy ibn Khatam reports: One day people complained, in the presence of God's Messenger, about poverty, deprivation, and unsafe desert roads. He replied: "A day will come when a woman will travel alone on her camel from Hira to the Ka'ba with fear of nothing but God alone. A day will come and the treasures of Chosroes (the Persian ruler) will be distributed among you. A day will come when people will travel around to find someone to pay the prescribed alms to, but in vain." When he predicted this, members of the Tayy tribe used to attack travelers, and the Persian Empire was enjoying its most splendid days. But I personally witnessed the first two predictions come true, and I am expecting the third also will prove to be true.[25]

'Adiy did not live long enough to see the third prediction come true. However, soon after his death, during the caliphate of 'Umar ibn 'Abd al-'Aziz, people became so rich that no one could be found to give the prescribed alms to in the vast lands of the Muslim state. Living standards were very high, and there was no discernible imbalance in the distribution of wealth.

- While the Prophet's Mosque was being built in Madina, everybody, including God's Messenger, worked to complete it as quickly as possible. Some cast sun-dried bricks, and others carried them to construction site. Meanwhile, 'Ammar ibn Yasir, one of the first Muslims, approached God's Messenger and, probably to attract his love and affection, said: "O God's Messenger, they loaded on me two sun-dried bricks." God's Messenger smiled and, while rubbing the dust off 'Ammar's face, said he would be martyred: "What a pity (Glad tidings for you, according to another version), O 'Ammar, a rebellious group will kill you."[26] 'Ammar was martyred about 40 years later at the Battle of Siffin by Mu'awiya's followers.

- God's Messenger was distributing the spoils of a war when a man with Mongol features told him to be just in distribution. To this impertinence, God's Messenger asked: "Who else will show justice if I am not just? If I do not show justice, then I have been lost and brought to naught." According to another version, he said: "If I am not just, then, (by following me) you (the people) have been lost and brought to naught."[27]

'Umar was furious with this man, and demanded that God's Messenger allow him to "cut off this hypocrite's head." But the Messenger only said: "In the future, a group of people with chubby faces, slanting eyes, and flat noses [like this man] will appear. They will recite so much of the Qur'an that, when compared to their recitation, yours will seem small to you. Nevertheless, what they recite will not have the slightest effect on them. They will leave the religion like an arrow shot from a bow. There will, moreover, be a large fatty growth on the arm of one of them."[28]

Years passed, and a group called the Kharijites appeared. Bearing these very characteristics, and basing themselves on a mistaken interpretation of the Qur'an, they rebelled. Caliph 'Ali met and defeated them at Nahrawan. A corpse with a fatty growth on its arm was taken to 'Ali. This event, besides proving the truthfulness and Messengership of Prophet Muhammad, fulfilled another prediction: "O 'Ali, I have fought for the descent of the Qur'an; you will fight against its misinterpretation."[29]

- One day God's Messenger slept in the house of Umm Haram, his foster aunt. He woke up smiling. Umm Haram asked why he was happy, and he answered: "I dreamed that like kings seated on thrones, a group of Muslims boarded ships and went off to war." Umm Haram asked him to pray that she would be included in this group. He did so, and said: "You will be among them."[30] Years passed. During Mu'awiya's caliphate, Muslims waged war upon Cyprus. Umm Haram was in the army accompanying her husband, 'Ubada ibn Samit. She died there, and her tomb has been visited ever since.

Predictions: The Distant Future

- Once God's Messenger declared: "When the end of time [the Last Day] approaches, the children of Kantura will appear. They will be slant-eyed, chubby-faced, and flat-nosed."[31] This description fits the Mongols, and some of the Kharijites, to whom it is traditionally thought to refer. God's Messenger predicted both the Mongol invasion and the destruction of the Muslim world, and the Western massacre of Andalusia's Muslims—two of the most tragic calamities to afflict the Muslim nation. Always concerned with his people's fate, he used such predictions to warn Muslims that deviating from the Straight Path will bring calamity. God uses wrongdoers and oppressors to chasten and correct His believing servants, and afterward turns against the oppressors and eradicates them.

- God's Messenger foresaw the conquest of Constantinople (present-day Istanbul): "Certainly, Constantinople will be conquered. How good is the commander who will conquer it, and how good his army!"[32] Hoping to be the object of the Prophet's praise, Muslim rulers and commanders from the time of Mu'awiya sought to conquer this city. During one campaign, Abu Ayyub al-Ansari, the noble Companion, was martyred and buried near the city walls.

Constantinople finally was conquered by the Ottoman ruler Mehmed the Conqueror. Besides this great commander and statesman, his two school friends Hasan of Ulubat and Kadı Hızır Çelebi, as well as his tutor Ak Shamsaddin, were also symbols of this conquest. One was in the army, and the others were in the departments of religious and scientific education. The prayer and praise of God's Messenger encompasses all of them.

- God's Messenger predicted and explained the principle reasons for the Ottoman State's destruction and condition of the Muslim world after the First World War: "Nations will call each other, as people make invitations to a meal, to make a concerted attack on you." Someone asked: "Will this happen because there are only a few of us?" God's Messenger answered: "No, your numbers will be vast, but you will be as powerless as wood-chips or straw carried in a flood. God will remove your enemies' fear of you and implant within you a fear of death and a love of the world."[33]

The prediction, which became reality during the First World War, also describes our current situation. We are divided into many factions, while our enemies seek closer unity based on mutual interests. In the past, they were afraid of us because we saw the grave as a bridal chamber, something to look forward to. But now, we are so attached to this world that we do all we can to escape death, even though we know this is impossible. We also have been the object of many betrayals. 'Uthman and 'Ali were victims of treachery, and the magnificent Ottoman

State was made sacrificial food for the carnivorous peoples of the world. It experienced uncountable betrayals by nations who had been so prosperous and peaceful under Ottoman rule.

- God's Messenger predicted the rise of communism in a hadith reported by Ibn 'Umar. Facing toward the east, he said: "Take care! Anarchy and subversion will appear from that direction, from where the Age of Satan will begin."[34] The Age of Satan, built upon atheism and hedonism, is the opposite of the Age of the Prophet, based on belief in and devotion to God. Communism, the unlawful outcome of capitalism, champions hostility to religion, piety, and all moral and traditional values. In another hadith, God's Messenger foretold that communism would arise as "a red wind."

- God's Messenger once declared: "The Euphrates will probably go dry, uncovering a treasure (a mountain, in another version) of gold beneath it. Whoever of you witnesses it, should refrain from taking any of it."[35] This hadith alludes to the great war expected to take place along the Euphrates. Although this river has seen many wars, among them the Iran–Iraq war, this hadith points to a much greater spasm of violence in the future. While we can take the hadith literally, we also can take it figuratively. For example, oil is known as "black gold." Or, maybe the water itself will become as valuable as gold and cause regional or even international wars. Maybe the income obtained from the dams on this river will attract international attention and cause great wars. In whichever case, God's Messenger warned that the Euphrates region is like dynamite at the heart of the Muslim world.

- God's Messenger averred that Christianity would be purified of its borrowed, pagan elements and join Islam, thus strengthening the Divine religion.[36] This will be a universal turning point in human history, and the believers, at a time when they are gripped by their enemies, will defeat and destroy the global representatives of unbelief.

- God's Messenger predicted that agricultural reform and developments in science and technology would enable farmers to produce a pomegranate that, on an individual bases, will be enough for twenty people, and that its rind will provide shade for people. He also prophesied that wheat produced in area the size of a house balcony will be enough to feed a family for a year.[37] With the advent of biotechnology and genetic manipulation, such wonders are probably not too far in the future.

- In another Tradition, God's Messenger describes the end of time: "Prior to Doomsday, people will discriminate when greeting others (preferring to greet only some), trade will be given so much currency and preference that a wife will help her husband in it, parents and relatives will no longer be visited, false evidence and false testimony will replace the truth, and writing will gain prominence."[38]

  All of this has come true. Today, trade is the most preferred way of making a livelihood, and women are exploited to advertise various products and services, and to attract customers. The rights of parents and relatives are no longer considered and, once they become old and most need attention and affection, they are often placed in old people's homes or nursing homes. The power of the modern press is unquestionable, and lying is now so widespread that few people can resist it. This is true at all levels, from business lies to false testimony in law suits.

- In a *hadith qudsi*, the Prophet relates from God: "At the end of time I will cause knowledge to be obtained by everyone, men and women, slave and free, and old and young."[39] Education is now open to almost everyone through schools, universities, and the media. Many intellectuals and scientists say that the next age will be the Age of Information.

- In another authentic Tradition, God's Messenger declares: "The Last Day will not come until the Qur'an is a means of shame and Islam is left without a powerful group to support it."[40] We have seen the truth of this prediction. For nearly a century, Muslims have been persecuted even in their own lands. While atheists and unbelievers have openly declared their unbelief everywhere, Islam has been the target of verbal, written, and even physical assault. Muslims have felt compelled to conceal their belief, and have become too ashamed to openly declare their belief.

- The Messenger predicted the developments in telecommunication and transportation. The above *hadith* continues: "The Hour will not come until the distances of time and space diminish." I have translated the word *taqarub* as "diminish."[41] It means "to approach each other" and implies that before the Day of Judgment, things which previously took a long time will be possible in a very short time.

    This *hadith*, in addition to predicting modern methods of transportation and telecommunication, implies that time is relative. The Earth is gradually taking an elliptical shape. This may cause some changes in the division and calculation of time. As for the relativity of time alluded to in the *hadith*, we know that time differs in some aspects (e.g., division, length, calculation, and the speed of its passage in or around every sphere or planet). If humanity manages to leave this solar system, the present conception of time will completely change. Thus, in a single word, God's Messenger makes several predictions, some of which have already come true, and also alludes to several scientific facts.

- God's Messenger also predicted: "A time will come upon people when almost everyone will eat from usury, to the extent that those who refrain from it will be exposed to its 'dust'."[42] God's Messenger points to two important facts:
    - A time will come when all formal transactions will involve interest. No one will be able to avoid it completely. However, those who do not enter into interest-based transactions will not be held accountable

for the interest they eat unintentionally, as long as they do their best to refrain from usury.

– God's Messenger may have meant by being exposed to its dust that a capitalist class would emerge and increase its wealth through interest. This would gradually lead the working class into deeper and deeper poverty, which would result in direct and bitter class warfare.

All these predictions have come true. How tragic it is that Muslim countries are in such a despised, degenerate state because, among other things, they are drowning in a swamp of interest despite the Qur'anic warning that anyone involved in interest-based transactions is *at war with God and His Messenger* (2:279). If only Muslims had been conscious of such Qur'anic statements, they would not be in such a miserable position.

• In the following authentic Tradition, God's Messenger points to another aspect of the present sad state of the Muslim world: "A time will come when believers conceal themselves as hypocrites do among you today."[43] At the time of the Prophet, hypocrites used to conceal themselves by going through the outward motions of the religious rituals. According to this *hadith*, Muslims will try to conceal themselves, even performing their religious obligations in secret. The same state was described in another *hadith*: "Sedition and deviation will occur. A Muslim will be disgraced for performing the prescribed prayers, just as a woman is disgraced today because of fornication."

• In another narration, God's Messenger predicted that oil would be discovered in Taleqan (Iran): "Good tidings to Taleqan, for God's treasuries are there, but not of gold and silver."[44] In the past, treasury meant gold and silver. For this reason, God's Messenger emphasized that Taleqan's treasuries would be something else. What comes to mind first today when told of such a treasury is oil. However, he might have implied resources of uranium or diamonds. If this is the case, the prediction has come true, for such resources have been discovered in and around Taleqan.

• "You will walk in the footsteps of those who preceded you so closely that if, for example, they put their heads in a lizard's hole, you would do the same." The Companions asked him if *those who preceded* you meant the Jews and Christians, and he answered: "Who else could it be?"[45] Muslims have been suffering from an identity crisis for two centuries. They are blind imitators of the West and have been caught up in vices that destroyed all previous civilizations.

Predictions: Scientific Developments

God's Messenger also made many predictions concerning various scientific developments, some of which have already come true. Out of the many examples, I will cite only a few to illustrate his accuracy in this regard.

• As related by Bukhari, God's Messenger declared: "God did not send down an illness for which He did not send a cure."[46] This *hadith*, in addition to declaring that every illness is curable, is the most comprehensive statement encouraging medical research. In another Tradition, the Messenger states that "there is a cure for every illness."[47]

Another version tells us: "Do not neglect to treat your diseases, for God does not send a disease for which He does not also send a cure. The only exception is old age."[48] Humanity may discover a cure for every illness, but will never be able to stop our journey from the world of spirits to the material world and then on to either Paradise or Hell through the stations of embryo, infancy, childhood, youth, old age, the grave, and the Resurrection. The Prophet encourages us to learn how to cure illnesses, but also warns us not to neglect preparing for the next world.

God encourages us to pursue scientific knowledge by relating the miracles of earlier Prophets. This brings such matters to the scientists' attention and thereby shows the limits to their aspirations. By allowing Jesus the inimitable miracle of bringing the dead back to life, He points out that we can cure everything but death.

The story of Moses' staff shows us that we can use inanimate things for various purposes, such as obtaining water from deep underground by using such simple things as a staff like a centrifuge. However, we will never cause a rock to bring forth abundant water by striking it with a staff, or to change a staff into a snake, both of which Moses did.

The Qur'an is Prophet Muhammad's greatest miracle, and marks the farthest limit in literary style and eloquence that humanity can attain. It also implies that writing and eloquence will have the greatest importance toward the end of time. The Prophets set examples and showed us the limits to which we may go in material as well as spiritual progress.

- The Messenger advised quarantine to contain outbreaks of contagious diseases: "If you hear that there is pestilence in a place, don't enter it; if pestilence breaks out where you are, don't leave it to escape the pestilence."[49] According to Ahmad ibn Hanbal, he also declared: "Keep away from the leper as you do from a lion."[50] In this *hadith*, God's Messenger advises us to protect ourselves against leprosy. Quarantine is again suggested here as a way to prevent the spread of leprosy.

- Imam Muslim narrates in his *Sahih* that God's Messenger declared: "If a dog licks your bowl, clean it seven times, first time with soil, and the other six with water."[51] This *hadith* contains the following medical principles related to bacteria:
  - Dogs may carry microbes of certain diseases that can be passed to people. This fact was discovered recently by scientists.
  - A dog's saliva and excrement may contain substances that can damage a person's health.

–   At the time of the Prophet, disinfection and steriliza-
    tion were unknown. Nevertheless, God's Messenger
    recommends that a bowl licked by a dog be cleaned
    with soil. Today we know that soil is a good antisep-
    tic that contains such substances as tetracycline.

In another *hadith* concerning dogs, God's Messenger
expresses a fundamental principle of ecology: "If dogs
were not a separate community, I would order their
killing."[52] This implies that every species is an indispensable element of ecological balance.

•   As recorded by *Sahih al-Tirmidhi* and *Sunan Abu Dawud*,
    God's Messenger declares: "The blessings of food lie in
    washing hands before and after eating."[53] This *hadith*
    emphasizes the importance of cleanliness. As we use our
    hands, germs accumulate and can be removed only by
    washing them. In another *hadith*, he advises us to wash
    our hands after we wake up since "You do not know where
    your hands have moved while you sleep."[54] At that time,
    no one knew about microbes.

•   As recorded in all six of the most authentic books of
    Tradition from as many as 40 Companions, God's
    Messenger established the principle of dental care: "If it
    didn't burden upon community excessively, I would com-
    mand them to clean their teeth with *miswak* [a tooth
    stick] before each of the five daily prayers."[55] Dental
    hygiene is of great significance not just for our teeth,
    but for our entire body. God's Messenger followed this
    practice, and so we should do likewise.

•   In relation to health and digestion, God's Messenger
    recommended: "In eating, apportion a third of your
    stomach to food, another third to water, and leave the
    last third empty. The bowl most distasteful to God is a
    full stomach."[56] In another similar *hadith*, he said: "What
    I fear concerning my community is a large belly, over-
    sleep, idleness, and the lack of certainty."[57]

    All of the points mentioned here are either antecedent
to or a result of the other. Those who are idle and heed-

less, who ignore self-control and self-criticism, are apt to become fat. This causes them to eat more food. A full stomach encourages more sleep, and the person begins to sleep for longer periods of time. Such people, now addicted to overeating and excessive sleeping, will never be able to acquire certainty and deep conviction in Islam. This is the case with most people today.

- Another Tradition concerning health is as follows: "Treat your eyes with kohl, for it nourishes the eyes and eyelashes."[58] Many medical authorities state that kohl does exactly that. Another substance, recommended by the Prophet and useful for health as an antibiotic and for its dermatological effect, is henna.[59] Henna is better and more effective as an antiseptic and sterilization agent than such substances as a tincture of iodine.

- Bukhari relates from Abu Hurayra that once God's Messenger said: "A black cumin seed contains a cure for every illness but death."[60] This *hadith* contains many truths related to therapy. A patient needs, particularly during convalescence, foods that are rich in proteins, calories, and vitamins, and that are easily digestible. Scientific investigations have recently shown that all these properties are found in black cumin.

- Bukhari relates from God's Messenger: "When a fly falls into your bowl, dip it completely in the food before taking it out. There is disease in one of the fly's wings, and cure in the other."[61] No one at that time knew that flies carry microbes. Moreover, when a fly drops into a bowl, it tries to hold one of its wings off the food so that it can take off again. Thus, it leaves bacteria on the food. But when it is submerged with a slight touch, the tiny bag on the other wing bursts and scatters the anti-bacteria to kill the germs already left. This is a very recent medical discovery.

- 'A'isha related that once Fatima bint Abu Khubash asked God's Messenger: "O God's Messenger, my blood does not stop. Should I abandon the prescribed prayers?" He replied: "No, you must not, for it is not menstrual blood but rather a hemorrhage."[62] Except by Prophethood, how could he have distinguished between a normal hemorrhage and menstrual blood?

- Tariq ibn Suwayd narrates: I used to suffer from an illness, and took alcohol as a remedy. When alcohol was banned, I asked God's Messenger whether I could continue using this remedy. He told me: "No, for it is not a remedy; rather, it is the disease itself."[63] Scientists now agree that even a single drop of alcohol is harmful to one's physical and spiritual health.

- God's Messenger proclaimed that ten things are intrinsically necessary for men and therefore ordered by Prophets. Circumcision is one of them.[64] Today, scientists admit that a man's foreskin is exposed and susceptible to infections, even cancer. Therefore, millions of people are circumcised in Europe and America.

We are convinced that the West will one day acknowledge the truth of Islam, and that the prediction made at the beginning of the twentieth century by Said Nursi will come true: "The Ottoman State is pregnant with a Western one, as the West is with an Islamic one. Both will give birth to what they are pregnant with."[65]

We have so far explained the truthfulness of Prophets, emphasizing the truthfulness of Prophet Muhammad. As mentioned, all predictions made by a Prophet eventually come true, for they never lie. They came to guide us to the Straight Path and to lead us to Paradise. Had they lied even once, they would have guided no one to the truth. However, their truthfulness, especially that of Prophet Muhammad, will be as clear as the sun in the Hereafter, where people will see everything as it is. There, all the tidings they gave about the next life, the Resurrection, the Place of Gathering, the Final Reckoning, the Bridge, Paradise, and Hell will be realized.

TRUSTWORTHINESS

The second attribute of Prophethood is *amana*, an Arabic word meaning *trustworthiness* and derived from the same root as *mu'min* (believer). Being a believer implies being a trustworthy person. All Prophets were the best believers and therefore perfect exemplars of trustworthiness. To stress this principle, God summarizes the stories of five Prophets using the same words:

> The people of Noah denied the Messengers. When their brother Noah asked them: "Will you not fear God and avoid evil? I am a trustworthy Messenger to you." (26:105-7)

Replace the name Noah with those of Hud, Lut, Shu'ayb, and Salih, and you have a summarized version of these five Prophets' trustworthiness.

Mu'min is also a Divine Name, for God is the ultimate *Mu'min*, the source of security and reliability. We put our trust in, confide in, and rely upon Him. He distinguished the Prophets by their trustworthiness, and our connection to Him through the Prophets is based entirely on their trustworthiness and reliability.

Trustworthiness is also an essential quality of Archangel Gabriel. The Qur'an describes Gabriel as *one obeyed and trustworthy* (81:21). We received the Qur'an through two trustworthy Messengers: Gabriel and Prophet Muhammad. The former conveyed it; the latter related it to us.

The Trustworthiness of God's Messenger

Prophet Muhammad was completely trustworthy toward all of God's creatures. He was loyal and never cheated anyone.

God chose the Messenger for his trustworthiness so that he would devote himself totally to delivering the Message truthfully. He was so concerned about his duty that he would repeat the verses while Gabriel was reciting them to him. God finally revealed:

> Move not your tongue concerning (the Qur'an) to make haste therewith. It is for Us to collect it, to establish it in your heart and enable you to recite it. So, when We have recited it to you, follow its recital. Then it is also for Us to make it clear to you. (75:16-19)

As the Qur'an was given to him as a trust, he conveyed it to people in the best way possible. He dedicated his life to this sacred cause, constantly aware of his responsibility. In the last year of his life, when he was delivering the Farewell Pilgrimage's sermon at Mount 'Arafat, he reiterated the Commandments of God once more. At the end of each sentence, he told the people: "In the near future, they will ask you about me." He then would ask them if he had conveyed the Message to them, to which they responded, each time, with great enthusiasm: "Yes, you have conveyed it!" He then would call upon God to witness their words.[66]

Specific Events

God's Messenger never thought of concealing even a word of the Qur'an. In fact, we read in the Qur'an several mild Divine admonitions for a few actions of his. If he wrote it, as some mistakenly claim, why would he have included such verses?

The Prophet was raised in a primitive society characterized by customs that contradicted reason as well as sociological and scientific facts. For example, as adopted children enjoyed the same legal status as natural children, a man could not legally marry his adopted son's widow or ex-wife. This practice was abolished, for adoption does not create a relationship comparable to that with one's biological parents. God solved this problem, as always, through the Messenger's life in order to separate a legal fiction from a natural reality, and to establish a new law and custom.

Zayd, an emancipated black slave and servant of God's Messenger, was also his adopted son. At the Prophet's request, Zayd married Zaynab bint Jahsh. Nevertheless, it soon became clear that the marriage would not last long. Admitting that he was spiritually and intellectually inferior to his wife, Zayd thought it would be better for him to divorce her. In the end, the Qur'an commanded Muhammad to marry her: *We gave her in marriage to you* (33:37).

Of course, doing so would violate a strong social taboo. As such, and because the Hypocrites would use this to defame him, he delayed announcing the Divine decree. God admonished him as follows:

Then you said to him on whom God bestowed grace and unto whom you had shown favor: "Keep your wife to yourself and fear God." But you hid in your heart that which God was about to make manifest because you feared the people [would slander you], whereas God had a better right that you should fear him. (33:37)

'A'isha later commented: "If God's Messenger could have concealed any Revelation, he would have concealed that verse."[67] If Muhammad had not been trustworthy, he would have done just that. However, such an act is contrary to his character and mission, and would mean that he had not delivered the Message. Furthermore, God prohibits him from doing this:

O Messenger, deliver what has been sent down to you from your Lord; for if you do not, you will not have fulfilled your task of His Messengership. God will protect you from men. God does not guide the unbelievers. (5:67)

So, God's Messenger passed on whatever was revealed to Him.

His Relations With Others

God's Messenger was trustworthy and encouraged others to follow his example. Once during the last ten days of Ramadan, his wife Safiyya visited him while he was keeping vigil in the mosque. As he was escorting her home, two Companions happened to pass by. The Messenger stopped them and, unveiling his wife's face, said: "This is my wife Safiyya." They said: "God forbid any evil thought about you, O Messenger of God." The Messenger was warning them against having evil thoughts about him, for that could cause them to lose their faith and enter Hell. He gave them and us a lesson, saying: "Satan continuously circulates within people's blood vessels."[68]

God's Messenger was an embodiment of trustworthiness. His own people, even before his Prophethood, called him al-Amin (the Trustworthy One). After his declaration, his enemies continued to entrust him with their precious goods.

He warned his people against lying, breaking their word, and breaching their trust. All of these were condemned as "signs of hypocrisy."[69] He was so meticulous in this matter that when he saw a woman call her child, saying: "Come on, I'll give you some-thing," he asked her if she was telling the truth. She replied that she would give him a date, to which God's Messenger responded: "If you were to give him nothing, you would have lied."

His concern in this matter extended even to animals. Once, annoyed at seeing a Companion trying to deceive his horse, he said: "Stop deceiving animals. Instead, be trustworthy with them."[70] Another time, while returning from a military campaign, a few Companions took some baby birds from a nest to pet them. The mother bird returned after a short while and, finding her babies gone, began to fly around in distress. When God's Messenger was informed, he was so upset that he ordered the birds to be returned immediately. Such an order was meant to show that representatives of trustworthiness should harm no living creatures.[71]

Each Companion was an embodiment of trustworthiness. By virtue of this and other laudable virtues, cities and states submitted to Islam. During 'Umar's caliphate, Abu 'Ubayda, the embodiment of justice, commanded the Muslim armies in Syria. When the Byzantine Emperor set out to recapture Hims, Abu 'Ubayda decid-ed to evacuate the city, for his forces were vastly outnumbered. He had the non-Muslim population assembled and announced: "We collected the protection tax from you because we had to defend you. Since we can't defend you against the coming Byzantine assault, we are returning the tax we collected." This was done. Pleased with the Muslim administration, Christian priests and Jewish rabbis flocked to the churches and synagogues to pray that God would cause the Muslim army to be successful.[72]

Such was the attitude of Muslim conquerors and administra-tors in the lands they ruled. Muslims stayed in Spain for eight centuries. If there were enough Christians left to acquire enough power to expel the Muslims later on, it was because of the Muslim administration's religious tolerance. Muslim rulers did not interfere with a conquered people's religion, language, or culture. If they had done so, there would have been no Christians left to recapture Spain, no Jews left to conquer Palestine, and no Christians left in the Balkans to engage in genocide. Nor would

Christians have been able to destroy peoples, cultures, and languages on an almost-global scale.

Islam emphasizes trustworthiness and security to such an extent that suspicion and gossip are forbidden:

> O you who believe! Avoid much suspicion, for suspicion in some cases is a grave sin. Do not spy on or gossip about one another. Would one of you like to eat the flesh of his dead brother? You would abhor it. Fear God, for verily God is the Acceptor of repentance, the Most Merciful. (49:12)

God's Messenger was so sensitive on this point that once when 'A'isha commented: "How long her neck is," he said: "You have gossiped about her and so ate of her flesh!"[73]

He always prayed: "O God, I seek refuge in You from hunger, for how bad a companion it is! I also seek refuge in You from betrayal, for what an evil confidant it is!"[74] He also had harsh words for those who betray and are disloyal: "When God gathers together on the Day of Judgment all the people preceding and to come, a banner will be raised on behalf of every disloyal person. It will be announced: 'This is because of the disloyalty of so and so!'"[75]

The heart of God's Messenger was closed to all evil, but open to all good. He lived in a climate of security, faithfulness, and trustworthiness. He never cheated, lied, betrayed people, just as he never gossiped about, slandered, or harbored evil suspicion about someone. In return, people relied on him and confided in him. His enemies slandered him, but no one ever accused him of lying and disloyalty. Those who turned their backs on him were deceived and dragged into wrong ways.

God's Messenger was totally reliable. His trustworthiness had two aspects: his relationship with people, and his relationship with God. The former manifested itself as complete reliability; the latter as perfect reliance on God. When combined, these two aspects ensure a peaceful atmosphere of steadfastness and security.

The Qur'an gives several examples concerning the Prophets' confidence in, and perfect reliance on, God. To cite only a few:

And recite to them the news of Noah, when he said to his people: "O my people! If my stay (with you) and my reminding (you) of the signs of God is unbearable to you, then I put my trust in God. So come together with your partners and come to an agreement on your plan! Then let not your affair be a worry to you. Pass your sentence on me, and give me no respite." (10:71)

[Hud said to his people:] "I call God to witness and bear you witness that I am free from all that you ascribe as partners in worship to God, beside Him. So, plot against me, all of you, and give me no respite. I put my trust in God, my Lord and your Lord. There's not a moving creature but He has grasp of its forelock. Verily my Lord is on a straight path." (11:54-56)

Indeed there has been an excellent example for you in Abraham and those with him, when they said to their people: "Verily we are free from you and from whatever you worship besides God; we have rejected you, and there has arisen between us and you hostility and hatred for ever, until you believe in God alone," except Abraham's saying to his father: "Verily I ask forgiveness (from God) for you, but I have no power to do anything for you before God. Our Lord! In you (alone) we put our trust, and to You (alone) we return in repentance, and to You (alone) is our final return." (60:4)

The nature of unbelief is deviation and opposition. Unbelievers see the world in darkness and feel alone in an alien world; believers see the whole universe as a cradle of brotherhood and sisterhood, and feel connected to everything. By its nature, unbelief severs relations and, as a result, unbelievers feel enmity against everything, especially believers. They cannot bear the believers' existence, so they try their best to eradicate belief. That is why all Prophets encountered severe opposition and, with their followers, suffered pitiless acts of cruelty. But due to their complete confidence in and perfect reliance on God, *they never lost heart because of what befell them in God's Way, nor did they weaken (in will) nor were they brought low* (3:146).

The Messenger's reliance on God made him fearless. He appeared in the heartland of a desert inhabited by one of the most uncivilized peoples. Despite their harsh treatment, and the strident hostility of one of his own uncles, he challenged the whole world and, through complete trust in God, carried his mission to victory. He had only a handful of supporters, and his victory came in a very short period—an unparalleled achievement. We can understand his fearless nature, which developed out of his absolute confidence in God, through the following anecdotes.

The Quraysh were so eager to kill him that just before his emigration to Madina they selected one man from each clan. These numbered roughly 200. Led by Abu Jahl and Abu Lahab, then besieged his house. God's Messenger told his cousin 'Ali to spend the night in his bed and, throwing some dust at the hostile men while reciting: *We have put a barrier before them and behind them, and thus covered them so that they cannot see* (36:9), he departed without being seen.[76] He left Makka with his closest friend, Abu Bakr, and reached Thawr cave, which is at the top of a steep mountain. Finding him gone, the Qurayshi chiefs sent out search parties. One of these climbed the mountain up to the cave. Abu Bakr became anxious, fearing for the life of God's Messenger. However, the latter comforted him: *Do not be anxious, for God is with us* (9:40), and added: "What do you think of the two men beside whom God is the third?"[77]

As related through various channels, during the military campaigns of Ghatfan and Anmar, a courageous chieftain named Ghowras unexpectedly appeared beside God's Messenger, who was lying under a tree. Unsheathing his sword, he asked him: "Who will save you from me now?" "God," the Messenger replied, and then prayed: "O God, protect me against him as You will." At that moment, Ghowras was knocked down and his sword slipped from his hand. God's Messenger picked it up and asked him: "Now, who will save you from me?" Ghowras began to tremble and pleaded for his life: "You are a noble, forgiving man; only forgiveness is expected of you." God's Messenger forgave him, and when Ghowras returned to his tribe, he said: "I have just come from the best of humanity."[78]

Trustworthiness is a cornerstone of belief:

> God commands you to give the trust to (the charge of) those
> qualified for them, and when you judge between men, to judge
> with justice. How excellent is the teaching which He gives you!
> Truly God is All-Hearing, All-Seeing. (4:58)

According to God's Messenger, breaching a trust is a sign of the end of time: "When a trust is breached, expect the end of time." When his Companions asked how a trust would be breached, he answered: "If a job or post is assigned to the unqualified, expect the end of time."[79]

Assigning qualified people to jobs or posts is a social trust and plays a significant role in public administration and social order. Its abuse causes social disorder. There should be order at all social levels, for some are to be given responsibilities by others. God's Messenger declared: "Each of you is a shepherd [manager], and each of you is responsible for your flock. The ruler is a shepherd responsible for his subjects. A husband is a shepherd responsible for his family. A woman is a shepherd responsible for her husband's house. A servant is a shepherd responsible for managing the duties or property his master entrusted to him."[80] If everyone in a society were to carry out their responsibilities, we would be living in a "society of trustworthy ones." Until that time, we can only imagine such utopias.

Trustworthiness is so essential an aspect of belief that God's Messenger once declared: "One who is not trustworthy is not a believer,"[81] and described a believer as one whom the people trust with their blood and property.[82] Furthermore, he said:

> Promise me the following six things and I will promise you
> Paradise: When you speak, speak the truth; when you give a
> promise, carry it out; when something is entrusted to you, do
> not breach it; keep chaste and don't engage in illicit sexual relations; don't look at what is forbidden; and don't grasp what is
> forbidden.[83]

Even looking with lust at one to whom you are not married is forbidden. God says: "[Such] a glance is like a poisonous arrow from Satan's quiver. Whoever refrains out of fear of Me, I inculcate belief so firmly in their hearts that they will taste it."[84]

To live in absolute security is only possible if trustworthy people are in power. If the Muslim world observes the Divine Trust and becomes the representative of trustworthiness and security in the world, a "new world order" based on justice and balance will be possible. Otherwise, humanity will continue to chase after mirages of justice, security, and happiness.

Through his truthfulness, trustworthiness, and other laudable virtues, God's Messenger left an indelible mark on people of all ages. His every word and deed proclaimed his Messengership, that he was sent to guide people to truth, to bring them out of the darkness of ignorance and savagery, slavery and immorality, into the light of knowledge, high morality and love, compassion and true freedom.[85]

COMMUNICATION

The third attribute of Prophethood is communication of Islamic truths, otherwise known as "enjoining good and forbidding evil." We say *Islamic* truths because every Prophet came with the same Divine Religion based on submission to God, and had as his sole mission the communication of this Message.

Just as God manifests His Mercifulness through the sun's warmth and light, He manifested His Mercy and Compassion for humanity through Prophets. He chose Muhammad, whom He sent as a mercy for all worlds, to establish eternally the Message of compassion and mercy. If he had not been sent to revive and revise the Messages of previous Prophets and then spread that knowledge throughout the world, we would be wandering in a terrifying desert of unbelief, misguidance, and ignorance.

Philosophers, sociologists, and psychologists always have sought answers to such vital questions as: "Who am I?" "Where do I come from?" "What is my final destination?" "What is the purpose of life?" "What does our dying mean?" and "Is death absolute non-existence or only a door to a new, eternal life?" All of us wrestle with such questions. But only through the enlightenment of the Prophets we can find true satisfaction and peace of mind. Through them, we understand that this earthly life is just a way station on our perpetual journeying from the world of spirits to the world of eternity, a field to be planted with seeds for harvesting in the eternal world. This world is reached through the intermediate realm of the grave. With this realization, we are relieved of our anxieties, and the world is transformed into a flowery garden of recreation and a gathering place of friends.

Prophets were sent to convey this Message and to illuminate the path to happiness in this world and the next. Now we will discuss three essential points regarding how a Prophet conveys the Divine Message.

A Comprehensive Invitation to God

The Prophets dealt with people and life in a holistic manner, appealing to each person's intellect, reason, spirit, and all outer and inner senses and feelings. They never ignored or neglected any human faculties.

The position of a Prophet in relation to Divine Revelation is similar to that of a corpse in the hands of a mortician: The individual can do nothing of his own volition.[86] God directs and guides a Prophet as necessary so that he can lead his people. Without this Divine direction, he would be unable to guide anyone. If he neglected their intellects, the end result would be a community of poor, docile mystics. If he neglected their hearts or spirits, a crude rationalism devoid of any spiritual dimension would be produced. As each individual is comprised of intellect, spirit, and body, each must be assigned its due part of the Message.

Human beings are active. Therefore, they should be led to those activities that form the real purpose of their lives, as determined by God and communicated by the Prophet. God did not create people only to have them to become passive recluses, activists without reason and spirit, or rationalists without spiritual reflection and activism.

Only when the intellect, spirit, and body are harmonized, and people are motivated to activity in the illuminated way of the Divine Message, can they become complete and attain true humanity. All Prophets sought this goal, and those who seek to follow them should strive for it: *Say (Muhammad): "This is my way: I call (people) to God with wisdom and insight, I and those who follow me"* (12:108).

A Prophet is totally dedicated to his mission, and thus is an altruist who lives for the happiness and good of others. His happiness lies in seeing people devote themselves to God in the hope of salvation, not in expecting some great reward for his services. He knows that his reward is with God alone. This indispensable fact is emphasized in the Qur'an: *O my people! I ask of you no wealth for it; my reward is from none but God* (11:29).

The Prophets were charged with conveying the Divine Message. They did their best, patiently faced many misfortunes and even torment, fulfilled their responsibilities, and then left the result to God. They knew with full certainty that only God brings about the desired result. These three fundamentals set the principles for all those who wish to call others to Islam.

The Method

Constant striving is an essential feature of delivering the Message, as well as an important element of the Prophetic method. A Prophet is, so to speak, obsessed with how to perform his duty. With that goal always uppermost, he considers all circumstances and does everything permitted. As he is not responsible for the results, he leaves them to God. He knows that he cannot cause anyone to accept the Message, for he is only sent to convey it as effectively as possible: *You [O Muhammad] guide not whom you like but God guides whom He wills. And He knows best those who receive guidance* (28:56).

Many Prophets lived with no one accepting their Message. However, they did not lose heart, weaken, or resort to such improper means as violence, terror, or deception even when faced with relentless hardship and torture. When the Prophet was severely wounded at Uhud, some Companions asked him to invoke God's curse on the enemy. Instead, he prayed for them, saying: "O God, forgive my people, because they don't know."[87] He did this while his face was covered with blood.

All Prophets reacted in the same way to the torments and false accusations they had to endure. For example:

> The leaders of Noah's people said: "We see you in clear deviation." He said: "O my people, there is no deviation in me. I am a Messenger from the Lord of the Worlds. I convey unto you the messages of my Lord, and give sincere advice to you. And I know from God that which you don't know." (7:60-62)

> The leaders of Hud's people, who were unbelievers, said: "We see you in foolishness; and think you are a liar." He replied: "O my people, there is no foolishness in me. I am a Messenger from the Lord of the Worlds. I convey unto you the messages of my Lord, and am a trustworthy adviser to you." (7:66-68)

Nothing changed during the history of Prophethood. The Prophets conveyed the Message for the sole purpose of God's pleasure. A Messenger was sent to every people:

> Whoever goes right, then he goes right only for his own soul's benefit. And whoever goes astray, then he goes astray only to his own loss. No laden soul can bear another's load. And We never punish until We have sent a Messenger. (17:15)

> And We have sent among every people a Messenger (saying): "Worship God (alone), and shun all false deities." (16:36)

After he received the first Revelation, God's Messenger returned home in a state of great excitement. While wrapped in his cloak, God ordered him:

> O you wrapped up in your cloak, arise and warn! Magnify your Lord. Cleanse your garments, and keep away from all pollution. Do not show favor, seeking worldly gain. Be patient for the sake of your Lord. (74:1-7)

He was also told:

> O you folded in garments! Keep vigil the night long, except a little; half of it, or a little less, or a little more, and recite the Qur'an in slow, measured rhythmic tones. We are about to address to you words of great gravity. (73:1-5)

Every Prophet conveyed God's Message to his people without becoming wearied or daunted. Their people's harshness did not deter them. For example:

> [Noah] said: "O my Lord! Day and night I have called my people. But my call has only added to their aversion. Every time I call on them to seek Your pardon, they thrust their fingers in their ears and cover themselves with their garments, persisting in sin and magnifying themselves in insolent pride. Further, I have called to them aloud. Further, I have spoken to them in public and in private, saying: 'Ask forgiveness from your Lord: for He is Oft-Forgiving.'" (71:5-10)

When a people rejects the Prophet sent to them and persists in unbelief and corruption, God's wrath usually falls upon them. The Qur'an contains accounts of several devastated peoples, and we see their ruins all over the world.

Consistent Effort

Communicating the Divine Message was the most essential characteristic of God's Messenger. We are worried when we are hungry or thirsty or have trouble breathing; he was worried if a day passed during which he could not convey the Divine Message to someone. He was so concerned about guidance and so pained by unbelief, that God advised him to take care of his health: *[O Muhammad] it may be that you will kill yourself following after them, with grief that they do not believe in this Message* (18:6).

God's Messenger invited all Makkans, both publicly and privately, to God's path. He called some extremely stubborn people, among them Abu Jahl, at least fifty times. He particularly sought his uncle Abu Talib's conversion, for he had raised him and protected him from the Makkan polytheists. In the eleventh year of his Prophethood, when Abu Talib was dying, God's Messenger again invited him to belief. However, the Makkan chiefs surrounded him to prevent this.

He was so grieved at Abu Talib's unbelief that he said: "I will ask forgiveness from God for you as long as I am not forbidden to."[88] A verse was revealed some time later, forbidding him to do this:

> It is not fitting for the Prophet and those who believe to ask (God) to forgive polytheists, even though they be near of kin (to them), after it has become clear to them that they are companions of the Fire. (9:113)

Abu Bakr, the Prophet's closest Companion, knew how much God's Messenger desired his uncle to be a believer. He took his aged father, who converted on the day of the Conquest of Makka, to God's Messenger and wept bitterly. When asked why he was sobbing, he explained: "O God's Messenger, I so wanted my father to be a believer and now he believes. But even more, I wanted Abu Talib to believe, for you desired it. However, God did not grant him belief. That is why I am weeping."[89]

One of the best examples of the Messenger's concern for everyone to believe was his invitation to Wahshi, who had killed his uncle Hamza at Uhud. After the conquest of Makka, God's Messenger sent for him to accept Islam. Wahshi returned the invitation with a letter, including the following verses:

> Those who invoke not with God any other deity, nor kill a soul that God has forbidden, except for just cause, nor commit illegal sexual intercourse—whoever does this shall receive the punishment. Their torment will be doubled on the Day of Judgment, and they will abide therein forever in disgrace. (25:68-69)

After the verse Wahshi added: "You invite me to accept Islam, but I have committed all the sins mentioned therein. I have lived immersed in unbelief, had illegal sexual intercourse and, in addition, killed your uncle, who was most beloved by you. Can such a person really be forgiven and become a Muslim?"

God's Messenger sent him a written reply, containing the following verse:

> God forgives not that partners should be associated with Him, but He forgives save that (anything else) to whom He wills. Whoever associates partners with God has invented a tremendous sin. (4:48)

Wahshi returned the letter with the excuse that the forgiveness promised in the verse depended on God's Will. Upon this,

God's Messenger sent him a third letter, in which the following verse was included:

> Say: "O My servants who have transgressed against their souls!
> Don't despair of the Mercy of God. God forgives all sins. He is
> the Oft-Forgiving, the Most Compassionate." (39:53)

Through this correspondence, God's Messenger opened Wahshi's heart to belief, and Wahshi could see himself included in the verse mentioned in the last letter. This correspondence enabled Wahshi to repent sincerely and become a Companion.[90] Nevertheless, Hamza's martyrdom had affected God's Messenger so deeply that he whispered to Wahshi: "Try not to present yourself to me too often. I might remember Hamza, and thus be unable to show you the proper affection."

Wahshi did his best to comply with this request. He would stand behind a pole and try to catch a glimpse of God's Messenger in the hope that he might be allowed to present himself. When God's Messenger died soon thereafter, Wahshi set out to find a way of atonement for his act. When the war of Yamama broke out against Musaylima the Liar, he hastened to the front lines with the spear he had used to kill Hamza. At the most critical point, he saw Musaylima trying to flee. Immediately, he threw his spear at the impostor and killed him. After this, Wahshi prostrated before God.[91] With tears flowing from his eyes, he was as if saying: "Will you now allow me to show myself to you, O God's Messenger?"

We cannot but wish that God's Messenger was present in spirit at Yamama and embraced Wahshi to show his pardon and full admission into his noble company.

Another fine example of God's Messenger's nobility and altruism, as well as his love for humanity and concern about people's guidance, is his acceptance of Ikrima as a Companion. Ikrima was one of the staunchest enemies of Islam and the Messenger, and an active participant in all plots to defeat him. He fled to Yemen with his wife on the day Makka was conquered, while many of his comrades chose conversion. His wife, Umm Hakam, convinced him to go to God's Messenger and ask forgiveness. Despite his previous hostility, Ikrima was welcomed by God's Messenger with the compliment: "Welcome, O emigrant rider!" After the conquest of Makka, there was no "emigration" in the true sense; God's Messenger was alluding to Ikrima's long journey from Yemen to Madina.

Ikrima was deeply affected by such nobility, and requested him to ask God's pardon for his sins. When the Messenger did so, Ikrima felt exhilarated and promised to spend for the sake of Islam double what he had spent fighting it. Ikrima fulfilled his promise at the Battle of Yarmuk, where he was wounded. Seeing his wife crying beside him in the tent, he told her: "Don't weep, for I won't die before I witness the victory." Some time later, his uncle Hisham entered and announced the Muslims' victory. Ikrima asked to be helped to stand up, and when they did so, whispered: "O God's Messenger, have I carried out the promise I gave you?" Then, he recited: *Make me die as a Muslim and join me to the righteous* (12:101), and submitted his soul to God.[92]

Throughout his life, God's Messenger grieved for the misfortunes of humanity. He ceaselessly called people to God's way. During his years in Makka, he walked the streets and visited the nearby annual fairs, always hoping to gain a few converts. Insults, derision, and torture did not deter him even once. When: *Warn your tribe of the nearest kindred* (26:214) was revealed, he invited his nearest relatives over for a meal. 'Ali later narrated the incident:

> God's Messenger invited his relatives to his house. After the meal, he addressed them: "God has commanded me to warn my nearest relatives. You are my tribe of the nearest kindred. I will not be able to do anything for you in the Hereafter unless you proclaim that there is no deity but God." At the end of his speech, he asked who would support him. At that time, I was a boy with puny legs and arms. When no one responded, I put aside the pitcher in my hand and declared: "I will, O Messenger of God!" The Messenger repeated the call three times, and each time only I answered him.[93]

The Messenger persevered, enduring relentless and in-creasingly harsh derision, degradation, beatings, and expulsion from the fairs. He was actually stoned by children in Ta'if.

Only in the twelfth year of his mission was he able to meet some Madinese at 'Aqaba (located outside of Makka). He told them of Islam, and they accepted it. The following year, 70 Madinese became Muslims at the same place. They swore allegiance to God's Messenger and promised to support him if he emigrated to Madina. He appointed Mus'ab ibn 'Umayr to teach them Islam. This was the beginning of a new phase in his life. By the time he emigrated to Madina the following year, every household had at least one Muslim.[94]

Further Remarks

An important point to note is that while communicating the Message, the Prophet set an excellent example of ardor in guiding people. The Companions did their best to imitate his technique. For example, Mus'ab ibn 'Umayr's technique was so effective and sincere that even the most stubborn Madinese, such as Sa'd ibn Mu'adh, became Muslims. Sa'd's initial reaction to Mus'ab's activity was harsh. But when the latter asked him politely: "First sit and listen. If you are not pleased with what I tell you, feel free to cut off my head with the sword in your hand," Sa'd's anger subsided. He parted from Mus'ab as a new Muslim.

God's Messenger continued to send Companions to neighboring cities. He sent Talha to Duwmat al-Jandal, and Bara' ibn A'dhib to Yemen. If a Companion was not successful, although this was rare, he sent another in his place. When Khalid and Bara' could not capture the Yemenis' hearts, God's Messenger sent 'Ali. Shortly thereafter, almost all of them became Muslims.[95]

Another important point is his conduct after the Treaty of Hudaybiya. Some of the Companions considered various conditions dishonorable (to the Muslims). However, in the ensuing atmosphere of peace, which followed years of disruption and war, many enemies of Islam reconsidered the Message. Eventually, even such leading opponents as Khalid and 'Amr ibn al-'As accepted Islam.[96]

God's Messenger welcomed Khalid with a compliment: "I was wondering how a sensible man like Khalid could remain an unbeliever. I had a strong conviction that you would one day accept Islam."[97] He comforted 'Amr ibn al-'As, who asked him to pray for God's forgiveness of him, and said: "Don't you know that those who accept Islam are cleansed of all their previous sins?"[98]

After the Treaty of Hudaybiyah, God's Messenger sent letters to the rulers of neighboring countries. He wrote to the Negus, king of Abyssinia:

> From Muhammad, God's Messenger, to the Negus Ashama, King of Abyssinia. Peace be upon you! On this occasion, I praise God, the Sovereign, the Holy One free from all defects, the Giver of security, the Watcher over His creatures. I bear witness that Jesus is a spirit from God, a word from Him, whom He bestowed upon Mary, who was chaste, pure, and a virgin. I call you to God, One with no partner.[99]

The Messenger urged the Negus to convert by first greeting him with peace. Since the Negus was a Christian, God's Messenger expressed his belief in the Prophethood of Jesus and affirmed Mary's virginity and purity, thus emphasizing the point of agreement between them.

The Negus received the letter, and, kissing it, put it to his head as a sign of respect. After reading it, he accepted Islam without hesitation and dictated the following to his secretary:

> To Muhammad, God's Messenger, from the Negus. I bear witness that you are the Messenger of God. If you command me to come to you, I will do it, but I am not in a position to make my subjects Muslim. O God's Messenger, I testify that what you say is all true.[100]

The Negus was so sincere that one day he told his confidants: "I would rather be a servant of Muhammad than a king." When he died, God's Messenger performed the funeral prayer for him in absentia.[101]

The following letter was sent to Heraclius, emperor of Byzantium:

> From Muhammad, the servant of God and His Messenger, to Heraclius, the greatest of the Byzantines. Peace be upon him

who follows the guidance. I invite you to Islam. Embrace Islam
and secure salvation, that God may give you a double reward.
If you turn away, you will be burned with, besides your own,
the sins of all those who turn away (among your people). Say:
"O people of the Book. Come to a word common between us
and you that we worship none but God, that we associate nothing in worship with Him, and that none of us shall take others
for lords beside God. If they turn away, say: 'Bear witness that
we are Muslims.'"(3:64)[102]

The Emperor was moved by the letter. He summoned Abu
Sufyan, who was then in Syria leading a Makkan trade caravan.
The following dialogue took place between them:

- What is this man's family status?
- A noble one.
- Did any of his ancestors claim Prophethood?
- No.
- Was there a king among his ancestors?
- No.
- Do the elite or the weak mostly follow him?'
- The weak.
- Has anyone apostatized after conversion to his religion?
- So far, nobody has.
- Do his followers increase or decrease?
- They increase daily.
- Have you ever heard him tell a lie?
- No.
- Has he ever broken his promise?
- Not yet, but I don't know whether he will in the future.

Although Abu Sufyan was at that time a ruthless enemy of
God's Messenger, he told the truth about him except in his last
words, which might raise doubts about the Messenger's future trustworthiness. The Emperor was inclined to acknowledge the faith, but
seeing the reaction of the priests near to him, only concluded: "In
the very near future, all these lands I am resting upon will be his."[103]
Imam Bukhari narrates that the bishop of the area accepted Islam.[104]

God's Messenger sent letters to other kings, among them
Muqawqis, the ruler of Egypt, who responded with some pres-

ents.[105] Chosroes of Persia tore up the letter, an incident predicting his empire's end, which took place during 'Umar's caliphate.[106]

When God orders Muhammad to communicate the Message, He addresses him as *Messenger* to show that he has the highest rank among the Prophets. All other Prophets are addressed by name; *Messenger* demonstrates that he is the foremost in conveying the Message. Islamic civilization, based upon the principles he conveyed, has attracted and astounded many, so much so that an interesting incident is recorded in *Mizancı Murad Tarihi* (History by Mizancı Murad): Auguste Comte, the atheist French philosopher, after visiting the remains of Islamic Spain, made a brief study of Islam. When he learned that Prophet Muhammad was unlettered, he said: "Muhammad was not a god, but he was not just a human being either."

However, quoting al-Busiri, we say: "The conclusion which we draw after all the information we have gathered about him is that he is a human being, but the best among God's creation."

Other Important Points

The following three points are important in conveying the Message of Islam: intelligence, practicing what they preach, and asking for no reward.

First, intelligence must be used to reach people on their own level. A Prophetic Tradition states: "We, the community of the Prophets, are commanded to address people according to their level of understanding." Those seeking to spread Islam should know how to approach and gain non-Muslims' attention. This point can be illustrated by many examples from the life of God's Messenger. Here are two of them:

God's Messenger won 'Umar's heart by appreciating his good sense. He told 'Umar: "I can't understand how a reasonable man like you can expect anything from inanimate objects like stones, wood, or soil." He also inspired confidence in 'Umar through his good conduct. His committed worship of God so influenced 'Umar that at last he came to God's Messenger, and was as obedient and reverent before him as a well-mannered child before a respected father.

One day, a young man (apparently Julaybib) asked God's Messenger for permission to fornicate, since he could not restrain himself. Those who were present reacted in various ways. Some scoffed at him, others pulled his robe, and still others readied themselves to hit him. But the compassionate Prophet drew him near and engaged him in conversation. He began by asking him: "Would you let someone do this with your mother?" to which the young man replied: "My mother and father be your ransom, O God's Messenger, I don't agree with that." The Prophet said: "Naturally, no one agrees that his mother should be a party in such a disgraceful act."

He then continued asking Julaybib the same question, but substituting *daughter, wife, sister, and aunt for mother*. Every time Julaybib replied that he would not agree to such an act. By the end of this conversation, Julaybib had lost all desire to fornicate. But God's Messenger concluded this "spiritual operation" with a supplication. Placing his hand on Julaybib's chest, he prayed: "O God, forgive him, purify his heart, and maintain his chastity."[107]

Julaybib became a model of chastity. Some time later he married through the intermediation of God's Messenger. Not long after that he was martyred in a battle after killing seven enemy soldiers. When his corpse was located, God's Messenger put his hand on his knee and said: "This one is of me, and I am of him."[108]

God's Messenger was so competent and successful in educating people that it is a conclusive proof of his Prophethood. The most uncivilized, crude, ill-mannered, ruthless, and ignorant people of that time were transformed into the most praiseworthy guides of humanity in a very short period.

I wonder whether even the largest, best-equipped group of professional educators, modern pedagogues, sociologists, psychologists, teachers and the like could achieve in 100 years anywhere in the modern civilized world even a hundredth of what God's Messenger accomplished in 23 years in the uncivilized desert of Arabia fourteen centuries ago. The modern efforts and techniques applied to remove so insignificant a bad habit as smoking with almost negligible success, when compared to the Prophet's lasting success in eradicating so many bad habits and views, prove that Prophet Muhammad was without parallel or equal when it came to educating people.

Second, those who want their words to influence people must practice what they preach. If they do not, how can they expect to succeed, for it is well known that actions always speak louder than words. The Qur'an is very explicit in this matter: *O you who believe, why do you say that which you do not do? Most hateful it is in the sight of God that you say what you do not do* (61:2-3).

God's Messenger was the living embodiment of his mission. He was the foremost in practicing Islam, devotion to God, and servanthood to Him. It was not uncommon for those who saw him to require no other proof to believe in his Prophethood. For example, 'Abd Allah ibn Salam, the renowned Jewish scholar of Madina, believed in him at first sight, saying: "There can be no lie in this face. One with such a face can only be a Messenger of God."[109]

'Abd Allah ibn Rawaha, a famous poet of that time, expressed this fact in the following couplet:

> *Even if he had not come with manifest signs,*
> *A single look at him suffices to inspire belief in him.*[110]

Those who believed in him were not foolish or unreasonable people. Among them were such people as the first four caliphs (Abu Bakr, 'Umar, 'Uthman, and 'Ali), all of whom administered a very great state. They were so profound in spirituality and deep in belief that 'Ali, for example, once said: "If the veil (between this material world and the immaterial world) were raised, my certainty (of the Unseen) would not increase."[111]

One reason why Prophet Muhammad is still loved deeply by hundreds of millions of people, regardless of unending hostile and negative propaganda, and why people all over the world embrace Islam daily, is that he practiced what he preached. For example, he invited people to worship God sincerely, and is himself the best example of such worship. He would spend more than half the night in prayer, crying and full of humility.

When asked why he went to such lengths that his feet would swell, and did so even though he was sinless, he would answer: "Should I not be a thankful slave of God?"[112]

'A'isha narrated that one night he asked her permission to get up and pray. He was so sensitive to the rights of his wives that he would seek their permission to perform supererogatory prayers. He prayed until daybreak and shed tears. He frequently recited the following verses:

> In the creation of the Heavens and the Earth, and in the alternation of day and night, are signs for those of understanding. Those that remember God standing, sitting, and lying down, and meditate upon the creation of the Heavens and the Earth. "Our Lord, You have not created this in vain. Glory be to You. Protect us from the punishment of the Fire. Our Lord, those whom You will admit to the Fire You have abased; for wrongdoers there are no helpers. Our Lord, we have heard a caller calling to faith: 'Believe in your Lord!' So we believed. Therefore, Our Lord, forgive our sins and erase our evil deeds. Take our souls in death in the company of the righteous. Our Lord, grant us what You promised to us through Your Messengers, and do not abase us on the Day of Resurrection. You never break the promise." (3:190-94)[113]

Again, 'A'isha reports:

> I woke up one night and could not see God's Messenger beside me. I was jealous, lest he had gone to another of his wives. As I just got up from bed, my hand touched his feet. I noticed that he was prostrating, praying: "O God, I seek refuge in Your pleasure from Your wrath, and in Your forgiveness from Your punishment; I also seek refuge in Yourself from You. I cannot praise You as You praise Yourself."[114]

His life was so simple that once 'Umar, upon seeing him, said: "O Messenger of God, kings sleep in soft, feather beds, while you lie on a rough mat. You are the Messenger of God and thereby deserve an easy life more than anyone else." God's Messenger answered: "Don't you agree that the world should be theirs and those of the Hereafter ours?"[115] God's Messenger lived for others. He desired a comfortable life for his nation, provided that his community would not be led astray by world attractions, but himself lived a very simple life.

Third, God's Messenger, like all Prophets, expected no reward for performing his mission. He suffered hunger, thirst, and every other hardship. He was forced into exile and made the target of assaults and traps. He bore all of these simply for the good pleasure of God and the good of humanity. Abu Hurayra once saw him praying while seated and asked if he were sick. The Messenger's reply caused Abu Hurayra to cry: "I am hungry, Abu Hurayra. Hunger has left me no strength to stand up for prayer."[116] Hunger was a common feature of Muslim life. One night, God's Messenger, Abu Bakr, and 'Umar met each other unexpectedly outside. When they asked one another why they were outside, all replied: "Hunger."[117]

Even though most of his Companions became wealthier in later years, the Messenger and his family never changed their very simple lifestyle. Fatima, his only surviving child, did all of the housework for her family by herself. Once when captives were distributed in Madina, she asked her father for a maid. He replied:

> O my daughter. I can give you nothing before I satisfy the needs of the people of the Suffa. However, let me teach you something that is better for you than having a servant. When you go to bed, say: "Glory be to God, All praise be to God, God is the Greatest" 33 times each. [Some Traditions say that the last phrase should be recited 34 times.] This is better for your next life.[118]

One day he saw her wearing a bracelet (or a necklace, according to another version) and warned her: "O my daughter, do you want people to say of my daughter that she is wearing a ring of Hellfire? Take it off immediately!"[119]

In addition to receiving no worldly benefit, God's Messenger bore many tortures. He often was beaten and left on the ground covered with dust, and only Fatima would run to his aid. Once he was being beaten at the Ka'ba, Abu Bakr ran to help him, shouting to those beating him: "Will you kill a man because he says: 'My Lord is God?'"[120]

INTELLECT

Intellect is another important attribute of Prophethood. In this context, it has a specific meaning: a composite of reasoning power, sagacity, intelligence, sound judgment, and wisdom far surpassing the ability of ordinary people through a sublime power of understanding. It encompasses and coordinates all human abilities, whether of the heart and soul or of the mind.

Under the influence of temporary trends, some reduce Islam to a rationalistic system. They regard reason as the ultimate authority, and make no distinction between the judgment of sound reason and the excesses and shortcomings of rationalism. All the principles of Islam, a revealed religion originating in an All-Encompassing Knowledge, can be confirmed by reason. However, a comprehensive understanding of Islam requires a Prophetic intellect to grasp the entire meaning of the universe and humanity. Islam admits reason's ultimate authority; not of human reason, which is limited by one's capacity and usually conflicts with another's, but of a Prophet's universal reason, for Islam is the name of the Divine universal order.

God manifests His Names through veils. His absolute Unity requires that we attribute effects directly to His creative Power. But His Transcendence, Grandeur, and Majesty require "natural" causes to veil His acts so that people do not ascribe to Him that which seems disagreeable to them. He raised the Prophets to communicate His Revelation. As we cannot receive Revelation directly, the Prophets functioned as a prism receiving and then reflecting Divine Revelation. They modulated the Revelation according to their audience's intellectual ability and the prevailing circumstances. In other words, the Prophetic intellect allows a Prophet to understand everything about his people and thus to answer all their questions and solve their problems.

If we study the Prophet's achievements, we see that he was a statesman and commander of the highest order. As the embodiment or most comprehensive manifestation of the Divine Attribute of Speech, he is the most influential orator we have ever seen. His words, regardless of their apparent simplicity, affect everyone, regardless of their intellectual simplicity. As human knowledge increases, we see that these supposedly simple words are, in fact, like an ocean whose depth is only appreciated the more deeply one dives into it, or like a rose with petals one within the other, each one full of meanings.

His level of understanding was so sublime that Wahb ibn Munabbih, who was well-versed in the Torah and Gospels, said: "When compared to that of God's Messenger, humanity's total mental capacity and perception is like a single sand particle compared to all the sand in a vast desert."[121]

Examples of His Intellectual Capacity

- Before his Prophethood, the Ka'ba was partly ruined by rain and the ensuing floods. The Quraysh restored it. However, clan warfare almost broke out over who would have the honor of restoring the sacred Black Stone to its proper place. Someone suggested that they refer the matter to whoever appeared first at the Ka'ba. To everyone's relief, this person was Muhammad. They told each other: "The Trustworthy One is coming!" After explaining the problem, he asked them to bring a piece of cloth, which he spread on the ground. Putting the Black Stone on it, he told each clan chief to hold a corner and lift the cloth. When the Black Stone was at the required height, Muhammad put it in its place. Clan warfare was thus averted.[122]

- God's Messenger always assessed a person's or an audience's spiritual and mental capacities accurately. He spoke directly to a particular individual at a particular time and under particular circumstances; he had no need for flattery or falsehood. One time Husayn, an eloquent speaker renowned for his persuasive rhetoric, sought to dissuade him from his mission. God's Messenger listened carefully to his argument and then initiated the following dialogue:

> - Husayn, how many deities do you worship?
> - Eight; one in the Heavens and the others on Earth.

- Which one do you call upon when misfortune befalls you?
- The one in the Heavens.
- Which one do you call when your goods are gone?
- The one in the Heavens.

God's Messenger asked a couple of similar questions, and, upon receiving the same answer to each question, asked: "According to you, the one in the Heavens alone answers your call. Yet you continue to associate partners with Him. Isn't this what I have been preaching? There is no deity but God. Become a Muslim and be saved."[123] This apparently simple argument defeated Husayn with his own logic.

- Bedouins are often called "people of the desert." Their way of life engenders many unique experiences: the loss of a camel, forgetfulness of where items have been placed, or being caught in a sandstorm. However many deities they worship, they always ask God, the One, the Unique Creator of the universe, and Powerful over all things, for help and rescue. Their inner sense and sound conscience tell them the truth under the enchanting desert sky or in the darkness, and they then acknowledge His Oneness. This happened with Hamza, who proclaimed: "O Muhammad, I have perceived in the darkness of the desert night, that God is too great to be restricted within four walls!"[124]

God's Messenger knew everyone's mood and thus took people "by the soul" when inviting them to Islam. For example, Ahmad ibn Hanbal reports from Abu Tamima that a Bedouin once asked God's Messenger if he was Muhammad. Receiving an affirmative answer, the Bedouin asked to what he was inviting people. The Messenger replied: "To God, the All-Majestic. I invite them to Him alone, without associating any partners with Him. He is God whom you call upon when a misfortune befalls you and He who removes it. It is to Him alone that you pray during drought and famine, and He sends rain and causes the grass to grow. It is also Him you entreat when you lose something in the vast desert, and He causes you to find it." These simple, accurate, and concise words caused the Bedouin to awake to the truth and embrace Islam on the spot.[125]

History records no other instance of an individual forming such a virtuous community so quickly and from such unpromising people and meager resources. Prophet Muhammad used the dynamics granted to him by God so effectively that historians and sociologists still cannot fully grasp all dimensions of his revolutionary Message. Its waves have swept through the ages, and continue to attract increasing numbers of people from all over the world into the peaceful ocean of Islam.

- The Prophet solved problems, as Bernard Shaw pointed out, as easily as one drinks coffee. Even when faced with the most unexpected emergencies, he remained calm and solved the problem to everyone's satisfaction. His whole life shows that he was a man of perfect balance, and that this balance was never lost.

Expanding on this last item, consider the following example. After the conquest of Makka, many former enemies proclaimed their conversion. Naturally, it was difficult for them to acquire sincere belief so quickly. So, God's Messenger sought to "reconcile their hearts" and increase their commitment by preferring them over the Muslims when distributing the war spoils after the Battle of Hunayn.

The spoils consisted of 24,000 camels, 40,000 sheep and goats, and 10,000 pounds of gold and silver. God's Messenger gave 300 camels and 250 pounds of gold and silver to Abu Sufyan and his family, 200 camels to Hakim ibn Hizam, and 100 camels each to Nusayr ibn al-Harith, Qays ibn Asiyy, Safwan ibn Umayya, Malik ibn Awf, Akra ibn Habis, and 'Uyayna ibn Hisn. Such generosity also did much to repair the Makkan chiefs' wounded pride.

Some younger Ansaris, despite their devotion to God's Messenger and Islam, became upset. They did not desire the spoils themselves; rather, they did not want to see such formerly staunch enemies of Islam, in their view, rewarded. This might have led to a dissident movement among the Muslims. When informed of the situation by Sa'd ibn 'Ubada, an Ansari leader, God's Messenger ordered them to assemble so he could address them. They did so, and he opened his speech in a dramatic way designed to attract and hold their attention, and to impress their souls: "O Community of the Helpers! I hear that you are displeased with me."

He continued in this powerful and impressive style, reminding them of God's blessings upon them through him. He asked: "Were you not in misguidance when I came to you? And has God not guided you to the truth through me? Were you not in poverty when I came to you? And has God not enriched you through me? Were you not in internal conflicts when I came to you? And has God not reconciled you through me?" They agreed to all of this, answering each question with: "True, O God's Messenger! We are indebted to God and His Messenger!"

After reminding them of these blessings, God's Messenger recounted their services to Islam, saying: "O Ansar! If you had desired, you could have answered me differently and said: 'Your people denied you, but we believed in you. You came to us with no one to defend you, but we admitted and protected you. Your people exiled you, but we embraced you. You came to us with nothing to subsist on, and we met all your needs.' If you had responded thus to me, you would have told the truth and no one would have stood up to contradict you."

He continued: "O Ansar! Even if you're upset with my actions, wouldn't you rather return home with God's Messenger while they return with camels and sheep? I swear by God, in Whose Hand of Power is my soul, that if all other people took a different direction than that of the Ansar, I wouldn't hesitate to go with the Ansar! Had it not been for the Emigration, I would have wished with all my heart to be one of the Ansar! O God, protect the Ansar and their descendants!" These words were enough for the Ansar to burst into tears, and all of them responded with one voice: "We are content with God and His Messenger! We desire nothing else!"[126]

Although uttered on the spur of the moment, this speech both quashed a potential dissident movement and reconquered the Ansar's hearts. Let's analyze this speech so that its wisdom can be better understood and appreciated.

- He addressed the Ansar only, for they were the offended party. This showed them special honor, and exerted a psychological influence upon them from the outset. It also prevented any ill-will among the Muhajirun, who had been forced to emigrate to Madina, or the new Muslims of Makka, many of whom still had to be won over.
- His speech, when considered in its Arabic original, is an extraordinarily eloquent rhetorical document.
- His opening was dramatic, for it was designed to win the audience's attention. Their attention never wavered, for the rest of his speech was just as dramatic and effective.
- He did not resort to flattery or diplomacy. Rather, he spoke in plain sincerity, which was vital in securing the desired influence upon the listeners.
- The spur-of-the-moment nature of his speech also was significant in obtaining the desired result. The freshness and force of such an unprepared address, on such occasions, is often more effective than a speech prepared in advance.

Those few examples illustrate the intellect of God's Messenger, and show that he did not speak or act of himself; rather, what he said and did carried the charge or force of one fulfilling a Divine mission.

Concise Speech

Another dimension of his intellect is the very concise nature of his speech. Remember that he is the leader not only of those who lived during his lifetime, but of every believer to come. He was sent to address people of every level, from ignorant seventh-century bedouins to those of the highest intellectual and scientific achievements, until the Day of Judgment. No one has yet been able to disprove what he said. Accordingly, after we scrutinize his Traditions and the Qur'an, we realize that they complement each other in style and content. Moreover, there is no contradiction between them and established scientific knowledge. Ever since the Revelation, billions of people have found in the Qur'an answers for their intellectual problems, cures for their spiritual diseases, and models for their behavior in all circumstances.

The enchanting, captivating, and informative words of God's Messenger that so enlightened his Companions intellectually and revived them spiritually have exerted the same influence on countless scholars, scientists, Qur'anic exegetes, Traditionists, jurists, spiritual guides, and specialists in science and humanities. Such people, the vast majority of whom have been non-Arab, have used the Qur'an and Sunna as the foundational sources of their academic studies and endeavors.

Even today, his words are enough to cause people to reform themselves and embrace Islam. He acknowledged this as one of God's blessings and, to emphasize it as so, would sometimes say: "I am Muhammad, an unlettered Prophet. No Prophet will come after me. I have been distinguished with conciseness of speech and comprehensiveness of meaning,"[127] and: "O people, I have been honored with conciseness of speech and giving the final judgment in all matters."[128]

The nightingale is said to convey the gratitude of plants and flowers to the All-Provider. Likewise, God's Messenger came to "sing" the praises of God in the "garden" of humanity and announce His Commandments with his enchanting "songs." His words opened ever-fresh flowers in all human hearts and reduced the words of others, regardless of their surface beauty, to nothing. Believers were purified by his words' deep serenity, exhilarated by the bright atmosphere created through his speeches, and by the love his personal conduct inspired. Through his words and deeds, God's Messenger removed the veils from the "face" of nature and embellished the "Book of the Universe" with Divine inscriptions.

Many famous rhetors, orators, and poets have preferred to listen to him or have benefited greatly from his words. Thousands of literary people have devoted their lives to studying his sayings, and have compiled multi-volumed books about or out of them. Many thinkers and scholars have quenched their "thirst" with the "water of life" found therein. In order to express the beauty and comprehensiveness of his words, we provide a slightly adapted version of a couplet uttered about the Qur'an:

> *Almost nothing of this world*
> *has come unveiled or pure,*
> *But the words of the Messenger*
> *preserve their purity undefiled,*
> *and still wait to be understood fully.*

As God's Messenger was unlettered, he was not influenced by his era's written culture. His conscience was so sound, his intellect so comprehensive, and his character so pure that only he could have received Divine Revelation. His mind and heart were fed by Divine Revelation exclusively. Each word and deed was a ray from that Revelation, a sign of his Messengership. Like a bright, crystal cup of clear, sweet water, his intellect was so pure that Divine Revelation entered it and emerged from it, drop by drop, in the form of words in their original clarity.

The primary expression of Divine Revelation is the Qur'an. It is also the primary source for Islamic law. Although it contains guidance pertaining to all aspects of human life, the number of questions and problems put to God's Messenger meant that a second form of Revelation was necessary. This took the form of inspiration, an implicit Revelation, to clarify Qur'anic verses or to establish new principles related to Islamic conduct. This, together with his daily words and conduct, forms the second source of Islamic law: the Sunna. This subject is discussed in the second volume of this book.

Every Prophet was supported by miracles relevant to his time and environment. For example, Moses' miracles had to appear as magic, for magic was widespread. Jesus' miracles took the form of healing, for medicine was in wide demand. Similarly, when Muhammad emerged as a Prophet, four things enjoyed popularity in Arabia: eloquence and fluency in writing and speaking, poetry and oratory, soothsaying and divination, and knowledge of the past and cosmology. The Qur'an challenged all known experts in these fields and forced them to surrender. Prophet Muhammad surpassed them through his wonderful eloquence, knowledge of the cosmos, and predictions.

As his Prophethood is universal and will exist until the Last Day, his eloquence and linguistic style will never be surpassed. His words, together with the Qur'an, supersede all literary works. Their excellence is everlasting and becomes increasingly vivid as their deeper meanings are discovered over the course of time. His words and the Qur'an are of such extraordinary nature and so full of meaning that millions of saints and people seeking Divine knowledge have obtained perfect knowledge of the Divine Essence, Attributes, and Names through them. The hidden truths of the Unseen worlds (e.g., angels, jinn, the Hereafter, Paradise, and Hell) are unveiled through them.

These two sources have also served as a pure, inexhaustible fountain of insight for countless jurists, Qur'anic interpreters, Traditionists, historians, scientists, sociologists, psychologists, and many others. The Qur'an and the Sunna have enlightened billions of people, and have shown them how to pray, fast, give alms, and make pilgrimage—even how to eat, drink, and speak. In short, it has shown them how to conduct themselves at every moment of their lives.

Some examples are the following:

• Imam Tirmidhi relates from Ibn 'Abbas, the Scholar of the Umma, that God's Messenger said to him:

> O young man, let me teach you a few principles: Observe the rights of God so that God will protect you. Observe His rights so that you always will find Him with you. When you ask something, ask it from God. When you seek help, seek it from God. Know that if everyone joined together to help you, they could only do that which God already preordained for you. If everyone joined together to hurt you, they could only

do that which God already preordained for you. The Pen of Destiny has been lifted, and everything has been ordained.[129]

This *hadith* encourages submission to God, and belief in His Unity and the truth of Destiny. We should not conclude that it excludes human free will; rather, it stresses one's action, prayer, and need to strive for the desired results. It balances this with a warning that since everything is ultimately in the hands of God, we should strive in accordance with His Commandments and seek the results only from Him.

- Imam Tirmidhi relates from Ibn 'Umar: God's Messenger said: "Live in the world as if you were a stranger or traveler. Regard yourself as one of the dead."[130] This succinct *hadith* encourages us to lead an austere, disciplined life based on awareness of God. It reminds us of our final destination by stressing this world's transience, and establishes the balance between this life and the next.

  We are travelers in this world. Mawlana Jalal al-Din al-Rumi, a thirteenth-century Turkish Sufi, says each individual is like a flute made of a reed separated from its group. We continually groan with the pangs of separation from the real Owner and our native land. We set out from the World of the Spirits and travel through the stations of our mother's womb, childhood, youth, old age, the grave, and the Resurrection. Finally, our journey ends either in Paradise or Hell. If we desire a pleasant journey and a safe arrival in Paradise, we must be aware of this life's transience and prepare for the eternal life. Although we can taste life's pleasures to a certain extent, provided they are not specifically forbidden, we should not overindulge or forget our true destination.

- Such authentic books of Tradition as *Sahih al-Bukhari*, *Sahih al-Muslim*, and *Sunan Abu Dawud* relate from 'Abd Allah Ibn Mas'ud that God's Messenger said: "Always tell the truth, for this guides to absolute piety and piety leads to Paradise. Those who always tell and pursue the truth are recorded by God as truthful. Don't lie, for this guides to sinfulness and sinfulness leads to Hellfire. Those who always tell and pursue lies are recorded by God as liars."[131]

Truthfulness is an indispensable attribute of Prophethood. Truthfulness opens the door of happiness in both worlds. No one can taste true bliss while living in the darkness of lies and lying. Lying is "an assertion contrary to God's knowledge," a pillar of unbelief, and the most manifest sign of hypocrisy. The current prevalence of lying is destroying our security and morality, and contaminating the whole community (especially its political circles) like a contagious disease. Any structure based on lying must eventually perish due to its very nature.

This *hadith* states that truthfulness leads to absolute piety, while lying leads to sinfulness. *Birr*, the Arabic word translated here as piety, encompasses every virtue, from sound thinking, truthfulness, and pure intention to honesty, decency, and good conduct. Its opposite, *fujur* (sinfulness), denotes every kind of deviation and evil, among them debauchery, indecency, and perversion.

• Bukhari and Muslim report from Ibn Mas'ud that God's Messenger said: "A man (or woman) is with him (her) whom he (she) loves."[132] This *hadith* is a source of hope and consolation for those unable to adhere completely to the Divine Commandments. Those who love the Prophets and saints will be in their company in the Hereafter. Therefore, whoever desires this should love them sincerely and follow them as best they can. Those who love the enemies of God will be with them in Hell.

Nu'ayman, a Companion, could not stop drinking alcohol. He was punished several times. When yet another Companion reproached him, God's Messenger warned that Companion: "Don't help Satan against your brother! I swear by God that he loves God and His Messenger."[133] Thus, those who are trying their best to reform them-

selves, as long as they continue to perform their obligatory duties and try to refrain from major sins, should be
encouraged, not reprimanded. This is a prerequisite of
their love for God and His Messenger.

- Ibn Hanbal related from Mu'adh ibn Jabal: God's
  Messenger said: "Fear God wherever you are. Do good
  immediately after a sinful act to erase it, and always be
  well-mannered in your relationship with people."[134] This
  concise *hadith* establishes the principles of a happy life
  and describes the way to eternal bliss. Fear of God is the
  basis of every virtue and good conduct, and leads to
  Paradise. Through this, people can erase their sins with
  good deeds, and being well-mannered elevates them to
  the rank of perfection.

- God's Messenger declares: "You are governed how you are
  (according to your beliefs and lifestyle.)"[135] This *hadith*
  expresses a principle of public and political administration:
  A country's political structure is shaped according to its
  people's tendencies, whether directly through democracy
  or indirectly through other ways. Both the natural and the
  social sciences have their own laws, which we call "God's
  creational and operational laws of the universe." According
  to these laws, if people immerse themselves in sin and evil,
  they inevitably will be ruled by evil people. If, by contrast,
  they prefer a virtuous life, their government will be good.

  The *hadith* stresses that laws have no sanction on their
  own; rather, their authority depends on those who apply
  them. Therefore, the character of government officials is
  of vital importance. If the people are righteous, their rulers
  or government officials will be righteous. If they are not,
  no one can expect a righteous administration. The ruling
  elite are like the cream rising to the surface of a liquid: milk
  has its own kind of cream, as do lime and alum. When
  Hajjaj, a despotic commander, was reminded of 'Umar's
  justice, he replied: "If you were like 'Umar's people, I
  would be like 'Umar."

The *hadith* also tells us to develop self-control and discern our own faults. Social harmony cannot be established if people tend to blame others. As emphasized in the Qur'an: *God will not change the condition of a people unless they change themselves* (13:11). We are the ones who determine our fate and make our own history.

- Bukhari, Muslim, and Abu Dawud relate from 'Umar that God's Messenger said: "Actions are judged according to intentions. One is rewarded for whatever one intends to do. Whoever emigrates for God and His Messenger has emigrated for God and His Messenger; whoever emigrates to acquire something worldly or to marry has emigrated for what is intended."[136] This *hadith* concerns a Companion who emigrated to marry Umm Qays. It is considered a cornerstone of Islamic law and the foremost standard for evaluating a believer's actions.

Intention is the spirit of our actions. For example, if we fulfill our religious duties without making a specific intention to do so, they are unacceptable to God. If we do not seek God's good pleasure, what we do is not rewarded by God. *Hijra* (sacred emigration in the way of God) can be considered a twin of jihad (holy struggle in the way of God).

Although there is no *hijra* after the conquest of Makka, it will continue elsewhere along with jihad until the Last Day. Believers may emigrate to preach Islam, as God's Messenger and his Companions did when they could no longer do this in Makka. Such emigrations are accepted as hijra when done purely for the sake of God. Intention can sometimes be rewarded without action. For example, if we sincerely intend to do something good but cannot, for some justifiable reason, we will be rewarded for what we intended to do.

Intention multiplies an action's reward, and transforms every action into a kind of worship. We cannot earn eternal happiness in this short worldly life. But by intending to worship God as if we were to live forever, we can become deserving of the eternal life of Paradise. Unbelievers whose hearts are closed to belief, according to the same principle, deserve the eternal punishment of Hellfire. Believers who sleep after the night prayer with the intention of getting up before dawn to pray *tahajjud* are recorded as having worshipped God for the whole night. This is why God's Messenger declared: "A believer's intention is more rewarding than his [or her] action."[137]

- Bukhari records that God's Messenger said: "The Muslim is one from whose tongue and hand Muslims are safe. The Emigrant is one who emigrates from what God forbids."[138] This short *hadith* expresses many truths. First of all, it describes the ideal or norm by beginning with *the Muslim*, as opposed to *a Muslim*. In this way, our Prophet draws attention to the qualities of perfect Muslims, not to those who are only nominal Muslims.

The word Muslim, derived from the infinitive *silm* (security, peace, and salvation), comes to mean one who desires and gives peace, security, and salvation. So, *the Muslims* are believers who embody peace, cause no trouble for anyone, from whom all are safe, and who are the most reliable representatives of peace and security. They strive to bring peace, security, and salvation to others, and dedicate themselves to disseminating their inner peace and happiness.

Our Prophet mentions the tongue before the hand, for slander, gossip, and insult often do far more damage than physical violence. If people can refrain from verbal assault, they can more easily refrain from physical assault. Moreover, self-defense against physical violence is often easier than that against gossip and slander. So, true Muslims always restrain their tongues and hands so that others will be safe from them.

In the same *hadith*, emigration means more than leaving one's family, house, possessions, and native land for the sake of God. To be capable of the latter, one must first emigrate from the material to the spiritual dimension of his or her being, from worldly pleasures to an altruistic life, and from selfish aims to living for a Divine cause. Therefore, obeying Divine prohibitions is directly related to being a good Muslim and to sacrificing one's life in the service of people purely for the sake of God.

• God's Messenger says: "Being a good Muslim causes people to abandon that which is of no use to them."[139] Such people practice *ihsan*, a term denoting that we worship God as if we see Him, fully aware that even if we cannot see God, He sees us all the time.[140] Those who reach this rank can say: "I was searching for Him in the outer world, but now I have come to understand that He is the Soul within my soul" or "I expected some news from beyond the world. However, the veil has been removed from my soul and I have seen myself."

To attain this degree, worshippers should abandon whatever is vain and useless. They should know that God is watching them, and that God's Messenger and discerning believers are aware of their deeds' true value. God says:

> Say: "Work, and (know that) God will behold your work, and so will His Messenger and the believers; then you shall be brought back to the Knower of what is hidden and what is open, and He will declare to you all that you have done." (9:105)

Good Muslims abandon heedlessness and indifference, do their work properly, put forth their best efforts in whatever they do, and are serious and reliable in all dealings and transactions. Flippancy and frivolity injure one's reliability and reduce one's dignity.

• Both Bukhari and Muslim relate that God's Messenger said: "Patience is shown at the moment of misfortune."[141] In the early days of his mission, God's Messenger forbade people to visit graves, as some un-Islamic practices were still observed. After such practices vanished, he encouraged his Companions to visit graves, and did so himself, for this encourages people to improve their moral conduct and strive for the next life.

During a visit to Madina's graveyard, God's Messenger saw a woman weeping bitterly and complaining about Destiny. When he sought to console her, the woman, who did not recognize him, angrily told him to go away, for: "You don't know what misfortune has befallen me!" When she later learned his identity, she hurried after him and, finding him at home, begged his pardon. God's Messenger told her: "Patience is shown at the moment of misfortune."

Patience is a key to success and triumph. It means to accept pain, trouble, misfortune, and similar unpleasant facts without complaint, or loss of self-control, trust, or belief in God and Destiny. Sometimes one can achieve patience in difficult circumstances by changing one's attitude, place, preoccupation, or immediate conditions. Performing *wudu'* (ritual ablution) or praying also may help one deal with sorrow.

There are several kinds of patience:

- Determination to avoid sins. This elevates one to the rank of the God-fearing, whom God takes into His care.

- Constant and regular worship of God. This causes one to acquire the rank of being a beloved of God.

- Acceptance of misfortune without complaint. This causes one to be included among the people of patience and those who put their trust in God.

- Dealing with exasperation. This means having a realistic understanding of what is required to achieve a specific result. For example, producing a loaf of bread requires that the field be cultivated, the crop harvested, the grain taken to a mill, and the dough shaped into loaves and baked in an oven. If, out of impatience or neglect, this procedure is not followed exactly and in this specific order, a loaf of bread will not be produced.

- Bukhari, Muslim, and Ahmad ibn Hanbal record that God's Messenger said: "The upper hand is better than the lower one."[142] In another *hadith*, God's Messenger explains that the upper hand gives to the poor and needy, while the lower hand takes from others. So, besides expressing the merits of charity, this *hadith* encourages people to work and earn their living.

  A subtle point: God's Messenger did not say *the one who gives and the one who receives*. Instead, he said *the upper hand and the lower hand*. This indicates that the act, not the person, is generally preferable. As a result, the recipient may sometimes be better than the giver.

  For example some people, like Bara' ibn Malik, appear to be very low but are so beloved in His sight that whatever they predict, and then swear on by God, comes true. Such people ask for nothing and are extraordinarily independent. God's Messenger advised Thawban not to beg. As a result, he would not even ask someone to pick up a whip he dropped while riding his camel. So, when seemingly "poor" believers of this quality receive from people, it cannot be said that they are inferior to those who give.

  Islam does not approve of begging either on the individual or the national level. It should never be forgotten that honor, dignity, and superiority always belong to God, His Messenger, and the believers. Therefore Muslims should not come under the control or authority of unbelievers, for this undermines their dignity and superiority.

- Imam Muslim relates from God's Messenger: On the Last Day, God will not talk to, pay attention to, or purify three types of people. A painful torment awaits them. These are the people who "trail their robes," who remind those they have favored of their favors, and who try to sell their goods by false oaths.[143]

  The *hadith* begins with *thalathatun* (three), meaning any three, unnamed, unworthy of being named. In other words, they may be met anywhere, and they and their actions are so despicable that Muslims should avoid them. God will ignore such people in the next world. This is a severe punishment, for, as stated in *Surat al-Rahman*, speech is one of the foremost and greatest favors of God to humanity. Besides, we will be in dire need of speaking on the Day of Judgment, when we try to justify ourselves. These people, however, will be told: *Be driven into it (the Fire)! Don't speak to Me!* (23:108).

On that day, everyone will be occupied with their own troubles, and there will be no refuge except God the Almighty. Everyone will hope that God will give them some personal attention, that He will look upon them with mercy and purify them. But those three sorts of people will have no hope of being purified and for-given, since God Almighty will not acknowledge them.

In the *hadith*, their punishment is announced before their sins are identified. God's Messenger thereby empha-sizes the gravity of their sins and warns everybody to refrain from them. The first and most grievous sin is "trailing one's robe," an Arabic idiom for arrogance.

Arrogance means to contest with God for the rule of the Earth. Human beings, despite their vast weakness, poverty, and powerless are nevertheless enchanted with themselves. They consider their abilities, skills, position, wealth, apparent accomplishments, and so on worthy of pride. This leads to self-conceit and self-pride. Though created from a drop of lowly "water" and unable to choose their time and place of their birth, family, color, and race, this self-pride grows despite their inability to satisfy their bodies' operative needs.

For example, they cannot satisfy their hunger, thirst, and sleep on their own. The only reason human beings survive is because God has endowed them with various talents and faculties. But people ignore this fact, attrib-ute their accomplishments to themselves, and so contest with God. Such arrogance eventually blinds them to innumerable signs pointing to God's Existence, Unity, and Absolute Sovereignty. In the words of the Qur'an:

> Those who behave arrogantly on the Earth in defiance of truth—I will turn them away from My signs: even if they see all the signs, they will not believe in them; even if they see the way of guidance and right conduct, they will not choose it for their way. For they rejected Our signs, and gave no heed to them. (7:146)

The second grave sin is reminding others of the favors you have done for them. This is closely related to arrogance, for those who consider what God has bestowed upon them as their own possessions and abilities tend to engage in this sin as well. Those who regard everything as a gift from God understand that they can benefit others only if He allows them to do so. As a result, those who do the favor actually feel indebted to those they have helped, for such actions allow them to receive a spiritual reward. This hadith encourages people to disinterested generosity and altruism, concerning which God's Messenger says:

> The generous are near to God, to Paradise, and to people, and distant from Hell. The miserly, however, are distant from God, from Paradise, and from human beings, but near to Hell.[144]

The last grave sin is deception in trade. According to the laws of Islam, merchants must disclose any defect in what they are selling. Swearing by God is also prohibited, especially in transactions. If merchants try to sell their goods through lies or false oaths, or stir up demand by swearing by God, they are committing a great sin deserving of severe punishment. This sin is closely linked to the two earlier ones, for it usually originates in miserliness and one's non-recognition of God. Besides being connected with unbelief in and distrust of God, these three sins poison society's life and indicate weak character. Hence, the severity of their punishment.

- Imam Bukhari records in his *Sahih* that God's Messenger said: "Whoever guarantees to me what is between their lips and what is between their legs, I will guarantee them Paradise."[145] As speech is one of the greatest favors of God, we should use our tongues only for good and useful acts, such as reciting the Qur'an, praying, telling the truth, and enjoining good and forbidding evil. We should be modest and well-mannered in our speech, and not engage in lying, profanity, slander, gossip, and so on. Words should be chosen carefully, for, as 'Ali said: "Your word is dependent on you until you utter it; once you utter it, however, you are dependent on it."

  Controlling one's sexual lust is very important for attaining human perfection and deserving Paradise. God has endowed us with many faculties and impulses so that we might evolve spiritually by restraining them and, channeling them into good deeds and virtues, attain higher spiritual ranks. By struggling to satisfy desires only in lawful ways, we can attain the rank of sainthood and gain superiority over angels. Since angels have no carnal desires and thus do not struggle against temptation, they do not evolve spiritually. However, because of our essential duality, we travel between the lowest (more wretched than Satan) and the highest (surpassing the angels) levels.

  Since Islam bans or blocks the ways leading to forbidden acts, one should refrain from such acts as displaying personal charm or beauty, gazing at the opposite sex, and being alone with someone of the opposite sex in such places that encourage illicit sexual relations. Like holding one's tongue, this requires strong willpower, self-discipline, and continuous struggle. Even though it seems at first sight to be too difficult, it will engender great spiritual pleasure, for the pleasure of labor and struggle lies in labor and struggle themselves. Those who are successful will be deserving of Paradise.

- Muslim records God's Messenger as having discussed forgiveness. He once asked:

"Listen. Shall I guide you to the things through which God blots out sins and elevates you to higher ranks?" When his Companions asked him to do so, he told them: "Perform wudu' (ritual ablution) as correctly as possible, even in the most adverse conditions; walk to the mosque for each prayer; and wait for the next prayer after praying. This is the ribat, this is the ribat (preparation, dedication)."[146]

The *hadith* begins with Listen to stress the importance of what follows. In this case, it is the five daily prayers.

The prescribed prayer is the pillar of Islam. Without it, Islam cannot be maintained. When believers pray correctly, they are protected from evil thoughts and deeds. It is also a sacred ladder for ascending to the Presence of God. But before we can climb it, we must perform wudu' as perfectly as possible. From the first step toward wudu', believers begin to gain reward. While performing it, they are relieved of the stress of daily life and cleansed of sins. When performed in difficult circumstances, believers receive an even greater exhilaration.

Adhan (the call to prayer) is both the call for believers to enter the Presence of God and the call to prosperity in both worlds. *Wudu'* is the preparation that believers must make before entering this Presence. By performing the supererogatory prayer before the prescribed one, believers complete their preparations and receive permission from the God's aide-de-camp: Prophet Muhammad. When the *muezzin* (caller to prayer) calls *iqama* (the beginning of the prayer), believers enter His Presence with total respect and reverence, converse with the Unique Owner of the universe, and petition Him for their needs and desires.

Believers pray five times a day, thereby having their sins erased and their potential to commit sins changed into "seeds of blessed trees of good and virtue." There is, however, one condition: The prayer must be performed with absolute sincerity, with pure intention to gain God's good pleasure only, and in full awareness of being in the Presence of the Creator and Owner of the universe, the All-Powerful, All-Knowing, All-Seeing, All-Hearing, and All-Overwhelming.

God's Messenger describes the prescribed prayer as ribat, which can be translated as "dedication to something or guarding the frontier." It appears in the Qur'an: *O you who believe! Persevere in patience and vie in such perseverance; be alert and prepared for jihad; and fear God, so that you may prosper* (3:200) and: *Against them make ready your strength to the utmost of your power, including horses dedicated to war* (8:60).

In the first verse, *ribat* means being alert and prepared; in the second, dedicated. By describing the prayer with this term, God's Messenger stresses the value and importance of struggling in God's way as well as the primacy of the prescribed prayers in Islam and a believer's life. In another *hadith*, he calls the former *the lesser jihad* and the latter *the greater jihad*. To succeed in the former, believers must be very attentive while performing the latter.

By describing the prescribed prayers as *ribat*, God's Messenger also emphasizes that Muslims should dedicate their lives to Divine worship and organize their daily activities around the five daily prayers. They should ensure that they can pray when necessary and with full attention. After each prayer, they should wait expectantly for the next one. Those who pray in such a manner will be cleansed of sins and, moreover, protected against committing more sins. Then they will experience, as another *hadith* says, something like a *mi'raj* (ascension to God's Presence).

- Bukhari relates that God's Messenger said: "God says: 'I have prepared for My righteous servants such things of which they have never seen, heard, or imagined.'"[147] Paradise is the place of surprises. The Qur'an tells us of its bounties using familiar words so that we can get some idea of them. But as Ibn 'Abbas points out: *They are given things in similitude* (2:25), means that these bounties are particular to Paradise in nature and taste; their appearance, however, is like that of their counterparts in the world. Believers will be rewarded in Paradise with ever-renewed bounties and, above all, will observe God free from any qualitative and quantitative dimensions. An instant of this observation will surpass, in delight and blessing, thousands of years of life in Paradise. But the greatest bounty of all in Paradise is that God will be pleased with believers forever.

To be worthy of Paradise, we must be righteous, upright in all our deeds, and do everything as perfectly as possible. Righteous believers do not lie or deceive others, and are completely reliable. God is confident that they will perform their religious duties as carefully as possible and obey His prohibitions. All other parts of creation are sure such believers will never hurt them. Such people do everything in full awareness that God Almighty is watching them. Since they have gained their Lord's good pleasure, they are counted among those whom God calls *My righteous servants*. That is, they are loved by God and, as a result: "He is their eyes with which they see, their ears with which they hear, their hands with which they hold, and their feet on which they walk."

God multiplies the good deeds of His servants and gives, in certain circumstances, millions of rewards for each deed. This is why believers will meet in Paradise such bounties as they could never have imagined while alive.

- In a *hadith* related by Sahih al-Bukhari and Muslim, God's Messenger says: "Paradise is surrounded by trouble and tribulation, and Hell is concealed in pleasure."[148] Paradise and Hell are, in essence, blessings for humanity. Fear of Hell causes us to observe God's prohibitions so that we may go to Paradise. However, being saved from Hell and becoming deserving of Paradise requires great self-discipline and strict intellectual and spiritual training.

The Qur'an says that people are tempted by love of the *opposite sex, children, hoarded treasures of gold and silver, splendid mounts, cattle, and plantations* (3:14). People have a natural attachment to life and its pleasures. Hell is an abode of torment placed within an attractive setting of enticing lures and pleasures. If we are captivated and live only to satisfy such desires, we are lured toward Hell. We can reach this destination easily, for the path to Hell passes through worldly attractions of every kind.

To reach Paradise, we first have to train ourselves to ignore worldly attractions. Hell is part of the way to Paradise, for we must travel to Hell without allowing any of its attractions to seduce us. This requires self-discipline and continuous struggle against temptation and the carnal self's desires. Whenever we are invited to enjoy such worldly luxuries as fame, wealth, and status, we must restrict ourselves to the boundaries set by Divine Commandments. We must continue to pray, fast, give alms, and (if possible) perform the pilgrimage to the Ka'ba.

In addition, we must engage only in fairness; honesty; truthfulness; kindness to the poor, the needy, and orphans; and enjoin good and forbid evil. We also must refrain from deception, usury, gambling, drinking alcohol, backbiting, hypocrisy, and every form of injustice. We should expect to be tested, for: God will test you with afflictions and *something of fear and hunger, and loss in goods or lives or in the fruits of his toil and earnings* (2:155). To reach Paradise, we must persevere, endure affliction, perform what is obligatory, avoid sin, and thank God for His bounties and blessings. Such virtuous acts are hated by our carnal selves.

• Imam Tirmidhi relates that God's Messenger said:

> I advise you to fear God and obey, even if a black slave becomes your leader. Those of you who live long enough will see great controversy, so adhere to my Sunna and the Sunna of the rightly guided caliphs. Cling to them stubbornly. Beware of newly invented matters in religion, for

every invented matter is an innovation. Every innovation is going astray, and every going astray is in Hellfire.[149]

The Arabic word translated here as "fear of God" is *taqwa*. Derived from *wiqaya* (protection), *taqwa* means to be in the safekeeping or protection of God. This has two aspects. The first is that believers fear God and obey Him by observing His commands and prohibitions. The second aspect is that, by studying nature and life and discovering the laws of God that control them, people acquire scientific knowledge and order their lives. Science cannot be established if people do not discover these laws.

To be under the safekeeping of God, true religion and science should be combined, for they are two expressions of a single truth. According to Muslim sages and scholars, the universe is "the Created Qur'an," where God's laws issuing from His Attributes of Will, Destiny, and Power are operative. The Qur'an, the collection of Divine laws issuing from God's Attribute of Speech, is "the composed universe" or "the universe in words."

The second point is that believers should not disobey their government without justifiable cause. Without a leader, a community is like a broken rosary whose beads have scattered everywhere. Such a situation of social and political conflict usually results in anarchy and destruction. The *hadith* also points out a truth that even modern democracies have proven unable to grasp: no racial discrimination. It is clearly stated that an emancipated black slave can lead the Muslim community. This was not only a theoretical assertion, but was testified to by the numerous and great black saints, administrators, and scholars who were respected and obeyed.

God's Messenger also draws attention here to his Sunna. As he is the most excellent example for all aspects of life, believers are to follow his example until the Last Day. Such adherence guarantees that Islam retains its original purity. Any deviation will result in social and doctrinal

splits and new importations into Islam, the religion perfected by God. Adherence to the way of the first four caliphs
also guarantees of Muslim unity and Islam's maintenance.

This *hadith* also contains a prediction that his first
four political successors would be rightly guided, and that
disobedience to them would cause internal splits. Islamic
history records the truth of this statement. Just look at the
uprisings during the caliphates of 'Uthman and 'Ali.

- Bukhari and Muslim relate that God's Messenger said:
  "Believers are not bitten twice from the same hole."[150]
  Believers have insight, perceptiveness, and intelligence,
  for they are distinguished by their sound reasoning and
  spiritual insight. The Muslim community has—and should
  have—the same perceptiveness and always be aware of
  potential dangers or problems. They may be deceived
  once, but the insight and awareness provided by belief
  should prevent them from being deceived twice. This
  hadith contains a significant warning for contemporary
  Muslims, who have been deceived for centuries by the
  West and the hypocrites of the East. Muslims must take
  control of their own affairs and re-examine the quality
  of their belief.

- One *hadith* recorded by Bukhari and Muslim calls educators to re-evaluate their methods: "Human beings are like
  ores containing silver or gold. Those who are promising
  and in leading positions in unbelief are better than others
  (in virtue) when they accept Islam and acquire a good
  understanding of it."[151] This *hadith* is very significant,
  especially with respect to education, which demands the
  imparting of insight and perceptiveness. The Prophet
  said: *This is my way: I call unto God with insight and sure
  knowledge, I and those who follow me* (12:108).

Insight implies knowing each individual's character,
potential, and shortcomings. Human beings are not alike in
character, capacity, ambition, and taste. For example, they
can be said to "contain coal, copper, silver, gold, and

diamonds." The first step in providing a good education is to recognize individual potentialities and figure out how to develop them. Just as you cannot obtain gold from a coal mine, you cannot develop "copper" people into "gold" people. Conversely, if you try to extract copper via the gold–ore extraction method, your efforts will be fruitless.

We also should note that those with great potential always distinguish themselves. For example, such leading opponents of Islam as 'Umar eventually embraced Islam and became leading figures of the Muslim community. This shows that their potential for virtue is refined and developed fully in the crucible of Islam.

- In another hadith, God's Messenger said: "Surely God grants the wrongdoer, the oppressor, a reprieve. But once He seizes him, He utterly destroys him."[152] Then he recited: *Such is the chastisement of your Lord when He chastises communities in the midst of their wrong: grievous, indeed, and severe is His chastisement* (11:102).

God gives the wrongdoers some time to repent and amend their behavior. If they do not take advantage of this opportunity, He punishes them severely.

God sometimes uses wrongdoers as a "sword of God" to punish the sinful. Muslims often become the target of wrongdoing powers when they deviate from Islam and abandon the Divine Commandments. This happens when God wills to punish them before the Day of Judgment.

For example, after the Muslims split into many competing factions nine centuries ago, they were exposed to the Mongol invasion and massacre. Likewise, they tasted the bitterness of overall defeat and subjugation during and after the First World War. This was because they were no longer practicing Islam in their lives and because they had surrendered intellectually, spiritually, and materially to un-Islamic trends coming from the West.

However, every misfortune befalling Muslims is, on account of resulting from sin, an occasion and means for self-purification and Divine forgiveness; the beginning of a new, more splendid revival. So, the near future will witness, if God wills, the collapse of tyranny and a magnificent revival of Islam and the Muslim world.

• In an authentic Tradition, God's Messenger says:

> God will shade seven (groups) of people under His shade on the Day when there will be no shade except His: the just ruler; young people who have grown up in worship of God, may He be glorified; those people who are greatly attached to mosques; two persons who love each other for God's sake, meet and then leave each other because of this love; men who refuse the invitations of beautiful women of rank,[153] saying: "I fear God"; those who spend in the way of God so secretly that when they give charity to the one on his left, the one on the right does not see it; and those whose eyes fill with tears when they mention God in seclusion.[154]

People will be drenched in sweat up to their necks because of the heat of the Day of Judgment. Those who wish for His shade must strive for it according to the instructions outlined in this *hadith*.

Justice is the foundation of social life, and a just ruler is a rare occurrence. Holy and blessed indeed are those young people who can control their carnal desires and devote themselves to the worship of God. Designing one's life according to the daily prayers is a laudable virtue that pleases God Almighty. Another important quality, especially in this world of individualism and selfishness, is to love each other for God's sake and regard the Earth as a "cradle of brotherhood and sisterhood." Chastity requires self-discipline, and is so meritorious that it elevates its practitioners to the highest ranks. Giving alms purely for God's sake and without display is almost as much encouraged in Islam as are belief and the prescribed prayers. Meditation and continuous self-supervision, accompanied by a healthy attitude of God-consciousness, prevent people from sinning and make them worthy of Paradise.

- God is kind and gives favors to everyone. Whatever people have is from God. Nevertheless, He bestowed special favors on each Prophet and community according to the dictates of the time. For example, Adam was favored with knowledge of the names (the keys to all branches of knowledge). Noah was endowed with steadfastness and perseverance; Abraham was honored with God's intimate friendship and being the father of numerous Prophets; Moses was given the ability to administer, and was exalted by being addressed by God directly; and Jesus was distinguished with patience, tolerance, and compassion. All Prophets have some share in these praiseworthy qualities, but each surpasses, on account of his mission, the others in one or more than one of those qualities.

Prophet Muhammad has all of the qualities mentioned above, except for being the father of Prophets. Moreover, because of the universal nature of his mission, he is further distinguished in the following five ways. As related by Bukhari, he says:

> I have been given five things not given to anyone before me: God helps me by implanting fear in the heart of my enemies at a distance of one month's walk; the Earth has been made a place of worship and means of cleansing for me, so whenever it is time to pray my followers can pray wherever they are; the spoils of war are lawful for me, although they were not lawful for anyone before me; I have the right to intercede (with God on behalf of believers); and, while every Prophet (before me) was sent to his people exclusively, I was sent to humanity.[155]

It is possible to deduce the following things from this *hadith*:

- Prophethood is a Divine favor bestowed by God on whomever He wishes.

- The five things mentioned in the *hadith* are exclusive to the Muslim community.
- To make your enemies fear you from great distances, maintain complete sincerity and devotion to the cause of God, as was done during the Era of Happiness when the Prophet and his true successors ruled the Muslims.
- As Islam recognizes no intermediaries between God and people, there is no church or organized and professional clergy. Although saintly people may be allowed to intercede for certain Muslims on the Day of Judg-ment, God's Messenger will enjoy the right of all-inclusive intercession for believers of every community.
- The spoils of war, forbidden to previous communities as a trial, are lawful for Muslims, because they must struggle in the way of God until the Last Day and convey the Message throughout the world.
- While the mission of previous Prophets was restricted to a certain people and time, God's Messenger was sent as a mercy for all worlds.

INFALLIBILITY

Infallibility is a necessary attribute of the Prophets. The original Arabic word translated here as *infallibility* is 'isma, which means "protecting, saving, or defending." It appears in the Qur'an in several derived forms. For example, when Prophet Noah asked his son to board the Ark during the Flood, the latter replied: *I will betake myself to some mountain; it will save me from the water. Noah replied: Today there is not a saving one [active participle] from the command of God* (11:43).

The wife of a high Egyptian official, named Potiphar in the Bible (Genesis 39:1), uses the same word in: *I did seek to seduce him, but he firmly saved himself guiltless* (12:32). The Qur'an calls believers to hold fast to the *rope of God* (the Qur'an and Islam) using the same word in a different form: *Hold fast all together to, and protect (against being divided), the rope of God* (3:103). Again, we see the same word in the verse: *God will defend (protect) you from people* (5:67).

The infallibility of Prophets is an established fact based on reason and tradition. This quality is required for several reasons. First, Prophets came to convey the Message of God. If we liken this Message to pure water or light (13:17, 24:35), the Archangel Gabriel (who brought it) and the Prophet (who conveyed it) also must be absolutely pure. If this were not so, their impurity would pollute the Message. Every falling off is an impurity, a dark spot, in the heart. The hearts or souls of Gabriel and the Prophet are like polished mirrors that reflect the Divine Revelation to people, a clean cup from which people quench their thirst for the pure, Divine water.

Any black spot on the mirror would absorb a ray of that light; a single drop of mud would make the water unclear. As a result, the Prophets would not be able to deliver the complete Message. But they delivered the Message perfectly, as stated in the Qur'an:

> O Messenger! Convey what has been sent to you from your Lord. If you did not, you would not have fulfilled His mission. God will defend you from people. God guides not the unbelieving people. (5:67)

> Today I have perfected your religion for you, and I have completed My favor upon you, and I have chosen and approved for you Islam as religion. (5:3)

Second, the Prophets teach their people all the commands and principles of belief and conduct. So that the people learn their religion in its pristine purity and truth, and as perfectly as possible to secure their happiness and prosperity in both worlds, the Prophets must represent and then present the Revelation without fault or defect. This is their function as guides and good examples to be followed:

> You have in the Messenger of God a beautiful pattern, an excellent example, for anyone who aspires after God and the Last Day, and who engages much in the remembrance of God. (33:21)

> There is for you an excellent example in Abraham and those
> with him ... there was in them an excellent example for you—
> for those who aspire after God and the Last Day. (60:4, 6)

A Prophet can do or say only that which has been sanctioned by God. If he could, he would have to repent even beyond his current lifetime. For example, Abraham will tell those who approach him for intercession on the Day of Judgment to go to Moses, saying he cannot intercede for them because he spoke allusively three times in his life.[156] Although this is not a sin, his repentance will continue in the Hereafter.

Third, the Qur'an commands believers to obey the Prophet's orders and prohibitions, without exception, and emphasizes that *it is not fitting for a believer, man or woman, when a matter has been decided by God and His Messenger, to have any option about their decision* (33:36). It also warns believers that *what falls to them when God and His Messenger have given a judgment is only to say: "We have heard and obeyed"* (24:51). Absolute obedience to a Prophet means that all of his commands and prohibitions are correct and beyond reproach.

Prophethood is so great a favor that all Prophets bore extreme hardship while fulfilling the duty of thanksgiving, and always worried about not worshipping God sufficiently. Prophet Muhammad often implored God as follows:

> Glory be to You. We have not been able to know You as Your
> knowledge requires, O Known One. Glory be to You. We have
> not been able to worship You as Your worship requires, O
> Worshipped One.

The Qur'anic verses that are sometimes understood (mistakenly) to reprimand certain Prophets for some faults or to show that they seek God's forgiveness for some sin, should be considered in this light. Besides, God's forgiveness does not always mean that a sin has been committed. The Qur'anic words 'afw (pardon) and maghfira (forgiveness) also signify a special favor and kindness, as well as Divine dispensation, in respect to lightening or overlooking a religious duty, as in the following verses:

If any is forced (to eat of them) by hunger, with no inclination toward transgression, God is indeed Oft-Forgiving, Most Merciful. (5:3)

If . . . you find no water, then take for yourselves clean sand or earth, and rub therewith your faces and hands. For God is All-Pardoning and Oft-Forgiving. (4:43)

Fifth, sins and pardoning have different types and degrees. These are: disobeying religious commandments, and forgiveness thereof; disobeying God's laws of creation and life, and forgiveness thereof; and disobeying the rules of good manners or courtesy, and the forgiveness thereof. A fourth type, which is not a sin, involves not doing something as perfectly as possible, which is required by the love of and nearness to God. Some Prophets may have done this, but such acts cannot be considered sins according to the common definition.

Tradition also proves the Prophets' infallibility. God says of Moses: *I cast love over you from Me (and made you comely and loveable) in order that you might be brought up under My eye* (20:39). Thus, as Moses was brought up by God Himself and prepared for the mission of Messengership, how could he possibly commit a sin?

The same is true of all other Prophets. For example, God's Messenger says of Jesus: "Satan could not touch Jesus and his mother at his birth." Jesus was protected from birth until his elevation to the Presence of God:

(Mary) pointed to the infant (Jesus). They asked: "How can we talk to an infant in the cradle?" Jesus said: "I am a servant of God. He has given me the Scripture and made me a Prophet. He has made me blessed wheresoever I may be, and enjoined on me prayer and charity as long as I live. He has made me kind to my mother, and not overbearing or a wretched rebel. So peace is on me the day I was born, the day that I die, and the day that I will be raised up to life again." (19:29-33)

Jesus, like all Prophets, was protected from sin from his birth. The Messenger, while still a child and not yet a Prophet, intended to attend two wedding ceremonies, but on each occasion was overpowered by sleep.[157] During his youth he helped his uncles repair the Ka'ba by carrying stones. Since the stones hurt his shoulders, his uncle 'Abbas advised him to wrap part of his lower garment around his shoulders for padding. But as soon as he did so, thereby leaving parts of his thighs exposed, he fell on his back and stared fixedly. An angel appeared and warned him: "This is not befitting for you,"[158] for later he would tell people to be well-mannered and observe Divinely ordained standards of conduct, including covering the thighs. In such ways was the future Prophet protected from his people's pagan rituals and practices.

God's Messenger says that "all children of Adam make faults and err, and the best of those who make faults and err are the repentant."[159] This implies that as human beings we are fallible by nature, not that we are condemned to make such mistakes. Whether by God's Will and special protection or, as will be explained below, by His showing the way to become free of error or sin, even the greatest saints who continue the Prophetic mission may be infallible to some degree.

God, the Almighty, promises to protect believers who obey Him in utmost respect and deserve His protection, and to endow them with sound judgment so that they can distinguish between the truth and falsehood, and right and wrong:

> O you who believe! If you obey God in utmost respect, He will establish in you a Criterion (to judge between right and wrong), purify you of all your evils, and forgive you. God is of grace unbounded. (8:29)

God made a covenant with the believers that if they obey Him and strive to exalt His Word, by proclaiming His religion, He will help them and establish them firmly in the religion, protecting them against all kinds of deviation (47:7). This protection from enemies and committing sins depends upon their support of Islam and the struggle to spread it so that only God is worshipped, and that no partners are associated with Him in belief or worship, or in the creation and rule of the universe. If believers keep their promise, *God will keep His (2:40); if they break it, God will cause them to fail* (17:8).

God protects His servants against sin in different ways. For example, he may place obstacles in their way, establish a "warner" in their hearts, or even cause them to suffer some injury so that they physically cannot sin. Or, He may put a verse in someone's mouth, as happened with a young man during 'Umar's caliphate.

The young man was so strict and attentive in his worship that he prayed every prayer in the mosque. A woman who lived on his way to the mosque had become enamored with him and so sought to seduce him. Although he resisted her gestures, the moment came when he took a few steps in her direction. Just at this moment, he felt he was reciting: *Those who fear God, when a thought of evil from Satan assaults them, bring God to remembrance, and lo! they see (aright)* (7:201). Overwhelmed with shame before God, and with love of God for preventing him from committing this sin, he fell down dead. When 'Umar was informed of this a few days later, he went to his grave and shouted: *"O young man. For those who fear the time when they will stand before the Lord, there will be two gardens!"* (55:46). A voice from the grave, whether that of the young man or an angel on his behalf, replied: "O Commander of the Believers, God has granted me the double of what you say."[160]

This is how God protects His sincere servants. He says in a *hadith qudsi*[161]:

> My servants cannot draw near to me through something else more lovable to Me than performing the obligations I have enjoined upon them. Apart from those obligations, they continue to draw near to Me through supererogatory acts of worship, until I love them. When I love them, I will be their ears with which they hear, their eyes with which they see, their hands with which they grasp, and their feet on which they walk. If they ask Me for something, I will give it to them immediately. If they seek refuge in Me from something, I will protect them from it.[162]

God guides His true servants to good and protects them from evil. The servants will and do what is good, and refrain from wickedness. They ask God for what is good, and whatever they ask is provided. They seek refuge in God from what is bad, and God protects them according to their request.

All Prophets were infallible, sinless, and lived completely virtuous lives. Although God sent numerous Prophets, the Qur'an specifically mentions only 28 of them. I think it would be proper here to count them in the words of Ibrahim Haqqi, an eighteenth-century Turkish saint and religious scholar, who also was an expert in anatomy and astronomy:

Some have regarded it a religious injunction to learn the names of the Prophets.

> God informed us of 28 of them in the Qur'an: Adam, Enoch, Noah, Hud, and Salih; Abraham, Isaac, and Ishmael, who was a sacrifice for God; Jacob, Joseph, Shu'ayb, Lot, and John the Baptist; Zachariah and Aaron, the brother of Moses, who spoke to God; David, Solomon, Elijah, and Job; Elisha, a relative of Jesus, who was a spirit from God; Dhu al-Kifl and Jonah, who was certainly a Prophet.

The Seal of Prophets is the Beloved of God—Muhammad, the Messenger of God. Scholars disagree on the Prophethood of Ezra, Luqman, and Dhu al-Qarnayn. Some regard them as Prophets, while others consider them saints of God.

Removing Doubts

Some Qur'anic verses appear to reprimand certain Prophets or entertain the possibility that a Prophet can sin, according to the usual definition of that word. Before clarifying specific examples, it may be appropriate to acquit the Prophets of such accusations.

Genesis 19:30-38 states that Prophet Lot's two daughters caused him to get drunk so that he would impregnate them. Such a charge against a Prophet is beyond belief. Lot's people (Sodom and Gomorra) were destroyed by God for their sexual immorality. Even the Bible says that Lot and his daughters were the only ones spared, because of their belief, good conduct, and decency. This supposed "sin" of Prophet Lot is worse than the sin of his people, which caused God to destroy them!

In Genesis 38:15-18, Judah,[163] a son of Jacob, is supposed to have engaged in sexual relations with his daughter-in-law. This woman, in turn, gave birth to twin boys. Some of the Israelite Prophets were descended from them. Genesis 49:4 also claims that Jacob's other son, Reuben, slept with his father's wife (Reuben's stepmother).

Neither the sons of Jacob, whom the Qur'an mentions as "grandchildren" whose ways should be followed, nor his wives could have engaged such a behavior.[164] Our Prophet explicitly declared that there is not a single case of fornication in his lineage back to Adam,[165] and that all Prophets are brothers descended from the same father.[166] Our Prophet is a descendant of Abraham, as were Judah and the other Israelite Prophets. Thus, how could any of them be the result of an improper sexual alliance?

II Samuel 11 records that Prophet David fell in love with the wife of a commander and committed adultery with her. According to the Bible, he then had her husband sent to the front line and, after he was killed, married her.

David is a Prophet who was given a Divine Scripture (the Psalms) and who is praised in the Qur'an for his sincere and profound devotion to God:

> Be patient with them, and remember Our servant David, the man of strength and abilities, who always turned to God in sincere devotion and submission. We made the mountains declare, in unison with him, Our praises, at eventide and at the break of day, and the birds gathered (in assemblies): all with him did turn to Him (in profound devotion). We strengthened his kingdom and gave him wisdom and sound judgment (in speech and decision). (38:17-20)

Though a king, he lived a simple life by his own labor. He had such a great awareness of God that he cried a great deal and fasted every other day. Our Prophet recommended this type of fast to some Companions who asked about the most rewarding type of supererogatory fasting.[167] Could such a noble Prophet ever commit adultery with a married woman, plot her husband's death, and then marry her?

In I Kings 11:1-8, despite God's command: "You must not intermarry with them, because they will surely turn your hearts after their gods," Prophet Solomon is accused of marrying many foreign women belonging to pagan nations and following their gods and goddesses (idols). Would a Prophet be able to commit such a grievous sin as following the idols and deities of other tribes?

If the Qur'an had not been revealed, we would not be sure whether the previous Prophets really were sincere, devout, and thankful servants of God. The Qur'an frees Jesus from his followers' mistaken deification of him and from his own people's denial of his Prophethood, and explains that God had no sons and daughters. It also clears the Israelite and non-Israelite Prophets of their supposed "sins" mentioned in the Bible. It presents Jesus as a spirit from God breathed into the Virgin Mary, Abraham as an intimate friend of God, Moses as one who spoke to God, and Solomon as a king and a Prophet who prayed to Him humbly:

> O my Lord, order me that I may be grateful for your favors,
> which You have bestowed on me and on my parents, and that
> I may work the righteousness that will please You. Admit me,
> by Your Grace, to the ranks of Your righteous servants. (27:19)

Solomon never worshipped idols or committed a sin. Despite being the greatest and most powerful king that ever lived, he remained a humble servant of God until his death.

Several other assertions are equally impossible to accept. For example: The Bible claims that although Prophet Isaac wanted to bless his older son Esau, he mistakenly blessed Jacob, for he could not see through his wife Rebaka's trick (Genesis 27). Also, the Bible claims that Prophet Jacob wrestled with God, who appeared to him in the form of a man (Genesis 32:24-30).

Individual Examples

A small minority of Muslim scholars have asserted that the Prophets may have committed insignificant sins (zalla: error or lapse). To prove their assertion, they cite some examples from the lives of Adam, Noah, Abraham, and Joseph.

Before elaborating upon this, it should be noted that lapses and sins have totally different definitions. Sin, for example, means disobedience to God's Commands. When the Prophets were faced with a question that they could not answer, they tended to wait for Revelation. On rare occasions, however, they used their own reason to decide the matter, as they were the foremost *mujtahids* (jurists of the highest rank who can deduce laws from the principles established by the Qur'an and the Sunna). They might have erred in their judgments or decisions. However, such errors, which were immediately corrected by God, are not sins.

Moreover, Prophets always sought God's good pleasure and tried to obtain whatever was best. If, for some reason, they could not obtain the best but had to settle for the better, a very rare event, this does not mean that they sinned. For example: Suppose you must decide whether to recite the Qur'an in 10 days while giving due attention to each verse, or recite it in 7 days to express your deep love of the Word of God. If you choose the first option without knowing that God's greater pleasure lies in the second, you cannot be considered guilty of a sin. So, a Prophet's preference of what is better instead of the best is not a sin. However, because of his position before Him, God might sometimes reproach him mildly.

Now, we will clarify some individual examples in the lives of certain Prophets.

Prophet Adam

Adam was in the Garden before his worldly life. While therein, God told him and his wife Eve not to eat of the fruit of a particular tree. They disobeyed Him in this matter, and so were expelled from the Garden and commanded to live on earth.

Although Qur'anic interpreters differ on what the prohibited fruit was, it was most probably the human inclination toward the opposite sex. Satan approached Adam and Eve, saying that it was *a tree of eternity and of a kingdom that would never decay, the fruit of which had been prohibited to them* (20:120). Most probably knowing that they were mortal, Adam and Eve must have desired eternity through offspring, as such a desire is inherent in people. This also can be deduced from:

> Then Satan whispered to them so that he might show to them that which was hidden from them of their shame. He said: "Your Lord forbade you this tree only lest you should become angels or become immortal." And he swore to them (saying): "Truly, I am a sincere adviser to you." Thus did he lead them by a deceit. When they tasted of the tree, their shame was shown to them and they began to cover (by placing) on themselves some leaves of the Garden. . . (7:20-22)

Even if we accept Adam's eating of the forbidden fruit as a lapse, it is difficult to regard it as deliberate or sustained disobedience or revolt against God, which might lead us to see the Prophets as fallible. First, Adam was not a Prophet while in the Garden. Second, this lapse was the result not of willful disobedience, but merely some sort of forgetfulness. Concerning this, the Qur'an says: *We had made a covenant with Adam before, but he forgot, and we found on his part no firm resolve* (20:115).

Sins committed because of forgetfulness will not be accounted for in the Hereafter. The Prophet said: "My community is exempt from being questioned about forgetting, unintentional errors, and what they are compelled to do."[168] The Qur'an teaches us this prayer: *Our Lord, don't condemn us if we forget or fall into error* (2:286).

Adam did not make this lapse deliberately. Although some have read into this verse Adam's lack of determination to fulfill his covenant with God, the context does not allow such an interpretation. Adam and Eve turned to God immediately after their lapse and, in sincere repentance, entreated Him: *Our Lord, we have wronged our own selves. If you don't forgive us and don't bestow Your Mercy upon us, we certainly shall be among the lost* (7:23).

Destiny had a part in Adam's lapse. God had destined him to be His vicegerent on Earth, even before his creation and settlement in the Garden. This is explicit in the Qur'an:

> Behold, your Lord said to the angels: "I will make a vicegerent on Earth." They asked: "Will you make therein one who will

make mischief and shed blood, while we celebrate Your praises and glorify You?" He said: "I know what you know not." (2:30)

God's Messenger also points to that truth in a hadith:

> Adam and Moses met each other in Heaven. Moses said to Adam: "You are the father of humanity, but you caused us to come down to Earth from the Garden." Adam replied: "You are the one whom God addressed directly. Did you not see this sentence in the Torah: 'Adam had been destined to eat of that fruit 40 years before he ate of it?'"

After reporting this meeting, God's Messenger added three times: "Adam silenced Moses."[169]

Adam's life in the Garden and his trial were preliminaries he had to pass through before his earthly life. He passed these tests. Being chosen and rescued from the swamp of sin and deviation, he was made a Prophet and honored with being the father of thousands of Prophets, including Prophet Muhammad, and millions of saints: *Then his Lord chose him; He relented toward him, and rightly guided him* (20:122).

Prophet Noah

Prophet Noah called his people to the religion of God for 950 years. When they insisted on unbelief and persisted in their wrongdoing, God told him to build the Ark. After completing this task, Noah placed therein, according to God's command, a male and female of each animal, all his family members (except for those whom God already had said He would punish), and the believers (11:40).

When the Ark was floating through the mountain-high waves, Noah saw that one of his sons had not boarded the Ark. He called to him, but his son rejected his call, saying: *I will betake myself to some mountain and it will save me from the water* (11:43). When Noah saw his son drowning, he called out to God: *My Lord, my son is of my family! Your promise is true, and You are the Most Just of Judges* (11:45). God replied: *O Noah, he is not of your family, for his conduct is unrighteous. Do not ask of Me that of which you have no knowledge. I give you counsel, lest you should act like the ignorant* (11:46).

Some scholars have regarded Noah's appeal as a sin. However, it is difficult to agree with them. Noah is mentioned in the Qur'an as one of the five greatest Prophets, and is described as resolute and steadfast. He thought his son was a believer.

It is well known that the religion of God tells us to judge according to outward appearances. Thus, those who profess belief and appear to perform the religious duties of primary importance (e.g., prescribed prayers and alms-giving) are treated as believers. This is why Prophet Muhammad treated the Hypocrites as if they were Muslims. Apparently, Noah's son hid his unbelief until the Flood, for it was Noah himself who had prayed beforehand that God *should forgive him, his parents, and all who entered his house in faith, and all believing men and believing women, and grant to the wrongdoers no increase but perdition* (71:28).

God accepted his prayer and told him to board the Ark with his family, except those who had already deserved punishment because of their willful insistence on unbelief. Noah's wife was among those who drowned. Noah did not ask God to save her, for he either knew or was informed that she was an unbeliever. He must have thought his son was a believer. As such, he felt compelled to express, in a manner befitting a Prophet, his astonishment that God had let him drown. This is why God replied to him as He did (11:46).

Noah, like every other Prophet, was kind-hearted and caring. Every Prophet sacrificed himself for the good of humanity and made tireless efforts to guide people toward the truth and true happiness in both worlds. Concerning Prophet Muhammad's attitude in this respect, God says: *You would nearly kill yourself following after them, in grief, if they believe not in this Message* (18:6).

Noah appealed to his people for 950 years, never once relenting. It is natural for a Prophet, a father, to show disappointment when he learns that his son is among the unbelievers who have been condemned to punishment in both worlds. But since God is the Most Just and Most Compassionate, Noah immediately turned to Him and sought refuge with Him, lest he should ask Him for that of which he had no knowledge:

> O my Lord, I seek refuge with you, lest I should ask You for that of which I have no knowledge. Unless You forgive me and have mercy on me, I shall be lost. (11:47)

Prophet Abraham

Abraham, the "intimate friend of God," was one of the greatest Prophets. God's Messenger took pride and pleasure in his connection with him, saying: "I am the one whose coming Abraham prayed for and Jesus gave glad tidings of, and I resemble my forefather Abraham more than anyone else."[170] He was thrown into fire because of his belief in One God, and the fire became, by God's Will and Power, coolness and a means of safety for him.

Like all Prophets, Abraham never even thought of worshipping that which was not God. Despite this fact, various erroneous and untrue stories have found their way into some Qur'anic commentaries. They have come from a misunderstanding of the following verses:

> When the night covered him over, he saw a star and said: "This is my Lord." But when it set, he said: "I don't love those that set." When he saw the moon rising in splendor, he said: "This is my Lord." But when it set, he said: "Unless my Lord guides me, I surely will be among those who go astray." When he saw the sun rising in splendor, he said: "This is my Lord; this is the greatest (of all)." But when the sun set, he said: "O my people, I am free from your ascribing partners to God. I have set my face toward Him Who created the Heavens and the Earth, a man of pure faith and one by nature upright. I am not among those who associate partners with God." (6:76-79)

These verses clearly show that Abraham tried, by way of analogy, to convince his people that no heavenly body could be God. Abraham lived among the Chaldeans of northern Mesopotamia, a people who knew a great deal about heavenly bodies and who worshipped them, along with many other idols. Abraham first argued with his father, telling him that no idol was worthy of worship: *Abraham once said to his father Azar: "Do you take idols for gods? Surely I see you and your people in manifest deviation"* (6:74).

Since Azar was the local idol maker, Abraham began his mission by opposing him. After that, he sought to guide his people to the truth. Since they had a great knowledge of heavenly bodies, God instructed him in such matters and showed him various hidden metaphysical realities so that he might attain complete certainty in belief and convince his people of their deviation:

> So also did We show Abraham the inner dimensions of, and the
> metaphysical realities behind, the Heavens and the Earth, that
> he might have certainty. (6:75)

While traveling in mind and heart through heavenly bodies, Abraham began by telling his people that a star could not be God because it sets. Although the superstitious might read fortunes into it or attribute some influence to it, true knowledge shows that it rises and sets according to God's laws, and that its light is extinguished in the broader light of day. So why should anyone worship stars?

His second step in this analogy was to show that the moon, although looking brighter and bigger than a star, could not be God. This is because it sets like a star, changes its shape from hour to hour, and depends on some other heavenly body for its light. At this point, Abraham openly declared that he had been guided by his Lord, and that those who did not worship only Him had gone astray.

Abraham's final analogy showed that the sun could not be worshipped as God, for despite its size and light, it also disappears from sight. Thus, worshipping created phenomena is pure folly. After rejecting the worship of creation, Abraham declared his faith:

> I have set my face toward Him Who created the Heavens and
> the Earth, a man of pure faith and one by nature upright. I am
> not among those who associate partners with God. (6:79)

So, it is a great mistake to infer from these verses that Abraham took heavenly bodies as God in the early phase of his life.

Abraham's second supposed fault or lapse is that he appealed to God to show him how He revives the dead. Concerning this, the Qur'an says:

> Behold! Abraham said: "My Lord, show me how You give life to the dead." He asked: "Do you not believe?" He said: "Yes, but to set my heart at rest." (2:260)

In a *hadith*, God's Messenger says that 70,000 veils separate God from humanity. This implies that our journey toward God is endless, and that people have different degrees of knowledge and understanding as well as varying capacities for spiritual and intellectual satisfaction. Since God is infinite, unbounded in His Attributes and Names, each individual can obtain only some knowledge of Him and attain some degree of satisfaction (according to his or her capacity).

Abraham had one of the greatest capacities, and therefore needed to increase in knowledge of God every day to attain full spiritual satisfaction. The Prophets, like every other human being, were in a constant process of spiritual and intellectual growth. Considering each previous stage of growth inadequate, they incessantly pursued further degrees of conviction. For this reason, God's Messenger asked God's forgiveness about 100 times a day and frequently entreated Him, saying:

> Glory be to You, we have not been able to know You as Your knowledge requires, O Known One! Glory be to You, we have not been able to worship You as Your worship requires, O Worshipped One!

Once Muhyi al-Din ibn al-'Arabi met Mawlana Jalal al-Din al-Rumi and asked him: "Who is greater: Prophet Muhammad, who says: 'Glory be to You, we have not been able to know You as Your knowledge requires, O Known One,' or Bayazid al-Bistami, who says [in an instance of entranced ecstasy]: 'Glory be to me, how exalted I am!'?" Mawlana's reply also answers those who try to find fault with Abraham: "Both utterances show to what extent our Prophet is greater than Bayazid. Our Prophet's heart or soul was like an ocean, so deep and vast that it could not be satisfied.

But Bayazid's soul, in comparison, was like a pitcher—easy to fill and quick to overflow."[171]

To remove any possible doubt of Abraham's conviction, God's Messenger once said: "If Abraham's conviction contained a doubt, we are more liable to doubt than him."[172]

Abraham's whole life was a constant struggle against unbelief and polytheism. On only three occasions did he ever use allusions. In other words, he chose to divert his audience's attention to something else by making indirect references to the truth. He did this either to avoid harassment or explain a religious truth in simpler terms. Since, however, some scholars consider these allusions to be lies, we must clarify them here.

The first allusion: When his people wanted him to accompany them to their religious celebration, he cast a glance at the stars and said he was sick.

Abraham was not physically sick, but the grief that he might be associated with his people's falsehoods was preying on his mind and soul. It was impossible for him to worship idols; rather, he was determined to destroy them. Once, to avoid participating in their ceremonies, he told them he was sick and, after they left, smashed their idols. This was not a lie, for he truly was sick of their idols and idolatry. This is why he did what he did. The Qur'an praises him for this:

> Among those who followed Noah's way was Abraham. He came unto his Lord with a pure, sound heart. He said to his father and his people: "What do you worship? Do you desire a falsehood, gods other than God? What, then, is your opinion of the Lord of the Worlds?" Then he cast a glance at the stars, and said: "I am indeed sick!" So they turned away from him and departed. Then he turned to their gods and asked: "Why don't you eat [of the offerings before you]? Why don't you speak?" Then he turned upon them, striking them with might (and breaking them). (37:83-93)

The second allusion: Abraham uses irony to make his point. As we read in the Qur'an:

We bestowed on Abraham his rectitude before, and were well acquainted with him. He asked his father and his people: "What are these images to which you are (so assiduously) devoted in worship?" They replied: "We found our fathers worshipping them." He said: "Clearly, both you and your fathers have deviated (from the truth)." They said: "Have you brought us the truth, or are you joking with us?" He replied: "No, your Lord is the Lord of the Heavens and the Earth, He who created them. I am a witness [to this truth]. By God, I have a plan for your idols after you go away and turn your backs." So he broke them to pieces, (all) but the biggest, that they might turn to it. They exclaimed: "Who has done this to our gods? He must indeed be some evil-doer!" They said: "We have heard a youth talk of them: Abraham." They replied: "Bring him before the people, that they may bear witness." They asked him: "Did you do this to our gods, Abraham?" He answered: "Maybe he did it. This is their biggest one. Ask them, if they can speak!" (21:51-63)

Some consider Abraham's final reply to be a lie. The truth is, it is an example of biting irony. Abraham wanted his people to understand that things that cannot speak or do them any harm or good are unworthy of worship. He was so successful in this attempt that his people, unable to refute his reasoning, could find no way to protect their idols other than by throwing him into the fire.

Abraham did not say that the idols had been broken by the biggest one. Look at his answer carefully. He said: "He did it," and then stopped—there is a significant stop in the reading of the verse—and then continued: "This is their biggest one!" Therefore, the phrase *He did it* alludes to the one who broke the idols, but diverted the audience's attention to the biggest one with: *This is their biggest one!*

Once, God's Messenger told an old woman that old people will not enter Paradise. When he saw that his words distressed her greatly, he clarified the irony: "Because they will enter it as young people."[173] This is, in a way, similar to what Abraham did and so is not a lie.

The third allusion: Abraham and his wife Sarah.

In a *hadith*, and also in the Bible (Genesis 20:2-14), we read that Abraham wanted his wife Sarah to reply to those who asked that she was his sister, not his wife.[174] According to the Bible, Abraham did this because he would have been killed if her true identity were known. This is not a lie, for as declared in the Qur'an, all believers are brothers or sisters to each other.

In conclusion, Abraham never lied. If he had done so, he would have been reproached by God. However, the Qur'an never mentions that God reproached him for lying. On the contrary, his allusions are mentioned where God praises him in the Qur'an. For this reason, the Prophetic Tradition about those allusions should not be treated literally.

Abraham's Supposed Lapse

Abraham began his mission by calling upon his father Azar, the local idol maker, to abandon idolatry and turn toward God, the Creator of the Heavens and the Earth. When his father refused to do so, he left him, saying that he would ask God to forgive him. He kept his promise: *Forgive my father, for he is one of those who go astray* (26:86).

Some consider this a lapse, for after all his father was an unbeliever. However, it is difficult to regard it as a lapse, for Abraham was a Prophet deputed by God to call people to the truth and salvation. Like every Prophet, it grieved him to see any of God's servants not following His way to happiness and salvation in both worlds. We can discern in the following verses just how much he desired his father to be guided:

> (Also) mention in the Book (the story of) Abraham: He was a man of truth, a Prophet. He asked his father: "My father, why do you worship that which cannot hear or see, and which cannot benefit you? There has come to me that knowledge which has not reached you, so follow me. I will guide you to a straight, even way. Don't serve Satan, for Satan is a rebel against the Most Merciful. O father, I fear lest a penalty afflict you from the Most Merciful, so that you become a friend to Satan." (19:41-45)

It was Abraham's duty to call people to worship God, despite their persistent rejection. Although the Qur'an openly stated that:

As to those who do not believe, it is the same to them whether you warn them or not, for they will not believe (2:6), God's Messenger never gave up warning them. Besides calling his father to the truth, Abraham prayed for him until, as stated in the Qur'an, he realized that his father was an enemy of God. When he was convinced of this fact, he dissociated himself from him. God mentions this not as a lapse on Abraham's part, but as a virtue, saying: *For Abraham was most tender-hearted, forbearing* (9:114).

God also mentions Abraham's conduct as an excellent example to follow:

> There is for you an excellent example (to follow) in Abraham and those with him. They said to their people: "We are free of you and whatever you worship besides God. We have rejected you, and there has arisen enmity and hatred forever between us and you, unless you believe in God and Him alone." But Abraham said to his father: "I will pray for forgiveness for you, although I have no power (to get) anything on your behalf from God." Our Lord! In You we have put our trust, and to You we turn in repentance; to You is the final return. (60:4)

As indicated above, Abraham prayed for his father's forgiveness because he had promised to do so (9:114). When he saw that his father was determined to persist in his unbelief, he dissociated himself from him and no longer sought his forgiveness.

Finally, it should be noted here that some Qur'anic interpreters do not consider Azar to be Abraham's father. Although it is not a defect on the part of Abraham to descend from an unbelieving father, for *God Almighty brings forth the living out of the dead, and brings forth the dead out of the living* (3:27), the Qur'an always uses the word ab (which in addition to father can mean *uncle, step-father, foster-father, or grandfather*) for Azar.

Although he was told not to seek forgiveness for Azar, the Qur'an mentions that in his old age he prayed: *Our Lord, forgive me, my parents, and all believers on the day that the Reckoning will be established* (14:41). In this prayer, he uses walid (the one who begot him) for father. It is therefore quite possible that Azar was not the one who begot him. According to the Bible, Abraham's real father was Terah. However, God knows best.

Prophet Joseph

Prophet Joseph is exalted in the Qur'an as an example of chastity. In his childhood, his envious brothers threw him down a well and left him there. A passing caravan found him and later sold him as a slave to a high official (probably a minister) of the Egyptian court. The Bible gives his name as Potiphar Genesis (37:36).

Joseph came from a family of Prophets. When someone told God's Messenger that he was a noble man, the Messenger alluded to this fact, saying: "The noble one, son of a noble one who is the son of a noble one who is the son of a noble one. This is Joseph, son of Jacob, son of Isaac, son of Abraham, the intimate friend of God."[175] Joseph was still a child in the well, when God revealed to him that he *would one day tell his brothers the truth of what they had done* (12:15). Therefore, from the beginning he was protected from all vice.

Joseph, an exceptionally handsome young man, soon came to the attention of his master's wife. Eventually, she fell in love with him. In the words of the ladies of the capital city, quoted by the Qur'an, Joseph *inspired her with passionate love* (12:30). She tried to seduce him by locking the doors and calling him to come to her. But Joseph, having been given knowledge, sound judgment, and discernment by God, replied immediately: *God forbid! Truly my Lord has treated me honorably. Assuredly, wrongdoers never prosper* (12:23).

Prophet Joseph had attained the rank of *ihsan*, which God's Messenger describes as the believer's ability to worship as if seeing God in front of him or her. In other words, at every instant he was aware of God watching him. He also was one whom God had made sincere, pure-hearted, and of pure intention. Therefore, it is inconceivable that he would betray God's blessings by succumbing to this temptation. If he had taken only one step in this direction, he would have become a wrongdoer. Or, if by "my lord" he meant his master, he would have been a wrongdoer if he had violated his master's trust.

While narrating the rest of the story, the Qur'an says:

> Certainly, she burnt inwardly because of him; and he burnt inwardly because of her until he saw the evidence of his Lord: thus We did that we might turn away from him all evil and shameful deeds. For he was one of Our servants, made beforehand sincere and pure. (12:24)

Unfortunately, the sentence translated here *as she burnt inwardly because of him; and he burnt inwardly because of her until he saw the evidence of his Lord*, has been misunderstood by some interpreters of the Qur'an to mean "she desired, and was moved toward him; and he desired, and was moved toward her, but just at that point he saw the evidence of his Lord and stopped." Some have embellished *the evidence of his Lord* with such flights of fancy as Jacob appearing with his hand on his lips and saving his son from a grave sin.

More than a misunderstanding, this is a slander against a Prophet who was honored and presented by God as "a most excellent model of chastity," and by God's Messenger as the noblest of all. To remove all such doubts, we will analyze hamma, which we have translated literally as "to burn inwardly," for this word has confused some interpreters.

Hamma literally means "to suffer, burn, be troubled inwardly, and be consumed with passion and longing." There is a principle in the sciences of morphology and semantics that the first and most common meaning of a word is preferred, unless an inconsistency or inconformity appears in the context. This principle, together with two other principles to be explained below, make it impossible to take hamma in its first meaning:

One: Joseph and this lady were worlds apart with respect to their beliefs, ambitions, characters, and ways of life. Therefore, each had his or her own suffering and anxiety, and each was consumed with completely different ambitions.

Two: The verse containing hamma is a parenthetical one explaining the virtue of belief and sincerity, which bring God's special favor and protection. It is not there merely as a part of the story. It also should be noted that there are stops after each phrase, which shows that they do not link a chain of events, but rather express three different realities. In this case, the exact meaning of the verse is as follows:

> She was burning inwardly because of her love for Joseph. This love got Joseph into great trouble; his chastity, good character and reputation might have been damaged. He had to escape this situation. At this juncture, God's evidence (His protection or something else) came to his aid and turned all evil away from him, for God already had made him one of His sincere and pure servants. He was not mukhlis (one purified and sincere due to self-discipline and spiritual training), but rather a *mukhlas* (one made by God sincere and pure).

Moreover, the verb hamma in this context does not indicate the beginning of an action, for we read in the previous verse that she already had started the action: *she locked the door and called Joseph to come to her* (12:23). But Joseph refused. So, to say that *hamma* has the meaning of "to start toward" for both Joseph and the woman contradicts the previous verse, as well as the next one: *So they both hurried to the door, and she tore the shirt from his back* (12:25). It is clear that Joseph ran to the door to escape, that she ran after him to catch him, and that she tore the shirt from his back.

Some, however, suggest that she desired Joseph and that he might have desired her if he had not seen his Lord's evidence. Since he had been protected from the beginning against sin, he could not have any desire for her. In either case, he neither felt something for her nor start toward her. Like every other Prophet, Joseph was infallible.

Prophet Muhammad

God's Messenger is superior to all other Prophets. This could not be otherwise, for he was sent as a mercy to all the worlds. The religion he relayed includes all essential tenets of the previously revealed religions as well as everything necessary to solve all human problems until the Last Day. In contrast, all earlier Prophets were sent to certain people and for a limited period.

Prophet Muhammad, in the words of Busiri: ". . . is the sun of virtues and the others are, in comparison to him, stars diffusing light for people at night." When the sun rises, both the moon and stars are no longer visible. Likewise, when the "Sun of Prophethood" (Prophet Muhammad rose to illuminate all the universe, starlight became unnecessary.

Like his predecessors, Prophet Muhammad was infallible. We see both in the Qur'an and history books that, although his enemies slandered him relentlessly, they never questioned his honesty and infallibility.

They said he was "mad"—he madly loved God and, again, madly desired and sought for the people to be guided. Thus he was "mad," but not in the sense of being crazy. They said he was a "magician" who charmed people—he did charm them, but with his personality, as well as with Islam and the Qur'an, both of which he brought from God. But he was not a magician. They said he was a "soothsayer"—he made hundreds of predictions, most of which have already come true and the others waiting to be proven. But he was not a soothsayer.

Like the already discussed Qur'anic expressions that, superficially, seem to cast doubt on the infallibility of some of the Prophets, there are several admonitions in the Qur'an regarding some actions of God's Messenger. Before analyzing them, however, we must remember that Prophets, like great jurists, also exercised their personal reason if no explicit or implicit ruling concerning the matter in question had been revealed.

Just as the Prophet's wives are not the same as other Muslim women with respect to reward and Divine punishment (see 33:30-32), God does not treat Prophets as He does other believers. For example, He admonished them when they drank water from Zamzam (a well in Makka) instead of from Kawthar (a fountain in Paradise). Such admonitions should never be regarded as the result of sin. Furthermore, these admonitions usually are really Divine compliments that show the greatness of Prophets and their nearness to God.

God's Messenger and the Prisoners Taken During the Battle of Badr

The small Muslim community of Makka was subjected to the most brutal tortures. Its members bore them patiently and never thought of retaliation, for the Qur'an ordered God's Messenger to call unbelievers with wisdom and fair preaching, to repel evil with what was better, and to forgive their faults and evil deeds. When the Muslims emigrated to Madina to live according to Islamic principles, they left everything behind. However, they continued to be harassed in Madina by both Makkan polytheists as well as a new group: Madina's Jewish tribes. Moreover, even though the Ansar (the Helpers) willingly shared all their possessions with the Emigrants, all Muslims experienced deprivation. In such straitened circumstances and because they had been wronged, God permitted them to resist the enemy onslaught. This was just before the Battle of Badr.

This battle was the Muslims' first military confrontation with the enemy forces. Although outnumbered, the believers won a great victory. Until then, if we do not accept the opinions of some Qur'anic interpreters that *Sura Muhammad*, which contains regulations on treating prisoners of war, was revealed before *Surat al-Anfal*, no Divine commandment had been revealed on how to treat captives. Muslims did not know if they were to kill enemy soldiers or take them as prisoners. Sa'd ibn Mu'adh, for example, was not pleased when he saw fellow Muslims taking prisoners; he was in favor of killing them in the first confrontation.

After the battle, the Prophet consulted with his Companions, as he always did where there was no specific Revelation, on how to treat the prisoners. Abu Bakr said: "O God's Messenger, they are your people. Even though they have wronged you and the believers greatly, you will win their hearts and cause their guidance if you forgive them and please them."

'Umar had a different idea. He said: "O God's Messenger, these prisoners are the leading figures of Makka. If we kill them, unbelief will no longer be strong enough to fight us again. Hand each prisoner over to his Muslim relative. Let 'Ali kill his brother 'Aqil. Let Abu Bakr kill his son 'Abd al-Rahman. Let me kill my relative so and so."

God's Messenger turned to Abu Bakr and said: *"You are like Abraham, who said: He who follows me is of me, and he who disobeys me—but You are indeed Oft-Forgiving, Most Compassionate* (14:36). You are also like Jesus, who said: *If You punish them, they are Your servants. If You forgive them, You are All-Mighty, All-Wise* (5:118). Then he turned to 'Umar and said: "You are like Noah, who said: *O my Lord, don't leave even one unbeliever on Earth*" (71:26). You are also like Moses, who said: *Our Lord, destroy their (Pharaoh's and his chiefs') riches and harden their hearts so they will not believe until they see the painful chastisement* (10:88). He followed Abu Bakr's advice.[176]

Every Prophet was sent to guide people to the way of God, and the mission of each was based on mercy. However, mercy sometimes requires, as in the case of Noah and Moses amputating an arm to ensure the body's health, or even that the body should undergo a major operation. Islam, being the middle way of absolute balance between all temporal and spiritual extremes and containing the ways of all previous Prophets, makes a choice according to the situation.

Prior to Badr, the Muslims were weak, whereas their enemies, in material terms, were strong, formidable, and organized. Thus, conditions may have required that *the Prophet should not have had prisoners of war until he became completely triumphant in the land* (8:67), for they were fighting for the cause of God, not for some worldly purpose. However, God Almighty already had decreed that ransom and spoils of war would be lawful for Muslims. The pure hearts of the Prophet and Abu Bakr must have felt that God would allow them to take spoils of war and ransom prisoners. Therefore, they released the prisoners in return for some ransom before the relevant verses were revealed:

> Had it not been for that decree, a severe penalty would have reached them for the ransom that they took. But if God made it lawful, they could enjoy what they took in war, lawful and good. (8:68-69)

This is mentioned more explicitly in another verse:

> When you confront the unbelievers (in battle), smite their necks. When you have thoroughly subdued them, bind them firmly.

> Thereafter (it is time for) either generosity (release without ran-
> som) or ransom (recommended). (47:4)

To conclude, the Muslims did not disobey a Divine commandment that had been revealed already, and so they did not
sin. already It was a decision reached after consultation.

The Prophet's Exempting the Hypocrites from the Expedition of Tabuk

The expedition of Tabuk took place in 9 ah (after hijra) during the
summer, when Arabia's heat is intense. The soldiers were sent to
face Byzantium, one of the two local superpowers. Against his custom, God's Messenger announced the expedition's target. Some
people asked to be excused, and God's Messenger excused those
whose excuses he regarded as justifiable. He did not check to see
whether they were telling the truth for, as a Muslim, he had to
judge according to outward signs and the affirmation of faith.[177]

Besides, as God veils people's shortcomings, God's Messenger
never reproached people directly. When he discerned a defect in an
individual or a fault common in his community, he would mount
the pulpit and give a general warning. He never mentioned any
names.

Many hypocrites offered bogus excuses. Despite this, God's
Messenger accepted their excuses. In this case: *God forgive you!
Why did you grant them exemption until those who told the truth
were manifest to you, and you knew the liars?* (9:43) was revealed.

Although some scholars hold that God reproached His
Messenger for exempting the Hypocrites, the truth is the reverse.
Imam Fakhr al-Din al-Razi and many others, among whom are
linguists, have correctly pointed out that God forgive you! is an
exclamation, [like *God bless you!* in English.] So, the true meaning
of the expression is *God give you grace!* As explained earlier, it is
not necessary for a sin to exist before forgiveness is granted. For
example, as we saw in verses 4:99, 5:3, and 4:43, forgiveness may
be juxtaposed with grace, for their meanings are closely allied.[178]

In addition, God's Messenger was motivated by kindness as
well as policy: kindness because, in the urgency of the moment,
he did not wish to refuse those who had real excuses; and poli-

cy, because those who were there just because they were obligated to be there would be a burden and a source of disorder. This is stated explicitly:

> If they had gone forth with you, they would have added nothing but mischief; they would have hurried through your ranks, seeking to cause sedition among you. (9:47)

God's Messenger knew who the Hypocrites were: *Surely you will know them by the tone of their speech* (47:30). In addition, God did not will that they should set out for war:

> If they had intended to go forth they would certainly have made some preparation therefor; but God was averse to their being sent forth; so He made them lag behind, and they were told: "Sit among those who sit (inactive)." (9:46)

That being so, the meaning of the verse in question is this: "God give you grace! If you had not excused them when they asked, the Hypocrites would have been clearly distinguished from the truthful." As we can see, the Prophet is not being reprimanded; rather, the verse expresses a Divine compliment and affection for him.

Surat al-'Abasa (He Frowned)

Prophethood is not just another job that anyone can do. Each person has two aspects: heavenly and earthly. We are shaped from dust and created from a lowly drop of "water," but nevertheless have been distinguished with the "breath of God." As a result, we can rise (or fall) to infinitely high (or low) levels. All Prophets were of the highest rank. God chose them and endowed them with all laudable virtues and the highest degree of intellectual and spiritual faculties.

To catch just a glimpse of the greatness of God's Messenger we should consider how, by God's Will and Power, he transformed a savage and backward desert people into the founders of the most magnificent civilization in human history. In addition, according to the rule that "one who causes something is like its doer," the reward of each believer's deeds, from the time of the Prophet to the Last Day, is added to the Prophet's reward, which causes him to grow in spirit incessantly.

Despite this, some classical Qur'anic commentaries and the like contain assertions based on borrowings or unreliable anecdotes incompatible with Prophethood. What is more tragic is that in the Muslim world itself, "researchers" influenced by either Orientalists or worldly temptations, have been less-than-respectful toward Prophethood, God's Messenger, and the Sunna. Deceived into mistaking "the sun's reflection for the sun itself," they regard themselves as free to criticize the Prophet and his Sunna. One of their pretexts is the initial verses of *Surat al-'Abasa*:

> He frowned and turned away because there came to him the blind man. But how can you know? Perhaps he might purify himself or be forewarned, and warning might profit him. As for him who regards himself as self-sufficient, to him you eagerly attend, though it is not your concern if he does not purify himself. But as for him who eagerly hastens to you, and is in fear [of God], you are heedless of him. (80:1-10)

According to what some Qur'anic interpreters have written, God's Messenger was once deeply and earnestly engaged in conveying the Message to pagan Qurayshi leaders when he was interrupted by a blind man. This man, 'Abd Allah ibn Umm Maktum, was so poor that usually no one took any notice of him. He desired to benefit from the teaching of God's Messenger, but the latter disliked the interruption and became impatient. As a result, these verses were revealed to reproach the Prophet.

This story is, however, highly questionable for several reasons:

 - The narration of the event and its participants are not the same in all reliable Tradition books as in some Qur'anic commentaries. In total, the various accounts mention seven people in addition to Ibn Umm Maktum.
 - Several verses explain how previous Prophets behaved toward poor people. It is inconceivable for a Prophet who always advised his followers to be with poor people to frown at or turn away from a poor blind man, especially when he came to listen to him.

- God's Messenger always rejected the calls of Qurayshi leaders to drive away the poor Muslims if he wanted them to believe in Islam.
- The Qur'an attaches great importance to how a believer behaves in the presence of God's Messenger. For example, they are "not to depart without asking for his leave when they are with him." They cannot enter his house without permission, will have their deeds reduced to nothing if they raise their voices above his, and will be punished in Hell if they ill-treat him. Given this, Ibn Umm Maktum should have been reprimanded for interrupting God's Messenger.
- Ibn Umm Maktum was the son of Khadija's uncle, and one of those who accepted Islam in its early days. He had a remarkable position in Islam. God's Messenger deputed to him the government of Madina twice while he was on military campaign. So, despite his blindness, he could not have been so rude as to interrupt God's Messenger while the latter was inviting the Qurayshi leaders to the truth. He was blind, not deaf.
- The reprimand contained in the relevant verses is too severe to be for the Prophet. The verbs to *frown* and *to turn away from* are never used in the Qur'an for a Prophet; in fact, they are not even used for ordinary believers. In this verse, they are used in their third person, singular form. In the absence of the Prophet, this means disrespect and debasement. Also, the following expressions are of the type used for the leaders of the unbelievers. Therefore, it is inconceivable that the target of this reprimand was the Prophet.
- The Qur'anic interpreters who mention this incident add to it that whenever God's Messenger saw Ibn Umm Maktum afterwards, he would say to him: "Greetings to you, O one because of whom my Lord admonished me." This addition is not to be found in reliable books of Tradition.

  – God's Messenger was very kind-hearted and gave all he
  had to bring his people to guidance. The Qur'an states: *It
  grieves him that the believers should perish. He is ardently anxious over them, and most kind and merciful to them* (9:128).
    After all these explanations, we choose to refer the truth of
the matter to God, who is the All-Knowing.

The Offer Made by the Thaqif Tribe

Before entering Islam, the Thaqif tribe tried to get some concessions from the Prophet, including some exemptions from various
religious duties—as if the Messenger were authorized to do so!
As even an ordinary Muslim would never think of granting such
a request, imagine the Prophet's reaction! The verses revealed
concerning this incident say:

> They sought to entice you from what we reveal unto you, to
> substitute against Us something different. Then, they would
> certainly have made you a trusted friend! Indeed, had We not
> given you strength and firmness, you might nearly have
> inclined to them a little. Then, We should have made you taste
> double (punishment) in this life, and double in death; and
> moreover you would have found none for you to help you
> against Us. (17:73-75)

    First, God's Messenger is the direct addressee and receiver
of the Divine Revelation. For this reason, God directly addresses him concerning collective and individual orders, prohibitions,
and responsibilities. This does not mean that God's Messenger
sometimes ignored what he was told to do. Being the embodiment, representative, and preacher of Islam, as well as the best
example, God's Messenger practiced them most strictly and
experienced the "whole history of Islam" in miniature measure.
    God used him, his time, and his Companions as a pattern
according to which the future expansion of Islam would be
shaped. He functioned as a seed from which all future Islamic civilizations, movements, and sciences—the universal tree of Islam—
would grow. For this reason, such verses should never be taken to
suggest that God's Messenger was reproached for doing some-

thing wrong. That blessed person, the Beloved of God and for whose sake God created all the worlds, is absolutely free of defect, fault, and shortcoming.

God's Messenger was extremely eager for the guidance of all people. To have some understanding of his love and affection for humanity and existence in general, reflect on what Said Nursi, the great saintly scholar of our time, said concerning his eagerness for the guidance and well-being of his nation:

> I have known nothing of worldly pleasures in my life of over eighty years. All my life has passed on battlefields, and at various other places of suffering. There has been no torment which I have not tasted and no oppression which I have not suffered. I care for neither Paradise nor fear Hell. If I witness that the faith of my nation (that is, all the Muslim peoples) has been secured, I will have no objection to being burnt in the flames of Hell, for my heart will change into a rose garden while my body is being burnt.[179]

God said to His Messenger, consoling him in the face of persistent unbelief: *You will nearly grieve yourself to death, following after them, if they don't believe in this Message* (18:6).

Having seen the eagerness of God's Messenger to guide people, the Thaqifi leaders tried to extract special concessions. They even added that if others objected, he might excuse it with the lie that his Lord had ordered him to do so. From a purely human point of view, it may seem good policy to make a small concession to fulfill a great mission. But the Messenger was not the author of Islam; his only responsibility was to convey it. The religion belongs to God. The verses in question emphasize this point.

His Marriage to Zaynab

During the pre-Islamic period, and still today, cultural, economic, and spiritual slavery was widespread. Islam came to destroy such slavery and sought to solve this social, as well as psychological, problem in stages. Since slavery has a deep psychological aspect, its abolition all at once could have resulted in even harsher conditions. For example, when Lincoln abolished slavery in the United

States, most slaves had to return to their owners because their ability to assume responsibility, to choose, and to manage their affairs as free people had been beaten out of them or had caused their leaders to be murdered.

Islam established, as a first step, strict principles on how to treat slaves, as seen in the following *hadiths*: "Those who kill their slaves will be killed. Those who imprison and starve their slaves will be imprisoned and starved. Those who castrate their slaves will be castrated,"[180] and "Arabs are not superior to non-Arabs; non-Arabs are not superior to Arabs. White people are not superior to black people; black people are not superior to white people. Superiority is only in righteousness and fear of God."[181]

As its second step, Islam enabled slaves to realize their human consciousness and identity. It educated them in Islamic values, and implanted in them a love of freedom. On the day of their emancipation, they were fully equipped to be useful members of the community as farmers, artisans, teachers, scholars, commanders, governors, ministers, and even prime ministers.

Another pre-Islamic practice, which still exists in the civil law codes of many contemporary countries, is allowing adopted children to enjoy the same legal status as natural children. As a result, a father could not legally marry his adopted son's widow or divorced wife. This practice was to be abolished, for neither adoption nor any other method of declaring someone a son can create a relationship comparable to that between children and their natural parents.

Zayd was a black African who had been kidnapped and enslaved as a child. Khadija, the first wife of God's Messenger, had purchased him in the Makkan slave market. After she married the Prophet, she gave Zayd to him as a gift. God's Messenger emancipated him and called him "my son." When Zayd's parents finally located him and came to Makka to get him, he refused to go with them, saying that he would rather stay with God's Messenger.

In order to show the equality between black and white people and demonstrate that superiority lies in righteousness and devotion to God, not in descent and worldly position, God's

Messenger married Zayd to Zaynab bint Jahsh of the Hashimite tribe. She was a very devoted and intellectual Muslim woman and had a noble character. God's Messenger had known her very well since her childhood. Although her family had wanted her to marry God's Messenger, they agreed to let her marry Zayd because God's Messenger desired it.

Zayd, however, admitted that he was spiritually inferior to his wife. He realized through his insight that her sublimity of character made her fit to be the wife of a far greater man than himself. He asked God's Messenger many times to allow him to divorce her, but each time God's Messenger advised him to remain married to her. Nevertheless, Zayd concluded that he was not his wife's equal and eventually divorced her.

After this, God told His Messenger to marry her, even though this would violate his society's norms. But as this marriage had been ordained in heaven, he submitted and married Zaynab:

> When Zayd had dissolved (his marriage) with her, We gave her in marriage to you, so that there may be no difficulty and sin for believers in marriage with the wives of their adopted sons if they divorce them. And God's command must be fulfilled. (33:37)

Although this marriage was very difficult for God's Messenger to enter into, God used it to abolish a mistaken custom and establish a new law and custom. The Messenger always was the first to practice the law or rule to be established and obeyed, so that it would have enough influence on others. His marriage to Zaynab was one of the most difficult commandments he had to carry out. That is why his wife 'A'isha remarked: "If the Messenger of God been inclined to suppress anything of what was revealed to him, he would surely have suppressed this verse."

As expected, the enemies of Islam and the Hypocrites slandered God's Messenger. Although some of their allegations have found their way into various Qur'anic commentaries, no such allegation or slander has ever affected—or will affect—his pure personality and chastity. All scholars agree that he lived happily with Khadija, a widow 15 years older than himself, with nothing to suggest any misconduct during their 25-year marriage (ending only with Khadija's death). Unlike young people, he did not burn with lust and carnal desires. This clearly shows that his subsequent marriages, which took place after he was 50 years old, a time when desire has subsided, were entered into for specific purposes.

In sum, like every other Prophet, God's Messenger has no blemish and is innocent of what they accuse him. Nor can his infallibility be doubted.

NO BODILY OR MENTAL DEFECTS

All Muslim theologians agree that Prophets have no bodily or mental defects. As they were extraordinarily attractive in personality and conduct, they were also graceful and charming in outward appearance. They were perfect in bodily structure, handsome, and well-built.

Anas says that God's Messenger was the most handsome of people. Jabir ibn Samura remarks: "Once during a full moon, we were sitting in the mosque. God's Messenger came in. I looked first at the shining moon, and then at his face. I swear by God that his face was brighter than the moon."[182]

Prophets must be free from all bodily defects, for their appearance should not repel others. In explaining the Divine wisdom of God's Messenger living for 63 years, Said Nursi writes:

> Believers are religiously obliged to love and respect God's Messenger to the utmost degree, and follow his every command without feeling any dislike for any aspect of him. For this reason, God did not allow him to live to the troublesome and often humiliating period of old age, and sent him to the "highest abode" when he was 63 years old. This was the average lifespan of the members of his community, thus making him the example in this respect also.[183]

Job's Afflictions

Despite this characteristic being common to all Prophets, false stories about Job and Moses, either borrowed from Israelite sources or misunderstandings of Qur'anic verses, have found their way into Qur'anic commentaries.

In a *hadith*, God's Messenger says: "The Prophets undergo the severest trials; the greatest misfortunes strike them. Then come other believers; the firmer their belief, the bigger their misfortune." Prophet Job is praised in the Qur'an as *a steadfast, excellent servant of God, one ever-turning to his Lord* (38:44). As can be deduced from the Qur'anic verses, and mentioned in the Bible, he was afflicted with a skin disease, which caused painful sores from the soles of his feet to the top of his head (Job 2:7). Influenced by Israelite stories, some Qur'anic commentators have added that worms lived in his sores or abscesses, and that the resulting offensive odor caused people to leave him.

These additions are completely groundless. If people really left him, this might have been due to his later poverty. In the beginning, Job was a rich, thankful servant of God; later on, he lost his wealth and children. As a Prophet, he could not have had a repulsive or disgusting appearance, with, at least, his face exempt from sores. Nor could his body have emitted an offensive smell.

Contrary to the Biblical account that he cursed the day of his birth (Job 3:1) and God openly (Job 7:20-21), and justified himself rather than God (Job 32:2), Job bore his afflictions for years without any objection. He prayed: *Affliction has visited me, and You are the Most Merciful of the Merciful* (21:83). God answered his prayer and removed his affliction, and restored to him his household and the like thereof along with them (21:84).

Moses' Speech Impediment

The Qur'an states that Moses, on receiving the order to go to Pharaoh, supplicated: *My Lord, open my breast (relieve my mind and enable me to bear everything), and ease for me my task. Loosen a knot upon my tongue so that they may understand my words* (20:25-28). Some commentators, influenced by Israelite sources and misunderstanding Moses' supplication, have asserted that he had a speech impediment. They say that a young Moses once pulled Pharaoh's beard. Angered, Pharaoh wanted to have him killed.

But his wife, trying to save the child, asked Pharaoh to test him to see whether he was fit to be judged or decide in his favor. Bringing a weighing scale, the put a piece of gold in one pan and some embers in the other. Moses put the embers in his mouth, which gave him a permanent stutter. So, according to these interpretations, Moses was asking God to remove his stutter.

An invented story cannot serve as the basis for interpreting a Qur'anic verse. If Moses had had such a speech impediment, he should have prayed for the knot—not a knot—to be loosened. What Moses was asking for was a greater ability to articulate God's Message in Pharaoh's presence, for he was not as eloquent as his brother Aaron (28:34; Exodus 4:10).

In conclusion, all Prophets were both physically and mentally perfect. Regardless of what others might claim, there is nothing in their lives to suggest even the slightest defect. However, some of them may have been superior to others in certain respects: *And those Messengers, some We have preferred above others; some there are to whom God spoke [directly], and some He raised in rank* (2:253). Prophet Muhammad is superior to all of them by virtue of being the last Prophet sent to both humanity and jinn. His Mission was not restricted to a certain people or a certain time; rather, it was directed toward all people and remains valid until the end of time.

CHAPTER 5

Prophet Muhammad as Husband
and Father

PROPHET MUHAMMAD AS HUSBAND AND FATHER

THE PROPHET AND HIS WIVES

Prophet Muhammad personifies the roles of perfect father and husband. He was so kind and tolerant with his wives that they could not envisage their lives without him, nor did they want to live away from him.

He married Sawda, his second wife, while in Makka. After a while, he wanted to divorce her for certain reasons. She was extremely upset at this news, and implored him: "O Messenger of God, I wish no worldly thing of you. I will sacrifice the time allocated to me, if you don't want to visit me. But please don't deprive me of being your wife. I want to go to the Hereafter as your wife. I care for nothing else."[1] The Messenger did not divorce her, nor did he stop visiting her.[2]

Once he noticed that Hafsa was uncomfortable over their financial situation. "If she wishes, I may set her free," he said, or something to that effect. This suggestion so alarmed her that she requested mediators to persuade him not to do so. He kept his faithful friend's daughter as his trusted wife.

His wives viewed separation from the Messenger of God as a calamity, so firmly had he established himself in their hearts. They were completely at one with him. They shared in his blessed, mild, and natural life. If he had left them, they would have died of despair. If he had divorced one of them, she would have waited at his doorstep until the Last Day.

After his death, there was much yearning and a great deal of grief. Abu Bakr and 'Umar found the Messenger's wives weeping whenever they visited them. Their weeping seemed to continue for the rest of their lives. Muhammad left a lasting impression on everyone. At one point, he had nine wives and dealt equally with all of them and without any serious problems. He was a kind and gentle husband, and never behaved harshly or rudely. In short, he was the perfect husband.

A few days before his death, he said: "A servant has been allowed to choose this world or his Lord. He chose his Lord."[3] Abu Bakr, a man of great intelligence, began to cry, understanding that the Prophet was talking about himself. His illness worsened daily, and his severe headache caused him to writhe in pain. But even during this difficult period, he continued to treat his wives with kindness and gentleness. He asked for permission to stay in one room, as he had no strength to visit them one by one. His wives agreed, and the Messenger spent his last days in Aisha's room.

Each wife, because of his generosity and kindness, thought she was his most beloved. The idea that any man could show complete equality and fairness in his relationships with nine women seems impossible. For this reason, the Messenger of God asked God's pardon for any unintentional leanings. He would pray: "I may have unintentionally shown more love to one of them than the others, and this would be injustice. So, O Lord, I take refuge in Your grace for those things beyond my power."[4]

What gentleness and sensitivity! I wonder if anyone else could show such kindness to his children or spouses. When people manage to cover up their lower inborn tendencies, it is as if they have done something very clever and shown tremendous willpower. But they sometimes expose these very defects unconsciously while bragging of their cleverness. The Messenger, despite showing no fault, sought only God's forgiveness.

His gentleness penetrated his wives souls so deeply that his departure led to what they must have felt to be an unbridgeable separation. They did not commit suicide, as Islam forbids it, but their lives now became full of endless sorrow and ceaseless tears.

The Messenger was kind and gentle to all women, and advised all other men to follow him in this regard. Sa'd ibn Abi Waqqas described his kindness as follows:

'Umar said: One day I went to the Prophet and saw him smiling. "May God make you smile forever, O Messenger of God," I said, and asked why he was smiling. "I smile at those women. They were chatting in front of me before you came. When they heard your voice, they all vanished," he answered still smiling. On hearing this answer, I raised my voice and told them: "O enemies of your own selves, you are scared of me, but you are not scared of the Messenger of God, and you don't show respect to him." "You are hard-hearted and strict," they replied.[5]

'Umar also was gentle to women. However, the most handsome man looks ugly when compared to Joseph's beauty. Likewise, 'Umar's gentleness and sensitivity seem like violence and severity when compared to those of the Prophet. The women had seen the Messengers gentleness, sensitivity, and kindness, and so regarded 'Umar as strict and severe. Yet 'Umar shouldered the caliphate perfectly and became one of the greatest examples after the Prophet. He was a just ruler, and strove to distinguish right from wrong. His qualities enabled him to be caliph. Some of his qualities might seem rather severe; however, those very qualities enabled him to shoulder very demanding responsibilities.

The Prophet's Consultation With His Wives

The Messenger discussed matters with his wives as friends. Certainly he did not need their advice, since he was directed by Revelation. However, he wanted to teach his nation that Muslim men were to give women every consideration. This was quite a radical idea in his time, as it is today in many parts of the world. He began teaching his people through his own relationship with his wives.

For example, the conditions laid down in the Treaty of Hudaybiya disappointed and enraged many Muslims, for one condition stipulated that they could not make the pilgrimage that year. They wanted to reject the treaty, continue on to Makka, and face the possible consequences. But the Messenger ordered them to slaughter their sacrificial animals and take off their pilgrim attire. Some Companions hesitated, hoping that he would change his mind. He repeated his order, but they continued to hesitate. They did not oppose him; rather, they still hoped he might change his mind, for they had set out with the intention of pilgrimage and did not want to stop half way.

Noticing this reluctance, the Prophet returned to his tent and asked Umm Salama, his wife accompanying him at that time, what she thought of the situation. So she told him, fully aware that he did not need her advice. In doing this, he taught Muslim men an important social lesson: There is nothing wrong with exchanging ideas with women on important matters, or on any matters at all.

She said: "O Messenger of God, don't repeat your order. They may resist and thereby perish. Slaughter your sacrificial animal and change out of your pilgrim attire. They will obey, willingly or not, when they see that your order is final."[6] He immediately took a knife in his hand, went outside, and began to slaughter his sheep. The Companions began to do the same, for now it was clear that his order would not be changed.

Counsel and consultation, like every good deed, were practiced by God's Messenger first within his own family and then in the wider community. Even today, we understand so little about his relationships with his wives that it is as if we are wandering aimlessly around a plot of land, unaware of the vast treasure buried below our feet.

Women are secondary beings in the minds of many, including those self-appointed defenders of women's rights as well as many self-proclaimed Muslim men. For us, a woman is part of a whole, a part that renders the other half useful. We believe that when the two halves come together, the true unity of a human being appears. When this unity does not exist, humanity does not exist—nor can Prophethood, sainthood, or even Islam.

Our master encouraged us through his enlightening words to behave kindly to women. He declared: "The most perfect believers are the best in character, and the best of you are the kindest to their families."[7] It is clear that women have received the true honor and respect they deserve, not just in theory but in actual practice, only once in history—during the period of Prophet Muhammad.

The Choice God's Messenger Gave to His Wives

His wives were given the choice of remaining with him or leaving:

> O Prophet, say to your wives: "If you desire the life of this world and its glitter, then come! I will provide for your enjoyment and set you free in a handsome manner. But if you seek God, His Messenger, and the Home of the Hereafter, verily God has prepared for you, the well-doers among you, a great reward." (33:28-29)

A few of his wives who wanted a more prosperous life asked: "Couldn't we live a little more luxuriously, like other Muslims do? Couldn't we have at least a bowl of soup everyday, or some prettier garments?" At first sight, such wishes might be considered fair and just. However, they were members of the family that was to be an example for all Muslim families until the Last Day.

The Messenger reacted by going into retreat. The news spread, and everyone rushed to the mosque and began to cry. The smallest grief felt by their beloved Messenger was enough to bring them all to tears, and even the smallest incident in his life would disturb them. Abu Bakr and 'Umar, seeing the event in a different light as their daughters were directly involved, rushed to the mosque. They wanted to see him, but he would not leave his retreat. Eventually, on their third attempt, they gained entry and began to rebuke their daughters. The Messenger saw what was happening, but only said: "I cannot afford what they want."[8] The Qur'an declared: *O wives of the Prophet! You are not like any other women* (33:32).

Others might save themselves by simply fulfilling their obligations, but those who were at the very center of Islam had to devote themselves fully, so that no weakness would appear at the center. There were advantages in being the Prophet's wife, but these advantages brought responsibilities and potential risks. The Messenger was preparing them as exemplars for all present and future Muslim women. He was especially worried that they might enjoy the reward for their good deeds in this world, and thereby be included in: *You have exhausted your share of the good things in your life of the world and sought comfort in them* (46:20).

Life in the Prophet's house was uncomfortable. For this reason, either explicitly or implicitly, his wives made some modest demands. As their status was unique, they were not expected to enjoy themselves in a worldly sense. Some godly people laugh only a few times during their lives; others never fill their stomachs.

For example, Fudayl ibn Iyad never laughed. He smiled only once, and those who saw him do so asked him why he smiled, for they were greatly surprised. He told them: "Today, I learned that my son 'Ali died. I was happy to hear that God had loved him, and so I smiled."[9] If there were such people outside of the Prophets household, his wives, who were even more pious and respectful of God and regarded as "mothers of the believers," would certainly be of a higher degree.

It is not easy to merit being together with the Messenger in this world and the Hereafter. Thus, these special women were put to a great test. The Messenger allowed them to choose his poor home or the world's luxury. If they choose the world, he would give them whatever they wanted and then dissolve his marriage with them. If they choose God and His Messenger, they had to be content with their lives. This was a peculiarity of his family. Since this family was unique, its members had to be unique. The head of the family was chosen, as were the wives and children.

The Messenger first called 'A'isha and said: "I want to discuss something with you. You'd better talk with your parents before making a decision." Then he recited the verses mentioned above. Her decision was exactly as expected from a truthful daughter of a truthful father: "O Messenger of God, do I need to talk with my parents? By God, I choose God and His Messenger."[10]

'A'isha herself tells us what happened next: "The Messenger received the same answer from all his wives. No one expressed a different opinion. They all said what I had said." They did so because they were all at one with the Messenger. They could not differ. If the Messenger had told them to fast for a lifetime without break, they would have done so, and endured it with pleasure. So, they endured hardship until their deaths.

Some of his wives had enjoyed an extravagant lifestyle before their marriage to him. One of these was Safiyya, who had lost her father and husband, and had been taken prisoner, during the Battle of Khaybar. She must have been very angry with the Messenger, but when she saw him, her feelings changed completely. She endured the same destiny as the other wives. They endured it because love of the Messenger had penetrated their hearts.

Safiyya was a Jewess. Once, she was dismayed when this fact was mentioned to her sarcastically. She informed the Messenger, expressing her sadness. He comforted her saying: "If they repeat it, tell them: 'My father is Prophet Aaron, my uncle is Prophet Moses, and my husband is, as you see, Prophet Muhammad, the Chosen One. What do you have more than me to be proud of ?'"[11]

The Qur'an declares that his wives are the *mothers of the believers* (33:6). Although fourteen centuries have passed, we still feel delight in saying "my mother" when referring to Khadija, 'A'isha, Umm Salama, Hafsa, and his other wives. We feel this because of him. Some feel more love for these women than they do for their real mothers. Certainly, this feeling must have been deeper, warmer, and stronger in the Prophet's own time.

The Messenger was the perfect head of a family. Managing many women with ease, being a lover of their hearts, an instructor of their minds, an educator of their souls, he never neglected the affairs of the nation or compromised his duties.

The Messenger excelled in every area of life. People should not compare him to themselves or to the so-called great personalities of their age. Researchers should look at him, the one to whom angels are grateful, always remembering that he excelled in every way. If they want to look for Muhammad they must search for him in his own dimensions. Our imaginations cannot reach him, for we do not even know how to imagine properly. God bestowed upon him, as His special favor, superiority in every field.

GOD'S MESSENGER AND CHILDREN

He was an extraordinary husband, a perfect father, and a unique grandfather. He was unique in every way. He treated his children and grandchildren with great compassion, and never neglected to direct them to the Hereafter and good deeds. He smiled at them, caressed and loved them, but did not allow them to neglect matters related to the afterlife. In worldly matters he was extremely open; but when it came to maintaining their relationship with God, he was very serious and dignified. He showed them how to lead a humane life, and never allowed them to neglect their religious duties and become spoiled. His ultimate goal was to prepare them for the Hereafter. His perfect balance in such matters is another dimension of his Divinely inspired intellect.

In a *hadith* narrated by Muslim, Anas bin Malik, honored as the Messenger's servant for 10 continuous years, says: "I've never seen a man who was more compassionate to his family members than Muhammad."[12] If this admission were made just by us, it could be dismissed as unimportant. However, millions of people, so benign and compassionate that they would not even offend an ant, declare that he embraced everything with compassion. He was a human like us, but God inspired in him such an intimate affection for every living thing that he could establish a connection with all of them. As a result, he was full of extraordinary affection toward his family members and others.

All of the Prophet's sons had died. Ibrahim, his last son born to his Coptic wife Mary, also died in infancy. The Messenger often visited his son before the latter's death, although he was very busy. Ibrahim was looked after by a nurse. The Prophet would embrace, kiss, and caress him before returning home.[13] When Ibrahim died, the Prophet took him on his lap again, embraced him, and described his sorrow while on the brink of tears. Some were surprised. He gave them this answer: "Eyes may water and hearts may be broken, but we do not say anything except what God will be pleased with." He pointed to his tongue and said: "God will ask us about this."[14]

He carried his grandsons Hasan and Husayn on his back. Despite his unique status, he did this without hesitation to herald the honor that they would attain later. One time when they were on his back, Umar came into the Prophet's house and, seeing them, exclaimed: "What a beautiful mount you have!" The Messenger added immediately: "What beautiful riders they are!"[15]

They may not have been aware that the Messenger had honored them. This special compliment was due to their future status as leaders and family heads of the Prophet's household. Among their descendants would be the greatest and most respected saints. His compliment was not only for his grandsons, but for all his offspring. For this reason, Abd al-Qadir Jilani, a well-known descendant of the Prophets household, said: "The Messengers blessed feet are on my shoulders, and mine are on the shoulders of all saints." This statement will probably stand for all saints to come.

The Messenger was completely balanced in the way he brought up his children. He loved his children and grandchildren very much, and instilled love in them. However, he never let his love for them be abused. None of them deliberately dared to do anything wrong. If they made an unintentional mistake, the Messengers protection prevented them from going even slightly astray. He did this by wrapping them in love and an aura of dignity. For example, once Hasan or Husayn wanted to eat a date that had been given to distribute among the poor as alms. The Messenger immediately took it from his hand, and said: "Anything given as alms is forbidden to us."[16] In teaching them while they were young to be sensitive to forbidden acts, he established an important principle of education.

Whenever he returned to Madina, he would carry children on his mount. On such occasions, the Messenger embraced not only his grandchildren but also those in his house and those nearby. He conquered their hearts through his compassion. He loved all children.

He loved his granddaughter Umama as much as he loved Hasan and Husayn. He often went out with her on his shoulders, and even placed her on his back while praying. When he prostrated, he put her down; when he had finished, he placed her on his back again.[17] He showed this degree of love to Umama to teach his male followers how to treat girls. This was a vital necessity, for only a decade earlier it had been the social norm to bury infant or young girls alive. Such public paternal affection for a granddaughter had never been seen before in Arabia.

The Messenger proclaimed that Islam allows no discrimination between son and daughter. How could there be? One is Muhammad, the other is Khadija; one is Adam, the other is Eve; one is Ali, the other is Fatima. For every great man there is a great woman.

Fatima, the daughter of the Messenger, is the mother of all members of his household. She is our mother, too. As soon as Fatima entered, the Messenger would stand, take her hands and make her sit where he had been sitting. He would ask about her health and family, show his paternal love for her, and compliment her.

He loved her like his own self, and Fatima, knowing how fond he was of her, loved him more than her own self. Her great mission was to be the seed for saints and godly people. She always watched her father and how he called people to Islam. She wept and groaned when the Messenger told her that he would die soon, and rejoiced when he told her that she would be the first family member to follow him.[18] Her father loved her, and she loved her father. The Messenger was totally balanced even in his love for Fatima. He trained her for the heights to which the human soul should rise.

The Messenger raised her, as well as all of his other family members and Companions, in a way to prepare them for the Hereafter. All of us were created for eternity, and so cannot be satisfied except through eternity and the Eternal Being. Therefore, we only want Him and long for Him, either consciously or unconsciously. The essence of all religions and the message of every Prophet was about the Hereafter. For this reason, the Messenger always sought to prepare his followers for the eternal peace and permanent bliss; meanwhile, his very existence among them was a sample of that peace and bliss they would taste in His presence.

He loved them and directed them toward the Hereafter, to the otherworldly and eternal beauty, and to God. For example, He once saw Fatima wearing a necklace (a bracelet, according to another version), and asked her: "Do you want the inhabitants of the Earth and the Heavens to say that my daughter is holding (or wearing) a chain from Hell?" These few words, coming from a man whose throne was established in her heart and who had conquered all her faculties, caused her to report, in her own words: "I immediately sold the necklace, bought and freed a slave, and then went to the Messenger. When I told him what I had done, he rejoiced. He opened his hands and thanked God: All thanks to God, Who protected Fatima from Hell."[19]

Fatima did not commit any sin by wearing this necklace. However, the Messenger wanted to keep her in the circle of the *muqarrabin* (those made near to God). His warning to her was based on *taqwa* (righteousness and devotion to God) and qurb (nearness to God). This was, in a sense, a neglect of worldly things. It is also an example of the sensitivity befitting the mother of the Prophet's household, which represents the Muslim community until the Last Day. To be a mother of such godly men like Hasan, Husayn, and Zayn al-'Abidin was certainly no ordinary task. The Messenger was preparing her to be the mother first of his own household (Ahl al-Bayt), and then of those who would descend from them, such great spiritual leaders as Abd al-Qadir al-Jilani, Muhammad Baha' al-Din al-Naqshband, Ahmad Rifa'i, Ahmad Badawi, al-Shadhili, and the like.

It was as if he were telling her: "Fatima, you will marry a man ('Ali) and go to a house from which many golden rings will emerge in the future. Forget the golden chain on your neck and concentrate on becoming the mother for the golden chains of saints who will appear in the spiritual orders of Naqshbandiya, Rifa'iya, Shadhiliyya, and the like." It was difficult to fulfill such a role while wearing a golden necklace. For this reason, the Messenger was more severe with his own household than with others. He reminded them of the straight path by turning their faces toward the other world, closing all the windows opening on this world, and telling them that what they need is God.

They were to lead their whole lives looking to the other world. For this reason, as a sign of his love, the Messenger purified his own household from all worldly rubbish and allowed no worldly dust to contaminate them. He turned their faces toward the exalted realms and prepared them for being together there.

"YOU ARE WITH THOSE WHOM YOU LOVE"

According to this *hadith*, if you love Prophet Muhammad you will be on his path, and those on his path will be together with him in the world beyond. To prepare his household and Companions for this gathering, the Messenger loved and embraced them. He used this love efficiently.

Bukhari and Muslim gave another example of how he educated them. 'Ali narrates that:

> We had no servant in our house, and so Fatima did all the housework by herself. We lived in a house with just a small room. There, she would light a fire and try to cook. She often singed her clothes while trying to increase the fire by blowing. She also baked our bread and carried water. Her hands became covered in calluses from turning the millstone, as did her back from carrying water. Meanwhile some prisoners of war were brought to Madina. The Messenger gave them to those who applied. I suggested to Fatima that she ask for a servant from her father. And she did.

Fatima continues:

> I went to my father, but he was not at home. 'A'isha said she would tell him when he came, so I returned home. As soon as we went to bed, the Messenger came in. We wanted to get up, but he did not let us and instead sat between us. I could feel the cold of his foot on my body. He asked what we wanted, and I explained the situation. The Messenger, in an awesome manner, replied: "Fatima, fear God and be faultless in all your duties to Him. I will tell you something. When you want to go to bed, say subhan Allah (All glory be to God), al-hamdu li-Allah (All praise be to God), and Allahu akbar (God is the greatest) 33 times each. This is better for you than having a maid."[20]

What he was actually saying through this conversation was:

I am turning your faces to the otherworldly realms. There are two ways for you to reach them and be together with me there: Fulfill your duties in perfect servitude to your Lord and fulfill your duties to your husband. If a maid takes your responsibilities, this may make you deficient. You must have two wings to fly to the higher ranks. How can a man or woman become a perfect slave of God? How can a person become a perfect human being and fulfill all of his or her obligations? It is your duty to find the answers to these questions. First of all, become a perfect slave of God. Then, become a perfect human being by performing your duties to 'Ali, a great man who represents all the saints who will descend from your family. If you do so, you will be with me in Heaven, where all the perfect things and perfect human beings shall come together.

I cannot help but digress to mention a fact about 'Ali. The Messenger gave him his daughter in marriage without hesitation, because he deserved to have such a wife and to be a Prophet's son-in-law. 'Ali was the king of saints, and was created in this nature. The Messenger told him: "O 'Ali, every other Prophet had his own offspring. However, mine will come from you."[21] 'Ali is the father of the Prophet's household, namely, his grandchildren and later descendants. For this reason, obeying 'Ali means obeying the Messenger, and obeying the Messenger means obeying God. Also, those who love 'Ali should love the Prophet and follow his Sunna.

WHY HE HAD MORE THAN ONE WIFE

Some critics of Islam, either because they do not know the reasons for these marriages or because they want to portray him as a self-indulgent libertine, have accused the Messenger of character failings that are incompatible with having even average virtue, let alone with the virtue of God's final Messenger and best example for humanity. The facts, all of which are easily available in scores of biographies and well-authenticated accounts of his sayings and actions, refute all such allegations and show that these marriages were part of a strictly disciplined life and yet another burden he had to bear.

The reasons behind his several marriages, while differing from case to case, all have to do with his role as the leader of the new Muslim community, and his responsibility to guide his followers toward the norms and values of Islam.

Muhammad married his first wife when he was 25 years old, 15 years before his Prophethood began. Given the cultural and moral climate in which he lived, not to mention his youth and other factors, he nevertheless enjoyed a sound reputation for chastity, integrity, and trustworthiness. As soon as he was called to Prophethood, he acquired enemies who made all sorts of charges. However, not even his fiercest enemies attacked his reputation, for doing so would have caused them to be ridiculed and discredited immediately. It is important to realize that his life was founded upon chastity and self-discipline from the outset, and so remained.

When he was 25 and in the prime of life, Muhammad married Khadija, a widow 15 years his senior. This marriage was very high and exceptional in the eyes of the Prophet and God. For 23 years, this devoted couple lived together in complete contentment and fidelity. The Prophet took no other wives while Khadija was alive, although public opinion and social norms would have allowed this. Even his enemies admitted that, during these years, they could find no flaw in his moral character. When she died during the eighth year of Prophethood, the Prophet found himself single once again, but this time with children. He remained unmarried for 4 or 5 years. All of his other marriages began when he was 53 years old or older, a age when very little real interest and desire for marriage remains, especially in Arabia where people grow old relatively earlier. Thus, allegations of licentiousness or self-indulgence are groundless.

People often ask how a Prophet can have more than one wife. There are three points to be made in answering this question. But, let's first see who is asking this question. Mostly, they are either Christians or Jews (People of the Book), or atheists. As such people usually know next to nothing about Islam, their question is based either on genuine ignorance or the desire to spread doubt among believers.

Those who neither believe in nor practice a religion have no right to reproach those who do. Such people are known for their casual relations and liaisons with numerous sexual partners and their refusal to follow any moral rules or ethics. Their disguised yet unrestrained self-indulgence, as well as their refusal to consider its consequences upon themselves and young people in general, not to mention their own children, has had serious social repercussions. Considering themselves free, they engage in what most societies consider to be immoral behavior: incest, homosexuality, polyandry (multiple husbands at the same time), and others. They never stop to consider what effect such practices have on the children of such unions.

When we understand this, we can take their criticisms for what they are: a desire, whether conscious or otherwise, to drag believers into the mess of moral confusion and viciousness in which they themselves are trapped.

One wonders why Jews and Christians attack the Prophet for his multiple marriages. Have they forgotten that the great Hebrew patriarchs, considered Prophets in the Bible and in the Qur'an and revered by Jews, Christians, and Muslims as exemplars of moral excellence, all practiced polygamy? Moreover, as in the case of Prophet Solomon,[22] they had far more wives than Prophet Muhammad, upon him be peace. One wonders if they are moved more by their anti-Islam bias than genuine concern or interest.

Polygamy did not begin with the Muslims. Furthermore, in the case of the Prophet of Islam, it was an essential part of conveying the message of Islam and bringing unbelievers into its fold. For example, a religion that encompasses every sphere of life cannot be shy when it comes to intimate matters. Such things can only be known by one's spouse. Therefore, there must be women who can give clear instruction and advice, as such matters cannot be left to the usual allusions, hints, and innuendoes. The Prophet's wives functioned as teachers who conveyed and explained to other women, as well as men, Islamic norms and rules for correct domestic, marital, and other private concerns.

Some marriages were contracted for specific reasons, such as:

- Since his wives were young, middle-aged, and elderly, the requirements and norms of Islamic law could be applied correctly to each stage of their lives and experiences. These provisions were learned and applied within the Prophet's household and then conveyed to other Muslims through his wives.

- Each wife was from a different clan or tribe, which allowed him to establish bonds of kinship and affinity throughout Arabia. This caused a profound attachment to him to spread among the diverse peoples of the new Muslim community, and also created and secured equality, brotherhood, and sisterhood among both in practical matters and in terms of religion.

- Both before and after the Prophets death, each wife proved to be of great benefit and service. They conveyed and interpreted Islam to their people in all its inner and outer experiences, as well as the qualities, manners, and faith of the man who was living embodiment of the Qur'an in every aspect of his life. In this way, their people learned the Qur'an, the Traditions, *tafsir* (Qur'anic interpretation and commentary), and fiqh (understanding of the Islamic law), and so became fully aware of Islam's essence and spirit.

- These marriages allowed Prophet Muhammad to establish kinship ties throughout Arabia, and thus to move freely wherever he wished and to be accepted as a member in each family. In addition, everyone so connected to him felt that they could approach him personally for guidance on any issue. The entire tribe also benefited from this connection; they considered themselves fortunate and took pride in their new relationship. For example, such relationships were established for the Umayyads (through Umm Habiba), the Hashimites (through Zaynab bint Jahsh), and the Banu Makhzum (through Umm Salama).

So far, what we have said is general and could, in some respects, be true of all Prophets. However, now we will give brief life sketches of these women, not in the order of marriage but from a different perspective.

Khadija was the Prophet's first wife. When they married, she was 40; he was 25. She was the mother of all his children except for his son Ibrahim, who did not survive infancy. But she was more than just his wife—she was his friend who shared his inclinations and ideals to a remarkable degree. Their marriage was wonderfully blessed, and they lived together in profound harmony for 23 years. Through every outrage and persecution heaped upon him by the Makkans, Khadija was his dearest companion and helper. He loved her deeply, and married no other woman while she was alive.

This marriage presents the ideal forms of intimacy, friendship, mutual respect, support, and consolation. Though faithful and loyal to all his wives, he never forgot Khadija; for the rest of his life, he often mentioned her virtues and merits. The Prophet did not remarry for 4 or 5 years after her death. Providing his children's daily food and provisions, bearing their troubles and hardships, caused him to be both a father and a mother. To allege that such a man was a sensualist or lusted after women is beyond belief. If there were even the least grain of truth in it, he could not have lived as history records that he did.

'A'isha, his second wife (though not in the order of marriage), was the daughter of Abu Bakr, his closest friend and devoted follower. One of the earliest converts to Islam, this man had long hoped to cement the deep attachment between himself and the Prophet by giving 'A'isha to him in marriage. His acceptance of this arrangement conferred the highest honor and courtesy on a man who had shared all the good and bad times with him throughout his mission.

'A'isha, who proved to be a remarkably intelligent and wise woman, had both the nature and temperament to carry forward the work of Prophetic mission. Her marriage prepared her to be a spiritual guide and teacher to all women. She became a major student and disciple of the Prophet and through him, like so many Muslims of that blessed time, she matured and perfected her skills and talents so that she could join him in the abode of bliss both as wife and as student. Her life and service to Islam after her marriage prove that such an exceptional person was worthy to be the Prophet's wife.

Over time, she proved to be one of the greatest authorities on *hadith*, an excellent Qur'anic commentator, and a most distinguished and knowledgeable expert (*faqih*) in Islamic law. She truly represented the inner and outer qualities and experiences of Prophet Muhammad through her unique understanding.

Umm Salama, of the Makhzum clan, was first married to her cousin. The couple had embraced Islam at the very beginning and emigrated to Abyssinia to avoid Qurayshi persecution. After their return, they migrated to Madina with their four children. Her husband participated in many battles and, severely wounded at Uhud, attained martyrdom shortly thereafter. Abu Bakr and 'Umar proposed marriage, aware of her needs and suffering as a widow with children but without means to support them. She refused, believing that no one could be better than her late husband.

Some time after that, the Prophet offered to marry her. This was quite right and natural, for this great woman, who had never shied from sacrifice and suffering for Islam, was now alone after having passed many years among the noblest Arab clan. She could not be neglected and left to beg her way in life. Considering her piety, sincerity, and all that she had suffered, she deserved to be helped. By marrying her, the Prophet was doing what he had been doing since his youth, namely, befriending those lacking friends, supporting those without support, and protecting those without protection.

Umm Salama also was intelligent and quick in comprehension. She had all the capacities and gifts to become a spiritual guide and teacher. After her marriage to the Prophet, she became a new student in the school of knowledge and guidance, one to whom all women would be grateful. Let us recall that, at this time, the Prophet was approaching the age of sixty. His marriage to a widow with four children and acceptance of all related expenses and responsibilities can be understood only in terms of his infinite reserves of humanity and compassion.

Umm Habiba was the daughter of Abu Sufyan who, for a long time, was the Prophet's bitterest foe and strongest supporter of unbelief. But despite this, his daughter was one of the earliest converts to Islam and emigrated to Abyssinia with her husband. Her husband died there, leaving her alone and desperate in exile.

At that time, the few Companions had problems supporting even themselves. She was faced with several options: conversion to Christianity in return for Abyssinian Christian support (unthinkable); return to her father's home, now a headquarters of the war against Islam (unthinkable); or go begging from household to household. This last option was just as unthinkable as the other two, but had the added disadvantage that if she were forced to do so, she would bring shame upon her family name, as it was one of the richest and noblest Arab families.

God recompensed Umm Habiba for all that she lost or sacrificed in the way of Islam. She had been reduced to a lonely exile and a grieving widow in an insecure environment among people who were racially and religiously different from her. The Prophet, learning of her plight, sent an offer of marriage through the king Negus. This noble and generous action is a practical proof of: *We have not sent you save as a mercy for all creatures* (21:107).

Through this marriage, Abu Sufyan's powerful family was linked with the person and household of the Prophet, a fact that caused them to rethink their opposition. It also is correct to trace this marriage's influence beyond Abu Sufyan's immediate family and to the Umayyads, who ruled the Muslims for almost a hundred years. This clan, whose members had been the most hostile to Islam, went on to produce some of Islam's most renowned warriors, administrators, and governors in the early period. It was his marriage to Umm Habiba that began this change: the Prophet's depth of generosity and magnanimity of soul surely overwhelmed them.

Zaynab bint Jahsh was a lady of noble birth and descent, as well as a close relative of the Prophet. She also was a woman of great piety, who fasted a great deal, kept long vigils, and gave generously to the poor. When the Prophet made known to her parents that he wished her to marry Zayd (at one time his adopted son), both she and her family were at first unwilling. The family had hoped to marry their daughter to the Prophet. Naturally, when they realized that it was the Prophet's wish that she marry Zayd, they all consented out of their love for the Prophet and his authority.

As mentioned above, the Messenger made this marriage to abolish several pagan customs: a freed ex-slave could not marry a free-born woman, racial prejudice (Zayd was black; Zaynab was not), an adoptive father could not marry his adopted sons ex-wife or widow. The marriage did not bring happiness to either person. Both were devout Muslims and loved the Prophet, but they were not compatible. Zayd several times asked the Prophet to allow him to divorce Zaynab, but the Prophet told him to be patient and not divorce her. Then, once when the Prophet was talking with some people, Gabriel came and a Divine Revelation was given to him.[23] This verse announced the Prophet's marriage to Zaynab as a bond already contracted: *We have married her to you* (33:37).

There was no lust involved here. Rather, it was such a severe trial that 'A'isha later said: "Had the Messenger of God been inclined to suppress anything of what was revealed to him, he would surely have suppressed this verse."[24]

Juwayriya bint Harith, daughter of the defeated Banu Mustaliq clan's chief, was captured during a military expedition. She was held, like other members of her proud family, alongside her clan's "common" people. She was in considerable distress when taken to the Prophet, not least because her kinsmen had lost everything and she really hated the Muslims. The Prophet understood her wounded pride and dignity, and how to heal them. He agreed to pay her ransom, set her free, and offered to marry her.

How gladly Juwayriya accepted this offer can easily be imagined. About 100 families were freed when the Ansar and the

Muhajirun learned that the Bani Mustaliq were now related to the Prophet by marriage. A tribe so honored could not be allowed to remain in slavery.[25] In this way, the hearts of Juwayriyah and all her people were won.

Safiyya was the daughter of Huyayy, a chieftain of the Jews of Khaybar, who had persuaded the Bani Qurayza to break their treaty with the Prophet. She had seen her family and relatives oppose the Prophet since her youth. In the Battle of Khaybar, she lost her father, brother, and husband, and she was among the captives.

The attitudes and actions of her family and relatives might have caused her to nurture a deep hatred of and desire for revenge against the Muslims. But 3 days before the Prophet's appearance in front of Khaybar's citadel, Safiyya had dreamed of a brilliant moon coming from Madina, moving toward Khaybar, and falling into her lap.

She later said: "When I was captured, I began to hope that my dream would come true." When she was brought before the Prophet, he generously set her free and offered her the choice of remaining a Jewess and returning to her people or entering Islam and becoming his wife. "I chose God and his Messenger," she said. They were married shortly thereafter.

Elevated to the Prophet's household and now a "mother of the believers," she experienced first-hand the Companions honorable and respectful treatment. She saw the refinement and true courtesy of those who had submitted their hearts and minds to God. Her attitude to her past experiences changed altogether, and she came to appreciate the great honor of being the Prophet's wife. This marriage also changed the attitude of many Jews, as they came to see and know the Prophet closely.

Sawda bint Zam'a was Sakran's widow. This couple had been among the first to embrace Islam and emigrate to Abyssinia. Sakran died in exile and left his wife utterly destitute. To relieve her distress, Prophet Muhammad married her, although he was facing great difficulties in meeting his own daily needs. This marriage took place some time after Khadija's death.

Hafsa was the daughter of 'Umar ibn al-Khattab, the future second caliph of Islam. Also an exile in Abyssinia and then an immigrant in Madina, she was widowed when her husband attained martyrdom in the path of God. She remained without a husband for a while. 'Umar wished for the honor and blessing of being close to the Prophet in this world and the Hereafter, just as Abu Bakr had, and so the Prophet married her to protect and help his faithful disciple's daughter.

Such were the circumstances and motives behind the Prophet's several marriages. There was no lust involved. Rather, he married them to provide helpless or widowed women with a dignified subsistence; to console and honor enraged or estranged tribespeople by bringing former enemies into some degree of relationship and harmony; to gain certain uniquely gifted individuals, in particular some exceptionally talented women, for the cause of Islam; to establish new norms of relationship between different people within the unifying brotherhood of faith in God; and to honor with family bonds the men who were to be his immediate political successors.

These marriages had nothing to do with self-indulgence, personal desire, or lust. With the exception of 'A'isha, all of his wives were widows, and all of his marriages (except for that with Khadija) were contracted when he was already an old man. Far from being acts of self-indulgence, these marriages were acts of self-discipline.

The Prophet was given a special Divine dispensation, one unique to his person, to have this number of wives. The Revelation restricting polygamy came after he had contracted all of these marriages. After that event, he also was forbidden to marry again.

CHAPTER 6

Prophet Muhammad as Educator

PROPHET MUHAMMAD AS EDUCATOR

THE EDUCATIONAL ATMOSPHERE

Consider the following verse:

> It is He who has sent among the unlettered a Messenger of
> their own, to recite to them His signs, to purify them, and to
> instruct them in Scripture and Wisdom, although they had
> been, before, in manifest error. (62:2)

Some of these words are very interesting. God is mentioned in the third person, because the ignorant, primitive, and savage Arabs did not know Him. As there was
no "He" in their minds, God first emphasizes the darkness of
their nature, their great distance from Him, and indicates that
they cannot be addressed directly by Him.

Then God calls them *unlettered*. They were not all illiterate,
but they had no knowledge of God and the Messenger. God, by
His infinite Power, sent to this trifling community a Messenger
with the greatest willpower, the most sublime nature, the deep-
est spirituality, and the highest morality, by means of whom He
would instruct them in how to become geniuses who would one
day govern humanity.

The word *among* shows that the Messenger was one of them,
but only in the sense of being unlettered. Being chosen by God, he
could not possibly belong to the Age of Ignorance (pre-Islamic
Arabia). However, he had to be unlettered so that God would teach
him what he needed to know. God would remove him from his people, educate him, and make him a teacher for all unlettered people.

The phrases *to recite to them His signs and to purify them* point
out that He teaches them about the meanings of the Qur'an and

of creation in a gradual manner, and informs them how to become perfect human beings by striving for spiritual perfection. He guides them to higher ranks by explaining the Qur'an and the universe to them, and showing them in minute detail how to lead a balanced and exemplary life in every sphere of activity.

The sentence *although they had been, before, in manifest error* indicates that God would purify and educate them even though they had gone astray. He did all of this through an unlettered Messenger and by teaching them the Qur'an. Throughout history and even today, this Book has met the needs of countless brilliant scientists, scholars, and saints.

After the Prophet, humanity saw his flag waving everywhere for centuries. Those who follow him, both now and in the past, reach the highest spiritual realms on wings of sainthood, piety, righteousness, knowledge, and science. Those who climbed the steps of good conduct and spirituality, and knowledge and science, both now and in the past, saw in each step the "footprints" of Prophet Muhammad and greet him with "God bless you."

They will do the same again in the near future. All so-called original ideas will disappear one by one, like candles blown out, leaving only one "sun"—the Qur'an—that will never set. Its flag will be the only one waving on the horizon, and every generation will rush to it, breaking the chains around their necks.

ISLAM ADDRESSES ALL HUMAN FACULTIES

As is explicit in the above-mentioned verse, the Messenger's method of education does not just purify our evil-commanding selves; rather, it is universal in nature and raises human hearts, spirits, minds, and souls to their ideal level. He respected and inspired reason; in fact, he led it to the highest rank under the intellect of Revelation.

The universal truths of the Qur'an also state this fact. Moreover, the Message touches all of our inner and outer senses, makes its followers rise on the wings of love and compassion, and takes them to places beyond their imagination. His universal call encompasses, in addition to the rules of good conduct and spirituality, all principles of economics, finance, administration, education, justice, and international law. He opened the doors of economic, social, administrative, military, political, and scientific institutions to his students, whose minds and spirits he trained and developed to become perfect administrators, the best economists, the most successful politicians and unique military geniuses.

If there had been any lack in his teaching of humanity, the aim of his Prophethood could not have been realized so fully. He said:

> Each Prophet before me built some part of this marvelous building, but there was a gap that needed to be closed. Every person passing by would say: "I wonder when this building will be completed." The one who completes it is me. After me, there is no longer any defect in the structure.[1]

The Qur'an affirms this: *This day I have completed your religion for you* (5:3). In short, the Prophet reformed, completed, and perfected the ways of life that had been lacking, had become deficient, or had deviated from the Will of God.

All previous Prophets were sent to a certain people and for a fixed time. However, as God chose Prophet Muhammad and Islam for all times and peoples, Islam is the perfection of His universal favor upon His creation. He fashioned Islam in such a way that it pleases everybody. Therefore, rather than trying to find fault with the Message and the principles relayed by the Messenger, people should seek these truths and principles in order to design their lives according to them.

The Prophet was a man who completed, perfected, and reformed. He transformed an illiterate, savage people into an army of blessed saints, illustrious educators, invincible commanders, eminent statesmen, and praiseworthy founders of the most magnificent civilization in history.

An educator's perfection depends on the greatness of his or her ideal and the quantitative and qualitative dimensions of his or her listeners. Even before Prophet Muhammad's death, the instructors and spiritual guides he dispatched were traveling from Egypt to Iran and from Yemen to Caucasia to spread what they had learned from him. In succeeding centuries, peoples of different traditions, conventions, and cultures (e.g., Persians and Turanians, Chinese and Indians, Romans and Abyssinians, Arabs and some Europeans) rushed to Islam. An educator's greatness also depends on the continuation of his or her principles. No one can deny that people all over the world accept Islam and adopt his principles. By God's Will and Power, most of humanity will embrace Islam soon.

Remember that the Messenger appeared among a wild and primitive people. They drank alcohol, gambled, and indulged in adultery without shame. Prostitution was legal, and brothels were indicated by a special flag. Indecency was so extreme that a man would be embarrassed to be called human. People were constantly fighting among themselves, and no one had ever been able to unify them into a strong nation. Everything evil could be found in Arabia. However, the Prophet eradicated these evils and replaced them with such deep-rooted values and virtues that his people became the leaders and teachers of the civilized world.

Even today we cannot reach their ranks. This has been acknowledged by such Western intellectuals as Isaac Taylor,[2] Robert Briffault, John Davenport, M. Pickhtall, P. Bayle, and Lamartine.[3]

God creates living things from lifeless things. He grants life to soil and rock. The Prophet transformed "rocks, soil, coal, and copper" into "gold and diamonds." Just consider the cases of Abu Bakr, 'Umar, 'Uthman, 'Ali, Khalid, 'Uqba ibn Nafi', Tariq ibn Ziyad, Abu Hanifa, Imam Shafi'i, Bayazid al-Bistami, Muhyi al-Din ibn al-'Arabi, Biruni, Zahrawi, and hundreds of thousands of others, all of whom were brought up in his school. The Messenger never allowed human faculties to remain undeveloped. He developed them and replaced weakness with marvelous competency. As a great thinker recalled:

> 'Umar had the potential to be a great man even before he embraced Islam. After his conversion, he became a powerful yet very gentle man who would not step on an ant or kill even a grasshopper.

We cannot eradicate such a small habit as smoking, despite all our modern facilities and practically daily symposia and conferences to combat it. Medical science says smoking causes cancer of the larynx, mouth, esophagus, windpipe, and lungs; however, people insist on smoking. On the other hand, the Messenger eradicated countless ingrained bad habits and replaced them with laudable virtues and habits. Those who saw them used to say: "My God, his followers are superior even to the angels." When these people pass over the Bridge above Hell with their light spreading everywhere, even the angels will ask in awe: "Are they Prophets or angels?" In fact, they are neither Prophets nor angels; they are the educated people of the Prophet's nation.

Prophet Muhammad had a holistic view of each individual. He took all of their mental and spiritual capacities and developed them, turning his own wretched people into paragons of virtue. His wisdom in assessing such potential is another proof of his Prophethood.

EDUCATING BY EXAMPLE

God's Messenger represented and expressed what he wanted to teach through his actions, and then translated his actions into words. How to be in awe of God, how to be humble, how to prostrate with deep feelings, how to bow, how to sit in prayer, how to cry to God at night—all of these he first did himself and then taught to others. As a result, whatever he preached was accepted immediately in his house and by his followers, for his words penetrated all of their hearts. After him, humanity saw his standard carried everywhere by people raised on the wings of sainthood, purification, devotion to God, and desire to be close to Him. Wherever they went, they walked in the footsteps of Prophet Muhammad. Others will do so in the future.

In the house of the Messenger there was a permanent sense of awe. Those who caught a glimpse of him could feel the allure of Heaven and the terror of Hell. He swayed to and fro during prayer, trembling with the fear of Hell and flying on wings of the desire of Heaven. All who saw him remembered God. Imam al-Nasa'i narrates: "While the Messenger was praying, a sound, like a boiling pot, was heard."[4] He always prayed with a burning and weeping heart. 'A'isha often found him in the presence of his Master, prostrating and trembling.[5]

His behavior inspired and benefited everyone around him. The children and wives of every Messenger had the same awe and fear, as the Messengers preached, ordered, related what they practiced and experienced, and gave examples through their actions. We can assess a person's impact through his or her behavior while at home. If all pedagogues gathered and merged their acquired knowledge about education, they could not be as effective as a Prophet.

Many of his descendants have shone among their respective generations like a sun, a moon, or a star. He brought up his Companions so perfectly that almost none of them became heretics.[6] None of his progeny has ever become a heretic, which is a distinction unique to him. Heretics and apostates have appeared among the households and descendants of many saintly people, but none of Muhammad's descendants have betrayed the roots of their household. If there have been a few exceptions unknown to us and history, they do not negate the rule.[7]

ESSENTIALS OF A GOOD EDUCATION

A real educator must have several virtues, among them the following:

First: Give due importance to all aspects of a person's mind, spirit, and self, and to raise each to its proper perfection. The Qur'an mentions the evil-commanding self that drags people, like beasts with ropes around their necks, wherever it wants to go, and goads them to obey their bodily desires. In effect, the evil-commanding self wants people to ignore their God-given ability to elevate their feelings, thoughts, and spirits.

The Qur'an quotes the Prophet Joseph as saying: *Surely the self commands evil, unless my Master has mercy* (12:53). Commanding evil is inherent in the self's nature. However, through worship and discipline, the self can be raised to higher ranks, to a position where it accuses itself for its evils and shortcomings (75:2), and then still higher where God says to it: *O self at peace! Return unto your Master, well-pleased, well-pleasing* (89:27-28).

Higher than the self at peace (at rest and contented) is the self perfectly purified. Those who rise to this degree of attainment are the nearest to God. When you look at them you remember God, for they are like polished mirrors in which all of His attributes are reflected. The Companions' desire to follow the training provided by Prophet Muhammad enabled almost all of them to reach this degree of moral and spiritual perfection; millions of people have followed and continue to follow their example.

Second: An education system is judged by its universality, comprehensiveness, and quality of its students. His students were ready to convey his Message throughout the world. The Message they conveyed, being universal in nature and valid for all times and places, found a ready acceptance among people of different races, religious background, intellectual levels, and age differences from modern-day Morocco and Spain to the Philippines, from the Russian steppes to the heart of Africa. Its principles remain valid. Despite numerous upheavals and changes, as well as social, economic, intellectual, scientific, and technological revolutions, his system remains the most unique and original, so much so that it is the hope of the future of humanity.

Third: An education system is judged by its ability to change its students. The example of smoking was mentioned earlier, as was that of how Islam and the Prophet's spread of it transformed the tribes of Arabia into their exact opposite within the space of just two or three decades. To those who deny or question his Prophethood, we challenge them to go anywhere in the world and accomplish, within 100 years, even one-hundredth of what he accomplished in the deserts of Arabia 1,400 years ago. Let them take all of the experts they can gather, and then we will wait to see their results.

When Prophet Muhammad was conveying the Message, Arabia was isolated from its neighbors by vast deserts. In terms of its cultural, intellectual, and moral life, it rightfully could be considered one of the most backward areas of the world. The Hijaz, where the Prophet was born, had experienced no social evolution and had attained no intellectual development worthy of mention. Dominated by superstitions, barbarous and violent customs, and degraded moral standards, people lived in savagery. They drank wine, gambled, and indulged in what even average societies consider immoral sexual activities. Prostitutes advertised their services by hanging a flag on the doors of their houses.[8]

It was a land without law and a government. Might was right, as in many areas today, and looting, arson, and murder were common. Any trivial incident could provoke intertribal feuding, which sometimes grew into peninsula-wide wars.

These were the people Prophet Muhammad appeared among. With the Message he relayed from God and his way of preaching it, he eradicated barbarism and savagery, adorned Arabia's wild and unyielding peoples with all praiseworthy virtues, and made them teachers of the world. His domination was not physical or military; rather, he conquered and subjugated them by becoming the beloved of their hearts, the teacher of their minds, the trainer of their souls, and the ruler of their spirits. He eradicated their evil qualities, and implanted and inculcated in his followers' hearts exalted qualities in such a way that they became second nature to all of his followers.

But this transformation was not limited only to the people of his own time and place, for this process continues even today wherever his Message spreads. It was not only quickly accepted in Arabia, Syria, Iraq, Persia, Egypt, North Africa, and Spain at its first outburst, but, with the exception of the now-vanished brilliant civilization of Islamic Spain, it has never lost its vantage ground. Since it first appeared, it has never stopped spreading.[9]

Many world-renowned individuals have been raised in the school of Muhammad. Certainly, we come across numerous great historical figures in other schools of education as well. God has honored humanity with great heroes, eminent states-men, invincible commanders, inspired saints, and great scientists. However, most of them have not made a deep impression on more than one or two aspects of human life, for they confine themselves to those fields.

But since Islam is a Divine way for all fields of life, a Divine system encompassing all aspects of life—"like a perfect work of architecture all of whose parts are harmoniously conceived to complement and support each other, nothing lacking, with the result of an absolute balance and solid composure," according the Muhammad Asad,[10] a Jewish convert—its students usually combine within themselves the spiritual and the rational, the intellectual and the material, the worldly with the otherworldly, the ideal with the real, and the scientific and the revealed (by God).

At its very outset, Islam abolished tribal conflicts and condemned racial and ethnic discrimination. The Prophet put the Qurayshi chiefs under Zayd's command (an emancipated black slave), and innumerable scholars and scientists, commanders, and saints appeared among conquered peoples. Among them was Tariq ibn Ziyad, an emancipated Berber slave who conquered Spain with 90,000 valiant warriors and laid the foundations of one of the most splendid civilizations of world history. After this victory, he went to the palace where the defeated king's treasury was kept. He said to himself:

> Be careful, Tariq. Yesterday you were a slave with a chain around your neck. God emancipated you, and today you are a victorious commander. However, you will change tomorrow into flesh rotting under earth. Finally, a day will come when you will stand in the Presence of God.

The world and its pomp could not attract him, and he continued to live a very simple life. What kind of education could transform a slave into such a dignified and honorable person?

However, his conquest of Spain was not his real victory. This came when he stood before the treasury of the Spanish king and reminded himself that one day he would die and face God. As a result of this self-advice, he took none of the treasure for himself.

'Uqba ibn Nafi' was another great commander who conquered northern Africa and reached the Atlantic coast. There he
stood and said: "O God, if this sea of darkness did not appear
before me, I would convey Your Name, the source of light, to
the remotest corners of the world."[11]

Before his conversion, 'Abd Allah ibn Mas'ud took care of
'Uqba ibn Abi Mu'ayt's sheep. He was a weak, little man who
everyone ignored.[12] After becoming a Muslim, however, he was
one of the most senior Companions. During his caliphate,
'Umar sent him to Kufa as a teacher. In the scholarly climate he
established there, the greatest figures of Islamic jurisprudence
grew up, among them Alqama, Ibrahim al-Nakha'i, Hammad
ibn Abi Sulayman, Sufyan al-Thawri, and especially Imam Abu
Hanifa, the founder of the largest Islamic legal school.

Ikrima was the son of Abu Jahl, the harsh and inflexible
leader of the Qurayshi unbelievers. Finally, after the Conquest of
Makka, he converted to Islam. This event so changed him that
he welcomed martyrdom 3 years later at the Battle of Yarmuk.
His son, Amir, was martyred with him.

Hansa was one of the finest poetesses before Islam. Becoming
a Muslim, she abandoned poetry because: "While we have the
Qur'an, I cannot write poems." She lost her four sons at the Battle
of Qadisiyya. This great woman, who had lamented her brother's
death before the appearance of Islam with a great poem, did not
lament this loss. Instead, she deepened her submission to God and
said only: "O God, all praise be to You. You have bestowed on me
while alive the possibility of offering you as martyrs my four sons
that you gave me."[13]

The school of Prophet Muhammad also produced the most
just rulers in history. Besides Abu Bakr, 'Uthman, 'Ali and many
others who succeeded them, 'Umar has been recognized in almost
every age as one of the world's most just and greatest statesmen.
He used to say: "If a sheep falls from a bridge even on the river
Euphrates and dies, God will call me to account for it on the Day
of Judgment."[14] When you compare the pagan 'Umar to the
Muslim 'Umar, you easily see the sharp contrast between the two
and understand how radically Islam changes people.

FURTHER REMARKS

Due to misconceptions and secular tendencies, especially in the West in recent centuries, most people define religion as blind faith, meaningless acts of worship, a consolation for life's problems. Such mistaken ideas have developed in Christendom partly due to Christianity's historical mistakes and shortcomings. Some secularized, worldly Muslims have compounded this mistake by reducing Islam to an ideology, a social, economic, and political system. They ignore one fact stated in the Qur'an, the Traditions, and throughout Islamic history: Islam, the middle way between all extremes, addresses itself to all human faculties and senses, as well as to each individual's mind, heart, and feelings, and encompasses every aspect of human life. That is why Prophet Muhammad stressed learning, trading, agriculture, action, and thought.

Moreover, he encouraged his people to do perfectly whatever they did, and condemned inaction and begging. For example, he said: "God loves a believing, skillful servant."[15] The Qur'an declares: *Say: "Work; and God will surely see your work, and the Messenger and the believers"* (9:105). As all of our actions will be displayed on the Day of Judgment, we cannot be careless and do something half-heartedly just to get rid of it. Moreover, The Messenger declares: "When you do something, God likes you to do it perfectly."[16]

Islam encourages people to work, and considers our lawful attempts to earn our living and support our family acts of worship. Unlike medieval Christianity, it does not idealize (nor even advise) life as a hermit. It forbids dissipation and luxury on the grounds that if we live a self-indulgent life here and neglect our religious duties, our prosperity in both worlds will be in jeopardy. The Messenger declares, in a concise saying that summarizes the essentials of a happy economic and social life and prosperity in both this world and the next:

> When you are involved in speculative transactions, occupied only with animal-breeding, content with agriculture, and abandon striving in the way of God to preach His religion, God will subject you to such a humiliation. He will not remove it until you return to your religion.[17]

This *hadith* gives a very accurate description of the pitiable condition of Muslims over the last few centuries. Speculative transactions signify the dying of a healthy economic life and the resort to unlawful, self-abandoned ways of earning one's living. Contentment with agriculture and animal breeding is the sign of laziness and abandoning scientific investigation—the Qur'an explicitly states that God created humanity as His vicegerent and entrusted us with knowledge of the names of things.

This means that we are to establish science and exploit natural resources by discovering the Divine laws of nature and reflecting on natural phenomena. However, while doing this, we should seek God's good pleasure and practice Islam.

The Qur'an contains many verses, such as: Say: *"Are they equal—those who know and those who don't know?"* (39:9), that emphasize the importance of knowledge and learning. It also warns that *among His servants, only those who have knowledge truly fear God* (35:28), meaning that true piety and worship is possible only through knowledge. Confining knowledge to religious sciences devoid of reflection and investigation inevitably results in contentment with animal breeding and agriculture, in idleness and the neglect of striving in the way of God. The ultimate result is misery, poverty, and humiliation.

The Messenger drew attention to this important fact in some other Traditions, such as: "An hour of reflection and contemplation is better than a year of (supererogatory) religious worship,"[18] and "A powerful believer is better and more lovable to God than a weak one."[19] Being powerful requires both spiritual and physical health as well as scientific and technical competence. Restricting the meaning of being powerful to physical strength shows one's total lack of understanding of what true power is based on.

In conclusion, being a good Muslim is possible only through being a good student in the school of Prophet Muhammad. This attitude was displayed by Ja'far ibn Abi Talib, the Prophet's cousin, who emigrated to Abyssinia to escape severe Qurayshi persecution. He once told the Negus, ruler of Abyssinia: "O king, we used to drink blood, eat carrion, fornicate, steal, kill each other, and plunder. The powerful used to oppress the weak. We used to do many other shameful and despicable things."[20]

Prophet Muhammad set the best example for his people in belief, worship, and good conduct—in short, in all aspects of life. His people considered having daughters a source of shame, and so buried them alive. When the Prophet came with the Divine Message, women enjoyed their rights fully. Once a girl came to The Messenger and complained: "O Messenger of God, my father is trying to force me to marry my uncle's son. I don't want to marry him." The Messenger sent for her father and warned him not to do this. The man promised that he would not do so. The girl then stood up and said: "O Messenger of God, I didn't intend to oppose my father. I came here only to find out whether Islam allows a father to marry his daughter to somebody without her consent."[21]

The Messenger warned his Companions not to beg. However poor and needy they were, the Companions did not beg from anybody. They were so sensitive in this matter that they even refrained from asking help. If, for example, one of them dropped his whip while on a mount, he would dismount and pick it up himself rather than ask someone to pick it up and hand it to him.[22]

Prior to Islam, people worshipped idols and did not give due respect to their parents. God's Message told them: *Your Master has decreed that you shall not worship any but Him, and to be good to parents* (17:23). This Divine decree changed them so radically that they began asking the Messenger if they would be punished if they did not return the looks of their parents' with a smile. The Qur'an ordered them *not to usurp an orphan's property* (17:34) and forbade theft. This made them so sensitive to others' rights that history does not record more than one or two thefts in that blessed period of the Prophet's rule.

Murder was extremely widespread in pre-Islamic Arabia. However, when the Prophet came with the prohibition: *Slay not the soul God has forbidden* (17:33), this evil was all but eradicated. The Messenger also forbade fornication. This ended all kinds of sexual immorality. However, we do find one incident of fornication during that period. It is as follows:

One day a pale and exhausted man came to the Messenger and exclaimed: "O Messenger of God, cleanse me!" The Messenger turned his face from him, but the man insisted, repeating his demand four times. At last, the Messenger asked: "Of what sin shall I cleanse you?" The man replied that he had fornicated. This sin weighed so heavily on his conscience that he desired to be punished. The Messenger asked those present: "Is he insane?" When told he was not, he told them to see if he was drunk. They examined him and found him sober. In the face of his insistent confession, the Messenger had to order the man to be punished. After it, he sat and wept.

A few days later, the man's partner appealed to the Messenger to cleanse her. Many times he turned away from her and sent her back. In utmost remorse, she insisted on being punished. The Messenger sent her back once more, saying: "You may be pregnant. Go and give birth to your child." The woman did so, and then returned with the same request. The Messenger excused her: "Go back, for perhaps your child needs feeding." After the child had been weaned, the woman came again. When someone reproved her while the punishment was being carried out, the Prophet frowned at him and said: "By God, this woman repented of her sin so much that if her repentance were shared out among all the people of Madina, it would be enough to cover them with forgiveness also."[23]

Prophet Muhammad established such a magnificent system and formed such an excellent community that not even a Plato, a Thomas Moore, a Campanella, or any other utopian has been able to imagine its equal. Among thousands of other examples, the following illustrates this fact:

Abu Hurayra, one of the poorest Companions, came to the Messenger. He had not eaten anything for some days. Abu Talha (an Ansari) took him home to feed him. But there was no food in his house except some soup that his wife had made for the children. She asked her husband what she should do, and they decided upon the following: They would put their children to bed without feeding them. As the soup was too little to satisfy all of them, only the guest should have it. While they were sitting at the table and getting ready to eat, Abu Talha's wife would knock the candle over, extinguishing it apparently by mistake. In the resulting darkness, they would act as if they were eating, although Abu Hurayra would be the only one eating. This is what they did. Abu Hurayra ate until he was satisfied, and then left, unaware of what had really happened.

The following day, they went to pray the morning prayer in the mosque. At the end of the prayer, the Messenger turned to them and asked: "What did you do last night, that caused this verse to be revealed in praise of you: *They prefer others above themselves, even though poverty be their portion.* (59:9)?"[24]

CHAPTER 7

The Military Dimension

THE MILITARY DIMENSION

I slam is the religion chosen by God for humanity's individual and collective welfare in this world and the next. It is based on belief in and worship of God, and does not countenance associating any partners with Him, whether in the form of something created, a person, or a concept. True belief and worship requires a deep concern for all animate and inanimate things. The deeper their belief in and submission to God is, the deeper is their concern for all creatures. Belief in God's Unity prevents humanity from enjoying and exercising absolute freedom in dealing with creatures.

Islam is derived from the Arabic root *s-l-m*, which means salvation, peace, and submission. In its religious context, it is the expression of God's Grace flowing in the universe's arteries, the Divine system to which all creatures (except humanity) have submitted willingly. The universe displays perfect order, for everything therein is *muslim*, in the sense that it submits to God's laws. Even people who reject belief in God or worship that which is not God are *muslims*, as far as their bodily existence is concerned. While we journey between being an embryo and a corpse, every bodily tissue and every limb follows the course prescribed for them by God's law.

The fundamental Islamic principle of Divine Unity implies that humanity necessarily must be in harmony with the surrounding world. The vast *muslim* universe displays a coherence and harmony of which our world is a part. Although our world is subject to laws special to itself and to the general "laws of nature," it is also in harmony with other laws governing surrounding phenomena. Human beings, unlike other creatures who tread "the path of nature," have free will. We bear the gift of freedom and the obligation to harmonize our life with nature. This harmony is also the path of our exaltation and progress, the path upon which God created human nature:

> Set your face to the religion, a man of pure faith—God's orig-
> inal nature in which He originated humanity. There is no
> changing God's creation. That is the right religion, but most of
> humanity know it not. (30:30)

To harmonize our lives with nature, we first should realize our personal integrity. To do this, we must apply our free will to our energies (e.g., desires, thoughts, and actions) to keep them within the limits established by God. If we do not recognize such limits, we might usurp another's property, seek illicit sexual relations, and indulge in other sins. If we do not recognize such limits with respect to our intellect, we may use it to deceive others. Our powers must be held in check, our intellect used with wisdom, and our desire and anger restrained by lawful behavior and moderation. In addition, we should remember that we are social beings; if we do not restrain ourselves as God demands, wrongdoing, injustice, exploitation, disorder, and revolution will occur in society.

God does not approve of wrongdoing and disorder. Rather, it is His Will that we live in peace and justice. Therefore, those who believe in God and worship Him faithfully are obliged to work for justice in this world. Islam calls this responsibility jihad.

JIHAD

Jihad has the literal meaning of exerting our best and greatest effort to achieve something. It is not the equivalent of war, for which the Arabic word is *qital*. Jihad has a much wider connotation and embraces every kind of striving in God's cause. A *mujahid* is one who is sincerely devoted to his or her cause; who uses all physical, intellectual, and spiritual resources to serve it; who confront any power that stands in its way; and, when necessary, dies for this cause. Jihad in the way of God is our struggle to win God's good pleasure, to establish His religion's supremacy, and to make His Word prevail.

A related principle, that of enjoining good and forbidding evil (*amr bi al-maʿruf wa nahy ʿan al-munkar*) seeks to convey the message of Islam and establish a model Islamic community. The Qur'an introduces the Islamic community as a model community required to inform humanity of Islam and of how the Prophet lived it: *Thus We have made you a community justly balanced, that you might be witnesses for all humanity, and the Messenger may be a witness for you* (2:143).

The Greater and Lesser Jihad

There are two aspects of jihad. One is fighting to overcome carnal desires and evil inclinations—the greater jihad. The other is encouraging others to achieve the same objective—the lesser jihad.

The Muslim army was returning to Madina after they had defeated the enemy, when the Messenger of God said to them: "We are returning from the lesser jihad to the greater one." When the Companions asked what the greater jihad was, he explained that it was fighting with the carnal self.[1]

The aim of either jihad is that the believer be purified of sins and so attain true humanity. The prophets were sent for this purpose. God says in the Qur'an:

> Thus We have sent unto you a Messenger from among you, who recites unto you Our revelations (and makes Our signs known to you), and who purifies you and instructs you in the Book and in the Wisdom, and also instructs you in what you don't know. (2:151)

Human beings are in some sense like raw minerals to be worked upon by Prophets, who purify and refine them by removing the seal from their hearts and ears, by lifting the veils from their eyes. Enlightened by the Prophets' message, people can understand the meaning of the laws of nature, which are signs of God's Existence and Unity, and can penetrate into the subtle reality behind things and events. Only through the guidance of Prophets can we attain the high status expected of us by God.

In addition to teaching the signs, Prophets also instructed their people in the Book and in Wisdom. As the Qur'an was the last Revelation to the Last Prophet, God means the Qur'an when He speaks of the Book, and the Sunna when He speaks of Wisdom. We must therefore follow the Qur'an and the Prophet's Sunna if we desire to be rightly guided.

The Prophet also teaches us what we do not know, and so humanity will continue to learn from the Prophet until the Day of Judgment. We learn from him how to purify ourselves of sin. By following his way, many great saints have attained their distinctions as saints. Among them, 'Ali says that his belief in the pillars of Islam is so firm that even if the veil of the Unseen were lifted, his certainty would not increase.[2] 'Abd al-Qadir al-Jilani is said to have had insight into the mysteries of the seventh heaven. These and many others, such as Fudayl bin 'Iyaz, Ibrahim bin Adham, and Bishr al-Khafi might well have been endowed with Prophethood, if God had not already set a seal on Prophethood.

The dark clouds of ignorance have been removed from our intellectual horizon through the guidance of Prophet Muhammad, and many more advances will be made in science and technology as a result of the light he brought from God.

Jihad is the legacy of the Prophets, and Prophethood is the mission of elevating men to God's favor by purifying them. Jihad is the name given to this prophetic mission, which has the same meaning as bearing witness to the truth. Just as judges listen to witnesses to settle a case, so those who have performed jihad have borne witness to God's Existence and Unity of God by striving in His way. The Qur'an says: *God bears witness that there is no god but He and so do the angels and the people of learning, maintaining justice. There is no god save He, the All-Mighty, the Wise* (3:18). Those who have performed jihad will also bear witness to the same truth in the heavenly court, where the case of unbelievers will be settled.

Those who bear witness to God Existence and Unity the remotest parts of the world and preach this truth. This was the duty of the Prophets as stated in the Qur'an, and it should be our duty as well:

> . . . Messengers who brought good news to humanity and who
> admonished them, so that they might have no argument
> against God after their coming. God is the All-Mighty and the
> All-Wise. God Himself bears witness by what He has revealed
> to you that it has been revealed with His knowledge; and so do
> the angels. There is no better witness than God. (4:165-66)

God has sent a Prophet to every people, so that every people can have an idea of Prophethood. As the term used to describe the activity of Prophethood, jihad is deeply engraved on the heart of every believer so that he or she feels a profound responsibility for preaching the truth in order to guide others to the Straight Path.

The lesser jihad, usually taken to mean fighting in God's cause, does not refer only to military struggle. The term is comprehensive, for it includes every action done for God's sake. Whether speaking or keeping silent, smiling or making a sour face, joining or leaving a meeting, every action taken to ameliorate the lot of humanity, whether by individuals or communities, is included in its meaning.

While the lesser jihad depends on mobilizing all material facilities and is performed in the outer world, the greater jihad means a person's fighting against his or her carnal soul. These two forms of jihad cannot be separated from each other.

The Messenger of God has taught us how to perform both forms of the jihad. He has established the principles of preaching the truth, which have application until the Day of Judgment. When we scrutinize the way he acted, we shall see that he was very systematic. This is actually another proof of his Prophethood and a wonderful example of following the way of God in behavior.

The believers kept their belief vigorous and active by means of jihad. Just as a tree keeps its leaves as long as it yields fruits, so believers can preserve their vigor as long as they perform jihad. Whenever you encounter a hopeless pessimist, you soon realize that he or she is one who has abandoned jihad. Such people have been deprived of the spirit, and are sunk in pessimism because they have abandoned preaching the truth. Whoever performs jihad unceasingly does not lose his or her enthusiasm and always tries to increase the scope of his or her activities. Every good deed results in a new one, so that believers never become deprived of a good: *As for those who strive for us We surely guide them to our path. God is with the good* (29:69).

There are as many paths leading to the Straight Path as the number of breaths drawn in creation. Whoever strives for His cause is guided, by God, to one of these paths and is save from going astray. Whoever is guided to His Straight Path by God lives a balanced life. They neither exceed the limits in their human needs and activities or in their worship and other religious observances. Such balance is the sign of true guidance.

All sacrifices made in fighting oppressive unbelievers, no matter how great, only constitute the lesser jihad of striving to discharge religious obligations as perfectly as possible. The greater jihad is much harder to accomplish, since it requires us to fight against our own destructive drives and impulses, such as arrogance, vindictiveness, jealousy, selfishness, self-conceit, and the carnal desires.

Although the person who abandons the lesser jihad is liable to spiritual deterioration, he or she may recover. Everything in the universe praises and glorifies God with each breath and is, accordingly, a sign of God's Existence and Unity. A person may be guided to the Straight Path through one of these signs. For this reason, it is said that there are as many paths leading to the Straight Path of God as the breaths of all His creatures. A person returning from the lesser jihad is vulnerable to worldly weaknesses. Pride, love of comfort and ease may captivate that person. Thus the Prophet warned us through his Companions by saying, while returning to Madina after a victory: "We are returning from the lesser jihad to the greater."

The Companions were fearless on the battlefields, and as sincere and humble as dervishes in worshipping God. Those victorious warriors used to spend most of their nights praying to God. Once, when night fell during battle, two of them took turns in standing guard. One rested while the other prayed. Having become aware of the situation, the enemy shot a shower of arrows at him.

He was hit and bled profusely, but did not abandon his prayer. When he finished his devotions, he woke his friend, who asked him in amazement why he had not done so sooner. He replied: "I was reciting *Surat al-Kahf*, and I did not wish the deep pleasure I found in this prayer to be interrupted."[3]

The Companions went into a trance-like state of ecstasy when in prayer, and would recite the Qur'an as if it were being revealed directly to them. Thus, they did not feel the pain caused by arrows which penetrated their bodies. Jihad, in its lesser and greater aspects, found complete expression in them.

The Prophet combined these two aspects of jihad in the most perfect way in his own person. He displayed monumental courage on the battlefields. 'Ali, one of the most courageous figures of Islam, confesses that the Companions took shelter behind the Prophet at the most critical moments of fighting.

Jihad's stages and main principles. The first Revelation to the Messenger was the command: *Read!* This command, coming at a time when there was nothing readily available to read, meant that believers should use their intellectual and spiritual faculties to discern God's acts in the universe and His laws related to its creation and operation. Through such discernment, believers seek to purify themselves and their minds of all ignorance-based superstitions and to acquire true knowledge through observation and contemplation.

We are not composed only of our minds. God has endowed us with many faculties, each of which needs satisfaction. So while feeding our minds with the Divine signs in the universe, we seek to cleanse our hearts of sin. We live a balanced life in awareness of Divine supervision, and continuously seek His forgiveness. In this way, we eventually conquer our desire for forbidden things and, through prayer, ask God to enable us to do good deeds.

Thus *Read!* signifies action. For the Messenger, who already was absolutely pure in spirit and devoid of superstition, it meant that it was time to start his mission as a Messenger of God. He was to recite the Revelation in public and instruct people about

His signs. By doing this, he would purify their minds of superstitions carried over from the Age of Ignorance, and their hearts of sin. He would enlighten them, intellectually and spiritually, by instructing them in the Revealed Book of God (the Qur'an) and His Created Book (the universe):

> We have sent among you, of yourselves, a Messenger who recites Our signs to you, purifies you, and instructs you in the Book and in the Wisdom, and also instructs you in what you don't know. (2:151)

After he received this first revelation, the Messenger returned home in great agitation. He was sleeping wrapped in a cloak, enwrapped by his people's suffering and this heavy responsibility, when God commanded him:

> O enwrapped one, keep vigil the night long, save a little (a half of it, or diminish or add a little), and chant the Qur'an in measure, for We shall charge you with a weighty word. (73:1-5)

The short period between the first revelation and the spreading of Islam, marked by such verses as those mentioned above, was a preliminary stage for the Messenger. He had to prepare himself to convey the Qur'an by keeping long night vigils and reciting the Qur'an in measure.[4]

In addition to conveying the Message, jihad, as discussed above, entails the believers' struggles with their carnal selves to build a genuine spiritual character, one overflowing with belief and inflamed with love. These two dimensions of jihad continue until the believer dies (the individual sphere) and until the Last Day (the collective sphere). Therefore, soon after this verse was revealed, the Messenger received the following revelation:

> O enshrouded one, arise and warn! Magnify your Master, purify your robes, and flee defilement! Do not show favor, seeking worldly gain! For the sake of your Master, be patient! (74:1-7)

These revelations ordered the Prophet to begin preaching Islam. He started with his family members and nearest relatives and, after *Warn your tribe of nearest kindred* (26:214) was revealed,

spread this call throughout his tribe. His subsequent public preaching was met with derision, threats, torture, enticing bribes if he
would stop, and boycott.

In Makka, the Messenger never resorted to or allowed retaliation. Islam came not to spread trouble or cause dissention,
but, in the words of Amir ibn Rabi', to bring people out of the
darkness of unbelief into the light of belief, to free them from
serving that which is not God so that they can serve the One
True God, and to elevate them from the pits of the Earth to the
heights of Heaven.[5]

As Islam literally means "peace, salvation, and submission,"
it obviously came to establish peace. This is estab-lished first in
our inner worlds, so that we are at peace with God and natural
environment, and then throughout the world and the universe.
Peace and order are fundamental in Islam, which seeks to spread
in a peaceful personal and collective atmosphere. It refrains from
resorting to force as much as possible, never approves of injustice, and forbids bloodshed:

> Whoever kills someone, other than in retaliation for murder or
> corruption on the Earth, in effect has killed humanity; whoev-
> er saves a life in effect has saved humanity. (5:32)

Coming to eradicate injustice and corruption, and to "unite"
the Earth with the Heavens in peace and harmony, Islam calls
people with wisdom and fair exhortation. It does not resort to
force until the defenders of their corrupt order, which is rooted in
injustice, oppression, self-interest, exploitation, and usurpation of
others' rights, seek to prevent its preaching in peaceful ways and
to suppress it. Thus, force is allowed in the following cases:

- If unbelievers, polytheists, or those who cause trouble
  and corruption actively resist the preaching of Islam and
  prevent others from listening to its message. As Islam is
  a Divine religion seeking to secure human well-being
  and happiness in both worlds, it has the right to present
  itself. If this is not allowed, theoretically, its opponents
  are given three alternatives: accept Islam, allow its preach-

ing in peaceful ways, or admit its rule. If they reject these alternatives, force is allowed.

However, there is an important point to mention. In order to use force, there must be an Islamic state. It was allowed only after the Prophet emigrated to Madina and established an independent state, for the Muslims had been wronged. The verses revealed to give this permission explain the Islamic view of just war:

> (Fighting is) permitted to those who are fought against, because they have been wronged. God is able to give them victory. Those who have been driven from their homes unjustly only because they said: "Our Master is God." For had it not been for God's repelling some people by means of others, cloisters and churches and synagogues and mosques, wherein the Name of God is much mentioned, would have been pulled down. God helps one who helps Him [His religion]. God is All-Strong, All-Mighty. Those who, if We give them power in the land, establish worship and pay zakat and enjoin the good and forbid the evil. And God's is the sequel of events. (22:39-41)

It is clear from these verses and from history that Islam resorts to force only to defend itself and establish freedom of belief. Under Muslim rule, Christians, Jews, Zoroastrians, Hindus, and adherents of other religions are free to practice their religion. Even many Western historians and writers have agreed that Christians and Jews experienced the most prosperous and happiest period of their history under Muslim rule.

• Islam, being the true religion revealed by God, never approves of injustice. As declared in: *We have written (decreed) in the Psalms after the Torah (and remind once more in the Qur'an) that My righteous servants will inherit the Earth* (21:105), God's righteous servants must submit the Earth to His rule, which depends on absolute justice and worship of the One God. They also are obliged to strive until persecution, as well as any worship of and obedience to false deities and unjust tyrants, is ended. Thus Muslims are to fight for the feeble and oppressed:

> How should you not fight for the cause of God and of the feeble and oppressed men and women and children, who cry: "Our Master! Bring us out of this town whose people are oppressors! Give us from Your presence some protecting friend! Give us from Your presence some defender!" (4:75)

Some Rules

As believers cannot transgress God's limits, they must observe His rules related to fighting. Some are deduced direct from the Qur'an and Sunna, and are as follows:

- A believer is *one from whom God has bought his or her life and wealth in exchange for Paradise* (9:111). They are dedicated solely to His cause and seek only His good pleasure. Therefore, whoever fights for other causes (e.g., fame, wealth, racial or ideological considerations) is excluded from God's good pleasure.

- *Fight in the way of God against those who fight you, but do not transgress. God does not love transgressors* (2:190). Believers are told not to fight neutral parties, and to reject unscrupulous methods or indiscriminate killing and pillage, which characterize all wars waged by non-Muslims. The excesses alluded to consist of, but are not limited to, fighting women and children, the old and the injured, mutilating enemy corpses, destroying fields and livestock, and other acts of injustice and brutality. Force is to be used only when unavoidable, and only to the extent absolutely necessary.

- When fighting cannot be avoided, the Qur'an tells believers not to avoid it. Rather, they must prepare themselves, both morally and spiritually, and take precautions. These are:
  - Strive for that spiritual stage when 20 Muslims can overcome 200 of the enemy:

> O Prophet! Exhort the believers to fight. Twenty steadfast men shall overcome 200; 100 hundred steadfast men shall overcome 1,000 unbelievers, because unbelievers have no understanding or sound judgment. (8:65)

> When those who will meet their Master exclaim: How often a small company has overcome a mighty host by God's leave! God is with the steadfast. (2:249)

To attain such a rank, Muslims must have an unshakable belief and trust in God and avoid all sins as much as possible. Belief and piety or righteousness are two unbreakable weapons, two sources of inexhaustible power: *Don't faint or grieve, for you shall gain the upper hand if you are true believers (3:139), and The sequel is for the righteous people* (7:128).

– In addition to moral strength, believers must equip themselves with the latest weaponry. Force is vital to obtaining the desired result, so believers cannot ignore it. Rather, they must be further advanced in science and technology than unbelievers so that the latter cannot use their superiority for their own selfish benefit. As Islam states that "right is might," believers must be able to prevent unbelievers and oppressors from showing that "might makes right":

> Make ready for them all you can of armed force and tethered horses, that thereby you may dismay the enemy of God and your enemy, and others beside them whom you don't know; God knows them. Whatever you spend in the way of God will be repaid to you in full, and you will not be wronged. (8:60)

An Islamic state should be powerful enough to deter the attacks of unbelievers and oppressors, as well as their plans to subject weaker people. It should be able to secure peace and justice, and to prevent any other power from causing trouble or corruption. This will be possible when Muslims equip themselves with strong belief and righteousness, and with scientific knowledge and the latest technology. They must combine science and technology with faith and good morals, and then use this force for the good of humanity.

Belief in God calls for serving people. Greater belief means a greater concern for the created's welfare. When Muslims attain this rank, *God will not allow unbelievers to defeat believers* (4:141). Otherwise, what the Prophet predicted will happen: "(The forces of unbelief) will unite to make a concerted attack upon you. They will snatch the morsel out of your mouths and pillage your table."[6]

– When fighting is necessary, Muslims must report for duty, for:

> O you who believe! What ails you that when you are told: "Go forth in the way of God," you sink down heavily to the ground? Are you so content with the life of the world, rather than the world to come? Yet the enjoyment of the life of the world, compared with the world to come, is a little thing. If you don't go forth, He will afflict you with a painful doom. He will replace you with another people; and you will not hurt Him. God is powerful over everything. (9:38-39)

> God loves those who battle for His cause in ranks, as if they were a solid structure. (61:4)

> O you who believe! Shall I show you something that will save you from a painful doom? You should believe in God and His Messenger, and strive for the cause of God with your wealth and your lives. That is better for you, if you only knew. He will forgive your sins and admit you into Gardens underneath which rivers flow, and to dwelling places goodly in Gardens of Eden. That is the mighty triumph; and other things

you love, help from God, and a nigh victory.
Give good tidings to believers. (61:10-13)

— A community is structured and functions like a body,
for it demands a "head" having "intellect." Therefore,
obedience to the head is vital for communal prosperity. When the Messenger was raised in Arabia, people
resembled a broken rosary's scattered beads and were
unaware of the need for obedience and the benefits of
collective life. The Messenger inculcated in them the
feeling of obedience to God, His Messenger, and their
superiors, and used Islam as an unbreakable rope to
unite them:

> O you who believe! Obey God, the Messenger,
> and those of you who are in authority. If you have
> a dispute concerning anything, refer it to God
> and the Messenger if you believe in God and the
> Last Day. That is better and more seemly in the
> end. (4:59)

> O you who believe! When you meet an army, hold
> firm and remember and mention God much, so
> that you may be successful. Obey God and His
> Messenger, and don't dispute with each other lest
> you falter and your strength departs. Be steadfast,
> and God is with the steadfast. (8:45-46)

The Companions' consciousness of obedience made
many previously impossible things possible. For
example, when he appointed the 18-year-old son of
his emancipated (black) slave as commander of an army
containing many elders, among them Abu Bakr, 'Umar,
and 'Uthman, no Companion objected.[7] In another
case, during a military expedition the commander
ordered his soldiers to throw themselves into a fire.
Even though this was not an Islamic order, some tried
to obey it. However, others prevented them from
committing suicide and persuaded them to ask the

Messenger whether they had to obey such un-Islamic orders.[8] Although it is unlawful to obey sinful orders, obedience to law is vitally important to a community's collective life, particularly if it wants to win a war. Believers must remain steadfast and are forbidden to flee the battlefield:

> O you who believe! When you meet unbelievers in battle, don't turn your backs to them. Whoever does so on that day, unless maneuvering for battle or intending to join a company, has incurred God's wrath, and his habitation will be Hell—an evil homecoming! (8:15-16)

Fleeing the battlefield is one of the seven major sins, for it causes disorder in the ranks and demoralizes the others. Their belief in God and the Hereafter cannot be firm, for their actions show they prefer this life to the Hereafter. Believers may leave the battlefield only to maneuver, as a tactic, or to join another company. In the Battle of Yarmuk (636), 20,000 valiant Muslims fought and defeated 200,000 Byzantines.[9] Qabbas ibn Ashyam, one of the heroes, realized that he had lost a leg (around noon) only when he dismounted from his horse hours later. His grandson later introduced himself to Caliph 'Umar ibn 'Abd al-'Aziz, saying: "O Caliph, I am the grandson of the one who lost his leg at noon but became aware of it only toward evening." During the Battle of Mu'ta (629), the Muslim army consisted of 3,000 soldiers; the opposing Byzantine forces had about 100,000 soldiers. The Muslims fought heroically, and both armies retreated at the same time. Despite this, the Muslims thought that they had fled the battlefield and so were ashamed to meet the Messenger. However, he welcomed and consoled them: "You did not flee; you retreated to join me. You will collect strength and fight with them again."[10] It happened just as he said, for just before his death the

Muslim army raided southern Syria; 2 years later, the Muslims dealt the Byzantines a deadly blow at Yarmuk.

MILITARY EXPEDITIONS

With the arrival of the Messenger in Madina, the struggle between Islam and unbelief entered a new phase. In Makka the Prophet had devoted himself almost exclusively to expounding Islam's basic principles and to his Companions' moral and spiritual training. After the Emigration (622), however, new Muslims belonging to different tribes and regions began to gather in Madina. Although the Muslims held only a tiny piece of land, the Quraysh allied itself with as many tribes as possible to exterminate them.

In these circumstances, the small Muslim community's success, not to mention its very survival, depended upon several factors. In order of importance, there were:

- Propagate Islam efficiently and effectively to convert others.
- Demonstrate the unbelievers' falsehoods so convincingly that nobody could doubt Islam's truth.
- Face exile, pervasive hostility and opposition, economic hardship, hunger, insecurity, and danger with patience and fortitude.
- Regain their wealth and goods usurped by the Makkans after they emigrated.
- Resist, with courage and weapons, any assault launched to frustrate their movement. While resisting, they should ignore the enemy's numerical or material superiority.

In addition to threats from Makka and its allies, the young community had to contend with Madina's three Jewish tribes, which controlled its economic life. Although they had been waiting for a Prophet, they opposed the Messenger because he was not Jewish. One of the first things the Messenger did in Madina was to sign a pact with the Jews.[11] Despite this, the Jews continued to harbor considerable ill-will toward the Messenger and plot against him and Islam. For example, the skilled Jewish poet Ka'b ibn Ashraf composed poems satirizing the Messenger and instigating his enemies.

In Madina, another hostile element began to emerge: hypocrisy. The Hypocrites can be divided into four broad groups, as follows:

- Those who had no faith in Islam but entered the Muslim community to cause trouble within its ranks.
- Those who understood political realities and so sought some advantage by seeming to convert. However, they maintained contacts with anti-Islamic forces in the hope that they could benefit from contacts with both sides and thus not be harmed.
- Those who had not made up their minds yet, but seemed to have converted because those around them were doing so.
- Those who accepted Islam as the true religion but found it difficult to abandon their inherited way of life, superstitions, and customs, as well as to exercise the self-discipline required by Islam.

In such severe circumstances, God's Messenger decided to dispatch military expeditions into the desert's heart. He had several goals in mind, some of which were as follows:

- Unbelievers tried *to extinguish the Light of God with their mouth, but, although they were averse, God willed to perfect His Light* (61:8). The Messenger wanted to prove that unbelievers could not exterminate Islam, and to show that Islam could not be ignored.
- Makka enjoyed a central position in Arabia. As the peninsula's most formidable power, all other tribes felt some sort of adherence to it. By sending military expeditions to neighboring areas, the Messenger wanted to display Islam's power and break the Quraysh's dominance. Throughout history, the concept of "might is right" has usually been a norm, for "right" is often too weak to rule. In Arabia, the Quraysh had might and wealth, and so neighboring tribes obeyed them. Islam came to make right prevail, and so the Messenger had to break Makka's grip.

- His Mission was not restricted to a fixed period or nation, for he was sent as a mercy for all the worlds. Thus he was charged with conveying Islam as far as possible. To succeed, he had to know what was going on in the peninsula. These expeditions served as vanguards providing him with the information he needed to pave the way for the preaching of Islam.

- One of the most effective ways to crush your enemies is to drive them to unpremeditated, premature actions, for this allows you to retain the initiative. The Messenger surely was informed of the Quraysh's contacts with 'Abd Allah ibn Ubayy ibn Salul, leader of Madina's Hypocrites. He also was alert to their possible attacks on Madina. After a Qurayshi military force entered Madina's suburbs and the returned to Makka with its plunder, the Messenger dispatched military expeditions to encourage the Quraysh to act before thinking. He then could thwart their plots.

- The Quraysh lived on trade with the international markets in Syria and Yemen, and so had to secure their trade routes. But now that the Muslims were in Madina, these routes could be threatened. While strengthening his position, the Prophet also was dispatching military expeditions to paralyze the Quraysh's hopes and plans of defeating him.

- Islam's commandments seek to guarantee security of life and property, chastity and belief, as well as physical, mental, and spiritual health. Given this, murder and theft, robbery and plundering, usurpation and interest (or usury), gambling, alcohol, illicit sexual relations, anarchy, and the propagation of atheism are forbidden.

    The Arabic word for belief, *iman*, means giving security. Thus a *mu'min* (believer) never cheats, and all are safe from a believer's tongue and hand. Believers do not lie, break their promise, or betray a trust. They do not earn their livelihood through stealing, usurpation, and interest-based transactions. In addition, they seek to harm no one, for they are convinced that those who kill even one person are like those who kill humanity.

When the Messenger was raised as a Prophet, Arabia had no security of life or property, chastity, health, or belief. One of his tasks, therefore, was to establish absolute security in every aspect of life. Once he said to Adiy ibn Khatam: "A day will come when a woman will travel, riding in a litter, from Hira to Makka and fear nothing except God and wolves."[12] By dispatching military expeditions, the Messenger sought to establish security therein and show everyone that only Islam would bring them security.

Expeditions

The first post-Emigration military expedition, led by Hamza, was sent toward Sif al-Bahr. It arrived just as a Qurayshi trade caravan was returning from Damascus. The Quraysh had usurped all the Emigrants' possessions and traded them in Damascus. The Messenger used this situation to display Muslim power and directly threaten Quraysh's economic well-being. No clash took place in this first confrontation, but the desert tribes witnessing the incident were inclined to acknowledge another source of power in the peninsula.

This expedition was followed by another one commanded by 'Ubayda ibn Harith. With the same purpose in mind, 'Ubayda went as far as Rabigh, a valley on the way to Makka. The 60 Muslim cavalrymen encountered a Qurayshi force of 200 armed men. An exchange of arrows took place and, fearing defeat, the Makkan force eventually withdrew toward Makka.[13]

Military expeditions, some led by the Messenger, now followed one another. In two of the expeditions he commanded, the Messenger went to Abwa and Buwat, respectively, with the intention of threatening Qurayshi trade caravans and intimidating the Quraysh.[14] In Abwa, he concluded a treaty with the Banu Damra tribe: neither side would fight the other, and Banu Damra would not aid the Muslims' enemies.

Shortly before the Battle of Badr (624), the Messenger sent an expedition of about 10 people, commanded by 'Abd Allah ibn Jahsh, to Nakhla, located a few miles from Makka on the way to Ta'if. He told them to follow the Quraysh's movements and gather information about their plans. While they were in Nakhla, a Qurayshi trade caravan coming from Ta'if halted there. Something happened unexpectedly, and the Muslims killed one Makkan and captured the rest (except one) and their belongings. These were taken to Madina.

This event occurred toward the end of Rajab and the beginning of Sha'ban. Therefore, it was uncertain whether the sanctity of Rajab, one of the four holy months, had been violated. The Quraysh, those Jews secretly allied with them, and the Hypocrites made full use of this possible violation in their anti-Muslim propaganda campaign. They claimed that the Muslims shed blood in a sacred month, a time when doing so is prohibited.

Since the incident had taken place without his approval, God's Messenger explained to its participants that he had not ordered them to fight. Other Muslims also reproached them. However, a Revelation consoled them on account of their pure intention with hope for God's mercy:

> They question you concerning the holy month, and fighting in it. Say: "Fighting in it is a heinous thing, but to bar from God's way, and unbelief in Him, denying entry into the Holy Mosque, expelling its people from it are more heinous in God's sight. Persecution is more heinous than killing." They will not cease to fight with you till they turn you from your religion, if they are able; and whoever of you turns from their religion and dies unbelieving—their works have failed in this world and the next. Those are the inhabitants of the Fire; therein they shall dwell forever. But the believers, and those who emigrate and struggle in God's way—those have hope of God's Mercy. God is All-Forgiving, All-Compassionate. (2:217-18)[15]

The verses answered the objections of the anti-Muslim forces. In short, fighting during the holy months is an evil act. However, those who had subjected the believers to continual and indescribable wrong for 13 years merely because they believed in the One God had no right or justification to raise such an objection. Not only had they driven the Muslims from their homes, they had placed the Holy Mosque beyond their reach, a punishment unknown in the Ka'ba's approximately 2,000-year known history. With such a record, who were they to raise such an outcry over a small incident, especially one that had taken place without the Prophet's approval?

A GENERAL EVALUATION

About 20 military expeditions preceded the Battle of Badr. Through these activities, the Messenger seized control of the desert and paralyzed Makka's morale. In addition, most of the desert tribes began to acknowledge Islam's power and come to some agreement with the Muslims. Only one expedition resulted in the Muslims actually killing or wounding enemy soldiers. To prove that Islam guaranteed security, they neither plundered caravans nor usurped the bedouins' property.

The Messenger formed an intelligence network to inform him of everything happening in the desert and in Makka. This system was so sophisticated that probably most of his Companions in Madina did not know, for example, that his uncle 'Abbas was left in Makka as an intelligence agent. When the Messenger set out on a military campaign, no one knew his real intention and destination.[16] He used couriers to communicate with his soldiers fighting at the front, and news reached him through a series of relay stations. With this system, his information was always up-to-date.

Only Emigrants participated in these expeditions. First of all, the Quraysh were at war with the Emigrants and did not want them to be sheltered in Madina. Besides, it was the Emigrants who had been forced out and made to leave all their possessions behind. As the Helpers had sworn allegiance to the Messenger, they were expected to realize on their own that they also should fight in the way of God.

The military genius of the Messenger showed itself in his choice of military commanders. His uncle Hamza led the first military expedition. Besides his courage and strength, Hamza had sound judgment, good opinions, and a high administrative ability. Until his community adopted his ideas and opinions, the Messenger chose to practice them through his relatives. Since his mission's military dimension was displayed for the first time in Madina, the Messenger put his own relatives on the front line until everyone became used to this. It should be noted, however, that these commanders were capable and eminent generals who were highly qualified for the post. In addition, they were wholly devoted to Islam.

Hamza was martyred at Uhud after killing more than 20 enemy soldiers. 'Ubayda ibn Harith, the Prophet's cousin, eventually died from wounds he received at Badr. Before he died, he asked the Messenger: "O the Messenger, I did not die fighting at the front. Am I considered a martyr?"[17]

The expedition sent to Nakhla was commanded by 'Abd Allah ibn Jahsh, the son of the Prophet's paternal aunt. In the second stage of the Battle of Uhud, he fought heroically. He came across Sa'd ibn Abi Waqqas and told him:

> "Come on and pray, and I'll say amen for your prayer. Then I'll pray and you say amen for mine." Sa'd prayed: "O God, make me encounter one of the strongest enemy soldiers, and let me defeat him." Ibn Jahsh said amen and then prayed: "O God, let me encounter one of the strongest enemy soldiers. After I wound him severely, let him kill me, and cut off my ears and nose and lips so that I shall come to Your Presence bleeding profusely. You will ask me: 'Abd Allah, where are your ears, nose, and lips?' and I'll respond: 'O God, I was ashamed to come to Your Presence with my members with which I had sinned, so I sacrificed them while fighting in the way of Your Beloved One.'"

When the battle ended, 'Abd Allah ibn Jahsh was found lying with his ears, nose, and lips cut off and his abdomen lanced.[18]

Lastly, by sending a series of military expeditions, the Messenger agitated the Quraysh into an unpremeditated action. On the pretext of recapturing their trade caravan, 1,000 Makkan soldiers left for Badr, some 90 miles toward Madina.

THE BATTLES

As Muslim power solidified in Madina, the Quraysh began to worry about a possible threat to their trade route to Syria. In a letter addressed to 'Abd Allah ibn Ubayy ibn Salul,[19] the Quraysh threatened to kill all Madinese men and enslave their women unless they expelled the Messenger. The Prophet put a timely end to this, and Ibn Ubayy did not pursue the matter. Next, when Sa'd ibn Mu'adh went to Makka to perform the minor pilgrimage ('umra), he was stopped at the Ka'ba's entrance and prevented from performing the circumambulation. The Makkans also sent quite regular invading parties.

The Battle of Badr

Given such incidents, the Muslims had to extend their control over the Syrian trade route to force the Quraysh and other unfriendly tribes to reconsider. It also was time for the Prophet to show the forces arrayed against him that the preaching of Islam could not be stopped or eradicated from its adherents' hearts, and that polytheism and unbelief would surrender to Islam.

At the beginning of 624, a large Qurayshi caravan en route to Makka from Syria, and escorted by no more than 40 security guards, arrived at a place within reach of the Muslims. It contained goods that had been purchased with the Emigrants' property. Naturally Abu Sufyan, the caravan's leader, feared a Muslim attempt to retrieve their stolen property. And so he sent a messenger to Makka asking for help and reinforcements.

This caused an uproar throughout Makka. Leading Qurayshi chiefs decided to fight the Prophet. About 1,000 fighters left Makka, amidst much pomp and show, to crush the Muslims' rising power. They also wanted, as always, to terrorize neighboring tribes to ensure their trade caravans' continued safety.

The Messenger, always informed of developments that could affect his mission, realized that if an effective step were not taken right then, the preaching of Islam might suffer a blow. Had the Quraysh taken the initiative and attacked Madina, the city's small Muslim community might have perished. Even if they only brought their caravan safely to Makka by dint of their military strength, the Muslims' political and military prestige would be undermined. Once this happened, their lives, property, and honor would be jeopardized.

Deciding to use his available resources, the Prophet left Madina. Although he may have wanted a decisive battle with the Quraysh, most Muslims wanted to capture the caravan and retrieve their property. The Prophet assembled the people and told them that the Qurayshi trade caravan was in the north and its invading army was in the south, moving toward Madina. He also informed them that God had promised that they would be able to seize either party.[20] It was for them to choose which target to attack.

Aware of the Prophet's intention, an Emigrant named Miqdad ibn 'Amr replied:

> O Messenger of God. Proceed as God has commanded you. We are with you wherever you go, even as far as Bark al-Ghimad. We shall not say, as the Children of Israel said to Moses: "Go forth, you and your Master, and fight. We shall remain here sitting." We rather say: "Go forth, you and your Master, and fight, and we shall fight on your side as long as the eyelid of any one of us keeps moving."[21]

Until the Battle of Badr, the Messenger had not sought military aid from the Ansar. This was the first time they would prove their commitment to Islam. Without addressing them directly, the Messenger again put the two alternatives before his audience. Realizing what the Messenger was doing, an Ansari named Sa'd ibn Mu'adh, the leader of the Aws tribe, rose and said:

> O Messenger of God. I think your question is directed to the Ansar. We believe in you, affirm that you are the Messenger of God, and bear witness to the truth of your teachings. We took the oath of allegiance to you that we would hear and obey you. O Messenger of God, do as you wish! By the One Who has sent you with the truth, if you were to take us to the sea and plunge into it, none of us should remain behind. So take us along to the battlefield with God's blessings.[22]

The decision was made to fight. This was also the decree of God, as mentioned above.

The Makkan army consisted of 1,000 fighters, including 600 soldiers in coats of mail and 200 cavalrymen, and was accompanied by singers and dancers. Dancing and drinking parties were held whenever it halted. The soldiers arrogantly vaunted their military power and numerical strength to the tribes and settlements it passed, and boasted of their invincibility.[23] Even worse, they were fighting for no lofty ideal; rather, they sought to defeat the forces of belief, truth, justice, and good morals.

The Muslim army was made up of 313 fighters: 86 Emigrants and 227 Ansar. Only two or three Muslims had horses, for resources were scarce. There were no more than 70 camels, so three or four persons took turns riding each camel. The Messenger took turns with two others. When they asked him to ride the camel and exclude them from the turns, the Messenger answered: "You are not stronger than me. And as for the reward, I need it just as much as you do."[24]

The Muslim soldiers were fully devoted to and ready to die for the cause of Islam. To accomplish what He had decreed, God made the Messenger dream that the number of Makkan soldiers was small, just as He made the number of the Muslims appear smaller in the eyes of the Makkans (8:44).

The two armies met at Badr. The Makkans outnumbered the Muslims by three to one and were far better equipped. However, the Muslims were fighting for the most sublime cause: to establish God's religion, based on belief, good morals, and justice. Deeply convinced of Islam's truth and eager to die for it, they were ready for battle.

Being the first to reach the battlefield, they positioned themselves around the wells. They also benefited from the heavy downpour of the previous night, for it provided them with an abundant supply of water that they quickly stored in large containers. The rain also compacted the loose sand in the upper part of the valley in which they pitched their tents. This allowed them to plant their feet firmly and move with less difficulty. In the valley's lower part, however, where the Quraysh army stationed itself, the ground was marshy. In addition to these Divine blessings, God sent a feeling of drowsiness over the Muslims and gave them a feeling of peace and security (8:11).

From their campsite, the Muslim army could see the whole battlefield. It was divided into three parts: one center and two flanks. The central force consisted of the leading Emigrants and Ansar who were foremost in devotion to the Messenger. Mus'ab ibn 'Umayr, a member of one of Makka's richest families who had accepted Islam as a youth, carried the standard of the Messenger. He was so handsome that when he would go out wearing his silk clothes, before his conversion, Makkan girls would stare at him from their windows. After he embraced Islam, however, he followed the Messenger wholeheartedly. He sacrificed whatever he had in the way of God, and was martyred at Uhud, during which he again bore the Prophet's standard. When he lost his right arm, he took the standard in his left hand; when he lost his left arm, he was left with a "head" to protect the Messenger, before whom he was finally martyred.[25]

The flanks were commanded by 'Ali and Sa'd ibn Mu'adh. 'Ali was famous for his courage and deep devotion to the Messenger. He had been only 9 or 10 years old when he told the Messenger: "I will help you," after the Messenger had gathered his kinsmen at the outset of his mission to seek their conversion and support.[26] On the night of the Prophet's Emigration, 'Ali had slept in the Prophet's bed so he could leave Makka in safety.[27] By the time those surrounding the house discovered this ruse, the Messenger had reached Thawr cave. 'Ali was wholly dedicated to the cause of God.

The Messenger took all necessary precautions and made the best possible preparations. He mobilized his resources and chose his best and most qualified men as commanders. He stationed his army at the valley's upper part. He then pitched his tent where he could see the whole battlefield and have his commands conveyed instantaneously. As the final prerequisite, he prayed with great earnestness and humility:

> O God, here are the Quraysh who in their vainglory seek to deny and cry lies against Your Messenger. O God, support us with the help You promised me. O God, were this small group of Muslims to perish, no one in the world would remain to worship You.[28]

After the prayer, he threw a handful of dust at the enemy saying: "May their faces be scorched."[29]

Badr was a severe test for the Muslims. They would either win or be martyred, for they were ordered not to flee. They could retreat in orderly fashion under strong enemy pressure, as a stratagem to seek reinforcements or to re-group with another party in the rear (8:15), but not because of cowardice and defeatism. Such a disorderly flight would reveal that they preferred their lives over Islam, a major and deadly sin.

The Battle Begins

In the Quraysh's first frontline were 'Utba ibn Rabi'a, his brother Shayba, and his son Walid. They challenged the Muslims to single combat. Three young Ansar went forward. "We will not fight Madina's farmers and shepherds!" 'Utba shouted arrogantly. This was, in fact, what the Messenger expected. He ordered 'Ali, Hamza, and 'Ubayda ibn Harith forward for single combat. Hamza fought and killed 'Utba, and 'Ali killed Walid with two blows. 'Ubayda, who was old, fought Shayba and was wounded on his knee. Hamza and 'Ali rescued him, killed Shayba, and carried 'Ubayda away.[30]

The Quraysh were shocked by such an unexpected beginning. The Muslims' belief, sincerity, and valor won them God's help. The Quraysh, who had exulted in their superiorty in number and weaponry, were decisively defeated by the ill-equipped Muslims. Seventy Qurayshis were killed. 'Awf and Mu'awwidh (two young Ansari brothers) joined with 'Abd Allah ibn Mas'ud to kill Abu Jahl, who the Messenger called the "Pharaoh of the Muslim Community."[31] Almost all Qurayshi leaders were killed: Abu Jahl, Walid ibn Mughira, 'Utba ibn Rabi'a, 'As ibn Sa'id, Umayyah ibn Khalaf, and Nawfal ibn Khuwaylid. Prior to the battle, the Messenger had indicated the spots where they would die, saying: "'Utba will be killed here; Abu Jahl here, Umayyah ibn Khalaf here," and so on.[32]

Seventy Qurayshis were captured. God allowed the Muslims to ransom them, and some were released. Those who were literate were to be released only after teaching the unlettered Muslims how to read and write. This policy had several benefits: captives who had expected execution gladly paid the ransom; Madina's low literacy rate was raised, making the newly literate Muslims more effective in preaching Islam and gaining people's respect; literate captives could learn about Islam and be in close contact with Muslims, which would bring more people into Islam; and the captives' families and relatives were so glad to see their presumed-dead family members that they became much more receptive to Islam.

The decisive victory made Islam a force to be reckoned with throughout Arabia, and many hardened hearts were inclined to accept Islam.

The Battle of Uhud

The victory of Badr alerted the peninsula's hostile forces. The Muslims were in a state of unease, and endured the wrath of most neighboring societies.

Madina's Jewish tribes were not eager to honor their agreements with the Messenger after his Emigration. During the Battle of Badr, they favored the Makkan polytheists; afterwards, they openly encouraged the Quraysh and other Arab tribes to unite against the Muslims. They also collaborated with the Hypocrites, who were apparently an integral part of the Muslim body politic.

To sabotage the spread of Islam, they began to fan the flames of old animosities between the Aws and Khazraj, the two tribes of Madinan Muslims. Ka'b ibn Ashraf, chief of Banu Nadir, went to Makka and recited stirring elegies for the Makkans killed at Badr to provoke the Quraysh into renewed hostilities. He also slandered the Muslims and satirized the Messenger in his poems.

The Jewish tribes' violation of their treaty obligations exceeded all reasonable limits. A few months after Badr, a Muslim woman was treated indecently by some Jews of Banu Qaynuqa, the most anti-Muslim Jewish tribe. During the ensuing fight, a Muslim was martyred and a Jew was killed. When the Messenger reproached them for this shameful conduct and reminded them of their treaty obligations, the Jews threatened him: "Don't be misled by your encounter with a people who have no knowledge of warfare. You were lucky. By God, if we fight you, you will know that we are men of war."

Finally, the Messenger attacked the Banu Qaynuqa, defeated them, and banished them from Madina's outskirts. In addition, upon the order of the Messenger, Muhammad ibn Maslama killed Ka'b ibn Ashraf and ended his trouble-making activities.[33]

The Reasons for the Battle

The Quraysh were still smarting from their defeat in the Battle of Badr. Their women were mourning their dead warriors almost daily, and encouraging the survivors to revenge themselves. In addition, the Jewish efforts to rouse their feelings of revenge were like pouring oil on flames. Within a year, the Quraysh attacked Madina with an army of 3,000 soldiers, including 700 in coats of mail and 200 cavalrymen.

Informed of the Makkans' march upon Madina, the Messenger consulted with his Companions about how to meet this threat.[34] He had dreamed that he was in his coat of mail with his sword notched, and that some oxen were being slaughtered. He interpreted this to mean that they should defend themselves within Madina's boundaries, and that a leading member of his kinsmen, together with some Companions, would be martyred.[35] He also knew that the Makkan army was coming to fight on open ground. Thus, if the Muslims defended themselves within Madina, the Makkan army could not mount a long siege. He stressed once more that Muslims represent peace and security, and that they should resort to force only to eliminate an obstacle to the preaching of Islam or to defend themselves, their faith, or their country.

However, several young people longed for martyrdom. Upset that they had not fought at Badr, they wanted to fight the enemy outside of Madina. The Messenger gave in to this ultimately majority demand. When these young people repented, upon warning from their elders about their insistence, and the elders informed the Messenger of this, the Messenger replied: "It does not befit a Prophet to take off his coat of mail once he has put it on."[36]

Having decided to follow the majority, the Messenger and 1,000 warriors left Madina for Uhud, a volcanic hill only a few miles from its western outskirts. Its main feature was a plain that stretched out before it. When they were only half way there, however, 'Abd Allah ibn Ubayy ibn Salul turned back with his 300 men.[37] This event, coming just before the battle began, caused such perplexity and confusion that the Banu Salama and Banu Haritha tribes also wanted to turn back. Eventually, they were persuaded to remain.

The Messenger advanced with the remaining ill-equipped 700 Muslims. He lined them up at the foot of Mount Uhud so that the mountain was behind them and the Qurayshi army in front of them. The enemy could launch a surprise attack from only one mountain pass. The Messenger posted 50 archers there under the command of 'Abd Allah ibn Jubayr. He told him not to let anyone approach or move from that spot, adding: "Even if you see birds fly off with our flesh, don't move from this place."[38]

Mus'ab ibn 'Umayr was the standard bearer, Zubayr ibn 'Awwam commanded the cavalry, and Hamza commanded the infantry. The army was ready to fight. To encourage his Companions, the Prophet brought forth a sword and asked: "Who would like to have this sword in return for giving its due?" Abu Dujana asked: "What is its due?" "To fight with it until it is broken," the Prophet said. Abu Dujana took it and fought.[39] Sa'd ibn Abi Waqqas and 'Abd Allah ibn Jahsh prayed to God to let them meet the strongest enemy soldiers. Hamza, the Prophet's uncle and "Lion of God," wore an ostrich feather on his chest. The verse revealed to describe the godly persons around previous Prophets pointed also to them:

> Many a Prophet there was, with whom a large number of God-devoted men fought. They fainted not for anything that befell them in the way of God, neither weakened nor abased themselves. God loves the steadfast. Nothing else did they say but: "Our Master, forgive our sins, and that we exceeded in our affair. Make our feet firm, and help us against the unbelievers." God gave them the reward of the world and the good reward of the Hereafter. God loves those who do good. (3:146-48)

In the first stage, the Muslims defeated the enemy so easily that Abu Dujana, with the sword the Prophet had given him, pushed into the center of the Qurayshi army. There he met Abu

Sufyan's (the Qurayshi commander) wife Hind. He tried to kill her but, "in order not to dirty the sword given by the Prophet with a woman's blood," spared her.[40] 'Ali killed Talha ibn 'Abi Talha, the enemy's standard-bearer. All who carried the Qurayshi standard were killed by 'Ali, 'Asim ibn Thabit, or Zubayr ibn 'Awwam. After that, such self-sacrificing heroes of the Muslim army as Hamza, 'Ali, Abu Dujana, Zubayr, and Miqdad ibn 'Amr flung themselves upon the enemy and routed them.

When the enemy began to flee, the Muslims gathered the spoils. The archers on the mountain pass saw this and said to themselves: "God has defeated the enemy, and our brothers are collecting the spoils. Let's join them." 'Abd Allah ibn Jubayr reminded them of the Prophet's order, but they said: "He ordered us to do that without knowing the outcome of the battle." All but a few left their posts and began to collect booty. Khalid ibn Walid, who had not accepted Islam yet and commander of the Qurayshi cavalry, seized this opportunity to lead his men around Mount Uhud and attacked the Muslims' flank through the pass. 'Abd Allah ibn Jubayr's depleted forces could not repel them.

The fleeing enemy soldiers came back and joined the attack from the front. Now, the battle turned against the Muslims. Both of these sudden attacks by superior forces caused great confusion among the Muslims. The enemy wanted to seize the Messenger alive or kill him, and so attacked him from all sides with swords, spears, arrows, and stones. Those who defended him fought heroically.

Hind, having lost her father and brothers at Badr, urged Wahshi, a black slave, to kill Hamza. When the scales turned, Hamza fought like a furious lion. He had killed almost 30 people when Wahshi's lance pierced him just above the thigh. Hind came forward and ordered Hamza's stomach split open. She then mutilated his body and chewed his liver.[41]

Ibn Kami'a martyred Mus'ab ibn 'Umayr, the Muslims' standard-bearer who had been fighting in front of him. Mus'ab resembled God's Messenger in build and complexion, and this caused Ibn Kami'a to announce that he had killed the Messenger. Meanwhile, the Messenger had been wounded by a sword and some stones. Falling into a pit and bleeding profusely, he stretched his hands and prayed: "O God, forgive my people, because they do not know (the truth)."[42]

The rumor of the Prophet's martyrdom led many Companions to lose courage. In addition to those like 'Ali, Abu Dujana, Sahl ibn Hunayf, Talha ibn 'Ubaydullah, Anas ibn Nadr, and 'Abd Allah ibn Jahsh, who fought self-sacrificingly, some Muslim women heard the rumor and rushed to the battlefield. Sumayra, of the Banu Dinar tribe, had lost her husband, father, and brother. All she asked about was the Messenger. When she saw him, she said: "All misfortunes mean nothing to me as long as you are alive, O Messenger!"[43]

Umm 'Umara fought before the Messenger so heroically that he asked her: "Who else can endure all that you endure?" That pride of womanhood took this opportunity to ask him to pray for her: "O Messenger of God, pray to God that I may be in your company in Paradise!" The Messenger did so, and she responded: "Whatever happens to me from now on does not matter."[44]

Anas ibn Nadr heard that the Messenger had been martyred. He fought so valiantly that he suffered 80 wounds.[45] They found Sa'd ibn Rabi' dying with 70 wounds on his body. His last words were: "Convey my greetings to the Messenger. I sense the fragrance of Paradise from behind Uhud."[46]

Besides Abu Dujana and Sahl ibn Hunayf, 'Ali stood in front of the Messenger and defended him. Three times the Messenger pointed to some of the enemy who were advancing toward them; each time 'Ali attacked and routed them.[47]

Despite the indescribable resistance of the Muslim warriors around the Messenger, defeat seemed inevitable until Ka'b ibn Malik, seeing the Messenger, shouted: "O Muslims! Good tidings for you! This is the Messenger, here!" The scattered Companions advanced toward him from all sides, rallied around him, and led him to the safety of the mountain.

The reasons for the setback at Uhud

Before explaining the reasons for this setback, it should be pointed out that the Companions, after the Prophets, are superior to everybody else in virtue. They are honored with being the comrades and trainees of Prophet Muhammad, the greatest of creation, the one for whose sake the universe was created and who was sent as a mercy for all the worlds. Therefore, according to the rule "the greater the blessing, the greater the responsibility," they had to be the most obedient to God and His Mess-enger.

We read, for example, *whoever of the Prophet's wives commits manifest indecency, the punishment for her will be doubled ... you are not like any other women* (33:30, 32). Likewise, even a small sin committed by a Companion deserves severe punishment. They are all included in those "foremost in belief and nearness to God," and their conduct is an example to be followed by later generations. Therefore, they must be pure in belief and intention, sincere in worship and devotion, upright in conduct, and extremely careful in refraining from sin and disobedience.

God raised the community of Muhammad *as the best community to enjoin the good and forbid the evil, and believe in One God* (3:110) and appointed them as *a middle nation so that they may be witnesses to humanity, and the Messenger may be a witness to them* (2:143). In the early years of the Madinan era, the Companions consisted of true believers and Hypocrites. Therefore, God wanted to sift His true witnesses against all humanity, and see who strove hard in His Way and remained steadfast (3:141-42). The Battle of Uhud, therefore, was a decisive test to sift out the sincere and steadfast from the hypocritical and wavering, and served to make the Islamic community more stable and formidable.

After these preliminary notes, we can summarize why the Muslims experienced a setback as follows:

- The Messenger, the commander-in-chief, thought they should stay within Madina. The younger Companions, inexperienced and excited, urged him to march out of the city. This was a mistake, even though for the sake of martyrdom in the way of God, since the Messenger tended to apply different tactics in battles and knew in advance that the Quraysh army was coming to fight in open field.

- The archers posted to defend the army left their posts. They misinterpreted the Messenger's order not to leave for any reason and went to collect booty.

- The 300 Hypocrites, one-third of the army, deserted half-way and returned to Madina. This undermined the morale of the Banu Salama and Banu Haritha tribes, who were persuaded only with difficulty not to leave. Moreover, a small group of Hypocrites demoralized the Muslims during the battle.

- Several Companions became impatient. They acted, in certain respects, inconsistently with the dictates of piety and were lured by material wealth.

- Some believers thought that as long as the Messenger was with them, and as long as they enjoyed God's support and help, the unbelievers could never beat them. However true this was, the setback taught them that deserving God's help requires, besides belief and devotion, deliberation, strategy, and steadfastness. They also perceived that the world is a field of testing and trial:

  > Many ways of life and systems have passed away before you; journey in the land, and see the end of those who did deny (the Messengers). This is an exposition for humanity, and a guidance and an admonition for the God-fearing. Don't faint or grieve, for you shall gain mastery if you are true believers. If a wound has touched you, a like wound already touched the (unbelieving) people (at Badr); such days We deal out in turn among humanity, that God may see who are the believers, and that He may take witnesses from among you; God loves not the evil-doers; and that God may prove the believers, and blot out the unbelievers. (3:137-41)

- Those who had not taken part in Badr sincerely prayed to God for martyrdom. They were deeply devoted to Islam and longed to meet God. Some, like 'Abd Allah ibn Jahsh, Anas ibn Nadr, Sa'd ibn Rabi', 'Amr ibn Jamuh, and Abu Sa'd Haysama tasted the pleasure of martyrdom; the martyrdom of the others was delayed. The Qur'an sings the praises of them as follows:

> Among the believers are men who were true to their covenant with God; some of them have fulfilled their vow by death (in battle), and some are still awaiting, and they have not changed in the least. (33:23)

- Any success or triumph lies with God, Who does whatever He wills and cannot be questioned. Belief in God's Unity means that believers must always ascribe their accomplishments to God and never appropriate anything good for themselves. If the decisive victory of Badr gave some Muslims a sort of self-pride, and if they imputed the victory to their own prudence, wise arrangement, or some material causes, this would have been part of the reason for their setback.

- Among the Qurayshi army were several eminent soldiers and commanders (such as Khalid ibn Walid, Ikrima ibn Abi Jahl, 'Amr ibn al-'As, and Ibn Hisham) who were destined by God to be great servants of Islam in the future. They were the ones most esteemed and respected among the people. For the sake of their future service, God may not have willed to hurt their feelings of honor completely. So, as expressed by Bediuzzaman Said Nursi, the Companions of the future defeated the Companions of the present.[48]

- The following verses explain the reasons for that setback together with its aftermath, and the lessons to be taken from it:

> Did you suppose you should enter Paradise without God displaying which of you have struggled and who are patient? (3:142)

> Muhammad is naught but a Messenger; Messengers have passed away before him. Will you, if he should die or is slain, turn back on your heels? Whoever should turn back on his heels will not harm God in any way;

and God will recompense the thankful. It is not given to any soul to die save by the leave of God, at an appointed time. Whoso desires the reward of this world, We will give him of this; and whoso desires the reward of the other world, We will give him of that; and We will recompense the thankful. (3:144-45)

God fulfilled His pledge to you when by His leave you blasted them, until you lost heart, and quarreled about the matter, and disobeyed, after He had shown you that you longed for. Some of you sought this world and some of you sought the next. Then He turned you from them, that He might try you; and He has pardoned you. God is bounteous to the believers. When you were going up, not twisting about for anyone, and the Messenger was calling you in your rear; so He rewarded you with grief after grief that you might not sorrow for what escaped you neither for what smote you. God is aware of the things you do. (3:152-35)

Those of you who turned away on the day two hosts encountered—Satan made them slip because of some of their lapses; but God has pardoned them. God is All-Forgiving, All-Clement. (3:155)

O believers, be not as the unbelievers who say concerning their brothers, when they journey in the land, or are upon expeditions: "If they had been with us, they would not have died and not been slain"—that God may make that an anguish in their hearts. For God gives life, and He makes to die; and God sees all that you do. If you are slain or die in God's way, forgiveness and mercy from God are a better thing than what they amass; if you die or are slain, it is unto God that you shall be mustered. (3:156-58)

If God helps you, none can overcome you; if He forsakes you, who can help you after Him? Therefore let the believers put all their trust in God. (3:160)

Why, when an affliction visited you, and you had visited twice over the like of it, did you say: "How is this?" Say: "This is from your own selves; God is powerful over everything." And what visited you, the day the two hosts encountered, was by God's leave, that He might mark out the believers and that He also might mark out the Hypocrites, to whom it was said: "Come, fight in the way of God, or repel!" They said: "If only we knew how to fight, we would follow you." They that day were nearer to unbelief than to belief. (3:165-67)

Count not those who were slain in God's way as dead. They are alive with their Master, by Him provided, rejoicing in the bounty that God has given them, and joyful in those who remain behind and have not joined them yet. No fear shall be on them, neither shall they sorrow, joyful in blessing and bounty from God, and that God leaves not to waste the wage of the believers. (3:169-71)

God will not leave the believers in the state in which you are, till He shall distinguish the corrupt from the good, and God will not inform you of the Unseen; but God chooses out of His Messengers whom He wills. Believe then in God and His Messengers; if you believe and avoid disobeying God, there shall be for you a mighty wage. (3:179)

The Last Stage of the Battle of Uhud and the Campaign of Hamra' al-Asad

After this confusion ended, his Companions rallied around the Prophet, who was wounded and had fainted. Many Companions also were wounded. They retreated to the mountain's safety. The Qurayshi army began to leave the battlefield, thinking they had revenged themselves for Badr. Seeing that they could not crush the Muslims' resistance, they mounted their camels and, leading their horses, headed for Makka.

The Messenger worried that the Makkans might return and launch another attack on Madina. On the second day of Uhud, therefore, he ordered those who had fought the day before to gather together and pursue the unbelievers. Some of the Banu 'Abd al-Qays, appointed by Abu Sufyan, tried to discourage this line of action by saying: "The people have gathered against you, therefore fear them." But this only increased the faith of the believers, who retorted: *God is sufficient for us; what an excellent Guardian He is!* (3:173).[49]

Most were seriously wounded; some could not stand and had to be carried by their friends.[50] At this highly critical moment, they girded up their loins and prepared to lay down their lives at the Messenger's behest. They accompanied him to Hamra' al-Asad, eight miles from Madina. The Makkan polytheists had halted and were talking about a second attack on Madina. However, when they saw the believers they had supposedly just defeated coming toward them, they could not muster sufficient courage and so continued on to Makka.

The Messenger's prudence and military genius turned a defeat into a victory. The enemy did not have enough courage to confront the Muslims' resolution yet again by marching upon Madina, and so retreated to Makka. God revealed the following verses in praise of the Muslim heroes:

> Those who answered God and the Messenger after the wound had smitten them—to all those of them who did good and behaved in utmost devotion to God, shall be a mighty wage; those to whom the people said: "The people have gathered against you, therefore fear them." But it increased them in faith, and they said: "God is sufficient for us; what an excellent Guardian He is!" So they returned with blessing and bounty from God, untouched by evil. They followed the good pleasure of God, and God is of bounty abounding. (3:172-74)

Toward the Battle of the Trench

The Jewish Banu Nadir tribe was originally the sworn ally of the Muslims in Madina. However, its members secretly intrigued with the Makkan pagans and the Madinan Hypocrites. They even tried to kill the Prophet while he was visiting them, breaking the laws of hospitality and their treaty. The Messenger asked them to leave their strategic position, about three miles south of Madina, and they agreed to do so. But when 'Abd Allah ibn

Ubayy, the Hypocrites' chief, promised them help in case of war, the Banu Nadir demurred.

The Muslim army then besieged them in their fortresses. The Banu Nadir, seeing that neither the Makkan polytheists nor the Madinan Hypocrites cared enough to help them, left the city. They were dismayed, but their lives were spared. Given 10 days to leave, along with their families and all they could carry, most of them joined their brethren in Syria and others in Khaybar.

While returning from Uhud, Abu Sufyan had challenged the Muslims to a rematch at Badr the following year.[51] But when the appointed time arrived, his courage failed him. As a face-saving device, he sent Nu'aym ibn Mas'ud (then an unbeliever) to Madina to spread the rumor that the Quraysh were making tremendous war preparations and gathering a huge and invincible army. However, when the Prophet reached Badr with an army of 1,500 fighters, there was no enemy to meet him. They stayed there for 8 days, waiting for the threatened encounter. When no sign of the Quraysh army appeared, they returned to Madina. This campaign was called *Badr al-Sughra* (Badr the Minor).

In 627, the Messenger was told that the desert tribes of Anmar and Sa'laba had decided to attack Madina. He went to Zat al-Riqa' with 400 fighters and, hearing that the enemy tribes had fled, returned to Madina.[52] After this, he marched upon the pagan Banu Mustaliq tribe, which had made preparations to fight the Muslims. He attacked and defeated them with 700 warriors.[53] On the way back to Madina, the Hypocrites tried, and failed, to cause dissension among the Emigrants and the Ansar. The verses sent down revealed all their secrets and how polluted their inner world was (63:1-11).

The Battle of the Trench

In 627, a group of the expelled Banu Nadir Jews, including Sallam ibn Abi al-Huqayq, Huyayy ibn Akhtab, and some of the Banu Wa'il, went to Makka. They met with the Quraysh, urged them to continue the fight, and promised their help and support. These Jews then went to Ghatafan and Qays Aylan tribes and, promising them help, encouraged them to fight against the

Messenger.[54] These intrigues resulted in a great anti-Muslim confederacy of Makkan polytheists, the desert tribes of central Arabia, the Jews (both already expelled and those still resident) in Madina, and the Hypocrites. The last two constituted a fifth column within Madina.

When the Messenger was informed of this anti-Muslim gathering of confederates through his intelligence service, he consulted his Companions. It was their unanimous view that they should remain in Madina and fight from there. Salman al-Farisi suggested digging a trench around the city. It took 6 days of feverish labor to dig this trench. The Messenger divided the Muslims into groups of ten and told them to compete with each other. It was a hard task, there was not much time, and hunger was rampant. Yet all the Companions worked enthusiastically. In order to not feel the hunger, each fastened a rock around his stomach and recited, while digging:

> *We are those people who*
> *Took the oath of allegiance to Muhammad;*
> *Therefore we shall fight in the way of God*
> *As long as we live.*
> *By God, if God had not enabled us to,*
> *We would have neither been guided*
> *Nor given alms, nor performed prayers.*
> *Send down unto us calmness and tranquility*
> *And make our feet firm if we confront the enemy!*[55]

The Messenger, digging alongside them with two rocks fastened around his stomach, answered them with the couplet:

> *O God, the real life is the life of the Hereafter*
> *So, forgive the Helpers and the Emigrants.*[56]

While digging the trench, the Companions unearthed a huge rock that they could not break. Informing the Messenger of this, he began to strike it with his pickaxe. In the light of the resulting sparks, he predicted: "I have been given the keys to Persia; my community will conquer it." He struck the rock a second time and, in the light of the resulting sparks, declared: "God is the Greatest. I have been given the keys to Byzantium. My community will conquer it."[57]

Madina Under Threat

The allies advanced against Madina in the hope of destroying the Muslims on an open battlefield. However, when they faced this new strategy, they took the first blow. Numbering around 20,000, they camped near the trench. The Madinans had no more than 3,000 soldiers. Moreover, the Jewish Banu Qurayza and the Hypocrite fifth columns already had contacted the enemy. As stated in Qur'an 33:12-20, when the Hypocrites first saw the enemy, they were already in a defeatist mood. Not content with disloyalty themselves, they tried to infect others, who made feeble excuses to withdraw. If the enemy could gain entrance, they would betray the city.

The Messenger once again displayed his sagacity and military genius: He kept the soldiers within the city and stationed them so that they could safeguard their homes against possible Banu Qurayza attacks. The most critical moment came when the Banu Qurayza sent a man into Madina to learn the conditions of the Muslim women. However, their hopes were frustrated when this man was killed by Safiyya, the Prophet's aunt.[58]

While the war was continuing with exchanges of arrows and stones, the Messenger engaged in diplomatic attempts to split the Allies. He contacted the Ghatafan's leaders and, offering them peace, urged them to withdraw their people. Nu'aym ibn Mas'ud, an Ally leader who before the battle had come to Madina to sow discord, already was inclining toward Islam. During the battle, he secretly entered Islam and followed the Messenger's order to stir up the Banu Qurayza. Nu'aym set them against the Quraysh by asserting that the Makkans would abandon them and so they should withhold their help until the Quraysh gave them hostages. Then he told the Quraysh that the Banu Qurayza would not fulfill their promise and would try to stall by asking for Qurayshi hostages to share their plight in case of defeat. This stratagem succeeded, and dissension grew among the Allies.[59]

The Messenger, supported by Sal mountain behind the city, had ordered a narrow point to be made in the trench, as he expected that leading Qurayshi horsemen would try to cross there. This is what happened, for some of the most renowned Qurayshi warriors tried to cross for single combat with Muslim fighters. Among them were 'Amr ibn 'Abd Wudd, Ikrima ibn Abi Jahl, Hubayra ibn Abi Wahb, Dirar ibn al-Khattab, and Nawfal ibn 'Abd Allah ibn al-Mughira.

Boasting of his strength and fighting ability, 'Amr dismounted from his horse and faced 'Ali, who was ordered by the Messenger to fight him. 'Amr advanced with his sword drawn. He brought his sword quickly against 'Ali, but it caught in 'Ali's shield. 'Ali struck him with such strength that dust rose around them. Then the words *Allahu akbar* (God is the Greatest) were heard: 'Ali had killed his opponent.[60] He also killed Dirar, Hubayra, and Nawfal.[61] No other Qurayshi horsemen or generals could get across at that spot.

The siege lasted 27 days. The Muslims suffered greatly from hunger, cold, unending barrages of arrows and stones, attempts and concentrated assaults to cross the trench, and betrayals and intrigues within Madina. The Qur'an describes this situation as follows:

> When they came against you from above and from below, and when your eyes swerved and your hearts reached your throats, while you thought thoughts about God; there it was that the believers were tried, and shaken most mightily. And when the Hypocrites, and those in whose hearts is sickness, said: "God and His Messenger promised us only delusion." And when a party of them said: "O people of Yathrib, there is no abiding here for you, therefore return!" And a party of them were asking leave of the Prophet, saying: "Our houses are exposed"; yet they were not exposed. They desired only to flee. (33:10-13)

After almost 4 weeks, during which the enemy was disheartened by it failure and the believers proved their steadfastness and loyalty, there was a piercing blast of cold wind from the east. The enemy's tents were torn up, their fires were extinguished, and sand and rain beat their faces. Terrified by the portents against them, and already riven by discord, they soon gave up. Hudayfa al-Yamani, sent by the Messenger to spy on the enemy's movements, heard Abu Sufyan shout: "Come on, we're going home!"[62]

The Muslims were victorious by God's help, for hidden forces (the angels) were helping them:

> O believers, remember God's blessing upon you when hosts came against you, and we loosed against them a wind, and hosts you didn't see. God sees the things you do. (33:9)

The Battle of the Trench was the last Qurayshi attempt to destroy Islam and the Muslims. Following their withdrawal in defeat and humiliation, the Messenger declared: "From this moment we will march upon them; they will no longer be able to raid us."[63]

After the Allies were routed and returned to their homes, the Messenger focused on to the Banu Qurayza, who had betrayed their agreement with the Messenger and allied themselves with the Quraysh. They also had given asylum to the Banu Nadir's leaders, like Huyay ibn Akhtab, who had been expelled from Madina and continued to conspire against the Muslims.

No sooner had the Messenger returned from this battle than Archangel Gabriel came and said: "I have not taken off my coat of mail, and I am going to the Banu Qurayza."[64] The Messenger ordered his Companions to march upon this Jewish tribe, and had his tent pitched opposite their fortresses. He would have forgiven them if they had asked, but they preferred to resist. The Messenger besieged them for 25 days. At last they asked for surrender terms, agreeing that they should submit to Sa'd ibn Mu'adh's judgment, who decreed the sentence according to the Torah. This was the end of the Banu Qurayza's conspiracies, as well as of the Jewish presence in Madina.[65]

Sa'd ibn Mu'adh, a leader of the Ansar, had been wounded in the Battle of the Trench. He prayed: "O God, if I am able to fight once more beside the Messenger, make me live. Otherwise, I am ready to die." He died a martyr shortly after the Jewish conspiracies ended.[66]

Toward the Conquest of Makka

As will be elaborated later, the treaty of Hudaybiya was a clear victory that opened a door to new and greater victories. The Makkan threat ended, and the Messenger sent envoys to neighboring countries to invite them to Islam. He also set out to solve the other problems he faced within Arabia.

Most of the Banu Nadir Jews had resettled in Khaybar. Together with them, the Jews of Khaybar continued to work against Islam in league, at various times, with either the Quraysh or the Banu Ghatafan. The Banu Nadir had been instrumental in forming the 20,000-man anti-Muslim alliance defeated during the Battle of the Trench. Seeking to end this continually hostile Jewish presence so that Arabia could be made secure for the future and free preaching of Islam, the Muslims acted.

The Banu Qurayza's punishment roused the Jews of Khaybar to ally themselves with the Banu Ghatafan and attack Madina.[67] They were making preparations for this when, after the treaty of Hudaybiya, the Messenger marched upon Khaybar. He made as if to attack the Banu Ghatafan, and forced them to shelter in their confines without daring to help the Jews in Khaybar. Then he suddenly turned toward Khaybar. The village's farmers, who had left their homes early with their farming tools, saw the Muslim army approach the city and began running and taking shelter in their formidable citadels.

The Messenger besieged Khaybar for 3 weeks. Toward the end of the siege, he gathered his soldiers and told them: "Tomorrow I will hand the standard to him who loves God and His Messenger and is loved by God and His Messenger. God will enable us to conquer Khaybar through him."[68] On the next day, almost everyone was hoping to receive the standard. However, the Messenger asked for 'Ali. Told that "he has sore eyes," the Messenger sent for him, applied his saliva to 'Ali's sore eyes, and gave him the standard.[69] 'Ali went to the fortress and, after a fierce battle, Khaybar was conquered. Among the prisoners was Safiyya, a noble woman and daughter of Huyay ibn Akhtab, the Banu Nadir's chief. By marrying her, the Messenger established a relationship with the conquered people.

The Battle of Mu'ta

In the peaceful atmosphere brought about by the treaty of Hudaybiya, the Messenger sent letters to neighboring kings inviting them to the fold of Islam. King Shurahbil of Busra, a Christian Arab, killed the envoy (Harith ibn 'Umayr). This was an unforgivable breach of international custom and the prestige of Islam, and could not remain unanswered. The Messenger formed an army of 3,000 men, with Zayd ibn Haritha as commander, and said: "If something happens to Zayd, Ja'far ibn Abi Talib will assume the command. If Ja'far is martyred, 'Abd Allah ibn Rawaha will assume the command. In case something happens to 'Abd Allah, choose one among you as the commander."

When the Muslim army reached Mu'ta, it confronted a 100,000-man Byzantine army. Obviously it would be a fierce battle. Each Muslim would have to fight about 33 of the enemy. In the meantime, the Messenger was in the mosque, relating the fighting to those around him. Zayd took the standard. He thrust himself into the enemy ranks and was martyred. The standard passed to Ja'far ibn Abi Talib. He also rose up to Paradise. 'Abd Allah ibn Rawaha took the standard and was martyred. Now the standard was in the hands of one of the "swords of God,"[70] meaning Khalid ibn Walid, who would, from then on, be called "the Sword of God."[71]

When it was night, Khalid stationed the troops at the rear in the front rank, and changed the wings, positioning those on the right to the left and vice versa. Seeing new troops before them in the morning, the Byzantine army was demoralized. When night fell, the sides parted with each other and retreated. The Muslim army returned to Madina with only 12 losses. Although this was a victory for the Muslims, they were ashamed to meet the Messenger. However, he welcomed and consoled them: "You didn't flee. You retreated to join me, and will go against them later."

The Conquest of Makka and its Aftermath

In 627, the Messenger had a dream or a vision that he and his Companions would enter the Holy Mosque of Makka in safety, with their heads shaven or trimmed, and without fear. As will be explained later, earlier they had been prevented from entering Makka and so made a treaty with the Quraysh at Hudaybiya. At first, the Muslims did not like the conditions, but the verses revealed after the treaty called it a clear victory.

The 2 years following this event proved the truth of these words. Such leading Qurayshi figures as Khalid ibn Walid and 'Amr ibn al-'As became Muslims, and Islam spread across Arabia. Jewish conspiracies were ended, and Islam crossed into other lands through the letters sent to neighboring kings. At the end of this period, the Banu Bakr (a Qurayshi ally) attacked the Banu Khuda'a (the Muslims' ally) and killed some of them. The truce between the Muslims and the Quraysh was now over. No longer able to resist the Muslims, Abu Sufyan came to Madina in the hopes of renewing it. However, the Messenger refused to meet with him.[72]

The Messenger began to prepare for war. As always, he kept the affair quite secret and no one, including his wives and closest friends, knew where the campaign would be. When Abu Bakr asked his daughter 'A'isha (a wife of the Messenger) where the Messenger intended to march, she told him that she did not know.[73] However, an Emigrant named Khatib ibn Abi Balta'a guessed his intention and sent a letter to the Quraysh informing them of the Messenger's preparations. The Messenger, learning of this through Revelation, ordered 'Ali and Zubayr to take the letter from the woman to whom Khatib had entrusted it. They did this successfully.[74]

The Messenger left Madina with 10,000 men. Two years before, they had numbered 1,600 when his attempted minor pilgrimage ('umra) resulted in the treaty of Hudaybiya. The resulting peaceful atmosphere caused many to reconsider and accept Islam.

The Companions did not know the destination until they were ordered to head for Makka. When they approached this holy city, the Messenger ordered each soldier to light a fire, for the Makkans would light a fire for every tent while traveling in the desert.[75] As a result, they estimated the Muslim army to consist of about 30,000 men. Having no realistic way to resist, they surrendered. Abu Sufyan, who had been invited by the Messenger to see the Muslim army, also advised this.

The Messenger did not desire bloodshed. Dividing his army into six columns, each one entered Makka through a different route. He ordered the commanders to avoid bloodshed unless they were attacked. To realize this goal and conquer Makka peacefully, he announced: "Those who shelter in the Ka'ba are safe, those who shelter in Abu Sufyan's house are safe, and those who stay in their own houses are safe."[76]

Being a Prophet of absolute mercy who came to secure the happiness of humanity both in this world and the next, the Messenger entered Makka, bowing on the back of his mule, as a victorious conqueror. He displayed no self-pride and had no thought of vengeance or retaliation. He proceeded toward the Ka'ba in complete modesty and absolute gratitude to God, who had made him victorious in his sacred mission. Stopping at the Ka'ba, he asked his enemies: "How do you expect me to treat you?" They replied: "You are a noble man, the son of a noble man." The Messenger stated: "This day there will be no reproach on you. God will forgive you; He is the Most Merciful of the Merciful. You can go away."[77]

This marked the end of polytheism in Makka. While he was destroying the idols at the Ka'ba, he recited: *Say: "Truth has come and falsehood has disappeared. Indeed falsehood is subject to disappearance"* (17:81).[78] Almost all Makkans now became Companions.

The Battle of Hunayn

The Arab tribes were waiting to see who would win before accepting Islam, saying: "If Muhammad prevails over his people, he is a Prophet." Consequently, after the Muslims' victory they began to enter Islam in throngs. This shocked the pagans, who organized a great gathering near Ta'if to coordinate their plans of attack.

The Hawazin and the Thaqif, famous for courage and archery, took the lead and prepared a great expedition against Makka. Informed of their movements by 'Abd Allah ibn Hadrad, whom he had sent to them, the Messenger left Makka with 12,000 Muslims who were enthusiastic over the 2,000 new conversions. To protect Makka and consolidate the new Muslims' belief by healing their wounded feelings, the Messenger did not want to fight within Makka.

The battle was joined at Hunayn, a valley between Makka and Ta'if. The new Muslims had more enthusiasm than wisdom, more a spirit of elation than of faith and confidence in the righteousness of their cause. The enemy had the advantage of knowing the ground thoroughly. They laid an ambush in which the Muslims' advance guard was caught or intentionally pushed by the Messenger, who might have planned to draw the enemy in under the guise of retreat. However, the retreat was confused and took place under a shower of enemy arrows.

The Prophet, calm as ever in his faith and wisdom in that hour of danger, spurred his horse forward. His uncle 'Abbas was on his right, and his uncle's son Fadl was on his left. While Abu Sufyan ibn al-Harith was trying to stop him, the Messenger was shouting: "Now war has been kindled. I am the Prophet, that is no lie. I am the descendant of 'Abd al-Muttalib."[79]

'Abbas shouted: "Companions who made the pledge of allegiance under the acacia tree!"[80] From all sides came the response: "*Labbayk!*" (At your service!), and they rallied to the Prophet. The enemy, now in the center of the Muslim army, was surrounded on all sides. The Messenger's courage, wisdom, and steadfastness changed a seeming defeat into a decisive victory. It was by God's help that the Muslims won the day. They completed the victory with an energetic pursuit of the enemy, capturing their camps, flocks and herds, and families, which they had boastfully brought with them in expectation of an easy victory.

The routed enemy took refuge in Ta'if. The Muslims' victory persuaded the desert tribes to accept Islam, and shortly thereafter the rebel tribes and Ta'if also surrendered and entered Islam.

The Expedition to Tabuk

The outcome of the Muslim–Byzantine encounter in Mu'ta shocked Arabia and the Middle East, for the Byzantines had not won, even though they had outnumbered the Muslims by thirty-three to one. Ultimately, thousands of people from the semi-independent Arab tribes living in Syria and adjoining areas converted to Islam. To avenge himself for Mu'ta and prevent the advance of Islam, Heraclius (the Byzantine Emperor) ordered military preparations to invade Arabia.

The Messenger, always aware of developments bearing on his mission, promptly decided to challenge the Byzantines on the battlefield. Any show of Muslim weakness might have revived the dying forces of Arabian polytheism and hostility, which had received a crushing blow at Hunayn. Such a development also could encourage the Hypocrites in and around Madina to cause serious damage to Islam from within. They already were in touch with the Ghassanid Christian prince and with the Byzantine Emperor, and had built a mosque—which the Qur'an calls the Mosque of Dirar (Dissension) (9:107)—near Madina to serve as their operational base.

Realizing the gravity of the situation, the Messenger publicly appealed to the Muslims to prepare for war and, against his usual practice, declared that the Byzantines were his target.

It was mid-summer. The scorching heat was at its peak, the harvest season had just arrived, and there was a shortage of material resources. Moreover, the enemy was one of the two current local superpowers. Despite this, the Companions responded ardently to his call and commenced their war preparations, all contributing much more than their financial means warranted. Huge amounts of money were donated by such wealthy Companions as 'Uthman and 'Abd al-Rahman ibn al-'Awf.[81] Those who could not be included in the Muslim army, due to shortages of riding animals and other necessary supplies, wept so bitterly and lamented their exclusion so pathetically that the Messenger was moved. God praised them in Qur'an 9:92. The occasion, in fact, served as a touchstone for distinguishing the sincere from the insincere, the believers from the Hypocrites.

In 631, the Messenger and 30,000 soldiers left Madina and marched to Tabuk, quite close to what was then Byzantine territory in Syria. The Byzantine Emperor, who had begun amassing a huge army, abandoned his plans and withdrew his army, for the Messenger arrived before he was expected and well before Byzantine troop concentrations were completed.[82]

The Messenger stayed in Tabuk for 20 days, and forced several buffer states under Byzantine hegemony to pay the poll tax (jizya) and live under his rule. Many Christian tribes embraced Islam willingly.[83] This bloodless victory enabled the Muslims to consolidate their position before launching a prolonged conflict with the Byzantines, and shattered the power of both unbelievers and Hypocrites in Arabia.

A GENERAL EVALUATION OF HIS MILITARY ACHIEVEMENTS

A significant point concerning the Messenger is that he was the most eminent commander in human history. To understand this dimension of his sacred mission, consider these following points:

- No other Prophet carried his mission to decisive victory in all aspects of life. Moses, who most resembles the Messenger, died while his people were still in the desert and unable to conquer Palestine after several decades of preaching. Jesus' mission sought mainly to infuse a spiritual and moral revival among the Jews, who were drowning in materialism. After his elevation to Heaven, his disciples conveyed his message to Rome, despite severe persecution. Unfortunately, the price to be paid was the degeneration of Jesus' original creed.

  When Prophet Muhammad died, he left behind a Muslim Arabia and dedicated Companions ready to convey Islam throughout the world. He achieved this end with a handful of self-sacrificing people who previously had not heard of belief or Scripture, and who had known nothing of civilized social life, world politics, good morals, and self-discipline. He transformed desert tribes engaged in civil wars and unending feuds, and equipped them with belief, sincerity, knowledge, good morals, love of humanity, compassion, and activism. They dedicated themselves to the Divine cause, and the result was an army of light. Rabi' ibn Amir, Muslim envoy to the Persian commander during the War of Qadisiya, said the religion the Messenger brought from God and preached

> . . . elevates people from the dark pits of worldly life to the high, boundless realm of the spirit; from the humiliation of worshipping false and human-made divinities to the honor and dignity of worshipping One God, the only Creator and Sustainer of the universe; and frees them from the oppression and depression brought about by false religions and human systems to the luminous and peaceful climate of Islam.

- God's Messenger never sought a worldly kingdom; he was sent to guide humanity to salvation in both worlds. His goal was to revive people, not to kill them. To achieve this, however, he had to arrange military expeditions and sometimes command armies. He sent out about 80 such expeditions, and actually commanded 28 of them. Fighting took place in almost half of these campaigns, and only around 1,000 people died: approximately 250 Muslims were martyred, and 750 non-Muslims were killed. He established Islam, brought absolute security to Arabia for the first time, and opened the way to global security at the cost of only 1,000 lives. This is, as so many of his other achievements are, unequalled in world history.
- The Messenger was the first to legislate an international law. Although the concept was known before Islam, international law was very limited. For example, there were no recognized rules concerning prisoners of war. The Messenger established a set of rules to bring a "discipline" to fighting. For example, the following is the order given by him and all his true successors to depart-

ing armies, an order obeyed to the letter by Muslims in their wars as Muslims:

> Always keep fear of God in your mind. Remember that you can't afford to do anything without His grace. Don't forget that Islam is a mission of peace and love. Don't destroy fruit trees or fertile fields in your paths. Be just, and spare the feelings of the vanquished. Respect all religious persons who live in hermitages or convents, and spare their edifices. Don't kill civilians, or violate women's chastity and the conquered's honor. Don't harm old people and children, or accept gifts from the civilian population. Don't billet your soldiers or officers in civilians' homes.[84]

- God's Messenger's preliminary precautions left nothing to chance. He always acted with great care, insight, and forethought, and so never met with any setbacks. He had no part in the reverse suffered at Uhud. Also, he was extraordinarily successful in getting information from the enemy without resorting to force or torture. For example, some Muslim soldiers who had captured an enemy soldier tried to force military information out of him. God's Messenger ordered his release and asked him how many camels his army slaughtered every day. Calculating how many camels are eaten by how many people in a day, he tried to work out how many soldiers were coming toward him.[85]

- The Messenger established a military intelligence service to provide him with all necessary information about the enemy. No news of his own movements, however, was ever leaked. Before setting out to conquer Makka, Khatib ibn Abi Balta'a secretly sent a letter with a woman to his relatives in Makka about the preparations. However, the Prophet was informed of this and sent 'Ali and Zubayr to intercept her, which they did.

Also, the Messenger kept his military preparations and ultimate destination a secret. He tended to march in one direction, and then turn toward his real destination later on. His tactics were characterized by speed, surprise attack, and flexibility. In most of his campaigns, he caught the enemy unprepared and overcame them relatively easily. For example, in the Battle of Khaybar, the Jews learned of his approach only because their farmers were abandoning their fields after seeing him in the early morning. They only had time to shelter in their citadels. When he marched upon Makka, his advance planning was so perfect that the Makkan polytheists surrendered unconditionally.

- In his position as a Prophet with a universal religion from God, he taught it so effectively that his Companions were always ready to sacrifice themselves. This was a main factor lying behind his victories. His Companions placed all of their reliance and confidence in him. Therefore, he inculcated fear in enemies' hearts, as he himself said: "I am supported by God through implanting fear in the hearts of my enemies from a distance of a month's walk."[86]

He used psychology to demoralize his enemies. Poets like Hassan ibn Thabit and 'Abd Allah ibn Rawaha wrote or recited verses to demoralize the enemy. While performing the minor pilgrimage one year after the treaty of Hudaybiya, he ordered his Companions to run around the Ka'ba to demonstrate their strength to the Makkans watching from the neighboring hills. While running, 'Abd Allah ibn Rawaha recited:

> *I start with the name of God,*
> *Apart from Whom there is no other god,*
> *And Muhammad is the Messenger of God.*
> *O unbelievers, and sons of unbelievers,*
> *clear out of his way.*

Pleased with his recitation, he said: "His words are more penetrating to the Quraysh than arrows."[87]

- The Messenger introduced new strategies and shattered the unity of allied enemy tribes. During the Battle of the

Trench, the Jewish Banu Qurayza broke their treaty with
the Muslims at a most critical moment and joined the
Qurayshi siege. Left between two hostile camps, he offered
peace to the Banu Ghatafan, a Qurayshi ally. This dis-
couraged the Banu Ghatafan from continuing the war.
He also engendered disagreement and mutual mistrust
between the Quraysh and the Banu Qurayza. During
the campaign of Khaybar, he pretended to march upon
the Banu Ghatafan, allies of the Jews of Khaybar. Thus
this tribe remained inactive and did not help the Jews.

- The Messenger did what he had to do, without hesitation
or irresolution, at each step of his life. He never retreated
or gave up hope during a battle. He stood steadfast during the critical moments of Uhud and Hunayn. He called
to his scattering Companions: "Do not scatter! I am
Muhammad, the Messenger of God. That is no lie!" When
the Jewish tribes in and around Madina refused to honor
their agreements, the Messenger marched upon them
immediately. He did the same thing against the Banu
Qurayza after the Battle of the Trench, without even stopping to take off his coat of mail, and against the Qurayshi
army a day after the setback at Uhud. Such incidents are
very significant in showing his resolution and invincibility.

- In almost every campaign, the Messenger took the initiative to attack and direct the battle. He did this even in set
battles (e.g., Badr, Uhud, and the Trench). His use of surprise strategies and effective tactics defeated the enemy.
He also used time and any opportunity most effectively.

- The Messenger usually changed his battle tactics and
strategy. For example, during Badr he launched an overall attack after demoralizing the enemy in single combat.
In Uhud's first stage, he rendered the enemy cavalry inactive through archers placed in the Aynayn mountain pass.
Using such eminent warriors as Hamza, 'Ali, Abu Dujana,
and Zubayr, he won the victory in the first stage. As for
the Trench, he faced the enemy with a long, deep trench

around Madina. Remaining within the city's confines, he forced the enemy to retreat after a 4-week siege.

• The Messenger was never short of necessary reinforcements or logistics, and always kept his lines of communication open. He brought up, along with such extraordinary statesmen as Abu Bakr and 'Umar and people of profound scholarship and spirituality, great soldiers and invincible commanders. His education featured three basic elements:

  – Continuous physical training. He urged his Companions to train in archery, wrestling, swimming, and riding horses. Sometimes he arranged and occasionally participated in competitions and footraces. He also stressed the need to preserve one's health and strength.

  – Good morals and being well-mannered.

  – Devotion to God with unshakable belief, submission, and reliance, and obedience to God, himself, and others in authority.

The Muslim army conveyed peace and security to the lands it conquered. Each soldier was absolutely dedicated to Islam. The only criterion for them to judge between people was belief in God. They did not feel true love for anybody who opposed God and His Messenger, even if they were their parents, children, or siblings (58:22). As a result, sometimes family members faced each other on the battlefield.

Belief and submission made the Muslim soldiers so powerful and fearless that neither the numerical strength of the enemy nor fear of death could prevent them from conveying the Divine Message. 'Abd Allah ibn Hudafa al-Sahmi, captured by the Byzantines, was told by a Christian priest that his life would be spared if he converted. He was given 3 minutes to decide. 'Abd Allah replied: "Thank you, father. You have given me 3 minutes to tell you about Islam."

CHAPTER 8

A Universal Leader

A UNIVERSAL LEADER

HIS APPOINTMENT OF COMPETENT PEOPLE

The Messenger appointed promising and competent Muslims to the work they could do best. He felt no need to change any appointment, for the person proved, through personal uprightness and competence, that he or she was the proper choice.

The Makkan period of Islam was inscribed in the Muslim community's memory as a time of unbearable persecution and torture. Abuse was not meted out only to the poor and unprotected Muslims (i.e., 'Ammar, Bilal, and Suhayb), but also to powerful Muslim members of the Qurayshi elite (i.e., Abu Bakr and 'Umar).[1] To protect his followers, the Messenger permitted those who were poor and unprotected to emigrate to Abyssinia. But he kept the powerful ones (i.e., 'Ali, Zubayr, Abu Bakr, 'Umar, and Sa'd ibn Abi Waqqas) in Makka, for Islam needed their support to spread and implant itself in Makka. These powerful Muslims went on to occupy the highest administrative positions of the Muslim state.

Abu Dharr was a poor, blunt, and upright bedouin who never restrained his faith or his feelings. When he heard Muhammad's declaration of Prophethood, he came to Makka and converted. The Messenger used to preach Islam secretly in the earliest stage of his Prophethood. Abu Dharr was very pious and austere. However, since public administration requires special skills, the Messenger did not accept his request for an administrative post, saying: "You cannot manage the people's affairs. Don't apply for such jobs, for we don't assign such jobs to those who apply for them."[2]

The Messenger refused Abu Dharr, but implied the caliphates of Abu Bakr, 'Umar, and 'Uthman. Holding the hands of Abu

Bakr and 'Umar, he said: "I have four viziers, two in the heavens and two in the world. Those in the heavens are Gabriel and Michael; as for those in the world, they are Abu Bakr and 'Umar."[3] Concerning the caliphate of 'Uthman, he declared: "It will be a trial for him."[4]

HE KNEW HIS PEOPLE

The Messenger knew his people more than they knew themselves. Like Abu Dharr, 'Amr ibn 'Abatha was a bedouin. He came to Makka and, meeting the Messenger, asked rudely: "What are you?" The Messenger replied very gently: "A Prophet of God." Such gentleness caused 'Amr to kneel down and declare: "I will follow you from now on, O Messenger." The Messenger did not want 'Amr to stay in Makka, for he would be unable to endure the torments inflicted upon the believers. So he told him: "Return to your tribe, and preach Islam among them. When you hear that I am victorious, come and join us."

Years later, 'Amr came to Madina's mosque and asked: "Do you recognize me, O Messenger?" The Messenger, who had an extraordinarily strong and keen memory (another dimension of his Prophethood) answered promptly: "Aren't you the one who came to me in Makka? I sent you back to your tribe and told you to join us when you heard that I was victorious."[5]

I mentioned the case of Julaybib earlier.[6] After this moral lesson, Julaybib became an honest, chaste young man. Upon the Messenger's request, a noble family gave him their daughter in marriage. Shortly afterwards, Julaybib took part in a battle and, after killing 7 enemy soldiers, was martyred. When his corpse was brought to the Messenger, he put his head on Julaybib's knees and said: "O God, this one is of me, and I am of him."[7] He had discovered Julaybib's essential virtue and foreseen his future service for Islam.

The conquest of Khaybar allowed the Messenger to demonstrate his unique ability to recognize each Muslim's potential, skills, and shortcomings. When the siege was prolonged, he declared: "Tomorrow I will hand the standard to one who loves

God and His Messenger and is loved by them."[8] This was a great honor, and all Companions earnestly hoped for it. He gave it to 'Ali, despite his youth, because of his great military and leadership skills. He took the standard and conquered the formidable stronghold of Khaybar.

Whoever the Messenger gave a job to performed it successfully. For example, he described Khalid ibn Walid as "a sword of God"[9]; Khalid was never defeated. Besides such great soldiers and invincible commanders as Qa'qa'a, Hamza, and Sa'd, the Messenger made 'Usama ibn Zayd commander over a great army containing such leading Muslims as Abu Bakr, 'Umar, 'Uthman, Talha, and Sa'd ibn Abi Waqqas. 'Usama was the approximately 17-year-old son of Zayd, the Messenger's black emancipated slave. His father had commanded the Muslim army at Mu'ta against the Byzantines, and was martyred.

The Messenger was 25 when he married Khadija bint Khuwaylid, a widow 15 years his senior. He did not marry another woman until her death in the tenth year of his Prophethood. All of his subsequent marriages, after the age of 53, were directly related to his mission. One important reason for this was that each wife had a different character and temperament, and so could convey to other Muslim women Islam's rules for women. Each one served as a guide and teacher for womanhood. Even such leading figures in subsequent generations as Masruq, Tawus ibn Kaysan, and 'Ata' ibn Rabah benefited considerably from them. The science of hadith is especially indebted to 'A'isha, who related more than 5,000 Traditions from the Messenger and was a great jurist.

Subsequent events proved how wise and apt were the Messenger's the choices, not least in the matter of marriage.

HIS WISDOM

Leaders gain the love and trust of their people and are followed by them in proportion to their ability to solve their problems. These can be personal or public, or related to individual's private life, or the community's social, economic, and political affairs.

Some leaders resort to force and terror, or sanctions or punishments (i.e., exile, imprisonment, loss of citizenship rights), torture, or spy into private affairs to solve their problems. But such solutions have only short-term benefits. In addition, they create a vicious circle in which the more people struggle to solve problems by such means, the more they entangle themselves in them.

The Messenger solved all problems so skillfully and easily that no one challenged him. Although his people were by nature quarrelsome, ignorant, wild, and rebellious, he delivered a Message to them that was so grave that *If We had sent down this Qur'an onto a mountain, you would have seen it humbled and rent asunder out of fear of God* (59:21). He transformed them into a harmonious community of peace, happiness, knowledge, and good morals. Reflect closely upon the utopias imagined in the West, such as *The Republic* (Plato), *Utopia* (Thomas Moore), and *Civitas Solis* (T. Campanella), and you will see that, in essence, they dreamed of Madina during the time of Prophet Muhammad. Humanity has never witnessed the equal of that society.

In the first volume, we described how he prevented an imminent clan war among the Quraysh while repairing the Ka'ba,[10] and how he prevented a possible disaster after the Battle of Hunayn.[11] In addition, he skillfully solved an impending Emigrant–Ansar conflict while returning from fighting the Banu Mustaliq. When an internal clash nearly broke out when the army halted by a well, the Messenger immediately gave the order to march.

MERGING TWO DIFFERENT COMMUNITIES

The emigration to Madina marks a turning point for Prophet Muhammad and for Islam. Belief, emigration, and holy struggle are three pillars of a single, sacred truth; three spouts of a fountain from which the water of life flows for the soldiers of truth. After drinking, they convey their message without becoming wearied and, when the opposition cannot be overcome, set out for a new land without regard for home, property, and family. The Prophet's emigration is so significant and sanctified that the virtuous people around him were praised by God as remain known as the Emigrants (Muhajirun). Those who welcomed them so warmly to Madina are known as the Helpers (Ansar). The Islamic calendar begins with this event.

Despite its significance, emigration is a difficult undertaking. When the Muslims resettle in Madina after years of persecution, they were destitute. Moreover, some were extremely poor, and others, who had earned their lives by trade, had no capital. The Muslims of Madina were mostly farmers, and the city's commercial life was controlled by Jews.

Another serious problem was that just before the Messenger's arrival, the Madinans had decided to make 'Abd Allah ibn Ubayy ibn Salul their chief. This plan naturally was abandoned, which made him a bitter enemy of the Messenger and an important foe. The Makkan polytheists still wanted to defeat the Prophet, and worked with him to achieve their goal. He told them: "Don't worry if he spreads Islam here. The main danger is that he might ally with the Christians and Jews against paganism. That is the real threat."

After he settled in Madina, the Messenger helped his people build a mosque. The importance of the mosque for the Muslim community's collective life is unquestionable. They meet there five times a day and, in the Presence of God, their Master, Creator, and Sustainer, increase in belief and submission to Him, the Prophet and Islam, and strengthen their solidarity. Especially in the first centuries of Islam, mosques functioned as places of worship and as centers of learning. The Prophet's Mosque in Madina was, in the time of the Prophet himself and his immediate political successors, also the center of government.

Immediately after settling in Madina, the Messenger established brotherhood between Muslims, particularly between the Emigrants and the Helpers. They became very close to each other. For example, Sa'd ibn Rabi' took his Emigrant "brother" 'Abd al-Rahman ibn 'Awf home and said: "Brother, you have left everything in Makka. This house, with everything in it, belongs to both of us. You don't have a wife here; I have two. Whichever

of them you like, I'll divorce her so that you may marry her."
'Abd al-Rahman answered him in tears: "Brother, may God bless
you with your wife! Please show me to the city bazaar so that I
may do some business."[12]

This brotherhood was so deep, sincere, and strong that the
Helpers shared everything with the Emigrants. This lasted for
some time. When the Emigrants had become accustomed to
their new environment, they asked the Messenger:

> O Messenger of God. We emigrated here purely for the sake of
> God. But our Helper brothers are so good to us that we fear we
> will consume in this world the reward of our good deeds, which
> we expect to get in the Hereafter. Also, we feel very indebted to
> them. Please ask them to let us earn our own living.

The Messenger sent for the Helpers and told them of the
situation. The Helpers unanimously objected, finding it unbearable to be separated from their brothers. To spare the Emigrants'
feeling of indebtedness, the Helpers agreed that the Emigrants
would work in their fields and gardens in return for wages until
they could build their own houses.[13]

As a second step in solving immediate problems, the Messenger
signed a pact with the Jewish community in Madina. This document, which some scholars describe as Madina's first constitution, confederated the Muslims and Jews as two separate, independent communities.[14] Since the Messenger took the initiative
in making this pact and acted as the final arbiter in all disputes,
Madina came under Muslim control.

To guarantee Muslims' security within this city-state, the
Messenger ordered the establishment of a new bazaar. Until
then, Madina's economic life had been controlled by the Jewish
community. After this, Jewish economic domination began to
decline, for they no longer monopolized Madina's commerce.

While the Muslim community was establishing itself and
growing in strength, it was forced to respond to internal and external attacks. After their victory of Badr, the Muslims fought the
Makkans again at the foot of Mount Uhud. Their easy victory during the battle's first part was followed, unfortunately, by a reverse

when the archers disregarded the Prophet's instructions. Seventy Muslims were martyred, and the Messenger was wounded.

The Muslim army took shelter on the mountain and prepared to fight back. Lacking enough courage for a further attack, the Makkan forces left. Nevertheless, they changed their mind halfway and decided to march upon Madina. Informed of this, the Messenger mobilized his troops. One of his orders was enough, even though they were ill or wounded. His every call was a breath of life for their souls, a breath that could revive old, rotten bones. Busiri says:

> *Were his value and greatness*
> *to be demonstrated by miracles,*
> *The bones that have rotted away*
> *were revived by calling his name.*

The half-crushed army set out to counter the enemy. Almost everyone was wounded, but no one wanted to stay behind. In describing the situation, one Companion said: "Some Companions couldn't walk. They said: 'We want to be present at the front where the Messenger has ordered us to go. Even if we cannot fight, we will stand there with spears in our hands.' They were carried on other people's shoulders or backs." Seeing the Muslim army marching toward them, Abu Sufyan ordered his troops to return to Makka.

In praising those heroes of Islam, the Qur'an says:

> Those to whom the people said: "The people have gathered against you, therefore fear them"; but it increased them in faith, and they said: "God is sufficient for us; an excellent Guardian is He." (3:173)[15]

CONSULTATION

The Messenger's wisdom was demonstrated when he consulted his Companions. This practice is so important in Islam that he never reached a decision, especially in public affairs, without it. Sometimes he even held counsel about his personal affairs. To cite only a few examples:

- 'A'isha accompanied the Prophet on the Banu Mustaliq campaign. At one halt, she lost her necklace and set out to find it. She returned to find that the army had left without her, as the camel drivers thought she was in her litter. Safwan, charged with collecting what was lost or left behind caravans, found her and brought her back to the army. In the ensuing scandal, her fidelity was questioned, mainly by the Hypocrites.

The Messenger knew she was innocent. However, since the Hypocrites used this incident to slander him, he consulted some of his Companions like 'Umar and 'Ali. 'Umar said that 'A'isha was undoubtedly chaste and pure, and that she had been slandered. When asked how he knew, he replied:

> O The Messenger, once you were praying. You stopped and explained that Archangel Gabriel had come and informed you that there was some dirt in your slippers. If there were some impurity in 'A'isha, God certainly would have informed you.[16]

The Messenger, who once said: "Whoever takes counsel, does not regret it in the end,"[17] always consulted those who could give informed advice on a particular matter.

- He consulted with his Companions before Badr, the first major post-Emigration military encounter, about whether the Muslims should fight the approaching Makkan army. The Muslim forces numbered 305 or 313, while the Makkans numbered around 1,000 men. One spokesman each for the Emigrants and the Helpers stood up and proclaimed their readiness to follow him wherever he might lead them.[18] During his life, all Companions continually promised to follow him in every step he took, and to carry out all of his orders. Despite this, the Messenger consulted with them about almost every community-wide matter so that this practice would become second nature.

- During Badr, the Muslim army was positioned some-where on the battlefield. Hubab ibn Mundhir, who was not a leading Companion, stood up and said:

  > O Messenger, if God has not ordered you to assume this place, let's arrange ourselves around the wells and then seal all but one to deny water to the enemy. Set up your camp at the side of that open well (from which we will take water), and we will encircle you.

  The Messenger adopted this view.[19]

- In 627, the Quraysh allied themselves with certain desert tribes and the Jewish Banu Nadir, who had emigrated from Madina to Khaybar. Forewarned of their plans, the Prophet asked for ideas about how to defeat the enemy offensive. Salman al-Farisi suggested digging a defensive trench around Madina, a stratagem unknown to the Arabs. The Messenger ordered it to be done. This war was forever after known as the Battle of the Trench.[20]

- The Muslims found the Treaty of Hudaybiya unpalatable, and were reluctant to obey the Prophet's order to sacrifice their sacrificial animals without making the pilgrimage. (One condition of the treaty was that they could not enter Makka that year.) The Messenger consulted with his wife Umm Salama. She replied: "O Messenger, don't repeat your order lest they disobey you and perish. Sacrifice your own animals and take off your pilgrim dress (*ihram*). When they understand the order is decisive, they'll obey you without hesitation." The Messenger did as she suggested.[21]

A MANIFEST VICTORY: THE TREATY OF HUDAYBIYA

The Messenger was a man of action. He never hesitated about putting his plans or decisions into action, for that would confuse and demoralize his followers. The Messenger always acted with deliberation and consulted others. But once he had decided or planned something, he carried it out immediately and had no second thoughts or a reason to regret his decision. Before acting, he took the necessary precautions, considered the probabilities, and consulted available experts. The ensuing finality of his decisions was an important reason for his victories and why his Companions followed him so completely.

One event worthy of further elaboration is the Treaty of Hudaybiya. The Messenger told his Companions that he had dreamed they would shortly enter the Holy Mosque in Makka in security, with their heads shaved or their hair cut short. His Companions, especially the Emigrants, were delighted. During that year, the Prophet set out for Makka with 1,400 unarmed men in pilgrim dress.

Informed of this event, the Quraysh armed themselves and the neighboring tribes to keep the Muslims out of Makka. They sent some 200 soldiers, led by Khalid ibn Walid and Ikrima ibn Abi Jahl, as far as Qura' al-Ghamim. Seeing the Muslims approaching, they returned to Makka to spread the news. When the Muslims reached Hudaybiya, about 12 miles from Makka, the Messenger told them to halt. Learning that there was a shortage of water, he threw an arrow down Hudaybiya's only well. Water began to gush and fill the well. Everyone drank some, performed *wudu'*, and filled their waterskins.[22]

As the Makkans refused to let the Muslims enter Makka, the Messenger sent Budayl ibn Warqa, a man from the Khuda'a tribe (the Muslims' ally), to announce that the Muslims had come for pilgrimage and thus were unarmed. The Quraysh, in reply, sent 'Urwa ibn Mas'ud al-Thaqafi. While talking to the Messenger 'Urwa tried to grasp his beard, a sign of jesting. Mughira ibn Shu'ba struck his hand, saying he would cut it off if 'Urwa tried such a thing again, for his hand was impure.

Mughira was 'Urwa's cousin, and had accepted Islam about 2 months earlier. In fact, only a few months ago 'Urwa had paid the blood money for a crime Mughira had committed. How Islam had changed Mughira! The Companions' commitment to their cause and devotion to the Messenger shocked 'Urwa, who returned to the Quraysh and said: "I have visited Chosroes,

Caesar, and the Negus. None of their subjects are so devoted to their rulers as his Companions are to Muhammad. I advise you not to struggle with him."[23]

The Quraysh did not heed his advice or give a warm welcome to Kharash ibn Umayya, whom the Messenger sent after 'Urwa. Kharash was followed by 'Uthman ibn al-'Affan, who had powerful relatives among the Quraysh. Although 'Uthman came to negotiate, the Makkans imprisoned him. When he did not return at the expected time, rumors circulated that he had been killed. At this point, the Prophet, sitting under a tree, took an oath from his Companions that they would hold together and fight to the death. He represented the absent 'Uthman by proxy in this oath.[24] Only Jadd ibn Qays, who hid behind a camel, did not take it.

The revelation that came on this occasion reads:

> God was well pleased with the believers when they were swearing allegiance to you under the tree, and He knew what was in their hearts, so He sent down peace of reassurance on them, and has rewarded them with a near victory. (48:18)

In that moment of tension, a cloud of dust appeared in the distance. This turned out to be a Makkan delegation led by Suhayl ibn 'Amr. When God's Messenger learned this, he took his name (easiness) as a good omen and told his Companions: "The situation has eased." Eventually, the Quraysh agreed to a truce and the Treaty of Hudaybiya was concluded.

Under this treaty, the Prophet and his followers could make pilgrimage the following year, not this one, at which time the Makkans would vacate the city for 3 days The treaty also stipulated a 10-year truce, that people or tribes could join or ally themselves with whoever they wished, and that Qurayshi subjects or dependents who defected to Madina would be returned. This last condition was not reciprocal, and thus was opposed in the Muslim camp. It shocked people like 'Umar, who questioned the Messenger about it. However, it really was of little importance. Muslims sent back to Makka were not likely to renounce Islam; on the contrary, they would be agents of change within Makka.

Just before the treaty was signed, Abu Jandal, Suhayl's son, arrived in chains and asked to join the Muslims. The Messenger had to return him to his father in tears. However, he whispered to him: "God will shortly save you and those of your like."[25]

Shortly after the treaty was signed, 'Utba ibn Asid (also known as Abu Basir) defected to Madina. The Quraysh sent two men to demand his return. On their way back to Makka, Abu Basir escaped, killed one man and wounded the other. The Messenger, citing the treaty's terms, did not allow him to stay in Madina. So he settled at Iyss, a place on the road from Makka to Syria. The Muslims held in Makka began to join Abu Basir. As this settlement grew, the Makkans perceived a potential threat to their trade route. This forced them to ask the Messenger to annul the relevant term and admit defecting Makkans to Madina.[26]

The Qur'an called the Treaty of Hudaybiya "a manifest victory": *We have given you a manifest victory* (48:1). This proved true for several reasons, among them:

- By signing this treaty after years of conflict, the Quraysh admitted that the Muslims were their equals. In effect, they gave up their struggle but did not admit it to themselves. Seeing the Makkans deal with the Prophet as an equal and a ruler, a rising tide of converts flowed toward Madina from all over Arabia.

- Many Qurayshis would benefit from the resulting peace by finally reflecting on what was going on. Such leading Qurayshis as Khalid ibn Walid, 'Amr ibn al-'As, and 'Uthman ibn Talha, all famous for their military and political skills, accepted Islam. 'Uthman was the person entrusted with the Ka'ba's keys, and after the conquest of Makka the Messenger honored him with the same task.

- The Quraysh used to regard the Ka'ba as their exclusive property, and made its visitors pay them a tribute. By not subjecting the Muslims' deferred pilgrimage to this condition, the Quraysh unwittingly ended their monopoly. The bedouin tribes now realized that the Quraysh had no right to claim exclusive ownership.

- At the time, there were Muslim men and women living in Makka. Not everyone in Madina knew who they were. Some were serving the Messenger as spies. Had a fight taken place in Makka, the victorious Muslim army might have killed some of them. This would have caused great personal anguish, as well as the martyrdom or identification of the Prophet's spies. The treaty prevented such a disaster.

The Qur'an points to this fact:

> He restrained their hands from you, and your hands from them, in the hollow of Makka, after He made you victors over them. God sees the things you do. They are the ones who disbelieved, and banned you from the Holy Mosque, and hindered the sacrificial animals from reaching their place of sacrifice. If it had not been for certain believing men and believing women (in Makka) whom you knew not—lest you should trample them and thus incur guilt for them unknowingly; that God may admit into His Mercy whom He will—(the believers and unbelievers) had been clearly separated, then We would have chastised the unbelievers among them with a painful chastisement. (48:24-25)

- The Prophet performed the minor pilgrimage the following year. The assertion: "There is no god but God, and Muhammad is the Messenger of God," rang throughout Makka. The Quraysh, camped on Abu Qubays hill, heard this portent of Islam's coming triumph. This was, in fact, God's fulfilling the vision He had given to His Messenger:

> God has indeed fulfilled the vision He vouchsafed to His Messenger: You shall enter the Holy Mosque, if God wills, in security, your heads shaved, your hair cut short, not fearing. He knew what you knew not, and, granted, besides this, a nigh victory. (48:27)

- The treaty allowed the Messenger to deal with others. In the post-treaty expeditions, the Muslims conquered the formidable Jewish citadels of Khaybar, telling them

either to convert or accept Muslim rule by paying tribute in lieu of protection (jizya). Their neighbors, as well
as other Arab tribes, were impressed with the Islamic
state's growing strength.

The Muslims faithfully observed the treaty's terms; however,
a tribe allied to the Makkans did not. The Banu Bakr attacked the
Banu Khuda'a, who were allied with the Prophet. So in December
629, the Messenger marched a 10,000-man army against Makka,
and captured it with almost no resistance on the first day of the
new year. The Ka'ba was purified of idols and, over the next couple of days, the Makkans accepted Islam. This was due to happen
because:

> He has sent His Messenger with the guidance and the religion
> of truth, that He may uplift it above every religion. God suf-
> fices as a witness. Muhammad is the Messenger of God, and
> those who are with him are hard against the unbelievers, mer-
> ciful to one another. You see them bowing, prostrating, seeking
> grace from God and (His) good pleasure. Their mark is on
> their faces, the trace of prostration. That is their likeness in the
> Torah, and their likeness in the Gospel is: as a seed that puts
> forth its shoot, and strengthens it, and it grows stout and rises
> straight upon its stalk, pleasing the sowers, that through them
> He may enrage the unbelievers. God has promised those of
> them who believe and do deeds of righteousness forgiveness
> and a mighty wage. (48:28-29)

ENDING RACISM

Racism is one of our age's severest problems. Everyone has heard
of how black Africans were transported across the Atlantic Ocean
in specially designed ships, thought of and treated exactly like
livestock. They were enslaved, forced to change their names and
religion and language, were never entitled even to hope for true
freedom, and were denied all human rights. The West's attitude
toward non-Westerners remained unchanged until recent times.
As a result, the political and social condition of Africans, even in
the case of their descendents who lived in the West amidst non-

black Americans or Europeans as theoretically equal fellow citizens, remained second-class (or even lower) citizens.

When the Messenger was raised as a Prophet, such racism was prevalent in Makka in the guise of tribalism. The Quraysh considered themselves (in particular) and Arabs (in general) superior to all other people. The Messenger came with the Divine Message and proclaimed that: "No Arab is superior to a non-Arab, and no white person is superior to a black person"[27]; Superiority is by righteousness and devotion to God alone (49:13); and: "Even if a black Abyssinian Muslim were to rule over Muslims, he should be obeyed."[28]

The Messenger eradicated color-based racism and discrimination so successfully that, for example, 'Umar once said of Bilal, who was black: "Bilal is our master, and was emancipated by our master Abu Bakr."[29] Zayd ibn Haritha, a black slave emancipated by the Messenger, was his adopted son before the Revelation banned such adoption. The Prophet married him to Zaynab bint Jahsh, one of the noblest (and non-black) Arab and Muslim women. In addition, he appointed Zayd commander of the Muslim army sent against the Byzantine Empire, even though it included such leading Companions as Abu Bakr, 'Umar, Ja'far ibn Abu Talib (the Messenger's cousin), and Khalid ibn Walid (the invincible general of the age).[30] He appointed Zayd's son Usama to command the army he formed just before his death. Included therein were such leading Companions as Abu Bakr, 'Umar, Khalid, Abu 'Ubayda, Talha, and Zubayr. This established in the Muslims' hearts and minds that superiority is not by birth or color or blood, but by righteousness and devotion to God.

During his caliphate, 'Umar paid Usama a higher salary than his own son, 'Abd Allah. When his son asked why, 'Umar replied: "I do so because I know that the Messenger loved his father more than me, and that he loved Usama more than you."[31]

THE LAST WORD

Prophet Muhammad had all the necessary leadership qualities for success in every aspect of life. But, more importantly, he was able to lead his community to success in every field. He is the source from which flowed all later developments related to command, statecraft, religion, spiritual development, and so on in the Muslim world.

In general, leaders should have the following qualities:

- *Realism.* Their messages and demands should not contradict reality. They should understand prevailing conditions as they actually are, and be aware of any advantages and disadvantages.

- *Absolute belief in their message.* Their conviction should never falter, and they should never renounce their mission.

- *Personal courage.* Even if left alone, they should have enough courage to persevere. When some of his pursuers reached the mouth of the cave in which they were hiding, Abu Bakr was afraid something would happen to the Messenger. However, the Prophet only said: Don't worry, for God is with us. (9:40)

- *Strong willpower and resolve.* They should never experience even one moment of hopelessness.

- *Awareness of personal responsibility.* Everything should be directed toward fulfilling this responsibility. In no way should they be seduced by the world's charms and life's attractions.

- *Farsighted and goal-centered.* Leaders should be able to discern and plan for potential developments. They should know how to evaluate the past, present, and future to reach a new synthesis. Those who frequently change their opinions only spread chaos in the community.

- *Personal knowledge of each follower.* Leaders should be fully aware of each follower's disposition, character, abilities, shortcomings, ambitions, and weak points. If they lack this knowledge, how can they fill vacant posts with the appropriate people?

- *Strong character and praiseworthy virtues.* Leaders should be determined but flexible while carrying out decisions, and know when to be unyielding and implacable or relenting and compassionate. They should know when to be earnest and dignified, when to be modest, and always be upright, truthful, trustworthy, and just.

- *No worldly ambitions or abuse of authority.* Leaders should live like the poorest members of their community. They should never discriminate among their subjects; rather, they should strive to love them, prefer them over themselves, and act so that their people will love them sincerely. They should be faithful to their community, and secure their community's loyalty and devotion in return.

The Messenger possessed all of these qualities, and many more as well. To cite only a few examples, he never even thought of abandoning his mission when confronted with great hostility and tempting bribes. Instead, he would tell them: "Say: 'There is no god but God,' and prosper in both worlds."[32] When his Companions complained about the harsh conditions and persecution in Makka, he answered:

> You show haste. A day will come and a woman will travel from Hira [a town in southern Iraq] to Makka alone on her camel (in security) and circumambulate the Ka'ba as an act of worship, and the treasuries of the Sassanid Emperor will be captured by my community.[33]

Once the Makkan leaders came to him and said: "If you meet with us on a day when others, especially those poor ones, are not present, we may talk to you about accepting your religion." They despised poor Muslims like Bilal, 'Ammar, and Habbab, and desired special treatment. The Messenger rejected such proposals without a second thought. The verses revealed addressed him as follows:

> Send not away those who call on their Master morning and evening, seeking His Face (6:52), and Persevere together with those who call on their Master morning and evening, seeking His Face. (18:28)

CHAPTER 9

Other Dimensions of
His Prophethood

OTHER DIMENSIONS OF
HIS PROPHETHOOD

HIS PRAYERS AND SUPPLICATIONS

The Messenger always prayed to God before any action. The books of Tradition (*hadith*) record no case in which he did not pray. As mentioned earlier, prayer is a mystery of servanthood to God, and the Messenger is the foremost in servanthood. This is made clear with every repetition of the declaration of faith: "I bear witness there is no god but God; I also bear witness that Muhammad is His servant and Messenger." Note that he is called servant before *Messenger*. Whatever he intended to do, he referred it to God through prayer.

God is the Creator of us and whatever we do. Although we should take necessary precautions and follow precedents to accomplish things in this material world, where cause and effect has a special place, we should never forget that everything ultimately depends on God for its existence. Therefore, we must combine action and prayer. This is also required by our belief in God's Unity.

The Messenger's knowledge of God can never be equaled. As a result, he was the foremost in love of, and paradoxically, in fear of Him. He was perfectly conscious that everything depends on God for its existence and subsistence. Whatever God wills, happens: *When He wills a thing, His command is to say to it "Be,"* *and it is* (36:82). Things exist and the universe operates according to the laws established by God and the fulfillment of prerequisites. Fully aware of this, the Messenger did what he had to and then, combining action with prayer, left the result to God with absolute confidence.

His supplications have been transmitted to us. When we read them, we see that they have deep meaning and accord exactly with the surrounding circumstances. They reflect profound belief, deep sincerity, absolute submission and complete confidence. Some examples are given below:

- When you go to bed, perform *wudu'* as you do before daily prayers and pray:

  > O God, hoping for (Your Mercy) and fearing (Your wrath), I submit myself to You, refer my affairs to You, and take refuge in You. There is no refuge or source of safety from Your wrath except You. I believe in the Book You sent down, and the Prophet you raised.[1]

- Without sins, a soul is like a polished mirror or a white cloth. Sins dirty the soul, and can be expunged only by repentance and asking His forgiveness. The Prophet used to pray the following, even though he was sinless: "O God, put between me and errors a distance as great as that which you have put between East and West. O God, cleanse me of my errors as a white garment is cleansed of dirt."[2] A whole volume could be written about the meaningful words used and the comparisons made here.

In addition to these supplications for specific cases, the Prophet also left behind comprehensive supplications of various lengths. We present some of them here:

- God, I ask You for all good, including what is at hand and what is deferred, what I already know and what I don't know. I take refuge in You from every evil, including what is at hand and what is deferred, what I already know and what I don't know.[3]

- God, nothing hinders what You grant, nor is anything granted that You hinder. No wealthy one can do us good, as wealth belongs to You.[4]

- God, I have not told anything, taken an oath, made a vow, or done anything that You did not previously will. Whatever You willed is, and whatever You didn't will is not. There is no strength or power save with You, and You are indeed All-Powerful over everything.[5]

• God, whatever prayer I have said, let it be for whomever You have mercy, and whatever curse I have called down, let it be for whomever You have cursed. Surely You are my Guardian in this world and the Hereafter. Make me die as a Muslim, and include me among the righteous.[6]

• God, I ask You for contentment after misfortune, a peaceful life after death, the pleasure of observing Your Face, and a desire to meet You. I take refuge in You from wronging others and from being wronged, from showing animosity and being subject to animosity, and from erring or committing unforgivable sins. If You leave me to myself, you leave me in weakness, need, sinfulness and error. I depend only on Your Mercy, so forgive all my sins, for only You can do so. Accept my repentance, for You are the Oft-Relenting, All-Compassionate.[7]

• God, You deserve most to be mentioned, and none but You deserve to be worshipped. You are more helpful than anyone whose help may be sought, more affectionate than every ruler, more generous than anyone who may be asked for something, and more generous than anyone who gives. You are the Monarch without partners, and the Unique One without like. Everything is perishable except You.

You are never obeyed but by Your permission, and never disobeyed but within Your knowledge. When somebody obeys You, You reward them; when someone disobeys You, You forgive them. You witness everything, being nearer to it than any other witness; and protect everything, being nearer to it than any other protector. You ordained the acts of all people and determined their time of death. You know what is in every mind, and all secrets are manifest to You.

The lawful is what You have made lawful; the forbidden is what You have forbidden. Religion is what You have laid down; the commandment is what You have decreed. The creation is Your creation, and the servants are Your servants. You are God, the All-Clement, All-Compassionate. I ask You, for the sake of the light of Your Face, by which the Heavens and Earth were illuminated, for the sake of every right belonging to You, and for the sake of those who ask of You, to forgive me just in this morning and in this evening, and to protect me, by Your Power, from Hellfire.[8]

- God, I seek refuge in You from all knowledge that gives no benefit, from a heart that does not fear You, from an unsatisfied soul, and from prayer that cannot be answered.[9]

- God, I ask You for steadfastness in my affairs, resolution in guidance, gratitude for Your bounties and acceptable service to You, and a truthful tongue and a sound heart. I seek refuge in You from the evil of what You know. I ask You for the good of what You know, and Your forgiveness for what You already know. Surely You are the Knower of the Unseen.[10]

- God, I ask You to enable me to do good, to refrain from vice, to love the poor, and to forgive me and have mercy on me. When You will people's deviation and dissension and disorder in public life, make me die before taking part in that disorder. I ask You for Your love and for the love of whom You love, and the love of the acts that will make me nearer to Your love.[11]

- God, I ask You for the good in the beginning and in the end, in its most comprehensive form with its beginning and result, its manifest and secret kinds, and for the highest rank in Paradise.[12]

- God, help me remember and mention You, thank You, and worship You most properly.[13]

- God, I ask You for guidance, fear of You, chastity, and independence of others.[14]

- God, bring all of our affairs to a good conclusion, protect us from disgrace and ignominy in the world, and from being tormented in the Hereafter.[15]

- God, we ask You for all of the good for which Your Prophet Muhammad asked You, and seek refuge in You from every evil from which Your Prophet Muhammad sought refuge in You.[16]

Prayer was a fundamental part of the Prophet's life. All the supplications quoted, together with many, have become keys in the hands of such great saints as Abu Hasan al-Shadhili, Ahmad al-Badawi, Ahmad al-Rifa'i, and 'Abd al-Qadir al-Jilani, who used them to knock on the door of God's Mercy.

THE PROPHET OF UNIVERSAL MERCY

The beginning of existence was an act of mercy and compassion without which the universe would be in chaos. Everything came into existence through compassion, and by compassion it continues to exist in harmony.

Muslim sages say that the universe is the All-Compassionate One's breath. In other words, the universe was created to manifest the Divine Name the All-Compassionate. Its subsistence depends on the same Name. This Name manifests itself first as the All-Provider, so that all living creatures can receive the food or nourishment they need to survive.

Life is God Almighty's foremost and most manifest blessing, and the true and everlasting life is that of the Hereafter. Since we can deserve this life by pleasing God, He sent Prophets and revealed Scriptures out of His compassion for humanity. For this reason, while mentioning His blessings upon humanity in *Surat al-Rahman* (the All-Merciful), He begins: *Al-Rahman. He taught the Qur'an, created humanity, and taught it speech* (55:1-4).

All aspects of this life are a rehearsal for the afterlife, and every creature is engaged in action toward this end. Order is evident in every effort, and compassion resides in every achievement. Some "natural" events or social convulsions may seem disagreeable at first, but we should not regard them as incompatible with compassion. They are like dark clouds or lightning and thunder that, although frightening, nevertheless bring us good tidings of rain. Thus the whole universe praises the All-Compassionate.

Muslim sages consider the Qur'an a "created book" issuing from His Attribute of Will. To write a book that people could not understand would be pointless. Therefore, He created Muhammad to tell people what the universe really means, and to relay His Commandments in the Qur'an through Muhammad so that we can know what is expected of us. Only by following these Commandments can we attain an eternal life of happiness. The Qur'an is the ultimate and most comprehensive Divine Revelation; Islam is the last, perfected, and universal form of Divine Religion; and Prophet Muhammad is the embodiment of Divine Compassion, one sent by God as a mercy for all worlds.

Prophet Muhammad is like a spring of pure water in the heart of a desert, a source of light in an all-enveloping darkness. Whoever appeals to this spring can take as much water as needed to quench their thirst, to become purified of all their sins, and to become illumined with the light of belief. Mercy was like a magic key in his hands, for with it he opened hearts that were so hardened and rusty that no one thought they could be opened. But he did even more: he lit a torch of belief in them.

The Messenger preached Islam, the religion of universal mercy. However, some self-proclaimed humanists say that Islam is "a religion of the sword." This is completely wrong. They make a great deal of noise when animals are killed or when one of their own is harmed, but are silent when Muslims are massacred. Their world is built on personal interest. It should be pointed out that abusing the feeling of compassion is just as harmful—sometimes even more harmful—than having no compassion at all.

Amputating a gangrenous limb is an act of compassion for the whole body. Likewise oxygen and hydrogen, when mixed in the proper ratios, form water, a most vital substance. When this ratio changes, however, each element resumes its original combustible identity.

Similarly, it is quite important to apportion compassion and to identify who deserves it, for "compassion for a wolf sharpens its appetite, and not being content with what it receives, it demands even more." Compassion for wrong-doers makes them more aggressive and encourages them to work against others. In fact, true compassion requires that such people be prevented from doing wrong. When the Messenger told his Companions to help people when they were just and unjust, they asked him to explain this seeming paradox. He replied: "You help such people by preventing them from engaging in injustice." So, compassion requires that those who cause trouble either be deprived of their means for, or prevented from, doing so. Otherwise, they eventually will take control and do as they please.

The Messenger's compassion encompassed every creature. In his role as an invincible commander and able statesman, he knew allowing blood-stained, blood-thirsty people to control others would be the most terrible form of tyranny imaginable. Therefore, out of compassion, he required that lambs should be able to live in security against wolves' attacks. He desired, of course, that everyone be guided. In fact, this was his greatest concern: *Yet it may be, if they believe not in this Message, you will consume yourself, following after them, with grief* (18:6).

But how should he deal with those who persisted in unbelief and fought him to destroy both him and his Message? He had to fight such people, for universal compassion encompasses every creature. This is why, when he was wounded severely at Uhud, he raised his hands and prayed: "O God, forgive my people, for they don't know."[17]

The Makkans, his own people, inflicted so much suffering on him that he finally emigrated to Madina. Even after that, the next 5 years were far from peaceful. However, when he conquered Makka without bloodshed in the twenty-first year of his Prophethood, he asked the Makkan unbelievers: "How do you expect me to treat you?" They responded unanimously: "You are a noble one, the son of a noble one." He then told them his decision: "You may leave, for no reproach this day shall be on you. May God forgive you. He is the Most Compassionate of the Compassionate."[18]

Sultan Mehmed the Conqueror said the same thing to the defeated Byzantines after conquering Istanbul 825 years later. Such is the universal compassion of Islam.

The Messenger displayed the highest degree of compassion toward the believers:

> There has come to you a Messenger from among yourselves; grievous to him is your suffering; anxious is he over you, full of concern for you, for the believers full of pity, compassionate. (9:128)

He lowered unto believers his wing of tenderness through mercy (15:88), and was the guardian of believers and nearer to them than their selves (33:6). When a Companion died, he asked those at the funeral if the deceased had left any debts. On learning that he had, the Prophet mentioned the above verse and announced that the creditors should come to him for repayment.[19]

His compassion even encompassed the Hypocrites and unbelievers. He knew who the Hypocrites were, but never identified them, for this would have deprived them of the rights of full citizenship they had gained by their outward confession of faith and practice. Since they lived among Muslims, their unbelief in eternal life may have been reduced or changed to doubt, thus diminishing their fear of death and the pain caused by the assertion of eternal non-existence after death.

God did not send a collective destruction upon the unbelievers, although He had eradicated many such people in the past: *But God would never chastise them while you were among them; God would never chastise them as they begged forgiveness* (8:33). This verse refers to unbelievers of whatever time. God will not destroy peoples altogether as long as those who follow the Messenger are alive. Besides, He has left the door of repentance open until the Last Day. Anyone can accept Islam or ask God's forgiveness, regardless of how sinful they consider themselves to be.

For this reason, a Muslim's enmity toward unbelievers is a form of pity. When 'Umar saw an 80-year-old priest, he sat down and sobbed. When asked why he did so, he replied: "God assigned him so long a life span, but he has not been able to find the true path." 'Umar was a disciple of the Messenger, who said: "I was not sent to call down curses on people, but as a mercy"[20] and:

I am Muhammad, and Ahmad (praised one), and Muqaffi (the Last Prophet); I am Hashir (the final Prophet in whose presence the dead will be resurrected); the Prophet of repentance (the Prophet for whom the door of repentance will always remain open), and the Prophet of mercy.[21]

Archangel Gabriel also benefited from the mercy of the Qur'an. Once the Prophet asked Gabriel whether he had any share in the mercy contained in the Qur'an. Gabriel replied that he did, and explained: "I was not certain about my end. However, when the verse: *(One) obeyed, and moreover, trustworthy and secured* (81:21) was revealed, I felt secure about it."[22] When Ma'iz was punished for fornication, a Companion verbally abused him. The Messenger frowned at him and said: "You have backbitten your friend. His repentance and asking God's pardon for his sin would be enough to forgive all the sinners in the world."[23]

The Messenger was particularly compassionate toward children. Whenever he saw a child crying, he sat beside him or her and shared his or her feelings. He felt a mother's pain for her child more than the mother herself. Once he said: "I stand in prayer and wish to prolong it. However, I hear a child cry and shorten the prayer to lessen the mother's anxiety."[24]

He took children in his arms and hugged them. Once when hugging his beloved grandsons Hasan and Husayn, Aqra ibn Habis told him: "I have 10 children, and have never kissed any of them." The Messenger responded: "One without pity for others is not pitied."[25] According to another report, he said or added: "What can I do for you if God has removed compassion from you?"[26]

He said: "Pity those on Earth so that those in the Heavens will pity you."[27] When Sa'd ibn 'Ubada became ill, the Messenger visited him at home and, seeing his faithful Companion in a pitiful state, began to cry. He said: "God does not punish because of tears or grief, but He punishes because of this," and he pointed to his tongue.[28] When 'Uthman ibn Mad'un died, he shed tears. During the funeral, a woman remarked: "'Uthman flew like a bird to Paradise." Even in that mournful state, the Prophet did not lose his balance and corrected the woman: "How do you know this? Even I don't know this, and I am a Prophet."[29]

A member of the Banu Muqarrin clan once beat his maidservant. She informed the Messenger, who sent for the master. He said: "You have beaten her without any justifiable right. Free her."[30] Freeing a slave free was far better for the master than being punished in the Hereafter because of that act. The Messenger always protected and supported widows, orphans, the poor and disabled even before announcing his Prophethood. When he returned home in excitement from Mount Hira after the first Revelation, his wife Khadija told him: "I hope you will be the Prophet of this Umma, for you always tell the truth, fulfill your trust, support your relatives, help the poor and weak, and feed guests."[31]

His compassion even encompassed animals. We hear from him: "A prostitute was guided to truth by God and ultimately went to Paradise because she gave water to a dog dying of thirst. Another woman was sent to Hell because she left a cat to die of hunger."[32] While returning from a military campaign, a few Companions removed some young birds from their nest to stroke them. The mother bird came back and, not finding its babies, began to fly around screeching. When told of this, the Messenger became angry and ordered the birds to be put back in the nest.[33]

Once he told his Companions that God reproached an earlier Prophet for setting fire to a nest of ants.[34] While in Mina, some of his Companions attacked a snake in order to kill it. However, it managed to escape. Watching this from afar, the Messenger remarked: "It was saved from your evil, as you were from its evil."[35] Ibn 'Abbas reported that when the Messenger saw a man sharpening his knife directly before the sheep to be slaughtered, he asked: "Do you want to kill it many times?"[36]

'Abd Allah ibn Ja'far narrates:

> The Messenger went to a garden in Madina with a few Companions. A very scrawny camel was in a corner. Seeing the Messenger, it began to cry. The Messenger went to it and, after staying beside it for a while, severely warned the owner to feed it properly.[37]

His love and compassion for creatures differed from that of today's self-proclaimed humanists, for he was sincere and balanced in this regard—a Prophet raised by God, the Creator and Sustainer of all beings, for the guidance and happiness humanity and jinn, and the harmony of existence. As such, he lived for others, and was a mercy for all the worlds, a manifestation of Compassion.

HIS MILDNESS AND FORBEARANCE

Mildness is another dimension of his character. He was a bright mirror in which God reflected His Mercy. Mildness is a reflection of compassion. God made His Messenger mild and gentle, thereby allowing him to gain many converts to Islam and overcome numerous obstacles.

After the victory of Badr, the Battle of Uhud was a severe trial for the young Muslim community. Although the Messenger wanted to fight on the outskirts of Madina, most Muslims desired to fight on an open battlefield. When the two armies met at the foot of Mount Uhud, the Messenger positioned 50 archers in 'Aynayn pass and ordered them not to move without his permission, even if they saw that the Muslims had won a decisive victory.

The Muslim army, having only one-third of the men and equipment of the enemy, almost defeated the Makkan polytheists in the initial stage. Seeing the enemy fleeing, these archers forgot the Prophet's command and left their post. Khalid ibn Walid, the Makkan cavalry's commander, saw this and, riding round the mountain, attacked the Muslims from behind. The fleeing enemy soldiers turned back, and caught the Muslims in a crossfire. They began to lose, more than 70 were martyred, and the Messenger was wounded.

He might have reproached those who had urged him to pursue their desires as well as the archers who had abandoned their post, but he did not. Instead, he showed leniency:

> It was by the mercy of God that you were gentle to them; if you had been harsh and hard of heart, they would have dispersed from about you. So pardon them and ask forgiveness for them and consult with them in the affair. And when you are resolved, then put your trust in God; surely God loves those who put their trust (in Him). (3:159)

This verse shows two prerequisite for leadership: mildness and leniency toward those who make well-intentioned mistakes, and the importance of consultation in public administration.

This mildness and forgiveness was a reflection of God's Names the All-Mild, All-Clement, and All-Forgiving. God does not stop providing for people despite their rebellion or unbelief. While most people disobey Him by indulging in unbelief, by explicitly or implicitly associating partners with Him, or transgressing His Commandments, the sun continues to send them its heat and light, clouds full of rain come to their aid, and the soil never stops feeding them with its fruits and plants. God's Clemency and Forgiveness are reflected through the Messenger's compassion, mildness, and forgiveness.

Like Abraham, whom he used to say that he resembled, the Messenger was mild, imploring, clement, and penitent (11:75), gentle to believers, and full of pity and compassion for them (9:128). Abraham was never angry with people, regardless of how much they tormented him. He wished good even for his enemies, and implored God and shed tears in His Presence. Since he was a man of peace and salvation, God made the fire into which he was thrown cool and safe (21:69).

Like him, the Messenger was never angry with anybody because of what they did to him. When his wife 'A'isha was slandered, he did not consider punishing the slanderers even after she was cleared by the Qur'an. Bedouins often behaved impolitely with him, but he did not even frown at them. Although extremely sensitive, he always showed forbearance toward both friend and foe.

For example, while he was distributing the spoils of war after the Battle of Hunayn, Dhu al-Huwaysira objected: "Be just, O Muhammad." This was an unforgivable insult, for the Prophet had been sent to establish justice. Unable to endure such offences, 'Umar demanded permission to kill "that hypocrite" on the spot. But the Messenger only replied: "Who else will show justice if I am not just? If I don't show justice, then I am lost and brought to naught."[38] According to another possible meaning of this expression, he said: "If I am not just, then, by following me, you people have been lost and brought to naught."[39] In addition, he implied that this man would later take part in a seditious movement. This came true during the caliphate of 'Ali: Dhu al-Huwaysira was found dead among the Kharijites after the Battle of Nahrawan.

Anas ibn Malik related that a Jewess offered a roasted sheep to the Messenger after the conquest of Khaybar. Just before he took the first bite, he stopped and told the others not to eat, saying: "This sheep tells me it has been poisoned." Nevertheless, a Companion named Bishr died immediately after his first bite (taken before the Messenger spoke). The Messenger sent for the woman and asked her why she had poisoned the meat. She replied: "If you're really a Prophet, the poison won't affect you. If you're not, I wanted to save people from your evil." The Messenger forgave her for her conspiracy to kill him.[40] According to some reports, however, Bishr's relatives demanded that she be punished, and she subsequently was.

Once when the Prophet was going home after talking to his Companions in the mosque, a bedouin pulled him by the collar and said rudely: "O Muhammad! Give me my due! Load up my two camels! For you will load them up with neither your own wealth nor that of your father!" Without showing any sign of being offended, he told others: "Give him what he wants."[41]

Zayd ibn San'an narrates:

> Before I embraced Islam, the Messenger borrowed some money from me. I went to him to collect my debt before its due time, and insulted him: "O you children of 'Abd al-Muttalib, you are very reluctant to pay your debts!" 'Umar became very angry with me and shouted: "O enemy of God! Were it not for the treaty between us and the Jewish community, I would cut off your head! Speak to the Messenger politely!" However, the Messenger smiled at me and, turning to 'Umar, said: "Pay him, and add 20 gallons to it, because you frightened him."

'Umar relates the rest of the story:

> We went together. On the way, Zayd said unexpectedly: "'Umar, you were angry with me. But I find in him all the features of the

Last Prophet recorded in the Torah, the Old Testament. It contains this verse: His mildness surpasses his anger. The severity of impudence to him increases him only in mildness and forbearance. To test his forbearance, I provoked him deliberately. Now I am convinced that he is the Prophet whose coming the Torah predicted. So, I believe and bear witness that he is the Last Prophet."[42]

This mildness and forbearance was enough for the conversion of Zayd ibn San'an, a Jewish scholar.

The Messenger was extremely meticulous in practicing Islam. Nobody could match his supererogatory prayers. Despite being sinless, he spent more than half the night praying and crying, and sometimes fasted two or three successive days. Every moment he took another step toward the "praised station" set for him by God. He was very tolerant toward others. Not wanting to burden his community, he did not perform the supererogatory prayers in the mosque. When people complained that an imam was prolonging the prayer, the Prophet mounted the pulpit and said: "O people! You cause people to dread the prayer. When you lead a prayer, don't prolong it, for for there are people among you who are sick or old or in urgent need."[43] Once his congregation complained about Mu'adh ibn Jabal, saying he prolonged the night prayer. The Prophet's love for Mu'adh did not stop him asking three times if he was a trouble-maker.[44]

The Messenger's mildness and forbearance captured hearts and preserved Muslim unity. As stated in the Qur'an, if he had been harsh and hard-hearted, people would have abandoned him. But those who saw him and listened to him were so endowed with Divine manifestations that they became saints. For example, Khalid ibn Walid was the Qurayshi general who caused the Muslims to experience a reverse at Uhud. However, when he was not included in the army that set out on the day after his conversion, he was so upset that he wept.

Like Khalid, Ikrima and 'Amr ibn al-'As were among those who did great harm to the Messenger and the Muslims. After their conversions, each became a sword of Islam drawn against unbelievers. Ibn Hisham, Abu Jahl's brother, converted to Islam shortly before the Messenger passed away. He was such a sincere Muslim that just before he was martyred at Yarmuk, he did not drink the water that Hudayfa al-'Adawi offered him. Rather, he asked that it be given to nearby wounded fellow Muslim groaning for water. He died, having preferred a fellow Muslim over himself.[45]

Such people attained high ranks in the enlightening atmosphere of the Messenger. They became his Companions, regarded and respected as the most virtuous people after the Prophets by almost all Muslims since the earliest days of Islam. Explaining their greatness, Said Nursi, the great twentieth-century Muslim revivalist, says:

> I wondered why even the greatest saints like Muhyi al-Din ibn al-'Arabi could not attain the rank of the Companions. One day God enabled me to perform in prayer a prostration that I could never repeat. I concluded that it is impossible to attain the Companions' ranks, for all of their prostrations were like that in meaning and merit.[46]

The Messenger brought up the Companions. Their greatness is shown in the fact that despite their small numbers, they successfully conveyed Islam to the furthest reaches of Asia and Africa within a few decades. In those areas, Islam became so deeply rooted that despite the concerted efforts by the superpowers of each era to extinguish Islam, it continues to gain new momentum and represents the only realistic alternative for human salvation. The Companions were transformed from their wretched pre-Islamic state to being guides and teachers of a considerable part of humanity until the Last Day, the vanguard of the most magnificent civilization in history.

In addition, the Messenger was absolutely balanced. His universal compassion did not prevent him from executing Divine justice, and his mildness and forbearance kept him from breaching any Islamic rule or humiliating himself. For example, during a military campaign Usama ibn Zayd threw an enemy soldier to the ground. When he was about to kill him, the man declared his belief in Islam. Judging this to be the result of a fear of imminent death,

Usama killed him. When informed of the incident, the Messenger reprimanded Usama severely: "Did you cleave his heart open and see (if what you suspected is true)?" He repeated this so many times that Usama said later: "I wished I had not yet become a Muslim on the day I was scolded so severely."[47]

Likewise, once Abu Dharr got so angry with Bilal that he insulted him: "You son of a black woman!" Bilal came to the Messenger and reported the incident in tears. The Messenger reproached Abu Dharr: "Do you still have a sign of Jahiliya?" Full of repentance, Abu Dharr lay on the ground and said: "I won't raise my head (meaning he wouldn't get up) unless Bilal put his foot on it to pass over it." Bilal forgave him, and they were reconciled.[48] Such was the brotherhood and humanity Islam created between once-savage people.

HIS GENEROSITY

The Messenger is the most polished mirror in which God's Names and Attributes are reflected to the highest degree. As the perfect manifestation of these Names and Attributes, an embodiment of the Qur'an and Islam, he is the greatest and most decisive and comprehensive proof of God's Existence and Unity, and of the truth of Islam and the Qur'an. Those who saw him remembered God automatically. Each of his virtues reflected a Name or Attribute of God, and is a proof of his Prophethood. Like his mildness and forbearance, his generosity is another dimension of his excellent, matchless personality, a reflection and proof of his Prophethood.

The people of Arabia were renowned for their generosity even in pre-Islamic times. When we look at that era's poetry, we see that the Arabs were proud of their generosity. However, their generosity was not for the sake of God or for an altruistic motive; rather, it was the cause of self-pride. But the Messenger's generosity was purely for God's sake. He never mentioned, and did not like to have mentioned, it. When a poet praised him for his generosity, he attributed whatever good he had or did to God. He never attributed his virtues and good deeds to himself.

The Messenger liked to distribute whatever he had. He engaged in trade until his Prophethood, and had considerable wealth. Afterwards, he and his wealthy wife Khadija spent everything in the way of God. When Khadija died, there was no money for her burial shroud. The Messenger had to borrow money to bury his own wife, the first person to embrace Islam and its first supporter.[49]

If the Messenger had desired, he could have been the richest man in Makka. But he rejected such offers without a second thought. Although God mandated that one-fifth of all war spoils should be at the Messenger's free disposal, he never spent it on himself or his family. He and his family lived austerely and survived on scanty provisions, for he always gave preference to others. For example, his share of the spoils of Hunayn was of 40,000 sheep, 24,000 camels, and 16 tons of silver.

Safwan ibn Umayya, from whom the Messenger had borrowed some weapons, gazed upon the spoils with greed and bewilderment. Aware of this, the Messenger gave him as many camels as he wanted. Astounded with such generosity, Safwan ran to his people and announced: "O my people! Accept Islam without hesitation, for Muhammad gives in such a way that only one who has no fear of poverty and relies fully on God can give!" Such generosity was enough to guide Safwan and his people, who had been among the bitterest enemies of Islam until just before that day, to the truth.[50]

The Messenger regarded himself a traveler in this world. Once he said: "What connection do I have with this world? I am like a traveler who takes shade under a tree and then continues on his way."[51] According to him, the world is like a tree under which people are shaded. No one can live forever, so people must prepare here for the second part of the journey, which will end either in Paradise or Hell.

The Messenger was sent to guide people to truth, and so spent his life and possessions to this end. Once 'Umar saw him lying on a rough mat and wept. When the Messenger asked him why he was weeping, 'Umar replied: "O Messenger of God, while kings sleep in soft feather beds, you lie on a rough mat. You are the Messenger of God, and as such deserve an easy life more than anyone else." He answered: "Don't you agree that the luxuries of the world should be theirs, and that those of the Hereafter should be ours?"[52]

Islam does not approve of monastic life. It came to secure justice and human well-being, but warns against overindulgence. Thus many Muslims have chosen an ascetic life. Although individual Muslims generally became rich after the Messenger passed away, others like Abu Bakr, 'Umar, and 'Ali preferred an austere life. This was partly because they felt the need to live as the poorest of their people, and partly because they strictly followed the Prophet's example. During his caliphate, Abu Bakr was offered a glass of cold water to break his fast during Ramadan. He brought the glass to his lips and suddenly began to weep. When asked why, he answered: "One day, the Messenger drank such a glass of cold water offered to him and wept. He said that God says: 'On that day, you will be questioned concerning every bounty.' We will be questioned about this water. I remembered that and wept."[53]

In the early days of his Caliphate, Abu Bakr earned his living by milking a woman's sheep. Some time later, he was given a small salary. While on his death-bed, he gave a pitcher to those around him and asked them to give it to the new caliph after his death. 'Umar succeeded him and, when he broke the pitcher, some coins came out, together with the following letter: "I lived according to the living standards of the poorest of Madina, and put in this pitcher the amount left of my salary. Therefore, these coins belong to the public treasury and must be returned there." On reading the letter, 'Umar wept and remarked: "O Abu Bakr, you have left an unbearable burden on your successors."[54]

The Messenger was, in the words of Anas, "the most comely and generous person."[55] Jabir ibn Samura reports:

> Once we were sitting in the mosque, and a full moon was shining above us. The Messenger entered. I looked first at the moon and then at his face. I swear by God that his face was brighter than the moon.[56]

The Messenger never refused anyone and, as Farazdak said, only said the word "no" when reciting the profession of faith while praying. Once, a bedouin came and asked the Messenger for something. The Messenger complied with his request. The bedouin continued to ask, and the Messenger continued to give until he had nothing left. When the bedouin asked again, he promised that he would give it to him when he had it. Angered by such rudeness, 'Umar said to the Messenger: "You were asked and you gave. Again you were asked and you gave, until you were asked once more and you promised!" 'Umar meant that the Messenger should not make things so difficult for himself. The Messenger did not approve of 'Umar's words. 'Abd Allah ibn Hudafa al-Sahmi stood up and said: "O Messenger, give without fear that the Owner of the Seat of Honor will make you poor!" Pleased with such words, the Messenger declared: "I was commanded to do so!"[57]

He never refused a request, for it was he who said: "The generous are near to God, Paradise, and people, but distant from the Fire. The miserly are distant from God, Paradise, and people, but near to the Fire,"[58] and: "O people! Surely God has chosen for you Islam as religion. Improve your practice of it through generosity and good manners."[59] His mercifulness rose up as moisture into the sky, and then rained as generosity so that hardened hearts would be fertile enough to grow "good trees whose roots are firm and whose branches are in the Heavens, and which yield their fruits every season by the leave of their Master."

HIS MODESTY

In society, each person has a window (status) through which he or she looks out to see others and be seen. If the window is built higher than their real stature, people try to make themselves appear taller through vanity and assumed airs. If the window is set lower than their real stature, they must bow in humility in order to look out, see, and be seen. Humility is the measure of one's greatness, just as vanity or conceit is the measure of low character.[60]

The Messenger had a stature so high that it could be said to touch the "roof of the Heavens." Therefore, he had no need to be seen. Whoever travels in the realm of virtues sees him before every created being, including angels. In the words of Said Nursi, the Messenger is the noble aide-de-camp of God. He lowered himself to stay in the world for a while so that people might find the way to God. Since he is the greatest of humanity, he is the greatest in modesty. This follows the well-knowing adage: "The greater one is, the more modest one is."

He never regarded himself as greater than anybody else. Only his radiant face and attractive person distinguished him from his Companions. He lived and dressed like the poorest people and sat and ate with them, just as he did with slaves and servants. Once a woman saw him eating and remarked: "He eats like a slave." The Messenger replied: "Could there be a better slave than me? I am a slave of God."[61]

One time when he was serving his friends, a bedouin came in and shouted: "Who is the master of this people?" The Messenger answered in such a way that he introduced himself while expressing a substantial principle of Islamic leadership and public administration: "The people's master is the one who serves them." 'Ali says that among people the Messenger was one of them. When he and Abu Bakr reached Quba while emigrating to Madina, some Madinese who did not know what the Prophet looked like tried to kiss Abu Bakr's hands. The only external sign distinguishing one man from the other was that Abu Bakr seemed older than the Messenger.[62]

While the Muslims were building their mosque in Madina, the Prophet carried two sun-dried bricks; everyone else carried one.[63] While digging the trench to defend Madina, the Companions bound a stone around their stomachs to quell their hunger; the Messenger bound two.[64] When a man seeing him for the first time began trembling out of fear, because he found the Prophet's appearance so awe-inspiring, the Messenger calmed him: "Brother, don't be afraid. I am a man, like you, whose mother used to eat dry bread."[65] Another time, an insane woman pulled him by the hand and said:

"Come with me and do my housework." He complied with her request.[66] 'A'isha reported that the Messenger patched his clothes, repaired his shoes, and helped his wives with the housework.[67]

Although his modesty elevated him to the highest rank, he regarded himself as an ordinary servant of God: "No one enters Paradise because of his or her deeds." When asked if this was true for him as well, he replied that he could enter Paradise only through the Mercy of God.[68]

His Companions always asked for his advice or permission before any action. Once 'Umar asked his permission to go for the minor pilgrimage. The Messenger allowed this, and even asked 'Umar to include him in his supplications. 'Umar rejoiced so much that later he would say: "If the worlds had been granted to me that day, I wouldn't have felt the same happiness."[69]

Humility was one of the Prophet's greatest qualities. As he attained a higher rank each day, he increased in humility and servanthood to God. His servanthood is prior to his Messengership, as seen in the declaration of faith: "I bear witness that there is no god but God; I also bear witness that Muhammad is His servant and Messenger." He preferred being a Prophet–slave to being a Prophet–king.

One day, while sitting with Archangel Gabriel, the Messenger mentioned that he had not eaten for several days. As soon as he said this, another angel appeared and asked: "O Messenger of God, God greets you and asks if you wish to be a Prophet–king or a Prophet–slave?" Gabriel advised him to be humble toward his Master. As humility was a fundamental part of his character, the Messenger replied: "I wish to be a Prophet–slave."[70] God praises his servanthood and mentions him as a servant in several verses: *When the servant of God stood up in prayer to Him, they (the jinn) were well nigh upon him in swarms (to watch his prayer)* (72:19), and:

> If you are in doubt concerning that which We have sent down on Our servant, then bring a sura of the like thereof, and call your witnesses beside God if you are truthful. (2:23)

After Khadija and Abu Talib died, the Messenger became convinced that he could no longer expect any victory or security in Makka. So before things became too critical, he sought a new base in Ta'if. As the townspeople were quite hostile, he felt that he had no support and protection. But then God manifested His Mercy and honored him with the Ascension to His Presence. While narrating this incident, God mentions him as His servant to show that he deserves Ascension through his servanthood:

> Glory be to him, Who carried His servant by night from the Holy Mosque to the Furthest Mosque, the precincts of which We have blessed, that We might show him some of Our signs. He is the All-Hearing, the All-Seeing. (17:1)

Humility is the most important aspect of the Messenger's servanthood. He declared: "God exalts the humble and abases the haughty."[71] 'Ali describes the Messenger as:

> He was the most generous person in giving, and the mildest and the foremost in patience and perseverance. He was the most truthful in speech, the most amiable and congenial in companionship, and the noblest of them in family. Whoever sees him first is stricken by awe, but whoever knows him closely is deeply attracted to him. Whoever attempts to describe him says: "I have never seen the like of him."[72]

THE ETHOS CREATED BY THE MESSENGER

It is difficult for us to understand Prophet Muhammad fully. As we tend to compartmentalize the universe, life, and humanity itself, we have no unitary vision. However, Prophet Muhammad perfectly combined a philosopher's intellect, a commander valor, a scientist's genius, a sage's wisdom, a statesman's insight and administrative ability, a Sufi master's spiritual profundity, and a scholar's knowledge in his own person.

Philosophers produce students, not followers; social or revolutionary leaders make followers, not complete people; Sufi masters make "lords of submission," not active fighters or intellectuals. But in Prophet Muhammad we find the characteristics of a philosopher, a revolutionary leader, a warrior and statesman, and a Sufi master. His school is one of the intellect and thought, revolution, submission and discipline, and goodness, beauty, ecstasy, and movement.

Prophet Muhammad transformed crude, ignorant, savage, and obstinate desert Arabs into a community of sincere devotees of a sublime cause, a society of gentleness and compassion, an assembly of sainthood, and a host of intellectuals and scholars. Nowhere else do we see such fervor and ardor combined with gentleness, kindness, sincerity, and compassion. This is a characteristic unique to the Muslim community, one that has been visible since its earliest days.

The "Garden" of Muhammad

Islam, the school of Prophet Muhammad, has been a "garden" rich in every kind of "flower." Like cascading water, God has brought forth from it such majestic people as Abu Bakr, 'Umar, 'Uthman, 'Ali, 'Umar ibn Abd al-'Aziz, Mahdi al-'Abbasi, Harun al-Rashid, Alp Arslan, Mehmed the Conqueror, Selim, and Sulayman. These were not only statesmen of the highest caliber and invincible commanders, but also men of profound spirituality, deep knowledge, oration, and literature.

The Messenger's blessed, pure climate produced invincible generals. Among the first generation we see such military geniuses as Khalid, Sa'd ibn Abi Waqqas, Abu 'Ubayda, Shurahbil ibn Hasana, and A'la al-Khadrami. They were succeeded by such brilliant generals as Tariq ibn Ziyad and 'Uqba ibn Nafi', both of whom combined military genius with human tenderness and religious conviction and devotion.

When 'Uqba, the conqueror of North Africa, reached the Atlantic Ocean, 2,000 miles away from Arabia, he cried out: "And now, God, take my soul! If this sea didn't stretch out before me, I would convey Your holy Name across it to other lands!" We can hardly imagine Alexander the "Great" thinking such thoughts as he set out for Persia. Yet as conquerors, the two men achieved comparable feats.

'Uqba's idealism and his "possibility" with respect to the Divine Will would be transmuted into irresistible action in this world. Alexander's empire crashed after his death; the lands 'Uqba conquered still retain Islam as their dominant worldview, creed, and lifestyle 14 centuries later, despite attempts to change this reality.

Tariq was a victorious commander, not only when he defeated the 90,000-man Spanish army with a handful of self-sacrificing, valiant men, but also when he stood before the king's treasure and said: "Be careful, Tariq! You were a slave yesterday. Today you are a victorious commander. And tomorrow you will be under the earth."

Yavuz Selim, an Ottoman Sultan who regarded the world as too small for two rulers, was truly victorious when he crowned some kings and dethroned others, and also when he silently entered Istanbul at bedtime, after conquering Syria and Egypt, to avoid the people's enthusiastic welcome. He also was victorious when he ordered that the robe muddied by his teacher's horse be placed over his coffin because of its sanctity—it had been "muddied" by the horse of a scholar.

During the rapid conquests after the Prophet, many conquered people were distributed among the Muslim families. Those emancipated slaves eventually became the foremost religious scholars: Hasan ibn Hasan al-Basri (Basra); 'Ata' ibn Rabah, Mujahid, Sa'id ibn Jubayr, and Sulayman ibn Yasar (Makka); Zayd ibn Aslam, Muhammad ibn al-Munkadir, and Nafi' ibn Abi Nujayh (Madina); 'Alqama ibn Qays al-Nakha'i, Aswad ibn Yazid, Hammad, and Abu Hanifa Nu'man ibn Thabit (Kufa); Tawus and ibn Munabbih (Yemen); 'Ata ibn 'Abd Allah al-Khorasani (Khorasan); and Maqhul (Damascus). They all opened as splendid, sweet-smelling flowers in the garden of Muhammad. They established the Islamic legal code and brought up thousands of jurists, who wrote and complied volumes that are still valued as legal references.

One of these jurists, Imam Abu Hanifa, founded the Hanafi legal school, which has hundreds of millions of followers today. He brought up such great scholars as Imam Abu Yusuf, Imam Zufar, and Imam Muhammad Hasan al-Shaybani, who taught

Imam Muhammad Idris al-Shafi'i. The notes Abu Hanifa dictated to Imam al-Shaybani were expounded centuries later by Imam Sarakhsi (the "Sun of Imams") in the 30-volume work *Al-Mabsut*.

Imam Shafi'i, who established the methodological principles of Islamic law, is regarded as reviver or renewer of religious sciences. However, when his students told Imam Sarakhsi that Imam Shafi'i had memorized 300 fascicles of the Prophetic Traditions, the latter answered: "He had the zakat (one-fortieth) of the Traditions in my memory." Imam Shafi'i, Abu Hanifa, Imam Malik, or Ahmad ibn Hanbal, and so many others, were brought up in the school of Prophet Muhammad.

And then there are such Qur'anic interpreters as Ibn Jarir al-Tabari, Fakhr al-Din al-Razi, Ibn Kathir, Imam Suyuti, Allama Hamdi Yazir, and Sayyid Qutb. In addition, there are such famous *hadith* collectors as Imam Bukhari, Muslim, Tirmidhi, Abu Dawud, Ibn Maja, Nasa'i, Ibn Hanbal, Bayhaqi, Darimi, Daraqutni, Sayf al-Din al-'Iraqi, Ibn Hajar al-Asqalani, and many others. They are all ever-shining stars in the luminous sky of Islamic sciences. All received their light from Prophet Muhammad.

According to Islam, God created humanity on the best pattern, as the most universal and all-embracing theater of Divine Names and Attributes. But people, because of their heedlessness, can fall to the lowest levels. Sufism, the inner dimension of Islam, leads people to perfection or enables them to reacquire their primordial angelic state. Islam has produced countless saints. As it never separated our metaphysical quest or gnosis from the study of nature, many practicing Sufis were also scientists. Such leading saints as 'Abd al Qadir al-Jilani, Shah Naqshband, Ma'ruf al-Karkhi, Hasan Shazili, Ahmad Badawi, Shaykh al-Harrani, Ja'far al-Sadiq, Junayd al-Baghdadi, Bayazid al-Bistami, Muhy al-Din al-'Arabi, and Mawlana Jalal al-Din al-Rumi have illumined the way to truth and trained others to purify their selves.

Being embodiments of sincerity, Divine love, and pure intention, Sufi masters became the motivating factor and the source of power behind the Islamic conquests and the subsequent Islamization of those lands. Figures like Imam Ghazali, Imam Rabbani, and Bediuzzaman Said Nursi are revivers or renewers of the highest degree, and combined in themselves the enlightenment of sages, the knowledge of religious scholars, and the spirituality of great saints.

Islam is the middle way. Its elaborate hierarchy of knowledge is integrated by the principle of Divine Unity. There are juridical, social and theological sciences, as well as metaphysical ones, all deriving their principles from the Qur'an. Over time, Muslims developed elaborate philosophical, natural, and mathematical sciences, each of which has its source in a Beautiful Name of God. For example, medicine depends on the Name All-Healing; geometry and engineering on the Names All-Just and All-Determiner, and All-Shaper and All-Harmonizing; philosophy reflects the Name All-Wise.

Each level of knowledge views nature in a particular light. Jurists and theologians see it as the background for human action; philosophers and scientists see it as a domain to be analyzed and understood; and metaphysicians consider it the object of contemplation and the mirror reflecting suprasensible realities. The Author of Nature has inscribed His Wisdom upon every leaf and stone, on every atom and particle, and has created the world of nature in such a way that every phenomenon is a sign singing the glory of His Oneness.

Islam has maintained an intimate connection between science and Islamic studies. Thus the traditional education of Islamic scientists, particularly in the early centuries, comprised most of contemporary sciences. In later life, each scientist's aptitude and interest would cause him or her to become an expert and specialist in one or more sciences.

Universities, libraries, observatories, and other scientific institutions played a major role in the continuing vitality of Islamic science. These, together with students who would travel hundreds of miles to study under acknowledged scholars, ensured that the whole corpus of knowledge was kept intact and transmitted from one place to another and from one generation to the next. This knowledge did not remain static; rather, it continued to expand and enrich itself. Today, there are hundreds of thousands of Islamic (mainly in Arabic) manuscripts in the world's libraries, a large number of which deal with scientific subjects.[73]

For example, Abu Yusuf Ya'qub al-Kindi (the "Philosopher of the Arabs") wrote on philosophy, mineralogy, metallurgy, geology, physics, and medicine, among other subjects, and was an accomplished physician. Ibn al-Haytham was a leading Muslim mathematician and, without doubt, the greatest physicist. We know the names of over 100 of his works. Some 19 of them, dealing with mathematics, astronomy, and physics, have been studied by modern scholars. His work exercised a profound influence on later scholars, both in the Muslim world and in the West, where he was known Alhazen. One of his works on optics was translated into Latin in 1572.

Abu al-Rayhan al-Biruni was one of the greatest scholars of medieval Islam, and certainly the most original and profound. He was equally well-versed in mathematics, astronomy, the physical and natural sciences, and also distinguished himself as a geographer and historian, a chronologist and linguist, and as an impartial observer of customs and creeds. Such figures as al-Kharizmi (mathematics), Ibn Shatir (astronomy), al-Khazini (physics), Jabir ibn Hayyan (medicine) are remembered even today. Andalucia (Muslim Spain) was the main center from which the West acquired knowledge and enlightenment for centuries.

Islam founded a most brilliant civilization. This should not be considered surprising, for the Qur'an begins with the injunction: *Read: In the Name of Your Master Who creates* (96:1). The Qur'an told people to read when there was very little to read and most people were illiterate. What we understand from this apparent paradox is that humanity is to "read" the universe itself as the "Book of Creation."

Its counterpart is the Qur'an, a book of letters and words. We are to observe the universe, perceive its meaning and content, and through those activities gain a deeper perception of the beauty and splendor of the Creator's system and the infinitude of His Might. Thus we are obliged to penetrate into the universe's manifold meanings, discover the Divine laws of nature, and establish a world in which science and faith complement each other. All of this will enable us to attain true bliss in both worlds.

In obedience to the Qur'an's injunctions and the Prophet's example, Muslims studied the Book of Divine Revelation (the Qur'an) and the Book of Creation (the universe) and eventually erected a magnificent civilization. Scholars from all over Europe benefited from centers of higher learning located in Damascus, Bukhara, Baghdad, Cairo, Faz, Qairwan, Zeituna, Cordoba, Sicily, Isfahan, Delhi and other great Islamic cities. Historians liken the Muslim world of the medieval ages, dark for Europe but golden and luminous for Muslims, to a beehive. Roads were full of students, scientists, and scholars traveling from one center of learning to another.

For the first 5 centuries of its existence, the realm of Islam was a most civilized and progressive area. Studded with splendid cities, gracious mosques, and quiet universities, the Muslim East offered a striking contrast to the Christian West, which was sunk in the Dark Ages. Even after the disastrous Mongol invasions and Crusades of the thirteenth century ce and onwards, it displayed vigor and remained far ahead of the West.

Although Islam ruled two-thirds of the known civilized world for at least 11 centuries, laziness and negligence of what was going on beyond its borders caused it to decay. However, it must be pointed out clearly that only Islamic civilization decayed—not Islam. Military victories and superiority, which continued into the eighteenth century, encouraged Muslims to rest on their laurels and neglect further scientific research. They abandoned themselves to living their own lives, and recited the Qur'an without studying its deeper meanings. Meanwhile, Europe made great advances in sciences, which they had borrowed from the Muslims.

What we call "sciences" are, in reality, languages of the Divine Book of Creation (another aspect of Islam). Those who ignore this book are doomed to failure in this world. When the Muslims began to ignore it, it was only a matter of time before they would be dominated by some external force. In this case, that external force was Europe. The unending attacks of the Western powers and colonialism contributed greatly to this result.

Every civilization has its own characteristics distinguishing it from others. The present modern civilization is, although having made great contributions to humanity's development in the fields of sciences and technology, is primarily materialistic and is considerably far from satisfying humanity's perennial needs. It is because of this that according to many Western sociologists such as Oswald Spengler it cannot last for long. Spengler has predicted its collapse on the grounds that it is against human nature and values. The bright world of the future will be built on the firm foundation of the wedding of sciences with faith, spirituality, and morality, and it will also attach due importance to basic human values and rights. Islam will make the greatest contribution to this world.

ENDNOTE: A Tribute to the Prophet

This is the tribute of Lamartine, a French historian, to the Prophet of Islam: "Is there any man greater than Muhammad?"

> Never a man set himself, voluntarily or involuntarily, a more sublime aim, since this aim was superhuman: To subvert superstitions which had been interposed between man and his Creator, to render God unto man and man unto God; to restore the rational and sacred idea of divinity amidst the chaos of the material and disfigured gods of idolatry then existing. Never has a man undertaken a work so far beyond human power with so feeble means, for he had in the conception as well as in the execution of such a great design no other instrument than himself, and no other aid except a handful of men living in a corner of desert. Finally, never has a man accomplished such a huge and lasting revolution in the world, because in less than two centuries after its appearance, Islam, in faith and arms, reigned over the whole of Arabia, and conquered in God's name Persia, Khorasan, Western India, Syria, Abyssinia, all the known continent of Northern Africa, numerous islands of Mediterranean, Spain, and a part of Gaul.

If greatness of purpose, smallness of means, and astounding results are the three criteria of human genius, who could dare to compare any great men to Muhammad? The most famous men created arms, laws, and empires only. They founded, if anything at all, no more than material powers which often crumbled away before their eyes. This man moved not only armies, legislation, empires, peoples, and dynasties, but millions of men in one-third of the then-inhabited world; and more than that, he moved the altars, the gods, the religions, the ideas, the beliefs, and the souls. On the basis of a Book, every letter of which has become law, he created a spiritual nationality which has blended together peoples of every tongue and of every race. He has left to us the indelible characteristic of this Muslim nationality, the hatred of false gods, and the passion for the One and immaterial God. This avenging patriotism against the profanation of Heaven formed the virtue of the followers of Muhammad: the conquest of one-third of the Earth to his creed was his miracle.

The idea of God's Unity proclaimed amidst the exhaustion of fabulous theogenies was in itself such a miracle that upon its utterance from his lips it destroyed all the ancient temples of idols and set on fire one-third of the world. His life, his meditations, his heroic reviling against the superstitions of his country, and his boldness in defying the furies of idolatry; his firmness in enduring them for thirteen years in Makka, his acceptance of the role of the public scorn and almost of being a victim of his fellow countrymen: all these and, finally his incessant preaching, his wars against odds, his faith in his success and his superhuman security in misfortune, his forbearance in victory, his ambition which was entirely devoted to one idea and in no manner striving for an empire; his endless prayer, his mystic conversations with God, his death and his triumph after death; all these attest not to an imposture but to a firm conviction. It was his conviction which gave him the power to restore a creed. This creed was twofold: God's Unity and the immateriality of God—the former telling what God is, the latter telling what God is not.

Philosopher, orator, apostle, legislator, warrior, conqueror of ideas, restorer of rational dogmas, of a cult without images; the founder of twenty terrestrial states and of one spiritual state, that is Muhammad. As regards all standards by which human greatness may be measured, we may well ask: Is there any man greater than he? (Tr.)

CHAPTER 10

The Sunna and Its Place
in Islamic Legislation

THE SUNNA AND ITS PLACE
IN ISLAMIC LEGISLATION

The science of *hadith* deals with Prophet Muhammad's life, especially his words and actions, and the actions he approved of in others. In this section, we will restrict ourselves to his own words and actions. These words and their meanings are his alone, for they were not included in the Qur'an, the Recited Revelation and whose meaning and wording belong to God exclusively. His actions include those whose rule and authority we are obliged to follow as laws, and his personal affairs, which are a source of spiritual reward and blessing if followed.

The science of *fiqh* (Islamic law) does not concern itself with the Prophet's personal affairs. The *fuqaha'* (jurists) consider that if those affairs touch upon the voluntary and purposed acts, they should be dealt with under the relevant law. However, if they are matters of the Prophet's personal likes and dislikes, which are not a basis for legislation, they are of no concern to the jurists. According to the *muhaddithun* (scholars of Hadith [Traditionists]), everything related to the Messenger is included in the meaning of Hadith (Tradition) and concerns them.

The Sunna is the record of the Messenger's every act, word, and confirmation, as well as the second source of Islamic legislation and life (the Qur'an is the first one). All scholars of religious sciences, and sometimes those of the natural scientists, use it to establish the principles of their disciplines and to solve difficulties. The Qur'an and authentic prophetic Traditions enjoin Muslims to follow the Sunna.

The Qur'an and the Sunna are inseparable. The Sunna clarifies the ambiguities in the Qur'an by expanding upon what is mentioned only briefly in it, specifies what is unconditional, enables generalizations from what is specifically stated, and particularizations from what is generally stated.

For example, how to pray, fast, give alms, and make pilgrimage was established and expounded in the Sunna. So were such principles or legislation that no one can inherit from the Prophet, killers cannot inherit from their victims, the meat of domestic donkeys and wild animals cannot be eaten, and men cannot marry a wife's female cousins if she is still living. Indeed, the Sunna is relevant to all aspects of Islam, and Muslims must design their lives according to it. For this reason, it has been studied and transmitted to each new generation with almost the same care as the Qur'an.

The Messenger ordered his Companions to obey his Sunna absolutely. He spoke distinctly, so they could understand and memorize his words, and encouraged them to convey his every word to future generations. Sometimes he even urged them to write his words down, for: "Whatever I say is true." The Companions were fully attentive to what his words and deeds and showed a great desire to mold their lives to his, even in the smallest details. They regarded his every word and deed as a Divine trust to which they must adhere and follow as closely as possible. Viewing his words as Divine gifts, they internalized, preserved, and transmitted them.

As truthfulness is the cornerstone of the Islamic character, the Companions did not lie. Just as they did not distort or alter the Qur'an, they did their best to preserve the Traditions and entrust them to future generations by either memorizing them or writing them down. Among the Hadith compilations made during the time of the Companions, three are very famous: *Al-Sahifa al-Sadiqa* by 'Abd Allah ibn 'Amr ibn al-'As, *Al-Sahifa al-Sahiha* by Hammam ibn Munabbih, and *Al-Majmu'* by Zayd ibn 'Ali ibn Husayn.

The Companions were extremely conscientious in relating the Traditions. For example, 'A'isha and 'Abd Allah ibn 'Umar would relate them word for word, not changing even one letter. Ibn Mas'ud and Abu al-Darda' would tremble, as if feverish, when asked to report a Tradition.

Caliph 'Umar ibn 'Abd al-'Aziz (ruled 717-20 ce) ordered that the orally preserved and circulated individual Tradition compilations be written down. Such illustrious figures as Sa'id ibn al-Musayyib, Sha'bi, 'Alqama, Sufyan al-Thawri, and Zuhri pioneered this sacred task. They were followed by the greatest specialists, who were entirely focused on the Traditions' accurate transmittal as well as studying their meaning, wording, and their narrators' careful critiques.

Thanks to these Traditionists, we have the second source of Islam in its original purity. Only through studying the Prophet's life and then conforming our own to it can we gain God's good pleasure and travel the way leading to Paradise. The greatest saints receive their light from this "sun" of guidance, Prophet Muhammad, and send it to those in darkness so that they may find their way.

THE SUNNA AND ITS ROLE

Sunna literally means "a conduct and a good or evil path to be followed." This is the meaning used in the following hadith:

> Those who establish a good path in Islam receive the reward of those who follow it, without any decrease in their reward. Those who establish an evil path in Islam are burdened with the sins of those who follow it, without any decrease in their burden.[1]

This term has different terminological connotations according to each group of Traditionists, methodologists, and jurists. Traditionists view it as including everything connected to the religious commandments reported from the Messenger and categorized, according to the Hanafi legal school (followers of Abu Hanifa), as obligations, necessities, practices particular to or encouraged by the Prophet as recommended and desirable.

Methodologists consider it to be every word, deed, and approval of the Messenger as related by his Companions. Jurists, who approach it as the opposite of innovation in religion, consider it a synonym for *hadith*. They use it for the Prophet's words, deeds, and approvals, all of which provide a basis for legislation and categorizing people's actions.

Derived from the word *haddatha* (to inform), hadith literally means "a tiding or information." Over time, it has assumed the meaning of every word, deed, and approval ascribed to the Messenger. Ibn Hajar says: "According to the Shari'a, the Hadith is everything related to the Messenger."

Another literal meaning is something that takes place within time. This is why some scholars of fine discernment write that *hadith* is that which is not Divine, eternal, or without beginning in time. This fine line separates Hadith from the Qur'an, as the latter is Divine, and eternal, and without beginning in time. The Messenger distinguished his words from the Qur'an: "It is two things only, nothing else: the Word and guidance. The best word is the Word of God, and the best guidance is the guidance of Muhammad."[2]

CATEGORIES OF THE SUNNA

The Sunna is divided into three categories: verbal, practical, and based on approval.

The Verbal Sunna

This category consists of the Messenger's words, which provide a basis for many religious commandments. To cite a few examples:

- "No bequest to the heir."[3] In other words, people cannot bequeath any of their wealth to their heirs, since they will naturally inherit the bulk of the estate. A bequest can be made to the poor or some social service institutions.
- "Don't harm (others), and don't return harm for harm."[4] That is, do not engage in any negative and damaging behavior toward others, and do not retaliate against them by returning bad for bad.
- "A tenth will be given (out of crops grown in fields) watered by rain or rivers; but a twentieth (out of those grown in fields) watered by people (irrigation or watering)."[5] The Qur'an enjoins charity, but goes into no detail about how to do so correctly. All such regulations were established by the Sunna.

- "A sea is that of which the water is clean and the dead animals are lawful to eat."[6] He gave this response when someone asked him if wudu' could be done with sea-water. This has provided a basis for many other rulings.

The Practical Sunna

The Qur'an usually lays down only general rules and principles. For example, it enjoins prayer and pilgrimage but does not describe in detail how to perform them. The Messenger, taught by God through inspiration or through Gabriel, provided this information through his actions. His life was one long, unique example to be followed by all Muslims. For example, he led the daily prayers before his Companions five times a day and ordered them to pray as he prayed.[7]

The Sunna based on approval. The Messenger corrected his Companions' mistakes usually by ascending the pulpit and asking: "Why has somebody done this?"[8] When he saw something agreeable in them, he gave his approval either explicitly or by keeping silent. For example:

- Two Companions traveling in the desert could not find enough water for wudu' before praying, and so used sand (tayammum). When they found water later on before the prayer's time had passed, one of them performed wudu' and repeated the prayer, and the other did not. When they asked The Messenger about it later, he told the one who had not repeated the prayer: "You acted in accordance with the Sunna." Then, he turned to the other one and said: "For you, there is double reward."[9]

- The Messenger ordered a march upon the Banu Qurayza immediately after the Battle of the Trench. He said: "Hurry up! We'll perform the afternoon prayer there." Some Companions, concluding that they should hasten and pray over there started out without delay. Others understood that they were to hasten to the Banu Qurayza's territory only, and that they could pray before departing. The Messenger approved of both interpretations.[10]

THE SUNNA IN THE QUR'AN

The Sunna is the main source of our religious life. It is promoted and encouraged by the Qur'an: *He Who raised among the unlettered ones a Messenger from them, reciting to them His revelations, purifies them and instructs them in the Book and the Wisdom* (62:2). According to most Qur'anic interpreters and Traditionists, *the Wisdom* signifies the Sunna. The Qur'an, being a miraculous exposition, contains nothing superfluous and does not exceed the proper terms. As *Wisdom* comes after *Book*, it must be something different. The Book is the Qur'an, and *the Wisdom* is the Sunna showing how the Qur'an is to be applied to our daily lives.

The Qur'an commands absolute obedience to the Messengers, for they have been sent to guide people to truth in every sphere of their lives. Our loyalty is to God, Who has sent His Messenger and told us to obey him, and not to that man personally: *We have not sent a Messenger save to be obeyed by God's leave* (4:64), and: *O you who believe! Obey God and His Messenger, and do not turn away from him* (8:20).

Obedience to God means unconditional obedience to what has been revealed in the Qur'an. Obedience to the Messenger means following his way of life as closely as possible by obeying what is enjoined and prohibited in the Qur'an and by the Messenger. The Sunna is a comprehensively detailed account of his life. He told his community: "Take care! I have been given the Book and its like together with it."[11]

As stated in 8:20, Muslims must not turn away from the Messenger. Therefore, disobeying, belittling, or criticizing the Sunna amounts to heresy or even apostasy. Many other verses emphasize the necessity of following the Sunna, such as: *O you who believe! Obey God and obey the Messenger and those in authority from among you* (4:59). The verse stresses obedience to God and to the Messenger. The repetition of *obey* in the imperative mood indicates that the Messenger is authorized to command or forbid, and that Muslims must do what he says. Besides, where obedience to those Muslims in authority is ordered, the Prophet has a far greater right to be obeyed.

Another verse states: *Obey God and His Messenger and do not dispute with one another, lest you should be dissolved (dispersed) and your strength fade away; and be steadfast* (8:46). Muslim strength and unity lie in submission to God and His Messenger. The Messenger established the Sunna by living the Qur'an, which means that it is the only way his community can follow. Based on this, we can say that the Sunna is both more comprehensive than the Qur'an and indispensable for leading an upright life in Islamic terms.

Muslims can obey God and show their love for Him only by obeying the Messenger or by following his Sunna: *Say (O Muhammad): "If you love God, follow me so that God loves you"* (3:31); *Surely there is for you in the Messenger an excellent example for him who aspires to God and the Hereafter, and mentions God oft* (33:21); and many other verses. Those who claim to love God or that God loves them, despite their non-adherence to the Sunna, are seriously deluded and astray.

Muslims must cling to the Sunna if they want to remain on the Straight Path and avoid deviation. For example: One day a woman said to ʿAbd Allah ibn Masʿud: "I have heard that you call down God's curse upon women who tattoo their bodies, pluck their facial hair, force their teeth apart in order to look more beautiful, and who change the creation of God."[12] Ibn Masʿud answered: "All of this is found in the Qur'an." The woman objected: "I swear by God that I have read the entire Qur'an, but I couldn't find anything related to this matter." Ibn Masʿud told her: "Our Prophet called God's curse upon women who wear wigs, who join somebody's hair to theirs, and who have tattoos on their bodies. Haven't you read: *Whatever the Messenger brings you, adopt it; whatever he forbids you, refrain from it* (59:7)?"[13]

The Qur'an also declares:

Nay, by your Master, they will never become believers until they choose you as judge to settle the matters in dispute between them. (4:65)

THE SUNNA IN THE TRADITIONS

The way of the Prophet is the way of God. As the Sunna is the way of the Prophet, those who reject it are, in essence, rejecting (and disobeying) God. As the Prophet stated: "Whoever obeys me, obeys God; whoever disobeys me, disobeys God."[14] Such disobedience is "rewarded" with Hell: "My nation will enter Paradise, except those who rebel." When asked who these rebels were, the Prophet answered: "Whoever obeys me will enter Paradise; whoever disobeys me rebels."[15]

The Sunna links all past, present, and future Muslims. It also enables Muslims to maintain their unity, as it forms a unique culture and system. Concerning this, the Messenger declared: "Those who survive me will witness many disputes and disagreements. Therefore, follow my way and the way of my rightly-guided and rightly-guiding successors. Hold firm to that way—cling to it with your teeth."[16]

Following the Sunna, on both the individual and the collective level, becomes vital when Islam is attacked and Muslims lose their supremacy. The Messenger stated that "at a time when the Muslim community breaks with Islam and consequently disintegrates, the one who holds firm to the Sunna gains the reward of a martyr."[17] Given this, those who criticize it should be asked, as the Qur'an asks unbelievers: *Where are you headed?*

THE SUNNA'S ROLE

The Sunna has two main functions. First, it enjoins and prohibits, lays down the principles related to establishing all religious obligations and necessities, and determines what is lawful or unlawful. Second, it interprets the Qur'an.

In each daily prescribed prayer, we recite: *Guide us to the Straight Path, to the path of those you have blessed, not of those who incurred (Your) wrath, nor of the misguided* (1:5-7). The verses mention, but do not specify, two groups of people. According to the Prophet, those who incurred God's wrath are Jews who have gone astray, and the misguided are Christians who have gone astray.[18]

The Jews killed many of their Prophets and caused trouble in many places. Although they had once followed Divine guidance and guided others to the Straight Path (during the times of Moses, David, and Solomon), over time many of them went astray and incurred both God's wrath and public ignominy. Those who follow this way also are included in *those who incurred (Your) wrath*. Such Jews are condemned harshly in the Bible as well. In fact, the Bible is much harsher toward them than the Qur'an. In many verses, the Qur'an reproaches such Jews and Christians very mildly and compassionately.

At first, the Christians obeyed Jesus and followed his way despite severe persecution. They heroically resisted all forms of hypocrisy and Roman oppression. But over time, many came under the influence of various Middle Eastern religions and philosophies as well as Roman paganism. By the time Christianity became the Roman Empire's official religion, it already was divided into many sects and had more than 300 Gospels in circulation. Although many remained devoted to the original creed of Jesus, many others contaminated these pure teachings with borrowed elements. The Qur'an therefore describes them as the misguided.

By making the above interpretation, the Prophet explained how people who had been blessed with Divine guidance could go astray and end up deserving God's wrath. Thus, he warned Muslims not to follow such Jews and Christians.

Out of many examples showing how the Sunna interprets the Qur'an, we also cite the following:

- When the verse: *Those who believed and did not mix their belief with wrongdoing: for them is security and they are those who are truly guided* (6:82) was revealed, the Companions, well aware what wrongdoing meant, asked the Messenger fearfully: "Is there one among us who has never done wrong?" The Messenger explained: "It's not as you think. It's as Luqman said to his son: *Don't associate any partners with God; surely, associating partners with God is a grave wrongdoing*" (31:13).[19]

- 'A'isha and Ibn Mas'ud are of the opinion that the mid-time prayer in: *Attend the prayers without any omission and the mid-time prayer* (2:238) is the afternoon prayer. Once 'A'isha ordered her servant to write a copy of the Qur'an for her and reminded her: "When you come to the verse: Attend the prayers without any omission, and the mid-time prayer, inform me." When this verse was to be copied out, 'A'isha dictated to her servant: "Attend the prayers without any omission, and the mid-time prayer, the afternoon prayer," and added: "This is what I heard from the Messenger."[20] Although there are some other interpretations, 'A'isha and Ibn Mas'ud were certain that it was the afternoon prayer.

In addition to interpreting the Qur'an's ambiguities, the Sunna fills in the details about those subjects that the Qur'an mentions only briefly. For example, the Qur'an orders Muslims to pray properly, but does not explain how they should pray. Although some leading interpreters deduce the prayer times from such verses such as: *Perform the prayer correctly at the two ends of the day and nigh of the night; surely the good deeds remove the evil deeds* (11:114), the exact prayer time was established by the Prophet as follows:

> On two occasions, Archangel Gabriel led me in the five daily prayers at the Ka'ba. On the first time, he prayed the noon prayer at noon, when an item's shadow was only as long as its base. When the shadow was as long as the actual item, he prayed the afternoon prayer. He prayed the evening prayer when it was time for a person to break the fast. He prayed the late evening (or night) prayer when dusk disappeared, and the dawn (or morning) prayer when those who intend to fast can no longer eat or drink. The second time, he prayed the noon prayer when an item's shadow was as long as the actual item, and prayed the afternoon prayer when it was twice as long as the actual item. He prayed the evening prayer at the same time he had prayed it previously. He prayed the night prayer after one-third of the night had passed, and the dawn prayer when it was lighter and the sun had still not risen. Then he turned to

me and said: "O Muhammad, each of the five daily prayers should be performed between these two periods of time, as the Prophets before you did it."[21]

The Messenger also taught his community everything related to prayer: its conditions; all obligatory, necessary, and commendable acts that validate and ennoble it; and all acts that invalidate and damage it. He passed on, both through words and actions, all that they needed to know about worship. This all-inclusive term is not limited to the actual prayers, but also includes such areas as fasting, alms-giving, pilgrimage, and many more. Just as he told his followers to "pray as you see me pray," he told them to "learn from me the rites and ceremonies of pilgrimage"[22] after he actually performed it with his Companions. If the Qur'an had gone into such exhaustive detail on such matters, it would have been many times its present size.

The Sunna also restricts general laws and commandments in the Qur'an. For example, it lays down general principles of inheritance. When the Prophet's daughter Fatima went to Abu Bakr, the first Caliph, and asked for her inheritance, Abu Bakr replied: "I heard the Messenger say: 'The community of the Prophets does not leave anything to be inherited. What we leave is for charity.'"[23] This hadith excludes the Prophets and their children from the laws of inheritance. Likewise, the Messenger decreed that "the killer (of his testator) would be disinherited."[24] In other words, if someone kills his or her parents, brother (sister), or uncle (aunt), they cannot inherit from them.

The Qur'an commands: *And the thief, male and female, cut off the hands of both, as a recompense for what they have earned, and a punishment exemplary from God; God is All-Mighty, All-Wise* (5:38). Whether this punishment is to be applied to every thief, or only to those who steal goods of a certain value, is not clear.

Also, in: O believers, when you stand up to pray wash your faces, and your hands up to elbows... (5:6), the hand extends to the elbow. But the Qur'an does not mention specifically what part of the hand should be cut, nor in what circumstances this punishment should be applied. For example, during 'Umar's caliphate there was a period of famine, and he did not apply this punishment.

The Qur'an decrees: *O you who believe! Consume not your goods among yourselves in vanity [through theft, usury, bribery, hoarding, and so on], except it be trade by mutual agreement* (4:29). Islam encourages trade as a livelihood, as long as it is carried out according to Islamic law. One condition, as stated in the verse, is mutual agreement. However, the Messenger decreed: "Don't sell fruits until their amount is definite in the tree [so that the amount to be given as alms can be determined]"[25] and: "Don't go to meet peasants outside the market to buy their goods [Let them earn the market prices of their goods]."[26]

In sum, the Qur'an contains general principles that are explained by the Messenger and then applied by him to daily life. God allowed His Messenger to issue rulings, as necessary, and ordered the believers: Whatever the Messenger brings you, adopt it; whatever he forbids you, refrain from it (59:7).

CHAPTER 11

Establishing the Sunna

ESTABLISHING THE SUNNA

THE SUNNA HAD TO BE ESTABLISHED

The Sunna as one of the two main sources of Islam was memorized, recorded, and carefully preserved so that it could be passed down without distortion or alteration. The Sunna is included in the meaning of: *We have sent down the dhikr [the collection of Divine instructions and recitations, the Divine guidance] in parts, and certainly We are its preserver* (15:9).

The Sunna, the unique example set by the Messenger of God for all Muslims to follow, shows us how to bring our lives into agreement with God's Commands and obtain His good pleasure. This being the case, the Messenger stood at the intersection of ignorance and knowledge, truth and falsehood, right and wrong, and this world and the other. He established, through his words as well as his actions and those of which he approved, the Divine way that all Muslims must follow.

The Sunna is the window opened on the Messenger of God, the sacred way leading to the blessings of Islam. Without it, Muslims cannot implement Islam in their daily lives, establish a connection with the Messenger, or receive his blessings. Those who ignore it run a grave danger of deviating and placing themselves outside Islam, for it is an unbreakable rope guaranteeing Muslim unity and elevating those who hold fast to it to Paradise.

There are several motives for establishing the Sunna. Among them are the following:

- God commands Muslims to follow the Sunna:

> Whatever the Messenger brings you, adopt it; whatever he forbids you, refrain from it; fear God and seek His protection, surely God is He Whose punishment is severe. (59:7)

Besides relaying the Qur'an, the Messenger expanded on it through the Sunna. The word *whatever* covers everything related to the Qur'an (the Revelation Recited) and the Hadith (the Revelation Unrecited). He only spoke what was revealed to him, or inspired in him, by God. Verse 59:7 tells Muslims to obey the Messenger so that they can become deserving of God's protection. Aware of this, the Companions paid close attention to his every word and were very careful in carrying out his commands.

- A Muslim can obtain God's good pleasure and attain true bliss in both worlds only by following the Sunna, for its sole purpose is to lead humanity to safety and eternal happiness. The Qur'an declares:

> Verily, there is for you a most excellent example in the Messenger of God, for him who aspires to God and the Last Day, and mentions God oft. (33:21)

- The Messenger encourages Muslims to learn his Sunna. The Companions knew what they needed to do to avoid eternal punishment and receive God's blessing, and so zealously memorized and recorded the Prophet's sayings. They heard him pray:

> [On the day when some faces will be radiant and some mournful], may God make radiant [with joy and happiness] the face of the one who has heard a word from me and, preserving (memorizing) it, conveys it to others.[1]

According to another version, he prayed:

> May God make radiant the face of the servant who has heard my speech and, committing it to memory and observing it in daily life, conveys it to others.[2]

- The Companions knew the Prophet would intercede for them only if they followed the Sunna:

> On the Day of Judgment, I will put my head on the ground and ask God to forgive my nation. I will be told:

"O Muhammad, raise your head and ask; you will be given whatever you ask. Intercede; your intercession will be accepted."[3]

The Messenger spoke distinctly and sometimes repeated his words so his audience could memorize them.[4] He taught them supplications and recitations that were not in the Qur'an with the same care and emphasis as he taught the Qur'an.[5] He continually urged his Companions to spread his words and teach others what they knew. If they did not, he warned them: "If you are asked about something you know and then conceal that knowledge, a bridle of fire will be put on you on the Day of Judgment."[6] The Qur'an also conveys this warning:

> Those who conceal what God has sent down of the Book and sell it for a little price, they do not eat in their bellies but the fire; God shall not speak to them on the Day of Resurrection, nor shall He purify them; for them is a painful torment. (2:174)

Keeping these words and warnings in mind, the Companions strove to memorize the Qur'an and the Sunna and to record the latter. They then lived their lives in accordance with Islamic principles and commands, and conveyed what they knew to others. They formed study and discussion groups to refine their understanding. The Messenger encouraged them to do this:

> If people come together in a house of God and recite from the Book of God and study it, peace and tranquillity descends upon them, (God's) Compassion envelops them, angels surround them, and God mentions them to those in His presence.[7]

Other motives

The Companions lived in an ethos that never lost its freshness. Like a growing embryo in the womb, the Muslim community grew and flourished, eventually including all areas of life. It was fed continuously with Revelation. Such factors, along with the

Sunna and the Companions' devotion to the Prophet, drove them to record or memorize whatever The Messenger said or did.

For example, when 'Uthman ibn Mad'un died, the Messenger shed as many tears as he had over Hamza's corpse. He kissed his forehead and attended the funeral. Witnessing this, a woman said: "How happy you are, 'Uthman. You have become a bird to fly in Paradise." The Messenger turned to her and asked: "How do you know that, while I, a Prophet, do not know? Unless God informs, no one can know whether someone is pure enough to deserve Paradise and whether he will go to Paradise or Hell." The woman collected herself, and said that she would never make such an assumption again.[8] Is it conceivable that she and the Companions present at the funeral should have forgotten that event? They did not forget it, as well as others that they witnessed during the Prophet's lifetime.

Another example: Quzman fought heroically at Uhud, and was finally killed. The Companions considered him a martyr. However, the Prophet told them that Quzman had gone to Hell. Someone later informed them that Quzman had committed suicide because of his wounds, and had said before he died: "I fought out of tribal solidarity, not for Islam." The Messenger concluded: "God strengthens this religion even through a sinful man."[9] Like others, that event and his final comment could never have been forgotten by the Companions, nor could they have failed to mention it whenever they talked about Uhud or martyrdom.

A similar incident took place during the conquest of Khaybar. 'Umar reports:

> On the day Khaybar was conquered, some Companions listed the martyrs. When they mentioned so-and-so as a martyr, the Messenger said: "I saw him in Hell, for he stole a robe from the spoils of war before it was distributed." He then told me to stand up and announce: "Only believers (who are true representatives or embodiments of absolute faith and trustworthiness) can enter Paradise."[10]

Each word and action of the Messenger refined the Companions' understanding and implementation of Islam. This motivated them to absorb his every word and action. When they settled in newly conquered lands, they conveyed their knowledge to the new Muslims, thereby ensuring that the Sunna would be transmitted from one generation to the next.

They were so well-behaved toward the Messenger that they would remain silent in his presence and let bedouins or others ask him questions. One day a bedouin named Dimam ibn Tha'laba came and asked rudely: "Which one of you is Muhammad?" They replied that he was the white-complexioned man sitting against the wall.

The bedouin turned to him and asked loudly: "O son of 'Abd al-Muttalib, I will ask you some questions! They may be injurious to you, so don't become annoyed with me." The Prophet told him to ask whatever was in his mind. He said: "Tell me, for the sake of God, your Master and the Master of those before you, did He send you to these people as a Prophet?" When the Prophet said that this was true, Dimam asked: "Tell me, for God's sake, is it God Who ordered you to pray five times a day?" When the Prophet said that this was true, Dimam continued questioning him in the same manner about fasting and alms-giving. Always receiving the same answer, Dimam announced: "I am Dimam ibn Tha'laba, from the tribe of Sa'd bin Bakr. They sent me to you as an envoy. I declare that I believe in whatever message you have brought from God."[11]

Like many others, this event too was not allowed to fall into oblivion; rather, it was handed down to succeeding generations until it was recorded in the books of Tradition.

Ubayy ibn Ka'b was one of the foremost reciters of the Qur'an. One day the Messenger sent for him and said: "God ordered me to recite *Surat al-Bayyina to you*." Ubayy was so moved that he asked: "Did God mention my name?" The Messenger's answer moved him to tears.[12] This was so great an honor for Ubayy's family that his grandson would introduce himself as "the grandson of the man to whom God ordered His Messenger to recite *Surat al-Bayyina*."

This was the ethos in which the Companions lived. Every day a new "fruit of Paradise" and "gift" of God was presented to them, and every day brought new situations. Previously unaware of faith, Divine Scripture, and Prophethood, these desert Arabs, gifted with a keen memory and a talent for poetry, were brought up by the Messenger to educate future Muslim generations. God chose them as His Messenger's Companions, and willed them to convey His Message throughout the world.

After the Prophet's death, they conquered in the name of Islam all the lands from Spain to China, from Caucasia to India, with unprecedented speed. Conveying the Qur'an and the Sunna everywhere they went, many of the conquered people joined their households and embraced Islam. The Muslims instructed these new Muslims in the Qur'an and the Sunna, thereby preparing the ground for all the leading Muslim scholars and scientists to come.

The Companions considered memorizing and transmitting the Qur'an and the Sunna as acts of worship, for they had heard from the Messenger say: "Whoever comes to my mosque should come either to learn the good or to teach it. Such people have the same rank as those who fight in the way of God."[13]

Anas reports that they frequently met to discuss what they heard from the Messenger.[14] Women also were taught by the Messenger, who set aside a specific day for them. His wives actively conveyed to other women whatever they learned from the Messenger. Their influence was great, for through them the Prophet established family ties with the people of Khaybar (through Safiyya), the Banu Amir ibn Sa'sa'a (through Maymuna), the Banu Makhzum (through Umm Salama), the Umayyads (through Umm Habiba), and the Banu Mustaliq (through Juwayriya). The women of these tribes would come to their "representative" among the Prophet's household ask her about religious matters.

In the last year of his Messengership, the Messenger went to Makka for what has become known as the Farewell Pilgrimage. In his Farewell Sermon at 'Arafat to more than 100,000 people, he summarized his mission and told his audience: "Those who are here should convey my speech to those who are not."[15] Some time later, the last verse to be revealed commanded the Muslim community to practice and support Islam: *Fear a day when you will be returned unto God and every soul shall be paid what it earned; they will not be wronged* (2:281).

THE COMPANIONS AND THE SUNNA

The Companions obeyed the Messenger in everything. They were so imbued with love for him that they strove to imitate him in every possible way. In fact, the Qur'an itself led them to do this, for it states that obeying the Messenger is directly related to belief:

> But no, by your Master! They will not believe till they make you the judge in disputes between them, then they shall find in themselves no impediment touching your verdict, but shall surrender in full submission. (4:65)

The following are only a few examples of their degree of submission.

- Shortly before his death, the Messenger raised an army, appointed Usama to command it, and told him to "advance only as far as the place where your father was martyred, and strengthen our rule there."[16] The Messenger took to his bed before the army departed. When Usama visited him, the Messenger prayed for him.

  The army was just about to set out when the Messenger died. Abu Bakr, his immediate political successor and the first caliph, dispatched the army without a second thought, despite uprisings in various parts of Arabia. He accompanied the soldiers to the outskirts of Madina and said: "By God, even if wolves attack us from all directions, I will not lower a flag hoisted by the Messenger."[17]

- The Messenger's death shocked and grieved Madina's Muslims. The subsequent election to choose the caliph caused some dissension among the Companions. Abu Bakr shouldered a very heavy task, for the army was waiting to be sent, reports of uprisings were coming in, and small groups were not satisfied with his election.

Just at this juncture, Fatima (the Prophet's daughter) asked him for her share in the land of Fadak. Abu Bakr did not want to offend her, but also was determined to remain faithful to the Sunna. He used to say: "I can't forsake anything that the Messenger did."[18] He had heard something from the Messenger, which Fatima had not: "We, the community of the Prophets, do not bequeath anything. Whatever we leave is charity."[19]

- After the conquest of Makka, people from all over Arabia embraced Islam. Of course, many were not as devoted to Islam as the Companions. Some apostatized and, following Musaylima the Liar, revolted against Madina. Others showed signs of revolt by refusing to pay the prescribed alms-tax. Abu Bakr fought such people until peace and security reigned in Arabia once again.

- 'Umar was known as "the one who submits himself to truth." Unaware of the Prophet's decree, he put forward his own judgment about how much money should be paid to compensate someone for a cut finger. A Companion opposed him: "O Commander of the Faithful! I heard the Messenger say: 'The blood money for both hands together is the same as that paid for a life. This amount is shared out equally among the fingers, as ten camels for each.'"[20] 'Umar instantly withdrew his ruling and said to himself: "O son of Khattab! Do you dare to judge, through your own reasoning, on a matter the Messenger decreed?"

- Abu Musa al-Ash'ari went to visit 'Umar in his office. He knocked on the door three times and then left, for no one answered. After Abu Musa left, 'Umar opened the door and asked who had knocked. Learning that Abu Musa had knocked, 'Umar sent for him and asked why he had left. Abu Musa answered: "The Messenger said: 'When you visit someone, knock on the door. If you are not allowed to enter after you knock for the third time, go away,'" 'Umar asked him if he could verify this hadith, which was unknown to him. Abu Musa brought Abu Sa'id al-Khudri, who testified to its truth. 'Umar conceded.[21]

- When 'Umar was stabbed while prostrating in the mosque, he was asked if he wanted to designate his successor. 'Umar answered: "If I designate, one who is better than me (Abu Bakr) did so. If I do not designate, one who is better than me (the Messenger) did not do so."[22] 'Umar was certain to follow the latter action. However, to prevent any possible disagreement, he left the matter to a consultative committee that he formed for this very purpose.

- When 'Umar saw Zayd ibn Khalid al-Juhani perform a supererogatory prayer after the afternoon prayer, he reproached him for doing what the Messenger had not done. Zayd told him: "Even if you break my head into pieces, I shall never give up this two rak'a prayer, for I saw the Messenger perform it."[23]

  Umm Salama, one of the Prophet's wives, reported that one day her husband could not perform the two rak'a supererogatory prayer after the noon prayer because he was busy with a visiting delegation. So, he prayed that prayer after the afternoon prayer.[24] Zayd must have seen the Messenger perform it at that time.

- 'Ali once drank water while standing. Maysara ibn Ya'qub criticized him: "Why are you drinking while standing?" 'Ali answered: "If I do so, it's because I saw the Messenger do so. If I drink while sitting, it's because I saw the Messenger do so."[25]

- Instead of washing the feet during wudu', Muslims can wipe the upper surface of light, thin-soled boots worn indoors (or inside overshoes[26]) with wet hands. Showing the Sunna's supremacy over personal reasoning, 'Ali said: "If I had not seen the Messenger wipe the upper surface of his light, thin-soled boots, I would deem it more proper to wipe their soles."[27]

- If a Muslim kills another by mistake, the killer's heirs must pay blood-money. 'Umar thought that a wife could not inherit any blood-money due her husband. However, Dahhak ibn Abi Sufyan informed him that when Ashyam ibn Dibabi had been killed, the Messenger had given some of the blood-money to his wife. 'Umar declared: "From now on, wives will inherit from the blood-money of their husbands."[28]

- Abu 'Ubayda ibn Jarrah commanded the Muslim armies fighting in Syria. When 'Umar went to visit him in Amwas, pestilence had broken out already. Before 'Umar entered the city, 'Abd al-Rahman ibn al-'Awf told him: "I heard the Messenger say: 'If you hear that pestilence has broken out in a place, don't enter it. If you are in such a place already, don't leave it.'"[29] 'Umar, so obedient to the Sunna, returned home without seeing his faithful friend for the last time.

FURTHER REMARKS ON THE SUNNA'S IMPORTANCE

The Qur'an declares:

> It is not for any believer, man or woman, when God and His Messenger have decreed a matter, to have the choice in the affair. Whosoever disobeys God and His Messenger has gone astray into manifest error. (33:36)

> . . . Those who believe in Our signs, those who follow the Messenger, the unlettered Prophet, whom they find written down with them in the Torah and the Gospel, enjoining the good and forbidding the evil, making lawful the good things and making unlawful the corrupt things, and relieving them of their loads and the fetters that were upon them. Those who believe in him and succor him and help him, and follow the light that has been sent down with him—they are the ones who prosper. (7:156-57)

The Traditions further declare:

- The best of words is the Book of God; the best way to follow is that of Muhammad. The worst affair is innovations (against my Sunna). Each innovation is a deviation.[30]

- "Everyone of my community will enter Paradise, except those who rebel." When they asked who these rebels were, he replied: "Whoever obeys me will enter Paradise; whoever disobeys me is a rebel."[31]
- In the case of my community, I am like someone who has lit a fire. Insects and butterflies flock to it. I hold you by the cloth [of your garments to keep you away from the fire], but you pull yourselves into it.[32]
- Don't let me find any of you seated in armchairs, who, when something I ordered or forbade is reported to them, respond: "We have no knowledge of it. So, we follow whatever we find in the Book of God."[33]
- Be careful! Surely I have been given the Book and its like together with it.[34]
- Those who outlive me will witness many controversies. Follow my way and that of the rightly guided successors (caliphs) who will guide to truth. Hold fast to it and cling to it stubbornly with your teeth. Refrain from newly invented things (in religion), for each such thing is an innovation, and each innovation is a deviation.[35]
- I have left to you two precious things that, if you hold fast to them, will never lead you astray: The Qur'an and the Sunna.[36]

RELATING THE TRADITIONS

The Companions and the immeiately following generations were meticulous in narrating or transmitting these Traditions.[37] They showed the utmost care and exactness in separating sound Traditions from those that had been fabricated (to meet personal or sectarian needs). After memorizing them word for word, they transmitted the sound ones to the following generations.

The Messenger's warning and the Companions' self-control

Islam is distinguished from unbelief by its firm rooting in truthfulness. True Muslims do not lie. The Companions and their successors proved their attachment to Islam though their personal sacrifice. They also feared God, lived austerely, and avoided life's comforts. Many great scholars and saints appeared among them, and their examples are still followed.

Along with the emphasis Islam puts on truthfulness, God's Messenger severely warned people not to lie about him: "Those who lie about me should prepare their abodes in the Fire"[38] and: "Whoever relates from me falsely is a liar."[39] In the face of such warnings, would the Companions, who had sacrificed their entire lives for the cause of Islam, even think of lying about the Messenger?

Based on these considerations, the Companions took great care when narrating Traditions so that no mistake or misunderstanding would occur. For example 'Ali, the cousin of the Messenger and the fourth Caliph after him, used to say: "I fear to narrate a Tradition from the Messenger so much that I would rather fall from Heaven than speak a lie on his behalf."[40]

'Abd Allah ibn al-Mas'ud, among the first four or five people to accept Islam and one of the most knowledgeable and nearest Companions, was similarly careful. When asked to report from God's Messenger, he began with: "The Messenger of God said," stopped and bowed his head, breathed deeply and unbuttoned his collar while his eyes filled with tears. After the narration, he added: "The Messenger of God said this, or something like this, or something more or less like this."[41]

Zubayr ibn 'Awwam, one of the ten Companions assured Paradise, narrated only a few Traditions from God's Messenger for fear of making a mistake. When his son asked him why, he replied: "I am so afraid that I might say something contrary to what the Messenger really said. For he declared: 'Those who lie about me intentionally should prepare their abodes in the Fire.'"[42] Anas ibn Malik, who served the Messenger for 10 years, said: "If I were not so afraid of making a mistake, I would relate many more narrations from the Messenger."[43]

'Abd al-Rahman ibn Abi Layla met 500 Companions. When he visited a place, people would say: "The man who met 500 Companions has come to our town." He had a great influence on Abu Hanifa and Imam Abu Yusuf. He reports: "I was personally familiar with 120 Companions. Sometimes all of them were in the same mosque. When they were asked about something, each would wait for the other to answer. If they were asked to narrate a Tradition, no one would dare to. Finally, one of them would place his trust in God and begin to narrate. He would always add: 'The Messenger said this, or something like this, or something more or less like this.'"[44]

Zayd ibn Arqam was one of the first people to embrace Islam. In the early days of Islam, the Messenger would meet with the Muslims secretly in his house. Zayd was appointed superintendent of the public treasury during the caliphates of 'Umar and 'Uthman. When he saw 'Uthman give items from the treasury to his relatives, he told him: "O Commander of the Faithful. People will suspect me and will no longer trust me. Allow me to resign." When 'Abd al-Rahman ibn Abi Layla asked him to narrate a Tradition, Zayd answered: "My son, I have become old and forgetful. Narrating about the Messenger is not something easy."[45]

Literal narration

Although the literal narration is better and always preferable, narration of meaning is allowed if the narrator has an expert command of Arabic, if the word used is appropriate in the given context, and if the original has been forgotten. However, the Companions always narrated Traditions literally despite this permission. For example, one day 'Ubayd ibn 'Umayr narrated: "A hypocrite resembles a sheep left between *rabidayn* (two flocks)." 'Abd Allah ibn 'Umar objected: "He did not say so. I heard the Messenger say: 'A hypocrite resembles a sheep left between *ghanamayn* (two flocks).'"[46] The meaning is the same; the difference is only between the words *rabidayn* and *ghanamayn*.

This same care was adopted by the scholars or narrators of the generation immediately following the Companions: the Tabi'un (those who follow). For instance, someone narrated in the presence of Sufyan ibn 'Uyayna: "The Messenger forbade leaving the juice (of grapes, dates, and the like) to ferment (*an yuntabadha*) in bowls made of pumpkin and lined with pitch." Sufyan objected: "I heard Zuhri narrate: 'The Messenger forbade leaving the juice (of grapes, dates, and the like) to ferment (an yunbadha) in bowls made of pumpkin and lined with pitch.'"[47] There is no difference in meaning, only in the verb's conjugation.

Bara ibn 'Adhib related:

> The Messenger advised me: Perform wudu' before going to bed. Then lie on your right side and pray: "O God, I have sub-mitted myself to You and committed my affair to You. I have sheltered in You, in fear of You, and in quest of You. There is no shelter from You except in You. I believe in Your Book You sent down, and Your Prophet You raised." To memorize this immediately, I repeated it to the Messenger and said at the end of it "Your Messenger You raised." He corrected the final sen-tence, saying: "and Your Prophet You raised."[48]

People dream when they sleep. True dreams constitute 1/46 of Prophethood, for the Messenger had true dreams during the first 6 months of his 23-year period of Prophethood. As they are related to Prophethood, not to Messengership,[49] the Messenger corrected Bara. This care was shown by almost all Companions, who studied the Traditions they heard from the Messenger and then discussed them. The Messenger told them: "Memorize and study the Traditions, for some are related to others. Therefore, come together and discuss them."[50]

Verification

The Companions strove to verify the meaning of every Tradition. None of them lied, for their fear of Divine punish-ment was too great. However, reporters might have misunder-stood the Tradition, missed an important point while receiving it from the Messenger, or misinterpreted it. With no intention to oppose the Messenger, they exerted themselves to understand his true purpose and discussed what they received from him.

A woman asked Caliph Abu Bakr if she could inherit from her grandchildren. He answered: "I have seen nothing in the

Qur'an that allows this, nor do I remember the Messenger saying anything on this point." Mughira ibn Shu'ba stood up and said: "The Messenger allowed the grandmother to receive one-sixth (of the estate)." Abu Bakr asked Mughira if he could produce a witness to testify to this. When Muhammad ibn Maslama testified to it, Abu Bakr gave the woman one-sixth of her grandson's estate.[51]

When the Messenger declared: "Those called to account for their deeds on the Day of Judgment by God will be ruined," 'A'isha asked: "What about the Divine declaration in the Qur'an: *Then they will be called to account (for their deeds), and it will be an easy act of giving account?*" The Messenger answered: "It is about presentation. Everyone will give account to God for their deeds. If those who did evil deny their evil deeds, God will inform them of their deeds. Such people will be ruined."[52]

As recorded in Bukhari, 'Umar narrates:

> I heard Hisham ibn Hakim pronounce some words of Surat al-Furqan somewhat differently from the way the Messenger taught me. I waited patiently until he had finished praying, and then asked him: "Who taught you such a recitation?" When he told me that he had learned it from the Messenger, I took him to the Messenger and explained the situation. The Messenger asked Hisham to recite the sura, which he did. The Messenger nodded, saying: "This is the way it was revealed to me." Then he asked me to recite, which I did. Again he nodded and said: "Thus it was revealed." He added: "The Qur'an is revealed in seven different ways. Recite it in the way easiest for you."[53]

The Companions were so devoted to the Sunna that they would travel long distances to learn just one *hadith*. For example, Abu Ayyub al-Ansari traveled from Madina to Egypt to check one hadith's exact wording. Among those who had received it from the Messenger, only 'Uqba ibn Amir was still alive and living in Egypt. Abu Ayyub arrived in the capital city and, calling on its governor Maslama ibn Mukhallad, found a guide to take him to 'Uqba. When he found this Companion in a street, he asked him about: "Whoever covers (hides) a believer's defect in the world, God will cover his (or her) defects in the Hereafter."[54] Being told by ʿUqba that his memory was correct, Abu Ayyub took his leave, saying: "I came just to ask about this *hadith*. I wouldn't like to make my intention impure [by staying] for some other reason."[55]

As related in Bukhari, Jabir ibn ʿAbd Allah traveled for a whole month just to receive a *hadith* directly from its narrator, ʿAbd Allah ibn Unays. Finding ʿAbd Allah, he said: "I've been informed that you relate a *hadith* that I didn't hear from the Messenger. Fearing that one of us may die before I learn it, I have come to you." Jabir learned the *hadith* and returned to Madina.[56]

Such journeys continued throughout the following centuries. Saʿid ibn al-Musayyib, Masruq ibn Ajda, and others made long journeys to learn a single *hadith* or even to confirm a single letter of one *hadith*. Kathir ibn Qays relates that one such lover of knowledge traveled from Madina to Damascus to learn one *hadith* from Abu al-Dardaʾ.[57]

The Tabiʿun exhibited the same degree of caution as the Companions when narrating a Tradition. As stated by Aʿmash, they would prefer the sky to collapse on them than to add so much as a wrong vowel to a *hadith*.[58]

The Ahl al-Sunna wa al-Jamaʿa agree on the absolute truthfulness of the Companions.[59] However, after internal conflicts broke out among the Muslims, the Tabiʿun began to scrutinize whatever *hadith* they heard and to inquire about their narrators' truthfulness. Muhammad ibn Sirin says: "Before, we didn't ask about the narrators. But after the internal conflicts broke out, we began to ask."[60]

People of weak character and ungrounded faith fabricated Traditions to promote their sectarian beliefs. The Nasiba (the Umayyads and their supporters who opposed ʿAli) forged Traditions in favor of ʿUthman and Muʿawiya and against ʿAli, and the Rafidites (Shiʿa extremists) forged Traditions against ʿUthman and Muʿawiya and for ʿAli. This caused meticulous, truth-seeking scholars to undertake a detailed and careful examination of each reported *hadith* and its narrators' character. Abu al-ʿAliya says:

We were no longer content with what was reported to us from a Companion. We traveled to receive it directly from the Companion or Companions who had narrated it, and to ask other Companions who knew about it.[61]

Imam Muslim relates that Bushayr al-'Adawi narrated a *hadith* to Ibn 'Abbas. Noticing that the latter was not paying attention, Bushayr asked in surprise: "Why aren't you listening to me? I'm narrating a *hadith*." Ibn 'Abbas answered:

In the past, our hearts would jump for joy and excitement when somebody began to narrate a hadith, saying: "The Messenger said." We would be fully attentive. But after people began to travel from place to place, we only receive from those whom we already know.[62]

Ibn 'Abd al-Barr, the great scholar of Muslim Spain (Andalusia), reports from Amir ibn Sharahil al-Sha'bi, one of the greatest Tabi'un scholars: Rabi' ibn Husayn related to Sha'bi the *hadith*:

Those who recite ten times: "There is no god but God, One, and He has no partner. His is the kingdom, and His is all praise. He gives life and causes death. He is powerful over everything," may earn as much reward as those who free a slave.

Sha'bi asked Rabi' who had narrated that *hadith* to him. He said that 'Abd al-Rahman ibn Abi Layla' had done so. Sha'bi then left and found Ibn Abi Layla, who was living in another city. Ibn Abi Layla testified to the *hadith*'s authenticity, saying he had heard it from Abu Ayyub al-Ansari.[63]

Such great scholars as Ibn Shihab al-Zuhri, Ibn Sirin, Sufyan al-Thawri, Amir ibn Sharahil al-Sha'bi, Ibrahim ibn Yazid al-Naha'i, Shu'ba, Abu Hilal, Qatada ibn Di'ama, Hisham al-Dastawa'i and Mith'ar ibn Qudam did their best to determine which Traditions were authentic and which were fabricated. When they were unsure of a Tradition's authenticity, they would consult each other. For example, Abu Hilal and Sa'id ibn Abi Sadaqa asked Hisham al-Dastawa'i about one Tradition's exact wording just to be sure. Shu'ba and Sufyan al-Thawri referred to Mith'ar a matter about which they did not have exact knowledge.[64] Such great scholars did not allow fabricated Traditions to spread. Whenever and wherever they heard people known for their sectarian views narrate a Tradition, these Traditionists would ask who had related this Tradition to them.

Those truth-loving and truth-seeking scholars did not refrain from revealing the weaknesses of their families or relatives. For example, Zayd ibn Unaysa warned Traditionists not to receive *hadith* from his brother, perhaps because of his forgetfulness, carelessness, or sectarianism.[65] When asked about his father, 'Ali ibn al-Madini, the first to write on the Companions, answered: "Ask others about him." When they insisted, he explained: "Hadith means religion. My father is weak on this point."[66]

Waki' ibn Jarrah, who was brought up in the school of Abu Hanifa and was a tutor of Imam Shafi'i, said: "As far as I know, I have never forgotten anything once I heard it. Nor do I remember anything that I had to repeat in order to memorize, if I only heard it once." Despite his keen memory, Imam Shafi'i once complained to Waki' about his poor memory. Waki' answered: "Refrain from sin. Knowledge is a light from God, and so cannot be granted to sinful people." When his father Jarrah was narrating a *hadith*, Waki' was always nearby. When asked why, he answered: "My father works in the state's finance department. I am afraid he might soften some Traditions in favor of the government. I accompany him to prevent such a lapse."[67]

While the Traditions were being written down, they also were being memorized by some of the greatest Traditionists of Islamic history. For example, Ahmad ibn Hanbal memorized around one million Traditions, including authentic, good, weak, and fabricated ones (some were identical in text but had different narration chains). His *Musnad* contains only 40,000 Traditions out of 300,000 Traditions.

Yahya ibn Ma'in memorized both authentic and fabricated Traditions. When Ibn Hanbal asked him why he did so, he replied: "I inform people of fabricated Traditions so they may choose the authentic ones."[68] Many scholars engaged in this activity and knew hundreds of thousands of them by heart. Among them, the most famous are Zuhri, Yahya ibn Sa'id al-Qattan,

Bukhari, Muslim, Daraqutni, Hakim, Dhahabi, Ibn Hajar al-ʿAsqalani, and Imam Suyuti.

Thanks to the tremendous efforts of such Traditionists, authentic Traditions were distinguished from fabricated ones. In addition to recording authentic Traditions in volumes and memorizing them, many Traditionists wrote on the narrators' character so people would know who was reliable or unreliable, careful or careless, profound and meticulous or superficial, and God-fearing or heedless.

When people warned them that revealing people's defects would bring shame upon those people, they would reply: "Hadith means religion. Therefore it should be given greater care than the hiding of the narrators' defects."[69] Yahya ibn Saʿid al-Qattan, renowned for being alert to sins, used to say: "In the presence of God I would rather have them as enemies than the Messenger."[70]

Ensuring Authenticity

There were several ways to tell whether a Tradition had been fabricated or not. One was to encourage the narrators to confess. This was not uncommon among those who had fallen into sectarianism and then, being guided to the truth, acknowledged the Traditions they had fabricated.

In addition, the Traditionists were extremely sensitive to lying. If it could be proven that a narrator had lied even once, all Traditions coming from that source were rejected. Narrators had to be completely truthful, have a keen memory, be very careful in practicing Islam, and not be involved in sectarianism. Moreover, if reliable narrators became forgetful or had similar mental difficulties, their Traditions were no longer accepted. For example, when Ibn Abi Lahiʿa, famous for his austerity and God-consciousness, lost the notebook from which he used to relate Traditions, Imam Bukhari restricted himself to those of his narrations confirmed or reinforced by other reliable narrators.

It is said that one's literary style is identical with that particular person. So if you are a careful reader, you can identify an author by his or her style and distinguish him or her from others. Traditionists dedicated themselves to Hadith, and were so could distinguish easily between the Prophet's sayings and those of everyone else, no matter how gifted.

Another way was to judge them according to the Qur'an and the *mutawatir hadith*. If three or more Companions reported a *hadith* from the Prophet, which was then handed down by several transmission chains of reliable narrators, it is *mutawatir*. Traditions reported from the Prophet by one Companion are called *ahadi*. Such Traditions usually were accepted as authentic after judged according to the Qur'an and *mutawatir* Traditions.

Although not an objective method, some saintly scholars saw the Messenger while awake and received directly from him. The *hadith qudsi*: "I was a hidden treasure. I wished to be known, and so created the universe" is reported to belong to this class.[71] Jalal al-Din al-Suyuti is reported to have met with the Messenger several times while awake. Before writing down a *hadith* he considered authentic, Imam Bukhari performed *wudu'*, referred it to the Messenger, and recorded it in his notebook only after receiving the Messenger's approval.[72] Some Traditionists saw the Companion who had narrated the hadith from the Prophet.

The Traditionists wrote multi-volume works about narrators, in which they detailed these people's biographies: where and when they were born, where they emigrated and lived, their teachers, from whom they received and to whom they narrated Traditions, and when and where they died.

The first book of this genre was 'Ali ibn al-Madini's *Kitab al-Ma'rifat al-Sahaba* (The Book of Knowledge about the Companions). Among the most significant are the following: Ibn 'Abd al-Barr's *Al-Isti'ab fi Ma'rifat al-Ashab* (The Comprehensive Book of Knowledge about the Companions), Ibn Hajar al-'Asqalani's *Al-Isaba fi Tamyiz al-Sahaba* (Finding the Truth in Judging the Companions), Ibn al-Athir's *Usd al-Ghaba* (The Lions of the Forest), Ibn Sa'd's *Al-Tabaqat al-Kubra'* (a most comprehensive biographical dictionary of the leading Companions and of the Tabi'un scholars), and *Tarikh Ibn 'Asakir* (History by Ibn 'Asakir), *Tarikh al-Bukhari* (History by Bukhari) and Yahya ibn Ma'in's *Al-Tarikh al-Kabir* (The Great History).

The greatest Traditionists, among them Bukhari, Muslim, Tirmidhi, Abu Dawud, Nasa'i, Ibn Maja, and Ahmad ibn Hanbal, collected authentic Traditions in voluminous books. Others, such as Maqdisi, collected fabricated Traditions. Still others, who came later, tested once more the authenticity of all previously collected Traditions.

For example, Ibn al-Jawzi (d. 597 ah) judged several Traditions in Ibn Hanbal's *Musnad* to be either weakly transmitted or fabricated, although he belonged to Ibn Hanbal's legal school. Later, Ibn Hajar al-'Asqalani made a detailed examination of the same Traditions and, with the exception of thirteen, proved their authenticity. Jalal al-Din al-Suyuti (d. 911 ah) scrutinized them once more and concluded that none were fabricated, although a few may have weak chains of transmission. He also reviewed Ibn al-Jawzi's *Al-Mawdu'at al-Kubra'* (A Great Collection of Fabricated Traditions) and sorted out the authentic ones. Thinking that the rest might not be fabricated either, he wrote *Al-Laa'li al-Masnu'a* (The Artifical Pearls).

Other great Traditionists compiled additional compendia. Such leading Traditionists as Bukhari and Muslim, tremendously exacting scholars, did not include many Traditions in their collections. Hakim's *Al-Mustadrak 'ala al-Sahihayn* (Addendum to The Two Collections of Authentic Traditions) is a voluminous appendix to Bukhari and Muslim. It was reviewed closely by Hafiz Dhahabi, who was famous for his keen memory.

In later centuries, books were written on widespread maxims, wise sayings, or proverbs regarded as Hadith. Sakhawi's *Maqasid al-Hasana* and 'Ajluni's *Kashf al-Khafa'* examined them one by one and explained which are truly Traditions and which are not. For example, apart from many authentic Traditions and Qur'anic verses encouraging people to learn, such popular sayings as: "Seek knowledge from the cradle to the grave" and "Seek knowledge even if it is in China" were tested by the Traditionists and shown not to be real Traditions.

After such tremendous studies, detailed examinations, and exacting verifications, we can state that the collections of authentic Traditions no longer contain fabricated Traditions. Those who continue to question the Traditions and Sunna act out of nothing more than religious, political, and ideological prejudice, as well as from biased Orientalist scholarship, to cast doubt on this vital source of Islam and its implementation in one's daily life.

Examples

Some examples of fabricated Traditions are the following:

- Abu Hanifa is perhaps the greatest Muslim jurist, and still shines like a sun in the sky of Islamic jurisprudence. But the saying attributed to the Prophet that "Abu Hanifa is the lamp of my nation" is not a *hadith*.[73] It must have been fabricated for sectarian considerations.

- "Have white cockerels" must have been forged by a white cockerel seller, even though we like white cockerels.[74]

- "Beware of the evil of one to whom you have done good" is another illogical saying wrongly attributed to the Prophet.[75] You can win somebody's heart by being good to him or her. If it were permissible to attribute a saying to the Prophet, I would say: "Do good to the one whose evil you fear," for it is said that "people are the slaves of the good done to them."

- Although rationality is a principle of Islam, Islam does not depend upon rationalism. No one can judge the Qur'an and the Prophet according to the dictates of individual reason. Islam is the collection of principles established by God, the Owner and Giver of all reasoning and intellect. Therefore, the saying: "Discuss among yourselves a saying attributed to me. If it agrees with the truth, confirm it and adopt it as a religious principle. It doesn't matter whether I have uttered it or not," is a fabrication.

- Another saying wrongly attributed to the Messenger is: "I was born in the time of the just king."[76] This was fabricated to exalt the Persian king Anushirwan. No one can confer honor on the Messenger, who himself brought honor to the whole of creation, most particularly to our world.

- Another widespread beautiful saying is also mistakenly thought to be a Tradition: "Cleanliness comes from belief." The meaning is true, but it was not reported from the Messenger through a sound chain of transmission. Instead, he said: "Purity (in body, mind, and heart) is half of belief, and *al-hamdu li-Allah* (all praise be to God) fills up the balance (where the good deeds will be weighed)."[77]

- Aqiq is a place located between Madina and Makka. During a journey, the Messenger told those traveling with him to: "Set up your tents at Aqiq." In Arabic, the word translated as *set up your tents is takhayyamu*. Since diacritical points were not used in writing during the early days of Islam, this word was confused with *takhattamu* (wear a ring). In addition, *aqiq* is used for cornelian. All this led to a false Tradition: "Wear a ring of cornelian," with the addition of "because it removes poverty."[78]

- "Looking at a beautiful face is an act of worship" is another false Tradition, one plainly slanderous against the Messenger.

- The saying: "Seek knowledge even if it is in China" is another false Tradition. It may have been fabricated to encourage learning. However, the Prophet has many sayings, and the Qur'an urges Muslims to learn or to seek knowledge: *Only those of His servants fear God who have knowledge* (35:28), and: *Say: "Are they equal—those who know and those who don't know?"* (39:9). In addition, the Prophet said: "Angels spread their wings beneath the feet of those who seek knowledge, because they are pleased (with them)."[79]

Some examples of authentic Traditions labelled as fabricated are the following:

- Imam Bukhari relates in his Sahih: This is in the Torah: "O Prophet, We have sent you as a witness, a bringer of good tidings and a warner, and a refuge for the unlettered. You are My servant and Messenger. I named you 'the one who places his trust in God.' He is not harsh and rude, nor one who shouts in the streets. He does not repel evil with evil; instead, he pardons and forgives. God will not take his soul until He guides the deviant people to believe that there is no god but God, and thereby opens blind eyes and deaf ears and hardened hearts."[80] Orientalists and their Muslim followers criticize this *hadith* because it was reported by ʿAbd Allah ibn ʿAmr ibn al-ʿAs, who sometimes narrated from Kaʿb ibn al-Akhbar. What they neglect to consider is that:

- This *hadith* does not contradict the characteristics of the Messenger described in the Qurʾan and other Islamic sources.

- Despite their distortions and alterations, the Torah and the Gospels still contain references to the Messenger. The Qurʾan points to this in several verses, among them: *Those who follow the Messenger, the unlettered Prophet whom they find written in the Torah and the Gospel with them* (7:157); and: *This is their like in the Torah, and their like in the Gospel is this* (48:29). Husayn Jisri, who lived during the first half of the twentieth century, found 124 allusions to the Messenger in the Torah and the Gospels. *The Gospel of Barnabas* explicitly mentions Prophet Muhammad.

- Kaʿb al-Akhbar was a Jew who accepted Islam. Many Christians and Jews embraced Islam, especially during its early spread in Africa and Asia. They brought with them their previous knowledge, but that which was contrary to Islam was either corrected or mostly rejected. Such Companions as ʿAbd Allah ibn ʿAbbas, Abu Hurayra, Anas ibn Malik, and ʿAbd Allah ibn ʿAmr ibn al-ʿAs listened to Kaʿb's narrations from the Torah. It was impossible for them to accept anything contrary to Islam. Would ʿAbd Allah ibn ʿAmr, an ascetic who was deeply devoted to Islam and the Prophet, lie or fabricate a Tradition when he knew the punishment for such an action?

• During a severe famine and drought, Caliph ʿUmar held the hand of ʿAbbas, the Prophet's uncle, and prayed: "O

God! While he was alive our Prophet prayed to You for rain, and You sent down rain. Now we take his uncle as the means to pray to You for rain, so send down rain."[81] Some criticize this Tradition based on Jahiz's objection. But Jahiz is not a Traditionist; rather, he sought to deny even the most authentic Traditions. His teacher was Nazzam, a materialist belonging to the Mu'tazila heterodox sect. Jahiz criticizes this Tradition in his *Al-Bayan wa al-Tabyin* as follows:

> In all the Traditions attributed to 'Umar with regard to praying for rain, there are defects making it difficult for us to accept their authenticity. In some versions, he prayed on the pulpit; in others, in an open area; and still in others, after a prescribed prayer. Such confusions show that those Traditions are not authentic.

The science of Hadith requires profound specialty. Jahiz is not a specialist. Neither is Ibn Abi al-Dunya, who, although a blessed ascetic, criticizes this Tradition in his book, which contains many mistakes and fabricated Traditions. Imam Ghazali is one of the few great revivers of the Islamic religious sciences and one of our greatest religious guides. Yet if you mention him as a reference in a disputed matter of Hadith, Traditionists will laugh at you. A doctor is not asked about engineering, and no one goes to a chemist for medical information or advice.

Second, using somebody or something as a means to reach God, provided you understand that the means do not affect the outcome, is allowed: *O you who believe! Fear God and seek a means to Him* (5:35). The Companions usually asked the Messenger to pray on their behalf. Once during a drought, they asked him to pay for rain. He did so, and it rained so heavily that they had to ask him to pray for it to stop. He prayed on the pulpit, and the people went to their houses in sunlight. After this explicit favor of God, the Messenger said: "I bear witness that

God is powerful over everything, and that I am His servant and Messenger."[82]

The Qur'an encouraged the Companions to ask the Messenger to seek God's forgiveness for them, emphasizing that his praying is a means of peace and tranquility:

> We never sent any Messenger, but that he should be obeyed, by the leave of God. If, when they wronged themselves, they had come to you, and prayed forgiveness of God, and the Messenger had prayed forgiveness for them, they would have found God All-Forgiving, All-Compassionate. (4:64)

and: *Pray for them; your prayers are a comfort for them* (9:103). Once a blind man complained to the Messenger about his blindness. The Messenger advised him to perform *wudu'*, pray two *rak'as*, and say:

> O God, I ask You and turn to You for the sake of Your Prophet Muhammad, the Prophet of mercy. O Muhammad, I turn to my Master for your sake for my need to be met. O God, accept his intercession with You on my behalf!

The man did so and recovered his sight.[83] In conclusion, nothing in the Tradition ruins its authenticity.

• It is reported in almost all of the six most authentic books of Tradition: "If a dog licks your bowl, clean it seven times; the first time with soil, the other six with water."[84] Some who are unaware of Hadith principles and medical developments doubt this *hadith*'s authenticity, despite its authentic chain of transmission and its being a proof of Muhammad's Prophethood. Had he not been a Prophet taught by God, how could he have known medical facts discovered only centuries later? We now know that dogs may carry microbes of certain diseases in their saliva and excrement, and that these can harm human health if they are transmitted.

Moreover, no one in the Propeht's era knew about disinfection and sterilization. The Messenger, being a Prophet taught by the All-Knowing, recommends soil to clean a bowl licked by a dog. Today we know that soil is a good antiseptic that contains such substances as tetracycline.

Some interpret *seven times* to mean as many times as needed to clean the bowl. Hanafi jurists regard it as sufficient to clean the bowl three times.

- Some contemporary critics, including the French convert Maurice Bucaille, were quick to criticize the following Tradition, reported by Abu Hurayra: "When a fly falls into one of your bowls, dip it completely in the food before taking it out, for there is disease in one wing [or side] and a cure in the other."[85] This Tradition's narrators are beyond reproach. It was included by Bukhari, Abu Dawud, Nasa'i, Darimi, and Ahmad ibn Hanbal.

  Like the previous Tradition, this one contains a proof of Muhammad's Prophethood. At that time, no one knew that flies carry germs. Moreover, we now know that when a fly falls into a bowl, it tries to hold one wing off the food so it can take off again. As a result, it leaves its bacteria in the food. But when it is submerged in the food with a slight touch, the tiny bag on the other wing or side (the word *janah* has both meanings) bursts open and scatters anti-bacteria to kill the germs left on the food.

- Another authentic, but criticized, Tradition mentioned in all the authentic books of Tradition is: "It is not worth setting out to visit [intending to gain spiritual reward] any mosque other than al-Masjid al-Haram [the Holy Mosque surrounding the Ka'ba], the Prophet's Mosque [in Madina], and al-Masjid al-Aqsa' [just south of the Dome of the Rock in Jerusalem]."[86] This Tradition is criticized for being reported by Companions who narrated from Ka'b al-Akhbar or that it sanctifies al-Masjid al-Aqsa'. This pretext is completely groundless, for it does not belong to the Jews. Our Prophet turned to it while praying in Makka.

It is also the symbol of Islam's terrestrial dominion. Our Prophet was first taken to al-Masjid al-Aqsa' during his Ascension and led prayer there before the souls of the previous Prophets. God declares that *He blessed the vicinities of this mosque* (17:1). This blessed land surrounding it was first captured by Prophet Yusha (Joshua) ibn Nun after the death of Moses. After Prophet Muhammad, it was recaptured during 'Umar's caliphate. Salah al-Din Ayyubi, one of the greatest Muslim commanders, retook it from the Crusaders. If the Messenger included it among the three mosques most blessed and worthy of visiting, despite difficulties of travel, it is because God sanctified it.

Despite their sanctity, however, it is a mistake to assume a special kind of prayer in those mosques. As reported by Ibn 'Abbas, a woman promised God that she would pray in al-Masjid al-Aqsa' if she recovered from her illness. She recovered and, before setting out, called on Maymuna (one of the Messenger's wives), who told her:

> Stay here, mind your house, and pray in the Mosque of the Prophet. I heard the Messenger say: "Prayer performed here is 1,000 times better than that performed in any other mosque, except that of the Ka'ba."[87]

- The Messenger declared: "Among my Community there will always be a group who support the truth, until the Command of God will come [the Last Day]. Those who oppose them will not be able to harm them."[88]

Despite being recorded in almost all authentic books of Tradition and proved by the long history of Islam, this Tradition has been subjected to unjustifiable criticism. Islam has resisted all attacks. No earthly power has been able to destroy it. Even after the concerted efforts to do so during the last 3 centuries, Islam is the only alternative, stronger and fresher than ever, for true human happiness and prosperity in both worlds.

God has preserved Islam through a devoted self-sacrificing community in every period. This community concentrated, in one period, in Damascus, and in another, in Baghdad or Istanbul; once around 'Umar ibn 'Abd al-'Aziz, and then around Imam Ghazali or Imam Rabbani. While concentrating around a particular person in one place, they may have come together, in another, around someone else. Nor will the world be lacking in such groups in the future.

• Another Tradition denied by some is: "When you get up from your bed, don't put your hand in a bowl [of food or drink] before washing it three times. You don't know where your hands have been while you were asleep."[89]

Ahmad Amin and Abu Rayya, under the influence of the Orientalist Goldziher, ridicule this Tradition, even though it contains principles of hygiene. People often suffer from allergies or an itch. They might have scratched the affected places while sleeping, thereby accumulating germs, particularly under their fingernails. If such people eat (from communal bowls) without washing their hands, other people may become infected.

The Messenger always depended on Revelation, whether explicit or implicit. His Companions, famous for truthfulness, followed him as closely as possible and narrated whatever they received from him. Meticulous, truth-loving Traditionists collected the Traditions reaching them through reliable, trustworthy, and upright narrators. Some authentic Traditions predict certain future events and scientific developments. Just as none of these have yet proven to be false, so too no one has been able to falsify any other authentic Traditions.

Creation still holds some mysteries, and will continue to do so, regardless of human scientific and other progress. Psychic events or supernormal phenomena like telepathy and second sight, necromancy and other transcendental experiences, give clues to the existence of worlds or dimensions different from our own. As it is possible to find references to this in the Qur'an, some Traditions also may be dealt with from this viewpoint.

- As recorded in authentic books of Tradition, Tamim al-Dari, a Christian convert, tells of a hairy creature called "Jassasa" whom he saw in a strange island, and of a gigantic man who lives in a cave and introduces himself as the Dajjal (Anti-Christ).[90] We cannot deny this Tradition on positivistic premises, just as we cannot deny that the breast of our Prophet was burst open.

- Another Tradition that we can deal with partly from the same viewpoint is that God enjoined 50 daily prayers during the Ascension of Prophet Muhammad. On his return, Moses warned him about the difficulty of such an order. After the Prophet's repeated appeals, God reduced the number to five.[91]

There are delicate points in this *hadith*. God is All-Forgiving. He knows how many prayers a day His servants can endure, and expects them to pray to Him for forgiveness and to realize their goals. Praying or supplicating is a mystery of servanthood to God and the cornerstone of servanthood. When servants perceive their poverty, inadequacy, and impotence, they come to depend on their Master's absolute and infinite Richness and Power, thereby acquiring immeasurable power and inexhaustible wealth. Servants should be reminded repeatedly of this so that they are not left to their carnal, evil-commanding, and self-conceited selves. If they are not so reminded, they are subject to incurable, unrecoverable helplessness and destitution.

As Prophet Muhammad is the last Prophet, he encompasses all aspects and dimensions of Prophethood and confirms all previous Prophets. If we compare Prophethood to a huge blessed tree with branches spreading throughout the universe, Prophet Muhammad represents it in its entirety. His Prophethood is rooted deeply in the mission of all earlier Prophets. Therefore, it is natural for him to benefit from his roots.

Moses preceded him, so desiring ease for his nation in carrying out its religious duties, Prophet Muhammad justifiably followed his advice. Although the greatest Prophet, he never allowed his followers to regard the others Prophets as inferior to him.

This matter requires further elaboration, as there is much to be said on it. However, this subject is beyond the scope of this book.

The Number of Authentic Traditions

Some Orientalists and their Muslim followers try to cast doubt on the Sunna's authenticity on the pretexts that some Companions narrate too many Traditions and that there are vast numbers of Traditions.

First, the Traditions are not limited to the Messenger's words. Rather, they cover his entire life: all his actions, likes and dislikes, and approvals or tacit confirmations of what his Companions said and did. He lived for 23 years among them as a Messenger of God. He taught them Islam down to its minutest details. He led the prayer five times a day, every detail of which was recorded, for he told them: "Pray as you see me praying." He fasted and explained all of its details to them, just as he did for alms-giving and pilgrimage. The essentials of belief and pillars of Islam (prayer, fasting, alms-giving, and pilgrimage) alone are the subjects of countless books.

Being a universal Divine system that includes everything related to human life, Islam has laws and regulations for individual and collective life: spiritual and material, social and economic, political and military, and all other aspects faced during one's daily life. He laid down principles related to all these. He constantly warned his Companions against deviation, and encouraged them to be deeper, more sensitive, and more careful servants of God.

He also told them about former nations and predicted future events. Abu Zayd 'Amr ibn Akhtab reported that sometimes the Prophet would ascend the pulpit after the dawn prayer and address the congregation until noon. He would continue talking after the noon and afternoon prayers, telling them what had happened from the beginning of the world until that time, and what would happen from then until the Last Day. Such addresses would include information on the upheavals of the other world, the grave, the Resurrection, the Great Mustering, balancing people's deeds, the Last Judgment, the Bridge, and Hell and Paradise.[92]

The Messenger commanded armies, heard and tried cases as a judge, sent and received envoys and delegations. He signed peace treaties, waged war, and dispatched military expeditions. He laid down rules of hygiene and principles of good conduct and high morality. His miracles number in the hundreds. As he set an example to be followed by Muslims, and because of the vital importance of Hadith in Islam as well as his Companions' love of him, his life was recorded from beginning to end.

He honored the universe with his Messengership, His servanthood to God, and his exalted, peerless personality. As honored witnesses of his life, the Companions recorded everything related to him. When they scattered throughout the lands conquered by Islam, new converts asked them to relate Traditions from the Messenger. They were so deeply devoted to him that they remained extraordinarily faithful to their memories of him.

Once during his caliphate, 'Umar passed by the house of 'Abbas, the Prophet's uncle, on his way to the Friday congregational prayer. A few drops of blood fell on his robe from the gutter. He became so angry that he pulled the gutter to the ground, saying to himself: "Who slaughtered an animal on this roof so that its blood should stain my robe when I'm going to the mosque?" He reached the mosque and, after the prayer, warned the congregation: "You are doing some wrong things. I was passing by such and such a wall on my way here, when some blood dropped onto my robe from the gutter. I pulled the gutter to the ground."

'Abbas was upset and sprang to his feet: "O 'Umar, what have you done!? I personally saw the Messenger put that gutter there in person." Now, it was 'Umar's turn to be upset. He said to 'Abbas in great agitation: "By God, I will lay my head at that wall's foot and you will put your foot on it to replace the gutter. Until you do that, I will not raise my head from the ground." Such was their devotion and faithfulness to the Messenger.[93]

The Messenger implanted such a zeal for learning in his followers' hearts that Islamic civilization, under the blessed shadow of which a considerable portion of humanity lived peacefully for centuries, was built on the pillars of belief, knowledge, piety, and brotherhood. In the lands through which the pure water of Islam flowed, innumerable flowers burst open in every field of science, and the scent diffused by them exhilarated the world.

Some of these flowers, like Ibn Hajar al-Asqalani, read in two or three sessions the entire collection of authentic Traditions compiled by Imam Muslim. Imam Nawawi dedicated himself so thoroughly to teaching and writing that he never married—he did not want to assign any time to anything other than knowledge. Imam Sarakhsi, a great Hanafi jurist, was imprisoned in a well by a king. During that time, he dictated his monumental 30-volume compendium, *Al-Mabsut*, to his students from memory. When his students told him that Imam Shafi'i, founder of the Shafi'i legal school and regarded by some as the second reviver of Islam, had memorized 300 fascicules of Traditions, he answered: "He knew the zakat (one-fortieth) of what I know."[94]

The works of Ibn Hajar al-Asqalani, Ibn Jarir al-Tabari, Fakhr al-Din al-Razi, Imam Suyuti, and others cover so many volumes that when divided among the days of their lives, we can see that they wrote about 20 pages every day. We cannot study or even read during our lives what each wrote during his lifetime.

Anas ibn Sirin, son of Muhammad ibn Sirin, one of the greatest Tabi'un scholars, says: "When I arrived in Kufa, 4,000 people were attending Hadith courses in mosques; 400 were experts in Islamic jurisprudence."[95] To understand what it meant to be an expert in Islamic jurisprudence, consider the following: Ahmad ibn Hanbal, whose *Musnad* contains 40,000 Traditions chosen from among the one million in circulation, was not considered an expert jurist by Ibn Jarir al-Tabari. Nor was he given the same status as Abu Hanifa, Imam Abu Yusuf, Imam Shafi'i, Imam Malik, and the like. The fact that some did not consider such a great figure an expert jurist shows just what intellectual and scholarly heights a jurisprudent had to reach to be regarded as an expert.

The general atmosphere was extremely propitious for the development of both religious and secular sciences, especially the science of Tradition. Every Muslim strove to acquire knowledge of Islam and recognize its Holy Prophet fully. People had a great aptitude for literature and languages, for poetry was widespread during the pre-Islamic period.

The Qur'an came, first of all, as an absolute and incomparable linguistic miracle. No literary or poetic expert denied its eloquence, and almost all of them gave up poetry after their conversion to dedicate themselves to the Qur'an and the Hadith. One of them, the poetess Hansa, became so deeply devoted to Islam that when her four sons were martyred at Qadisiyah, she praised God, saying: "O God, You gave me four sons, all of whom I have sacrificed in the way of Your Beloved (Prophet). Praise be to You, to the number of thousands."[96]

Life was quite simple in the desert. This enabled people to commit themselves to Islamic sciences. Also, they had very keen memories. For example, the Messenger once asked Zayd ibn Thabit to learn Hebrew; within a couple of weeks, he could read and write letters in Hebrew.[97] Ibn Shihab al-Zuhri, Qatada ibn Diama, Sha'bi, Ibrahim ibn Yazid al-Nakha'i, Imam Shafi'i, and many others publicly said that they never forgot a word after they memorized it. They could do this after either reading or hearing something only once.

When Imam Bukhari arrived in Baghdad, ten leading persons in Islamic sciences tested his knowledge of Hadith and memory. Each recited ten Traditions, changing either the order of the narrators in a chain of transmission or the chains with each other. For example, the famous Tradition: "Actions are judged according to intentions..." has the following chain (in descending order): Yahya ibn Sa'id al-Ansari, from Muhammad ibn Ibrahim al-Taymi, from Alqama ibn Waqqas al-Laysi, from 'Umar ibn al-Khattab. When they were finished, Imam Bukhari corrected the chains one by one from memory and repeated each Tradition with its own sound chain of transmission. The scholars then admitted his learning and knowledge of Hadith.[98] Ibn Khuzayma went so far as to say: "Neither Earth or Heaven has seen a second person as knowledgeable as you in this field."[99]

Imam Bukhari never sold his knowledge for worldly benefits. When the ruler of Bukhara invited him to his palace to teach his children, the great Imam refused, saying: "Knowledge cannot be debased by being taken to a ruler. If the ruler desires knowledge, he should personally come to knowledge." The ruler replied by asking him to assign one day a week to his children. Bukhari refused again, saying: "I'm busy with teaching the Umma of Muhammad. So, I cannot waste my time teaching your children." The ruler exiled him, and this greatest figure in the science of Hadith spent his last days in exile.[100]

Recording the Traditions

The first written compilations of Traditions were made during 'Umar ibn 'Abd al-'Aziz's caliphate, at the beginning of the second Islamic century (719-22). However, it should be remembered that all Traditions that would be collected and arranged in books were in oral circulation. In addition, most of them already had been recorded in individual collections.

The overwhelming majority of Arabs were unlettered. When the Revelation began, a desire to learn to read and write was aroused and encouraged by the Prophet. Remember that he released literate prisoners captured at Badr only after each of them had taught ten Muslims to read and write.[101] Moreover, the Revelation began with the command:

> Read, in the name of your Master, Who has created. He created man from a clot suspended (on the wall of the womb). Read, Your Master is the All-Munificent, Who taught (to write) with the pen. He taught man what he had not known. (96:1-5)

Despite the importance attached to knowledge and learning, in the early period of his Messengership the Prophet did not allow his Companions to write down what he said. For example, he said: "Don't write down what I say. If you have written down something received from me that is not part of the Qur'an, destroy it."[102] He did not want the Companions to confuse the Qur'anic verses with his own words. The Qur'an was still being revealed and recorded on sheets or fragments of leather or wood; it would assume its final book form at a later date.

This was an understandable precaution, for he wanted to be sure that later generations would not mistake his words for those of God. This is clear from a Tradition narrated by Abu Hurayra: "The Messenger once came near us while some friends were writing down what they had heard him say. He asked what they were writing, and they replied: 'What we heard you say.' The Messenger warned: 'Do you know that the communities preceding you went astray because they wrote down that which is not found in the Book of God?'"[103]

Another reason for this prohibition is that most of the Qur'anic Revelations came on specific occasions. Thus, some of its verses are concise and clear while others are ambiguous. Allegorical verses appear beside explicit and incontrovertible ones. As a purely Islamic community was still evolving, some commandments came to replace earlier ones.

The Messenger also had to address, on various occasions, people with widely varying temperaments and levels of understanding, as well as "new" and "old" Muslims. For example, when a new Muslim asked what the best deed was, he answered that it was belief and performing the five prescribed prayers. However, during a time when jihad had priority, he said it was jihad in the way of God. Further, since Islam is for all time and all people, he frequently resorted to allegories, similes, parables, and metaphors.

These and other factors might have led him to forbid certain individuals to record his words. If everyone had kept a personal account and been unable to distinguish between the real and the metaphorical, the concrete and the abstract, the abrogated and the abrogating, the general and the particular and occasional, the result would have been chaos and misunderstanding. For this reason, 'Umar sometimes warned people not to narrate Prophetic Traditions carelessly.

However, many Traditions state that the Messenger allowed his Companions to write down his words. A time came when the Companions attained the intellectual and spiritual maturity to distinguish between the Qur'an and the Hadith. Therefore, they could give the proper attention and importance to each, and understand the circumstances relevant to each Tradition. And so the Messenger encouraged them to record his Traditions.

Abu Hurayra relates: "'Abd Allah ibn 'Amr ibn al-'As is the only Companion who has as many Traditions as I do. I didn't write them down, but he did."[104] 'Abd Allah reported that he wrote down whatever he heard from the Messenger. Some people told him: "You're writing down everything coming from God's Messenger's mouth. He is a human being; sometimes he is angry and other times he is pleased." 'Abd Allah referred the matter to God's Messenger, who pointed to his mouth and said: "Write down, for I swear by Him in Whose hand is my life that only truth comes out from this."[105]

Whether angry or pleased, God's Messenger *never spoke on his own; out of personal caprice or whim. Whatever he spoke, is a Revelation [explicit or implicit] revealed* (53:3-4). As his every word and action had some bearing on Islam, they had to be recorded. The Companions did this holy task either through memorizing or recording what they heard or saw. As a result, his life is the most complete biography ever produced. Every aspect, even its minutest details, has been handed down throughout the generations. This is why we should feel indebted to the Companions and the two or three generations after them, especially the great Traditionists, who recorded and then transmitted his words and actions.

Someone once complained to the Messenger: "O Messenger of God, we hear many things from you. But most of them slip our minds because we cannot memorize them." The Messenger replied: "Ask your right hand for help."[106] In other words, write down what you hear. When Rafi' ibn Khadij asked the Messenger whether they could write down what they heard from him, he was told that they could.[107] As recorded in al-Darimi's *Sunan*, the Messenger advised: "Record knowledge by writing."[108] During the conquest of Makka, the Messenger gave a sermon. A Yemeni man named Abu Shah, stood up and said: "O Messenger, please write down these [words] for me." The Messenger ordered this to be done.[109]

'Ali had a sheet, which he attached to his sword, upon which was written narrations about the blood-money to be paid for injuries, the sanctification of Madina, and some other matters.[110] Ibn 'Abbas left behind a camel-load of books, most of which deal with what he had heard from the Messenger and other Companions.[111] The Messenger sent a letter to 'Amr ibn Hazm, which dealt with blood-money for murder and injury, and the law of retaliation.[112] This letter was handed down to Abu Bakr ibn Muhammad, his great-grandson.

Likewise, a scroll transferred from the Messenger to Abu Rafi' was handed down to Abu Bakr ibn 'Abd al-Rahman ibn Harith, one of the Tabi'un.[113] A leading scholar of that generation, Mujahid ibn Jabr, saw 'Abd Allah ibn 'Amr's compilation *Al-Sahifat al-Sadiqa*. Ibn al-Athir, a renowned historian, writes that it contained about 1,000 Traditions, half of which were recorded in authentic books of Tradition, with the chain from 'Amr ibn Shu'ayb, from his father, and from his grandfather, respectively.

Jabir ibn 'Abd Allah al-Ansari also left behind a voluminous book containing the sayings he had heard from the Messenger.[114] *Al-Sahifa al-Sahiha* is another important source of Hadith from the earliest period. Hammam ibn Munabbih, its compiler, followed Abu Hurayra whenever he went and wrote down the Prophetic sayings reported by him. This compilation, recently published by Muhammad Hamidullah, has been carbondated to a period thirteen centuries ago. Almost all of its Traditions can be found either in *Musnad ibn Hanbal* or the *Sahihayn* of Bukhari and Muslim.

After these first simple compilations, Caliph 'Umar ibn 'Abd al-'Aziz, who reigned between 719-22, decided that all oral and written authentic Traditions should be compiled systematically into books. He ordered Abu Bakr ibn Muhammad ibn 'Amr ibn Hazm, governor of Madina, to supervise this task. Muhammad ibn Shihab al-Zuhri, renowned for his profound learning and keen intelligence, undertook the task and acquired the honor of being the first official compiler of Traditions.[115]

But such an honor was not restricted solely to him: 'Abd al-Malik ibn 'Abd al-'Aziz ibn Jurayj (Makka), Sa'id ibn Abi 'Aruba (Iraq), Awza'i (Damascus), Zayd ibn Qudama and Sufyan al-Thawri (Kufa), Hammad ibn Salama (Basra), and 'Abd Allah ibn al-Mubarak (Khorasan) also were involved.

This period of official and systematic compilation was followed by the period of classification by such great Traditionists as Abu Dawud al-Tayalisi, Musaddad ibn Musarhad, al-Humaydi, and Ahmad ibn Hanbal, who brought out their *Musnads*. 'Abd al-Razzaq ibn Hammam and others formed their *Musannafs*, and Ibn Abi Dhi'b and Imam Malik produced their *Al-Muwattas*. Yahya ibn Sa'id al-Qattan and Yahya ibn Sa'id al-Ansari also should be mentioned among the pre-eminent figures of this period.

Then came the period of such great Traditionists as Bukhari, Muslim, Abu Dawud, Nasa'i, Tirmidhi, and Ibn Maja, who produced the well-known, six most authentic books of Tradition. These celebrated persons, and such other illustrious people like Yahya ibn Ma'in, included in their collections what they believed to be the most authentic Traditions after judging them according to the strictest criteria.

For example, Imam Bukhari sought a Tradition from a man renowned for his reliability and piety. When he saw that man hold his hat toward his animal as if it contained something to eat, in an attempt to entice it to come to him, he asked the man if the hat contained some food for the animal. When told that it did not, Bukhari took no Traditions from him. In his view, one who could deceive an animal in this way might also deceive people. Such were the exacting criteria applied when judging the reliability of narrators.

In short, the Prophetic Traditions were either written down or memorized during the time of the Companions. When the first Islamic century ended, they were circulating widely in both oral and written form. Caliph 'Umar ibn 'Abd al-'Aziz tasked eminent scholars with producing the first official compilation in different cities. Authentic Traditions were distinguished from fabricated ones according to the most stringent care and criteria. After they were classified, one of the most systematic and accurate compilations or collections was undertaken by the most prominent Traditionists of that time.

Later on, new authentic books of Traditions were produced. Also, such illustrious critics of Tradition as Ibn Hajar al-Asqalani, Ibn Abd al-Barr, Dhahabi, Ibn al-Jawzi, and Zayn al-Din al-'Iraqi reviewed all Traditions and wrote large compendiums about their narrators.

As a result of such scholarly activity, the Sunna has reached us through the most reliable channels. No one can doubt the authenticity of this second source of Islam, which approaches the Qur'an in purity, authenticity, and reliability.

CHAPTER 12

The Companions and
the Tabi'un

THE COMPANIONS AND THE TABI'UN

THE COMPANIONS

These people constitute the first pure and blessed channel through which the Qur'an and the Sunna were transmitted. God is the All-Trustworthy and Inspirer of Trust. The Qur'an describes Archangel Gabriel as trustworthy and as one obeyed and having power (81:20-21). Prophet Muhammad was renowned for his trustworthiness.

The Qur'an was entrusted to the Companions, who memorized and recorded it so that it could be transmitted. This blessed community, praised in the Torah and Gospel, was the living embodiment of almost all laudable virtues and sought only God's pleasure. In addition to the Qur'an, they absorbed the Sunna, lived disciplined lives in strict accordance with the Prophet's example, and exerted all their efforts to both represent and transmit it with complete accuracy.

According to Ibn Hajar al-Asqalani, scholars define a Companion as "a believer who saw and heard the Messenger at least once and died as a believer."[1] Even though some scholars have stipulated that a "potential" Companion should have lived in the Messenger's company for one or even two years, most scholars say it is enough to have been present in his radiant atmosphere long enough to derive some benefit.

The Companions varied in rank and greatness. Some believed in the Messenger from the first, and conversions continued until his death. The Qur'an grades them according to precedence in belief and to conversion before and after Makka's conquest (9:100; 57:10).

The same gradation also was made by the Messenger. For example, he reproached Khalid for offending 'Ammar, saying: "Don't bother my Companions."[2] He also frowned at 'Umar when he annoyed Abu Bakr, and asked: "Why don't you leave my Companions to me? Abu Bakr believed in me when all of you denied me." Abu Bakr knelt down and explained: "O Messenger of God, it was my fault."[3]

Hakim al-Nisaburi divided them into twelve ranks, and most scholars accept his ranking:

- The four Rightly Guided Caliphs (Abu Bakr, 'Umar, 'Uthman, and 'Ali), and the rest of the ten who were promised Paradise while still alive (Zubayr ibn al-'Awwam, Abu 'Ubayda ibn al-Jarrah, 'Abd al-Rahman ibn 'Awf, Talha ibn 'Ubayd Allah, Sa'd ibn Abi Waqqas, and Sa'id ibn Zayd).
- Those who believed prior to 'Umar's conversion and met secretly in Arqam's house to listen to the Messenger.
- Those who migrated to Abyssinia.
- The Helpers (Ansar) who swore their allegiance to the Messenger at al-'Aqaba.
- The Helpers who swore their allegiance at al-'Aqaba the following year.
- The Emigrants who joined the Messenger during the hijra before his arrival in Madina from Quba, where he stayed for a short while.
- The Companions who fought at Badr.
- Those who emigrated to Madina between the Battle of Badr and the Treaty of Hudaybiya.
- The Companions who swore allegiance under a tree during the expedition of Hudaybiya.
- Those who converted and emigrated to Madina after the Treaty of Hudaybiya.
- Those who became Muslims after the conquest of Makka.
- Children who saw the Messenger any time or any place after the conquest of Makka.[4]

Muslim scholars of the highest rank, whose minds are enlightened by scientific knowledge and whose souls are illumined by religious knowledge and practice, agree that Prophets are the greatest members of humanity. Immediately after them come the Companions of the Last Prophet, who is the greatest Prophet.

Although some Companions may have the same rank as previous Prophets in a particular virtue, no one can equal a Prophet in general terms. Some of the greatest saints or scholars can compete with or excel some of the Companions in particular virtues. But even a Companion of the lowest rank, such as Wahshi (who killed Hamza), is still greater, in general terms, than all who come after the Companions. All Muslim scholars, Traditionists, theologians, and saints agree upon this.

FACTORS IN THEIR GREATNESS

Relation to Messengership

Prophethood is greater than sainthood, and Messengership is greater than Prophethood. Every Prophet is a saint, but no saint is a Prophet. Although every Messenger is a Prophet, not every Prophet is simultaneously a Messenger. Prophet Muhammad is the last and greatest Prophet and Messenger. The Companions are related directly to his Messengership and connected with him due to his Messengership. All who come after the Prophet, however great they may be, are connected with him on account of sainthood only. Therefore, a Companion is greater than a saint to the degree that Messengership is greater than sainthood (the distance between them cannot be measured).

The Benefits of Company

Nothing can compare with the enlightenment and spiritual exhilaration gained from a Prophet's actual presence or company. No amount of reading what an intellectual, especially a spiritual, master has written can benefit you as much as learning directly from a Prophet. Thus the Companions, particularly those who were with him most often and from the very beginning, benefited so much that they were elevated from crude, ignorant, and savage desert people to the rank of being humanity's religious, intellectual, spiritual, and moral guides until the Last Day.

To be a Companion, one would have to go back to the Makka or Madina of the seventh century ce, listen to the Messenger attentively and observe him speaking, walking, eating, fighting, praying, prostrating, and so on. Since this is impossible, no one can attain the rank of the Companions, who were endowed with Divine coloring in the Messenger's presence.

Truthfulness

Islam is based on truthfulness and the absence of lies. The Companions embraced Islam in its original, pristine purity. For them, being a Muslim meant abandoning all previous vices, being purified in the radiant atmosphere of Divine Revelation, and embodying Islam. They would rather die than tell a lie. The Messenger once declared that if apostasy were as repugnant to a person as entering fire, then that person must have tasted the pleasure of belief. The Companions tasted this pleasure and, being sincere Muslims, could not lie, as this was almost as serious as apostasy. We have trouble understanding this point fully, for people in our own time regard lying and deceit as skills, and almost all virtues have been replaced by vices.

The Atmosphere Created by Revelation

The Companions were honored with being the first to receive the Divine Messages through the Prophet. Every day they were given original messages and invited to a new "Divine table" full of the ever-fresh "fruits" of Paradise. Every day they experienced radical changes in their lives, were elevated closer to God's Presence, and increased in belief and conviction. They found themselves in the verses of the Qur'an, and could learn directly whether or not God approved of their actions.

For example, whenever and wherever *Those who are with him are hard against the unbelievers, merciful one to another. You see them bowing, prostrating, seeking blessing from God and good pleasure.*

Their mark is on their faces, the trace of prostration (48:29) was revealed, eyes turned primarily to Abu Bakr, 'Umar, 'Uthman, and 'Ali. After all, they were famous for being with the Messenger from the very beginning, their hardness toward unbelievers, their mercy to fellow Muslims, and for frequent and long bowing and prostration before God while seeking His good pleasure.

When *Among the believers are men who were true to their covenant with God; some of them have fulfilled their vow by death, and some are still awaiting, and they have not changed in the least* (33:23) was recited, everyone remembered the martyrs of Uhud, especially Hamza, Anas ibn Nadr, and 'Abd Allah ibn Jahsh, as well as others who had promised God to give their lives willingly in His Way.

While God explicitly mentioned Zayd ibn Haritha in: *So when Zayd had accomplished what he would of her . . .* (33:37),[5] He declared in 48:18 that He was well pleased with the believers when they swore fealty to the Messenger under a tree during the expedition of Hudaybiya.

In such a blessed, pure, and radiant atmosphere, the Companions practiced Islam in its original fullness and pristine purity, based on deep perception, profound insight, and knowledge of God. So, even an ordinary believer who is aware of the meaning of belief and connection with God, and who is trying to practice Islam sincerely, can grasp some glimpse of the purity of the first channel through which the Sunna was transmitted to the next generation.

The Difficulty of the Circumstances

The reward of a deed changes according to the circumstances in which it is done and the purity of the doer's intention. Striving in the way of God in such severe circumstances as fear, threats, and shortage of necessary equipment, and purely for His sake, is far more rewarding than the same action performed in a free and promising atmosphere.

The Companions accepted and defended Islam in the severest circumstances imaginable. The opposition was very inflexible and unpitying. In Muhyi al-Din ibn al-'Arabi's *Musamarat al-*

Abrar, Abu Bakr is reported to have told 'Ali after the Prophet's death that the early Companions did not go out except at the risk of their lives—they always feared that a dagger would be thrust at them. Only God knows how many times they were insulted, beaten, and tortured. Those who were weak and enslaved, such as Bilal, 'Ammar, and Suhayb, were tortured almost to death. Young people like Sa'd ibn Abi Waqqas and Mus'ab ibn 'Umayr, were beaten, boycotted, and imprisoned by their families.

Yet none of them ever thought of recanting or opposing the Messenger. For the sake of God, they forsook everything they had—their homes, native lands, and belongings—and emigrated. The believers of Madina welcomed them enthusiastically, protected them, and shared with them everything they had. They fulfilled their covenant with God willingly, sold their goods and souls to God in exchange for belief and Paradise, and never broke their word. This gained them so high a rank in the view of God that no one can attain it until the Last Day.

The severity of circumstances, along with other factors, made the Companions' belief strong and firm beyond compare. For example, the Messenger once entered the mosque and saw Harith ibn Malik sleeping there. He woke him up. Harith said: "May my father and mother be sacrificed for your sake, O Messenger of God! I am ready to carry out your orders!" The Messenger asked him how he had spent the night. Harith answered: "As a true believer." The Messenger said: "Everything that is true must have a truth (to prove it). What is the truth of your belief?" Harith replied: "I fasted during the day and prayed to my Master in utmost sincerity all night long. Now I am in a state as if I were seeing the Throne of my God and the recreation of the people of Paradise in Paradise." The Messenger concluded: "You have become an embodiment of belief."[6]

The Companions became so near to God that "God was their eyes with which they saw, their ears with which they heard, their tongues with which they spoke, and their hands with which they held."

The Companions in the Qur'an

Ibn Hazm voices the opinion of many leading scholars: "All of the Companions will enter Paradise."[7] It is possible to find proofs in the Qur'an testifying to this assertion. The Qur'an describes the Companions as follows:

> Muhammad is the Messenger of God. Those who are with him are hard toward the unbelievers, merciful to one another. [They kept so long vigils that] you see them bowing, prostrating, seeking blessing, bounty (of forgiveness and Paradise) and good pleasure (of God). Their mark is on their faces, the trace of prostration. This is their likeness in the Torah and in the Gospel: as a seed that puts forth its shoot, and strengthens it, and it grows strong and rises straight upon its stalk, pleasing the sowers, that through them it may enrage the unbelievers. God has promised those of them who believe and do deeds of righteousness forgiveness and a mighty wage [He will reward them in Paradise with the things that neither eyes will ever have seen nor ears heard]. (48:29)

And as:

> The Outstrippers, the first Emigrants and Helpers, and those who followed them in doing good—God is well-pleased with them, and they are well-pleased with Him; He has prepared for them gardens underneath which rivers flow, therein to dwell forever; that is the mighty triumph. (9:100)

Abu Hurayra never missed a discourse of the Messenger. He was always with him, and stayed in the antechamber of the Prophet's Mosque. He suffered hunger almost all the time. Once he went to the Messenger and told him that he had eaten nothing for days. Abu Talha took him as a guest, but unfortunately there was little in his house to eat. So, he asked his wife Umm Sulaym to

> ". . . put the children to bed early, and put on the table whatever we have to eat. When we sit at the table, put out the candle pretending to make its light brighter. No one sees in the dark whether one is really eating or not. I will act as if I am eat-

ing, and thus our guest can satisfy his hunger." After the dawn prayer, the Messenger turned to them, smiled, and said: "What did you do last night? This verse was revealed concerning you:

> Those who made their dwelling in the abode [Madina], and in belief, before them [the Emigrants] love whoever has emigrated to them, not finding in their breasts any need for what they have been given, and preferring others above themselves, even though poverty be their portion. Whoever is guarded against the avarice of his own soul, those—they are the prosperous." (59:9)[8]

We also read of the Companions:

> God was well-pleased with the believers when they were swearing fealty to you under the tree, and He knew what was in their hearts, so He sent down peace, calm and tranquility upon them, and rewarded them with a nigh victory. (48:18)

The Companions swore many oaths of allegiance to the Messenger, promising to protect him and carry, by God's Will, Islam to ultimate victory as best they could. They kept their promise at the cost of all their belongings and lives. Most were martyred either during the Prophet's lifetime or while conveying Islam throughout the newly conquered lands. It is still possible to find, in almost every part of the Muslim world, tombs where several Companions are buried. They also raised numerous scholars in jurisprudence, Traditions, Qur'anic interpretation, as well as in history and the biography of the Prophet. The Qur'an states:

> Among believers are those who were true to their covenant with God; some have fulfilled their vow by death, and some are still awaiting, and they have not changed in the least. (33:23)

The Companions in Hadith

The Prophet also praised the Companions and warned Muslims not to attack or insult them. For example, Bukhari, Muslim, and other Traditionists relate from Abu Sa'id al-Khudri that the Messenger warned:

Don't curse my Companions, don't curse my Companions. I swear by Him in Whose hand is my life that even if you had as much gold as Mount Uhud and spent it in the way of God, this would not be equal in reward to a few handfuls of them or even to half of that.[9]

The Companions have such a high value because they accepted, preached, and protected Islam in the severest circumstances. Besides, according to the rule that "the cause is like the doer," the reward gained by all Muslims from that time until the Last Day is being added to the Companions' record, without taking away any of the doers' rewards. Had it not been for their efforts to spread Islam wherever they went, no one would know of it or be able to become Muslim. So, all Muslims after the Companions should feel indebted to them and, rather than thinking of criticizing them, should pray for them:

> As for those who came after them, they say: "Our Master, forgive us and our brothers who preceded us in belief, and put not into our hearts any rancor toward those who believe. Our Master, surely You are the All-Gentle, the All-Compassionate." (59:10)

Tirmidhi and Ibn Hibban quote the warning of 'Abd Allah ibn Mughaffal, which he heard from the Messenger:

> Oh God, Oh God! Refrain from using bad language about my Companions! Oh God, Oh God! Refrain from using bad language about my Companions! Don't make them the target of your attacks after me! Whoever loves them loves them on account of his love of me; whoever hates them hates them on account of his hatred of me. Whoever hurts them hurts me; whoever hurts me "hurts" God.[10]

Imam Muslim relates in his Sahih that the Messenger declared:

> Stars are means of security for the heaven. When they are scattered, what was promised for Heaven befalls it. I am the means of security for my Companions. When I leave the world, what was promised for my Companions will befall them. My Companions are means of security for my nation. When they leave the world, what was promised for my nation will befall it.[11]

As recorded in Bukhari, Muslim, and other authentic books of Tradition, the Messenger declared:

> The best people are those living in my time. Then come those who follow them, and then come those who follow them. Those will be followed by a generation whose witness is sometimes true, sometimes false.[12]

The time of the Companions and the two succeeding generations was the time of truthfulness. People of great righteousness and exacting scholars appeared during these first three generations. Later generations contained many who lied and perjured themselves to reinforce false beliefs or attain worldly aims. It was natural for liars and members of heterodox sects (as it is for biased Orientalists and their Muslim followers) to lie about the Companions and the pure Imams of the two generations succeeding them, as they were strongholds of Islam and strengthened its pillars.

Abu Nu'aym quotes 'Abd Allah ibn 'Umar as saying:

> Whoever desires to follow a straight path should follow the path of those who passed away: The Companions of Muhammad. They are the best of his Umma, the purest in heart, the deepest in knowledge, and the furthest from any false display of piety. They are a community whom God chose for His Prophet's company and His religion's conveyance. Try to be like them in conduct and follow their way. They are the Companions of Muhammad. I swear by God, the Master of the Ka'ba, that they were on true guidance.[13]

As recorded by Tabarani and Ibn al-Athir, 'Abd Allah ibn Mas'ud, one of the first people to embrace Islam in Makka and sent to Kufa as a teacher by 'Umar, said: "God looked at the hearts of His true servants and chose Muhammad to send to His creatures as a Messenger. Then He looked at the hearts of people and chose his Companions as the helpers of His religion and the viziers of His Prophet."[14] He also said:

> You may excel the Companions in fasting, praying, and in striving to worship God better. But they are better than you, for

they paid no attention to the world and were most desirous of the Hereafter.[15]

The Companions Who Excelled in Narrating Traditions

God Almighty created people with different dispositions and potentials so that human social life would be maintained through mutual help and the division of labor. Therefore, some Companions were good farmers, successful tradesmen or businessmen, students, military commanders, and administrators. Some, especially the *Ashab al-Suffa* (those who stayed in the antechamber of the Prophet's Mosque) never missed a teaching of the Messenger and tried to memorize his every word.

These Companions later narrated to people whatever they heard from or saw about the Messenger. Fortunately, they outlived the others by God's Will and, together with 'A'isha, constituted the first, golden channel through which the Sunna was transmitted. The following is a brief description of their characters and lives:

Abu Hurayra was from Yemeni tribe of Daws. He became a Muslim in the early days of 7 ah at the hands of Tufayl ibn 'Amr, the chief of his tribe. When he emigrated to Madina, the Messenger was busy with the Khaybar campaign. He joined him in Khaybar. The Messenger changed his name, 'Abd al-Shams, to 'Abd al-Rahman, saying: "A man is not the slave of either the sun or moon."

Abu Hurayra was very poor and modest. One day the Messenger saw him cradling a cat and nicknamed him Abu Hirr (the father or owner of a cat). People soon began to call him Abu Hurayra. However, he liked to be called Abu Hirr, since this title was given to him by the Messenger.[16]

He lived with his non-Muslim mother. Always praying her conversion, one day he asked the Messenger to pray for this. He did so, and before he lowered his arms, Abu Hurayra ran to his house, so sure was he that the Messenger's prayer would be accepted. When he arrived, his mother stopped him at the door so that she could finish ghusl (total ritual ablution). She then opened the door and declared her conversion. After this, Abu Hurayra requested the Messenger to pray that believers should love him and his mother. The Messenger did so.[17] Therefore, love of Abu Hurayra is a mark of belief.

This Companion had an extraordinarily keen memory. He slept the first third of night, prayed and did his daily supererogatory recitations in the second third, and went over the Traditions he had memorized in order never to forget them in the last third. He memorized more than 5,000 Traditions. He never missed a discourse of the Messenger, sought to learn his Traditions, and was a lover of knowledge.

One day he prayed: "O God, grant me knowledge I will never forget." The Messenger heard him and said: "O God, amen."[18] On another day, he told the Messenger: "O Messenger of God, I don't want to forget what I hear from you." The Messenger asked him to take off his cloak and spread it on the ground. The Messenger then prayed and emptied his hands onto the cloak as if filling them with something from the Unseen. He ordered Abu Hurayra to fold up the cloak and hold it to his breast. After narrating this incident, Abu Hurayra used to say: "I folded it up and held it to my breast. I swear by God that [since then] I have not forgotten anything I heard from the Messenger."[19]

Abu Hurayra paid no heed to the world. He usually fasted 3 or 4 days successively because of poverty. Sometimes he writhed with hunger on the ground and said to those passing by: *Istaqra'tuka*, which has a double meaning: "Will you not recite to me some Qur'an?" and "Will you not feed me?"[20] Ja'far Tayyar understood him better than anybody else and took him as a guest.[21]

Abu Hurayra patiently endured such hardship for the sake of Hadith. To those who sometimes warned him that he was narrating too many Traditions, he replied sincerely: "While my Emigrant brothers were busy in the bazaar and my Helper brothers with farming, I tried to keep my soul and body together to keep company with the Messenger."[22] Sometimes he said: "Were it not for the verse: *Those who conceal the clear signs and the guidance that We*

*have sent down, after We have shown them clearly in the Book, they shall
be cursed by God and the curses* (2:159), I would narrate nothing."[23]

Some claim that other Companions were opposed to Abu
Hurayra's narrating. This claim is groundless. Many Companions,
among them Abu Ayyub al-Ansari, 'Abd Allah ibn 'Umar, 'Abd
Allah ibn 'Abbas, Jabir ibn 'Abd Allah al-Ansari, Anas ibn Malik,
and Wasila ibn Aslam, narrated Traditions from him. Some asked
Abu Ayyub why he narrated from Abu Hurayra despite his earlier
conversion, to which he would reply: "He heard from the Messenger
many things we did not hear."[24]

Many leading Tabi'un also received numerous Traditions
from him, including Hasan al-Basri, Zayd ibn Aslam, Sa'id ibn
al-Musayyib (who married Abu Hurayra's daughter so that he
could benefit from him more), Sa'id ibn Yasar, Sa'id al-Makburi,
Sulayman ibn Yasar, Sha'bi (who received Traditions from 500
Companions), Muhammad ibn Abi Bakr, and Qasim ibn
Muhammad (who is accepted as a link in the chain of Nakshbandi
spiritual guides). Hammam ibn Munabbih and Muhammad ibn
Munkadir are the most famous of the 800 people who received
Traditions from him.[25]

'Umar appointed Abu Hurayra as governor to Bahrayn.
However, when he made a small amount of wealth by trade during
his period of office, 'Umar had him investigated. Although he was
found innocent and requested to return to office, Abu Hurayra
declined, saying: "That is enough for me as a governor."[26]

Abu Hurayra, despite claims to the contrary by such
Orientalists as Goldziher and their Muslim followers like Ahmad
Amin, Abu Rayya, and 'Ali 'Abd al-Razzaq, was never anti-'Ali
and pro-Umayyad. He should have supported 'Ali in the internal conflicts so that sedition would be crushed, but chose to
remain neutral, for: "Seditions will appear, during which the
one who sits [silent] is better than the one who stands [to par-
ticipate]; the one who stands is better than him who walks [to
participate], and the one who walks is better than him who runs
[in them]."[27] This hadith might not have been related to the internal conflicts during 'Ali's caliphate, but Abu Hurayra thought
that it was and so remained neutral.

Abu Hurayra opposed the Umayyad government. He once stood in front of Marwan ibn Hakam and narrated the *hadith*: "The destruction of my community will be in the hands of a few callow (young) men from the Quraysh."[28] Marwan responded: "May God's curse be upon them," pretending not to understand who was meant. Abu Hurayra added: "If you like, I can inform you of their names and characteristics."

He was frequently heard to pray: "O God, don't make me live until the sixtieth year."[29] This supplication was so famous that whoever saw Abu Hurayra recalled it. He had heard from the Messenger that some inexperienced, sinful young men would begin to rule the Muslims in 60 ah. He died in 59 ah, and Yazid succeeded his father Mu'awiya one year later.

There is no proof that 'A'isha was opposed to Abu Hurayra's narrating. Both 'A'isha and Abu Hurayra lived long lives and, except for the following incident, she never criticized his narrations. Once when he was narrating Traditions near her room while she was praying, she finished her prayer and came out, only to find that he had left. She remarked: "The Messenger's Traditions should not be narrated in this way, one after another,"[30] meaning that they should be narrated slowly and distinctly so that the listeners could understand and memorize them.

Some claim that Imam Abu Hanifa said: "I don't take the opinions of three Companions as evidence in jurisprudence. Abu Hurayra is one of them." This is simply a lie. Allama Ibn Humam, one of the greatest Hanafi jurists, regarded Abu Hurayra as a significant jurist. Besides, there is nothing to prove that Abu Hanifa said that.

Abu Hurayra narrated more than 5,000 Traditions. When gathered together, they make perhaps a volume 1.5 times as long as the Qur'an. Many people have memorized the Qur'an in 6 months or even quicker. Abu Hurayra had a very keen memory and spent 4 years with the Messenger, who prayed for the strength of Abu Hurayra's memory. It would be tantamount to accusing Abu Hurayra of deficient intelligence to claim that he could not have memorized so many Traditions. In addition, all of the Traditions he narrated were not directly from the Messenger. As leading Companions like Abu Bakr, 'Umar, Ubayy ibn Ka'b, 'A'isha, and Abu Ayyub al-Ansari narrated from him, he also received Traditions from them.

While Abu Hurayra was narrating Traditions in the presence of Marwan ibn Hakam at different times, the latter had his secretary record them written secretly. Some time later, he asked Abu Hurayra to repeat the Traditions he had narrated to him earlier. Abu Hurayra began: "In the name of God, the All-Merciful, the All-Compassionate," and narrated the same Traditions with exactly the same wording.[31] So, there is no reason to criticize him for narrating so many Prophetic Traditions.

'Abd Allah ibn 'Abbas was born 4 or 5 years before the Hijra. He had a keen intelligence and memory, and was an inspired man. The Messenger prayed for him: "O God, make him perceptive and well-versed in the religion, and teach him the hidden truths of the Qur'an."[32] During his lifetime, he came to be known as "the Great Scholar of the Umma," "the Sea" (One Very Profound in Knowledge), or "The Translator (Clarifier) of the Qur'an."[33]

He was a very handsome, tall man endowed with great eloquence. His memory was such that he memorized an 80-couplet poem by 'Amr ibn Rabi'a at one reading. Besides his profound knowledge of Qur'anic interpretation, Tradition, and jurisprudence, he also was well-versed in literature, particularly in pre-Islamic poetry. In his *Tafsir*, Ibn Jarir al-Tabari relates either a couplet or verse from him in connection with the interpretation of almost each Qur'anic verse.

He was greatly loved by the Companions. Despite his youth, 'Umar appointed him to his Advisory Council, which consisted of elder Companions. When asked why he had done this, 'Umar tested their level of understanding of the Qur'an. He asked them to explain:

> When comes the help of God, and victory, and you see men entering God's religion in throngs, then proclaim the praise of

Your Master, and seek His forgiveness; for He is Oft-Returning
[in grace and mercy]. (110:1-3)

The elders answered: "It orders the Prophet to praise God
and seek His forgiveness when he sees people entering Islam in
throngs after the help of God and victory came." 'Umar was not
satisfied, and so asked Ibn 'Abbas the same question. He replied:
"This *sura* implies that the death of the Messenger is near, for
when people enter Islam in throngs, it means that the mission
of Messengership has ended." 'Umar turned to the council and
explained: "That's why I include him among you."[34]

Ibn 'Abbas was famous for his deep insight, profound learning, keen memory, high intelligence, perceptiveness, and modesty.
When he entered a gathering place, people would stand in respect
for him. This made him so uncomfortable that he told them:
"Please, for the sake of the help and shelter (you gave the Prophet
and the Emigrants), don't stand for me!" Although one of the
most knowledgeable Muslims, he showed great respect to scholars. For example, he helped Zayd ibn Thabit mount his horse by
holding the stirrup steady and explained: "We have been told to
behave like this toward our scholars." In return, Zayd kissed his
hand without his approval and remarked: "We have been told to
behave like this toward the Messenger's relatives."[35]

As noted above, Ibn 'Abbas did not like people to stand for
him to show respect. However, when he was buried, something
occurred that was as if the dead had stood in respect for him and
the spirit beings welcomed him. A voice was heard from beneath
the grave: *O soul at peace! Return unto your Master, well-pleased, well-
pleasing! Enter among My servants! Enter my Paradise!* (89:27-30).[36]

Ibn 'Abbas brought up many scholars in every branch of
religious knowledge. The Makkan school of jurisprudence was
founded by him. Such leading Tabi'un scholars as Sa'id ibn Jubayr,
Mujahid ibn Jabr, and Ikrima acknowledged: "Ibn 'Abbas taught
us whatever we know." He narrated about 1,600 Traditions.

'Abd Allah ibn 'Umar was the only one of 'Umar's nine
sons to be called Ibn 'Umar (the son of 'Umar). This shows that
he had greater worth to be called 'Umar's son or to be men-

tioned with the name of 'Umar. Although 'Umar is the second greatest Companion, 'Abd Allah may be regarded superior in knowledge, piety, worship, and devotion to the Sunna. His care in following the Prophet's example was such that Nafi', Imam Malik's tutor, narrates: "While we were descending 'Arafat, Ibn 'Umar entered a hole. When he came out, I asked him what he had done there. The Imam answered: 'While descending 'Arafat, I was behind the Messenger. He went down into that hole and relieved himself. I felt no need to do that now, but I don't like to oppose him.'"[37] Also, no one ever saw him take more or less than three swallows of water, for he saw the Messenger drink water in three swallows.

Ibn 'Umar was born in the early years of Islam. He saw his father beaten severely by the Makkan polytheists many times.[38] When the Muslims emigrated to Madina, he was about 10 years old. The Messenger did not let him fight at Badr because he was too young. When he was also prevented from fighting at Uhud, he returned home so grief-stricken that he spent the whole night asking himself: "What sin have I committed that they did not include me in the army fighting in the way of the Messenger?"[39]

Ibn Khalliqan relates from Sha'bi:

> Once in their youth, 'Abd Allah ibn Zubayr, his brother Mus'ab ibn Zubayr, 'Abd al-Malik ibn Marwan, and 'Abd Allah ibn 'Umar were sitting near the Ka'ba. They thought that each should ask God for something special in the hope that the prayer would be accepted. Ibn Zubayr prayed: "O God, for the sake of Your Grandeur, Honor, and Majesty, make me a ruler in Hijaz." Mus'ab stretched out his arms and prayed: "O God, for the sake of Your Honor, Majesty, and Grandeur, of Your Throne and Seat, make me a ruler in Iraq." 'Abd al-Malik raised his hands and prayed: "O God, I ask You to make me a ruler over all the Muslims and secure, through me, Muslim unity even at the cost of some lives." When 'Abd Allah prayed, he asked: "O God, don't take my soul before You guarantee Paradise for me."[40]

The prayers of the first three were accepted: 'Abd Allah ibn Zubayr ruled for a while in Hijaz and was eventually martyred by Hajjaj the Tyrant, the notorious Umayyad governor. Mus'ab ruled in Iraq for a short time. 'Abd al-Malik succeeded his father, Marwan, as caliph and secured Muslim unity, though at the cost of many lives and much bloodshed.

As for Ibn 'Umar, Imam Sha'bi remarks: "Whether the Imam's prayer was accepted or not will be clear in the Hereafter." Sha'bi knew something: "Ibn 'Umar never opposed the Prophet's descendants or supported the Umayyads. Hajjaj was afraid of him. Once, Hajjaj gave a sermon before the noon prayer that was so long that the noon prayer's time was almost over. Ibn 'Umar warned him: 'O Governor, time is passing without waiting for you to finish your sermon.' Hajjaj was full of rancor and enmity for Ibn 'Umar. Finally, during a pilgrimage he found someone to prick Ibn 'Umar's heel with a poisonous spear while he was in pilgrim attire. The poison eventually killed him."[41]

'Abd Allah ibn Mas'ud, one of the first five or six people to embrace Islam, also narrated a considerable number of Traditions. As a youth, he tended the flocks of such Qurayshi leaders as Abu Jahl and 'Uqba ibn Abi Mu'ayt. After his conversion, he would no longer be separated from the Messenger. He entered the Prophet's house without asking to do so and so frequently that people thought he was a family member. During military or non-military expeditions, he carried the Prophet's water bag, wooden sandals, and mat upon which he slept or sat. Eventually, he became known as "the caretaker of the pattens (sandals, like shoes), couch, and water bag."[42]

Ibn Mas'ud worked some wonders. For example, while he was once being tortured in Makka, he became invisible to his torturers. The Messenger called him "the son of the mother of a slave," and advised his Companions: "Whoever wants to recite the Qur'an as if it were being revealed for the first time, let him recite it according to the recitation of the son of the mother of a slave."[43]

One day the Messenger asked him to recite some of the Qur'an to him. Ibn Mas'ud excused himself: "O Messenger of God, shall I recite it to you while the Qur'an is being revealed to you?" However, the Messenger insisted: "I would prefer to hear it from others." Ibn Mas'ud began to recite *Surat al-Nisa'*. When he reached verse 41: *How then will it be, when We bring forward from every nation a witness, and bring you as a witness against those?*, the Messenger, whose eyes were full of tears, stopped him, saying: "Stop, please. This is enough."[44]

Ibn Mas'ud, who was short and weak, once climbed a tree because the Messenger asked him to do so. Those present laughed at his legs. The Messenger warned them, saying: "Those legs will weigh more than Mount Uhud according to the measure of the Hereafter in the other world."[45]

Caliph 'Umar sent him to Kufa as a teacher and with a letter, in which he said: "O people of Kufa! If I did not prefer you over myself, I would not have sent Ibn Mas'ud to you."[46] Ibn Mas'ud lived in Kufa during the caliphate of 'Umar and trained many scholars. Such great Tabi'un scholars as Alqama ibn Qays, Aswad ibn Yazid al-Naha'i, and Ibrahim ibn Yazid al-Naha'i grew up in the ethos established by Ibn Mas'ud. One of the people attending Alqama's courses asked him who had been his teacher. When Alqama answered that he had learned from 'Umar, 'Uthman, 'Ali, and Ibn Mas'ud, the man responded: "Good! Good!"

Ibn Mas'ud continued to stay in Kufa during 'Uthman's caliphate. However, after 'Uthman summoned him to Madina to investigate a groundless complaint about him, Ibn Mas'ud did not want to go back to Kufa, as he was already very old. One day a man ran to him and said: "Last night I dreamed that the Messenger was telling you: 'They have afflicted you much after me, so come to me.' You answered: 'Alright, O Messenger of God. I will not leave Madina any more.' A few days later Ibn Mas'ud became ill. 'Uthman visited him, and the following conversation took place between them:

> – Do you have any complaints?
> – I have many complaints.
> – Of what?
> – Of my sins while going to God.
> – Is there something you desire?
> – God's mercy.
> – Would you like me to send for a doctor?

– The "doctor" has made me ill. So, there is nothing the doctor you will send for can do for me."

Ibn Mas'ud spent about 20 years in the company of the Messenger. He narrated approximately 800 Traditions.[47]

* * *

Besides those four great Companions, 'A'isha, Abu Sa'id al-Khudri, Jabir ibn 'Abd Allah, and Anas ibn Malik are the other Companions who narrated many Traditions.

'A'isha lived with the Messenger for 9 years. She had great talents, a keen intelligence and memory, and a deep in-sight and perceptiveness. She had a great curiosity to learn new things, and asked the Messenger to explain those matters that she found it hard to understand.

Abu Sa'id al-Khudri lived in the mosque's antechamber and was always with the Messenger. He lived a long life, and a time came when he was regarded as the most knowledgeable person of Madina.

Jabir ibn 'Abd Allah is the son of 'Abd Allah ibn 'Amr ibn Haram al-Ansari, who was martyred at Uhud. After the Messenger's death, he lived in Madina (where he lectured in the Prophet's Mosque), Egypt, and Damascus. Such leading Tabi'un scholars as 'Amr ibn Dinar, Mujahid, and 'Ata' ibn Abi Rabah attended his lectures.[48] People gathered around him in Damascus and Egypt to learn of the Messenger and his Traditions.

Anas ibn Malik served the Messenger for 10 years in Madina. After the Messenger's death, he lived a very long life, during which he must have taught the Prophetic Traditions to those around him.

All the Traditions recorded in *Kanz al-'Ummal*, including authentic and defectively transmitted ones, number 46,624. Among the Traditionists of early Islamic ages, many people memorized more than 100,000 Traditions, including fabricated ones. Given this fact, it cannot be claimed by the Sunna's detractors and doubters that the number of Traditions narrated from certain Companions is too great for them to have memorized and narrated.

THE TABI'UN

In many of the places where the Qur'an praises the Companions, it also mentions the blessed generations fol-lowing in their way. For example:

> The Outstrippers (the first to embrace Islam and excel others in virtue), the first of the Emigrants and the Helpers, and those who followed them in doing good, God is well-pleased with them and they are well-pleased with Him. He has prepared for them gardens underneath which rivers flow, therein to dwell forever; that is the mighty triumph. (9:100)

The Tabi'un, first of all, must be among those praised together with the Companions. Like them, they were well-pleased with God regardless of whether He sent them good or bad, blessing or misfortune. Conscious of their servanthood before God, they worshipped Him in deep respect and reverence.

Like the Companions, they loved Him deeply and trusted Him completely. The Messenger praised them, saying: "Good tidings for those who have seen me and believed in me, and good tidings for those who see those who saw me."[49]

The Tabi'un followed in the Companions' footsteps and showed them due respect. They felt no rancor and enmity against any believer, and wished everyone well:

> As for those who came after them, they say: "Our Master, forgive us and our brothers, who preceded us in belief, and put not into our hearts any rancor towards those who believe. Our Master, surely You are the All-Gentle, the All-Compassionate." (59:10)

As described in 9:100, this blessed generation followed the Companions in doing good (*ihsan*). In addition to meaning respect, being well-wishing and altruistic, one hadith says that ihsan also means: "Doing good (*ihsan*) is that you worship God as if you were seeing Him; if, however, you do not actually see Him, surely He sees you."[50]

This generation came at a time when conspiracies and hypocrisy caused great internal dissension. At this critical juncture, they protected, defended, and practiced Islam in deep consciousness and devotion. They became the referents of: *Our Master, in You we trust, to You we turn, and to You is the homecoming* (60:4).

Some of them performed 100 *rak'as* of nightly prayers, recited the whole Qur'an every 2 or 3 days, always did their obligatory prayers in congregation in a mosque, always slept (like Masruq) in prostration before the Ka'ba, and did not laugh loudly during their whole lives.

Uways al-Qarani is generally regarded as the greatest Tabi'un. Although old enough to have seen the Prophet, he had no opportunity to do so. One day while sitting with his Companions, the Messenger advised them: "If you see Uways al-Qarani, ask him to pray for you."[51] During his caliphate, 'Umar asked Yemeni pilgrims about Uways. When he was found one year among the pilgrims, 'Umar requested him to pray for him. Uncomfortable at being identified, Uways was never seen again among people until he was martyred at the Battle of Siffin fighting for 'Ali.[52]

There were many illustrious Tabi'un, among them Masruq ibn al-Ajda', 'Ata' ibn 'Abi Rabah, Hasan al-Basri, Muhammad ibn Sirin, 'Ali Zayn al-'Abidin, Qasim ibn Muhammad, and Muhammad ibn Munkadir, who were peerless in knowledge, piety, and righteousness.

Muhammad ibn Munkadir was called al-Bakka' (the one who cries much), due to his fear of God. Once his mother told him: "O my son, if I had not known you since childhood, I would think you are crying for some sin. Why do you cry so much?" He said that he did so because he was deeply conscious of God's Majesty, of the terror of the Day of Judgement, and of Hell.[53] When asked on his death-bed why he was crying, he replied: *I am afraid I'll be included in the meaning of the verse: Yet there will appear to them from God that they never reckoned with* (39:47).

Masruq ibn al-Ajda' worshipped God very earnestly. He used to sleep in prostration before the Ka'ba. When they suggested that he should lie down during his last illness, he answered: "By God, if someone appeared and told me that God wouldn't punish me, even then I would continue to pray with the same earnestness as before."[54] He did so because he was following the Prophet, who, when asked by 'A'isha why he tired himself so much with praying, answered: "Shall I not be a thankful servant?"

Sa'id ibn Jubayr was a student of Ibn 'Abbas. He spent the day preaching Islam and the night praying. He fought against Hajjaj on the side of 'Abd al-Rahman al-Kindi. When finally he was seized, the soldiers taking him to Hajjaj spent a night in a monastery in a big forest. Sa'id wanted to pray in the forest. The soldiers let him, thinking that wild animals would tear him to pieces. The soldiers watched him pray through a window, and saw wild animals gather around him also to watch.

When his captors used torture to force him to swear allegiance to Hajjaj, he always refused: "You are in the wrong, wronging the Prophet's descendants. I'll never take the oath of allegiance to you." Before he was executed, he recited the verse Muslims recite during the animal sacrifice: *I have turned my face to Him who originated the Heavens and the Earth, a man of pure faith; I am not of those who associate partners with God* (6:79). When they turned his face away from the prayer direction, he recited: *To God belong the East and the West; Wherever you turn, there is the Face of God* (2:115). They struck his neck with a sword and from his lips came out: "There is no god but God, and Muhammad is the Messenger of God."[55]

Such were the people who received the Traditions from the Companions and transmitted them to succeeding generations. Among them, the following few are also worth some fuller mention to recognize that blessed generation more closely:

Sa'id ibn al-Musayyib, the Tabi'un's foremost Tradition-ist, jurist, and Qur'anic interpreter, was born in 15 ah. He met most of the Companions, including 'Umar, 'Uthman, and 'Ali. Sa'id was renowned for his reflection and memory, as well as for his piety, righteousness, and profound devotion. These characteristics caused everyone to consider him, even during his lifetime, the greatest Traditionist of his time.

At the early age of around 20, Sa'id began to give opinions and deliver legal verdicts, just as Hasan al-Basri had done in Basra. The Companions admired him greatly. 'Abd Allah ibn 'Umar once remarked: "If the Messenger had seen that young man, he would have been very pleased with him."[56]

He was extremely careful about performing his daily prayers in congregation in the mosque. He used to say: "I always have said the opening *takbir* of the daily prayers just after the imam for 50 years."[57] He did not neglect any item of the Sunna. Once when he was ill and doctors advised him to stay in 'Aqiq valley for a month, he objected: "Then how can I come to the mosque for the night and dawn prayers?" He was not content to perform the prescribed prayers anywhere except in the Prophet's Mosque.[58]

He did not swear allegiance to Caliph Walid. Although Hisham, governor of Madina, had him beaten daily until the stick was broken, he did not yield. When his friends, such as Masruq and Tawus, advised him to give an oral consent to Walid's caliphate to end the beatings, he always replied: "People do what we do. If we consent, how will we be able to explain this to them?"[59]

Sa'id had married Abu Hurayra's daughter in order to be nearer to him and to improve his knowledge and understanding of Abu Hurayra's Traditions. When Caliph 'Abd al-Malik appealed to him that his son Hisham be allowed to marry Sa'id's daughter, he refused and, in the face of increasing pressure and threats, offered her to Ibn Abi Wada', who stayed in the *madrasa*.[60]

Imam Shafi'i considered all of Sa'id's Traditions unquestionably authentic, even if the Companion from whom he had received it was not mentioned. This means that for Imam Shafi'i, Sa'id was of the same rank as the Companions in knowledge and narration of the Prophetic Traditions. Among those who received Traditions from him, 'Ata' ibn Abi Rabah, Qatada, Muhammad al-Baqir ('Ali's great-grandson), Zuhri, and Yahya ibn Sa'id al-Ansari are worthy of special mention.

Alqama ibn Qays al-Nakha'i. During the time of the Tabi'un, Basra was honored by, in particular, Hasan al-Basri; Yemen by Tawus ibn Qaysan; Madina by Sa'id ibn al-Musayyib; and Kufa by Alqama ibn Qays al-Nakha'i. Kufa was first enlightened by 'Abd Allah ibn Mas'ud during 'Umar's caliphate, and then directly by 'Ali, when he moved the caliphate there. This gave Alqama a splendid opportunity to meet many Companions and to learn about the Messenger's life and Traditions at first hand.

Alqama is the founder of the Kufa school of Islamic religious sciences. Those who saw him remembered 'Abd Allah ibn Mas'ud, for he followed the latter's footsteps in prayer, conduct, and in practicing Islam. 'Amr ibn Shurahbil, among the great scholars who narrated Traditions from Alqama, frequently suggested to those near him: "Let's go to the one who resembles Ibn Mas'ud the most in conduct and attitudes."[61] Ibn Mas'ud represented the Messenger wholly. As the Messenger desired to listen to Ibn Mas'ud recite the Qur'an, so Ibn Mas'ud liked to listen to Alqama.[62]

Imam Abu Hanifa, generally accepted as the greatest Muslim jurist and a man famous for his piety and austerity, admired Alqama so much that he would say: "Alqama is probably more profound in [knowledge] of Tradition and jurisprudence than some Companions."

One day, someone came to Alqama and insulted him greatly. The illustrious scholar showed no indignation and, after the man had finished, recited the verse: *Those who hurt believing men and believing women, without their having earned it, have laid upon themselves calumny and manifest sin* (33:58). The man retorted: "Are you a believer?" Alqama answered humbly: "I hope so."[63]

Alqama struggled with falsehood in his time, and did not obey the misguided Umayyad administrators. As he received Traditions from hundreds of Companions, many leading figures among his own and succeeding generations narrated from him. Alqama brought up the most illustrious scholars of the Kufan school, people such as Aswad ibn Yazid al-Nakha'i, Ibrahim al-Nakha'i, and Hammad ibn Abi Sulayman, and provided Kufa with a propitious ethos for bringing up Sufyan al-Thawri, Abu Hanifa, and many others.

'Urwa ibn Zubayr ibn al-'Awwam's father was one of the ten for whom Paradise was promised while alive. 'Urwa's grandmother was Safiyya, the Prophet's paternal aunt, and his mother was Asma' bint Abu Bakr, who spent much of her life with

'A'isha. 'Urwa can be considered a student of his aunt 'A'isha. He also was taught by Sa'id ibn al-Musayyib, who was 7 or 8 years his senior.

'Urwa was one of the seven greatest jurists of his time. He transmitted most of the Traditions narrated by 'A'isha. He also received Traditions from 'Ali, 'Umar, Ibn 'Abbas, Abu Ayyub al-Ansari, and many other Companions. Many illustrious figures of succeeding generations, among them Qatada ibn Di'ama, Ibn Shihab al-Zuhri, Yahya ibn Sa'id al-Ansari, and Zayd ibn Aslam, narrated from him.

Like his contemporaries, 'Urwa was extremely pious. For example, one of his feet became infected with gangrene and he had to have it amputated. While it was being amputated with a saw, he did not complain, but only said: *We have encountered weariness from this journey of ours* (18:62).

When one of his four sons died some time later, he stretched his arms before the Ka'ba and glorified God, saying: "O God, You gave me four limbs, two arms and two legs, and four sons. You have taken one from both groups and left to me the remaining three. Many thousands of thanks to You!"[64] 'Urwa was certainly included in the meaning of: *God is well-pleased with them, and they are well-pleased with Him* (98:8).

Muhammad ibn Muslim ibn Shihab al-Zuhri, known as Ibn Shihab al-Zuhri, narrated one-fourth of the Prophetic Traditions coming from the Tabi'un. His father, Muslim, had struggled against the Umayyads, particularly Hajjaj. As a result, the Umayyad government usually kept him under surveillance. He did not, as alleged, support the Umayyads.

Like others honored by God as the most reliable narrators of the Prophetic Traditions, Ibn Shibab al-Zuhri had an extraordinarily keen memory. He memorized the Qur'an before he was 7 years old (it took him only 8 days). When he was 18 years old, he began to practice *ijtihad* (ruling on Islamic religious or legal matters based on principles laid down in the Qur'an and Sunna). He forgot nothing: "I have betrayed nothing that God put in my heart as a trust."[65]

Ibn Shihab al-Zuhri received his first education from Sa'id ibn al-Musayyib, who taught him for 8 years. He was also taught by 'Ubaydullah ibn 'Abd Allah ibn 'Utba, one of the seven leading jurists of the time. His life was wholly dedicated to Hadith: "I shuttled between Hijaz and Damascus for 40 years for the sake of Hadith."[66]

Some accuse him of flattering the Umayyads. This lie is contradicted by historical facts. It is true that he tutored Caliph Hisham's sons. However, this is not a fault and does not mean that he supported the Umayyads. He should, in fact, be praised for trying to guide the future rulers of the Muslim community to truth.

In his first meeting with Ibn Shihab al-Zuhri, Caliph 'Abd al-Malik reminded him that his father had supported 'Abd Allah ibn Zubayr in his dispute with the Umayyads for many years. But Ibn Shihab al-Zuhri never feared to speak the truth to the Umayyad rulers. Some Umayyads alleged that 'Ali was referred to in:

> As for him among them who took upon himself the greater part of it, a mighty chastisement awaits him, coming after: Those who came with slander are a band of you; do not reckon it evil for you; rather it is good for you. Every man of them shall have the sin that he has earned charged to him. (24:11) [This verse was revealed on the occasion of the slander against 'A'isha.]

This was, of course, a great lie against 'Ali. Ibn Shihab al-Zuhri openly stated in the Umayyad court that this verse refers to 'Abd Allah ibn Ubayy ibn Salul, leader of Madina's Hypocrites. When the Caliph frowned, Ibn Shihab al-Zuhri retorted: "May you be left without a father! I swear by God that if a herald were to announce from heaven that God allows lying, I would not lie at all!"[67]

Although Ibn Shihab al-Zuhri defended 'Ali to the Umayyads, he was accused of fabricating pro-Umayyad Traditions by Ya'qubi, a Shi'ite historian. Abu Ja'far al-Iskafi, another Shi'ite historian, made the same claim against Abu Hurayra. According to Ya'qubi's false account, Caliph 'Abd al-Malik had Jerusalem's Masjid al-

Aqsa' repaired to encourage the Muslims to circumambulate it instead of the Ka'ba. He asked Ibn Shihab al-Zuhri to fabricate a Tradition to that effect, which (it was claimed) he did: "It is not worth traveling [for prayer] except to the three mosques: Masjid al-Haram, Masjid al-Aqsa', and my Masjid here [in Madina]."

Earlier in this book, I argued in favor of this Tradition's authenticity. In fact, Ya'qubi laid himself open to ridicule through such an unreasonable account, for:

- No Jewish, Christian, or Islamic history book has recorded that Masjid al-Aqsa' has been circumambulated as the Ka'ba is.

- The Qur'an extols it and the Muslims therefore revere it; it does not need a fabricated Tradition to secure this reverence.

- Caliph 'Abd al-Malik, Caliph 'Umar, Nur al-Din al-Zangi, and Salah al-Din al-Ayyubi all had it repaired.

- Ibn Shihab al-Zuhri could not have met 'Abd al-Malik during his reign and fabricated a *hadith* for him at a time when his own father (along with 'Abd Allah ibn Zubayr) was fighting against the caliph.

- Ibn Shihab al-Zuhri was not a famous Traditionist at this time. He only began to compile the Traditions in a formal manner during the Caliphate of 'Umar ibn 'Abd al-'Aziz.

- 'Abd al-Malik was not the sort of man to attempt such an absurd fraud. Before his caliphate, he was very pious, an authority on Traditions, and well-acquainted with the scholars of his generation. Although he did not succeed, as caliph, in retaining his former reputation among scholars for piety, he could not have lowered himself so far to fabricate a *hadith*.

Despite its absurdity, Goldziher used Ya'qubi's account to defame Ibn Shihab al-Zuhri, the first formal compiler of the Traditions and a narrator of one-fourth of them. "Modern" researchers in the Muslim world, such as Ahmad Amin, 'Ali Hasan 'Abd al-Qadir, and Abu Rayya, who are spokesmen for the Orientalists, repeat the same claims.

The science of Hadith is founded on the most secure and sound pillars, and its original sources are there for anyone who wants to study them. Goldziher and his followers, on the other hand, base themselves on folkloric and poetical books, such as *'Iqd al-Farid* and *Al-Aghani* (Songs), and on books dealing with animals, like *Kitab al-Hayawan*. These books, and all similar ones, have nothing to do with Hadith and have no scientific approach.

Ibn Shihab al-Zuhri is one of the greatest Hadith authorities. Leading Hadith experts, such as Ibn al-Madini, Ibn Hibban, Abu Khatim, Hafiz al-Dhahabi, and Ibn Hajar al-Asqalani, agree upon his indisputable authority. He received Traditions from many Companions, and numerous scholars among the first and second generations after the Companions narrated from him.

Among the Tabi'un are many others worthy of mention, like Aswad ibn Yazid al-Nakha'i, Nafi' (who taught Imam Malik, founder of the Maliki legal school), and Tawus ibn Qaysan, who did not sleep for 40 years between the night and dawn prayers. However, the scope of this book does not allow me to go into further detail.

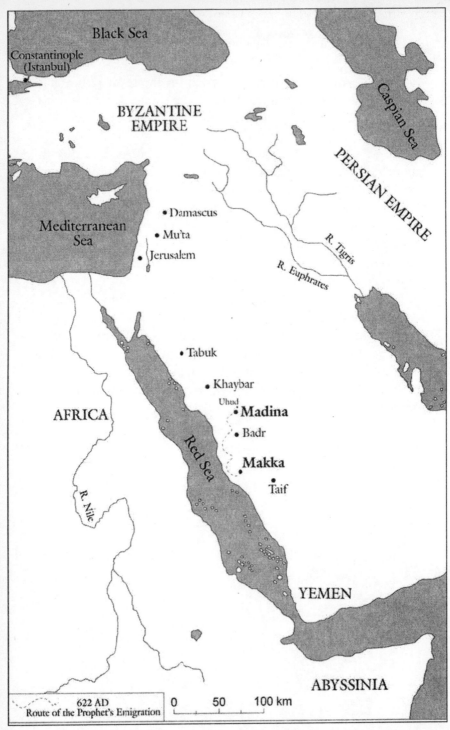

Arabia, 7th century AD

NOTES

INTRODUCTION

1   In any publication dealing with the Prophet Muhammad, his name or title is fol-
    lowed by the phrase "upon him be peace and blessings," to show our respect for
    him and because it is a religious requirement to do so. A similar phrase is used for
    his Companions and other illustrious Muslims: "May God be pleased with him (or
    her)." However, as this practice might be distracting to non-Muslim readers, these
    phrases do not appear in this book, on the understanding that they are assumed
    and that no disrespect is intended.

2   Maurice Bucaille is a French physician and scientist who accepted Islam about 25
    years ago. Roger Garaudy is one of the ideologues of communism of our age, and
    a previous general secretary of the French Communist Party. He chose Islam about
    20 years ago.

3   Majnun and Layla are two legendary figures in who loved each other very deeply. (Tr.)

4   Qadi Iyad, *Shifa' al-Sharif*, 1:173.

5   400Ahmad ibn Hanbal, *Musnad*, 2:76.

6   Al-Ajluni, *Kashf al-Khafa'*, 2:232.

7   Ibn Jarir al-Tabari, *Jami' al-Bayan 'an Ta'wil Ay al-Qur'an*; Ibn Kathir, *Al-Bidaya wa
    al Nihaya*, 3:139.

8   *Sahih al-Muslim*, "Fitan, 22-25"; *Ibn Hanbal*, 1:4.

9   Ibn Kathir, *Al-Bidaya*, 4:76.

10 Ibn Kathir, *Al-Bidaya*, 4:54; al-Haythami, *Majma' al-Zawa'id*, 6:115.

11 Ibn Hanbal, 5:235.

CHAPTER I
THE PROPHET SENT AS A MERCY

1   Darimi, *Sunan*, "Muqaddima," 7-8.

2   Busiri, in his famous *Qasida al-Bur'a* (Eulogy of Bur'a) mentions this incident, say-
    ing: "A cloud hovers over his head and protects him from the sun."

3   Ibn Hisham, *Sira*, 1:191.

4   *Sahih al-Bukhari*, "Tafsir," 1:111; *Sahih al-Muslim*, "Iman," 355.

5   Ibn Kathir, *Al-Bidaya*, 3:241.

6   Muttaqi al-Hindi, *Kanz al-'Ummal*, 11:384.

7   *Behold, Allah took the Covenant of the Prophets, saying: "I give you a Book and Wisdom.
    Then a Messenger comes to you, confirming what is with you. Believe in him and help
    him." Allah asked: "Do you agree, and take this Covenant as binding?" They replied:
    "We agree." He said: "Then bear witness, and I am with you among the witnesses."*

8   *Bukhari*, "Buyu'," 50; *Ibn Hanbal*, 2:174.

9   Ibn Kathir, *Al-Bidaya*, 2:223.

10 *Bukhari*, "Bad'u al-Wahy," 3.

11 Ahmad ibn Hanbal, *Musnad*, 5:451.

12   *Mukhtasar Tafsir Ibn al-Kathir*, 1:140.
13   *Bukhari*, al-Anbiya', "Bab Khalq Adam," 2.
14   Ibn Hisham, *Sira*, 1:228-34.
15   *Kanz al-'Ummal*, 14:39-40; Ibn Kathir, 3:83.
16   Ibn Kathir, 3:80-81; Ibn Hisham, 1:313.

CHAPTER 2
WHY PROPHETS ARE SENT

1   *Bukhari*, "Maghazi," 78; *Muslim*, "Salam," 50,51; *Abu Dawud*, "Tib," 19.
2   Tabari, *Jami' al-Bayan*, 24:33; Ibn Hanbal, 1:499.
3   *Bukhari*, "Marda," 19; *Muslim*, "Dhikr," 10.
4   Ibn Hisham, *Sira*, 2:60-63; Ibn Kathir, *Al-Bidaya*, 3:166.
5   Ibn Maja, "Manasik," 84; *Abu Dawud*, "Manasik," 56.
6   *Bukhari*, "Fada'il al-Ashab," 1; *Muslim*, "Fada'il al-Sahaba," 208-9.
7   *Bukhari*, "Fada'il al-Ashab," 1; *Muslim*, "Fada'il al-Sahaba," 212.
8   Ibrahim al-Halabi, *Sira*, 1:218.
9   'Ajluni, *Kashf al-Khafa'*, 2:83.
10   Ibn Sa'd, *Tabaqat*, 3:350; Haythami, *Majma' al-Zawa'id*, 1:295.
11   Abu Nu'aym, *Hilyat al-Awliya' wa Tabaqat al-Asfiya'*, 1:30-31.

CHAPTER 3
CHARACTERISTICS OF PROPHETS

1   Ibn Kathir, *Al-Bidaya*, 2:350.
2   *Bukhari*, "Hajj," 42; Ibn Kathir, *Al-Bidaya*, 2:350.
3   Ibn Hisham, *Sira*, 2:285.
4   *Bukhari*, "Tawhid," 36; *Muslim*, "Iman," 326.
5   *Bukhari*, "Riqaq," 17; *Muslim*, "Zuhd," 28.
6   Muttaqi al-Hindi, *Kanz al-'Ummal*, 7:199.
7   *Ibn Hanbal*, 2:231; Haythami, *Majma' al-Zawa'id*, 9:18-19.
8   Haythami, 9:21.
9   Bediuzzaman Said Nursi, *The Words*, "The First Word," 5.
10   *Abu Dawud*, "Adab," 152; *Ibn Hanbal*, 5:253.
11   *Bukhari*, "Iman," 47; *Muslim*, "Iman," 5:7.
12   'Ali al-Qari, Al-Asrar al-Marfu'a, 286.
13   Imam Malik, Muwatta, "Hajj," 246; Hindi, Kanz al-'Ummal, 5:73.

CHAPTER 4
THE ESSENTIALS OF PROPHETHOOD

1   *Muslim*, "Jihad," 101; *Bukhari*, "Anbiya'," 54.
2   Bukhari, Bad'u al-Wahy, 6.
3   *Ibn Hanbal*, 5:323.

4   *Tirmidhi*, "Qiyamah," 60; *Ibn Hanbal*, 1:200.
5   Hindi, *Kanz al-'Ummal*, 3:344.
6   *Bukhari*, "Adab," 69; *Muslim*, "Birr," 105; *Abu Dawud*, "Adab," 80.
7   *Bukhari*, "Maghazi," 79; *Muslim*, "Tawba," 53.
8   *Abu Dawud*, "Adab," 82.
9   It is not stated exactly why the Prophet was angry. However, we can make several guesses: Some questions may have contained unbecoming things or sounded unnecessary, or he might have seen some doubts in their hearts about his knowledge and so wanted to lay them to rest.
10 *Bukhari*, "Fitan," 15.
11 *Muslim*, "Janna," 76, 77.
12 *Ibn Hanbal*, 4:360-64.
13 Ibn Kathir, *Al-Bidaya*, 4:348; Bayhaqi, *Dala'il al-Nubuwwa*, 5:102.
14 Ibn Hajar, *Al-Isaba fi Tamyiz al-Sahaba*, 3:36.
15 *Bukhari*, "Fada'il al-Madina," 8; *Muslim*, "Fitan," 9.
16 *Bukhari*, "Sawm," 3; *Muslim*, "Fitan," 27.
17 *Bukhari*, "Manaqib," 22; *Abu Dawud*, "Jihad," 97.
18 *Ibn Maja*, "Jana'iz," 65; *Muslim*, "Fada'il al-Sahaba," 15; *Ibn Hanbal*, 3:197.
19 The death of God's Messenger touched Fatima so deeply that she gave voice to her grief in the following verses:

> *What else does the one who has smelt the soil of*
> *Muhammad's tomb need?*
> *Does one really need the smell of anything else?*
> *I have been struck by such misfortunes that if they*
> *had fallen upon days,*
> *They would have changed into nights!*

20 *Bukhari*, "Sulh," 9; *Ibn Hanbal*, 5:49.
21 Haythami, *Al-Majma' al-Zawa'id*, 9:404-5.
22 *Bukhari*, "Manaqib al-Ansar," 39; *Muslim*, "Jihad," 127.
23 *Bukhari*, "Maghazi," 29; *Muslim*, "Jihad," 123, 124, 125.
24 Ibn Kathir, *Al-Bidaya*, 4:116; *Ibn Hanbal*, 4:303; Ibn Hisham, *Sira*, 3:230.
25 *Bukhari*, "Manaqib," 22.
26 *Bukhari*, "Salat," 63; *Muslim*, "Fitan," 70, 72, 73; *Ibn Hanbal*, 12: 161, 164.
27 *Bukhari*, "Adab," 95; *Muslim*, "Zakat," 142; *Ibn Hanbal*, 3:56.
28 *Bukhari*, "Adab," 95; *Muslim*, "Zakat," 142; *Ibn Hanbal*, 1:356.
29 *Ibn Hanbal*, 3:82.
30 *Bukhari*, "Jihad," 3:8; *Muslim*, "'Imara," 160-61.
31 *Bukhari*, "Jihad," 95, 96; *Abu Dawud*, "Malahim," 10; *Ibn Maja*, "Fitan," 36; *Ibn Hanbal*, 5:40, 45.
32 Hakim, *Mustadrak*, 4:422; *Ibn Hanbal*, 4:335.
33 *Abu Dawud*, "Malahim," 5; *Ibn Hanbal*, 5:278.
34 *Bukhari*, "Fitan," 16; *Muslim*, "Fitan," 45; *Ibn Hanbal*, 2:50, 72.
35 *Bukhari*, "Fitan," 24; *Muslim*, "Fitan," 30; *Abu Dawud*, "Malahim," 12:13.
36 *Muslim*, "Iman," 244-47.

37 *Muslim*, "Fitan," 110; *Tirmidhi*, "Fitan," 59; *Ibn Hanbal*, 4:182.
38 *Ibn Hanbal*, 1:407, 408; Hakim, *Mustadrak*, 4:98, 448.
39 Darimi, *Muqaddima*, 27.
40 Hindi, *Kanz al-'Ummal*, 14:244.
41 Haythami, *Majma' al-Zawa'id*, 7:324.
42 *Ibn Maja*, "Tijara," 58; *Ibn Hanbal*, 2:494; *Nasa'i*, "Buyu'," 2.
43 Hindi, *Kanz al-'Ummal*, 11:176.
44 *Ibid.*, 14:591.
45 *Muslim*, "'Ilm," 6; *Bukhari*, "Anbiya'," 50.
46 *Bukhari*, "Tib," 1.
47 *Abu Dawud*, "Tib," 10; *Muslim*, "Salam," 69.
48 *Tirmidhi*, "Tib," 2; *Ibn Maja*, "Tib," 1; *Ibn Hanbal*, 4:278.
49 *Bukhari*, "Tib," 30; *Muslim*, "Salam," 98.
50 *Bukhari*, "Tib," 19; *Ibn Hanbal*, 2:443.
51 *Muslim*, "Tahara," 91.
52 *Abu Dawud*, "Adahi," 21; *Ibn Maja*, "Sayd," 2; *Ibn Hanbal*, 4:85.
53 *Abu Dawud*, "At'ima," 11; *Tirmidhi*, "'At'ima, 39; *Ibn Hanbal*, 5:441.
54 *Muslim*, "Tahara," 87; *Abu Dawud*, "Tahara," 49; *Tirmidhi*, "Tahara," 19.
55 *Bukhari*, "Jumu'a," 8; *Muslim*, "Tahara," 42; *Abu Dawud*, "Tahara," 25; *Tirmidhi*, "Tahara," 18; *Nasa'i*, "Tahara," 6; *Ibn Maja*, "Tahara," 7; *Ibn Hanbal*, 1:80.
56 *Tirmidhi*, "Zuhd," 47; *Ibn Hanbal*, 4:132.
57 Hindi, *Kanz al-'Ummal*, 3:460.
58 *Abu Dawud*, "Tib," 14; *Tirmidhi*, "Tib," 9.
59 *Ibn Maja*, "Tib," 29; *Tirmidhi*, "Tib," 13.
60 *Bukhari*, "Tib," 7; *Muslim*, "Salam, "88.
61 *Bukhari*, "Bad'u al-Khalq," 17; Tib, 58; *Abu Dawud*, "At'ima," 48.
62 *Bukhari*, "Wudu'," 63; *Muslim*, "Hayd," 62; *Abu Dawud*, "Tahara," 109.
63 *Muslim*, "Ashriba," 12; *Ibn Maja*, "Tib," 27.
64 *Muslim*, "Tahara," 49; *Abu Dawud*, "Tahara," 27.
65 Said Nursi, *Tarikhca Hayat* (Biography), 56.
66 *Abu Dawud*, "Manasik," 56; *Ibn Maja*, "Manasik," 84; Ibn Kathir, *Al-Bidaya*, 5:173.
67 *Bukhari*, "Tawhid," 22; *Muslim*, "Iman," 288.
68 *Bukhari*, "I'tiqaf," 8; *Ibn Maja*, "Siyam," 65.
69 *Abu Dawud*, "Adab," 80; *Ibn Hanbal*, 3:447.
70 *Bukhari*, "Iman," 24; *Muslim*, "Iman," 107.
71 *Abu Dawud*, "Jihad," 112, "Adab," 164; *Ibn Hanbal*, 1:404.
72 *Abu Dawud*, "Adab," 164; *Ibn Hanbal*, 1:404.
73 Ibn Kathir, *Tafsir*, 7:359; *Al-Targhib wa al-Tarhib*, 4:285.
74 *Abu Dawud*, "Witr," 32; *Nasa'i*, "Isti'adha," 19:20; *Ibn Maja*, "At'ima," 53.
75 *Muslim*, "Jihad," 9.
76 Ibn Hisham, *Sira*, 2:27.
77 Bukhari, *Tafsir*, 9; *Ibn Hanbal*, 1:4.
78 *Bukhari*, "Maghazi," 29, "Jihad," 83; *Muslim*, "Fada'il," 13.
79 *Bukhari*, "'Ilm," 2; *Ibn Hanbal*, 3:361.

[80]   *Bukhari*, "Jumu'a," 10; *Muslim*, "'Imara," 20; *Abu Dawud*, "'Imara," 1.

[81]   *Ibn Hanbal*, 3:135.

[82]   *Tirmidhi*, "Iman," 12; *Ibn Maja*, "Fitan," 2.

[83]   *Ibn Hanbal*, 5:323.

[84]   Hindi, *Kanz al-'Ummal*, 5:328.

[85]   One of Avicenna's students once told him that, with his extraordinary understanding and intelligence, he could claim Prophethood and easily gather many followers. Avicenna said nothing. Some time passed, and then during the winter they undertook a journey. Avicenna awoke from his sleep one morning at dawn, woke his student and asked him to bring some water for him to drink. The student put him off and made excuses. However much Avicenna persisted, the student would not leave his warm bed. At that moment, the call to prayer was made: *God is the Greatest... I bear witness that there is no god but God. I bear witness that Muhammad is the Messenger of God...* Avicenna, taking advantage of this opportunity, finally answered his student's question:

> Remember when you encouraged me to proclaim my Prophethood and that many people would follow me? Consider this: You have been my student for years and have benefited from my lessons, but you wouldn't even leave your warm bed to get some water for me. But this man, who calls us to prayer as others have done for the last 400 years, follows the (real) Prophet. He left his warm bed, as he does every morning together with hundreds of thousands of others, climbed the minaret and proclaimed God's Unity and Muhammad's Messengership. Now do you understand my position vis-à-vis the Prophet?! (Tr.)

[86]   This simile is coined with respect to the Prophet's submission to Revelation. He fulfills whatever he is commanded by Revelation.

[87]   Qadi Iyad, *Shifa' al-Sharif*, 1:105; *Bukhari*, "Anbiya'," 54; *Muslim*, "Jihad," 105.

[88]   Ibn Kathir, *Al-Bidaya*, 3:153.

[89]   Ibn Hisham, Sira, 4:48; *Ibn Hanbal*, 3:160; Ibn Hajar, *Al-Isaba*, 4:116.

[90]   Haythami, *Majma' al-Zawa'id*, 7:100-1.

[91]   *Bukhari*, "Maghazi," 21; Ibn Hisham, *Sira*, 3:76-77.

[92]   Hakim, *Mustadrak*, 3:241-43; Ibn Hajar, *Al-Isaba*, 2:496.

[93]   Ibn Hanbal, 1:159; Haythami, 8:302-3.

[94]   Ibn Hisham, *Sira*, 2:73.

[95]   Ibn Kathir, *Al-Bidaya*, 5:120-21.

[96]   *Ibid.*, 4:272.

[97]   *Ibid.*, 4:273.

[98]   *Ibid.*, 4:271.

[99]   *Ibid.*, 3:104.

[100]   *Ibid.*, 3:105.

[101]   *Bukhari*, "Jana'iz," 4:65; *Muslim*, "Jana'iz," 62-67.

[102]   *Bukhari*, "Bad'u al-Wahy," 6.

[103]   *Ibid.*

[104]   *Ibid.*

[105]   Ibn Kathir, *Al-Bidaya*, 5:324.
[106]   *Bukhari*, "'Ilm," 7:1; Ibn Hanbal, 1:243.
[107]   *Ibn Hanbal*, 5:256-57.
[108]   *Muslim*, "Fada'il al-Sahaba," 131.
[109]   Ibn Hisham, *Sira*, 163-64.
[110]   Sa'id al-Hawwa, *Al-Rasul*, 1:9. For a different version, see Ibn Hajar, *Al-Isaba*, 2:307.
[111]   'Ali al-Qari, *Al-Asrar al-Marfu'a*, 286.
[112]   *Bukhari*, "Tahajjud,"6; *Muslim*, "Munafiqin," 81.
[113]   Ibn Kathir, *Tafsir*, 2:164.
[114]   *Muslim*, "Salat," 221-2; *Abu Dawud*, "Salat," 148; "Witr," 5.
[115]   *Bukhari*, "Tafsir," 287; *Muslim*, "Talaq," 31.
[116]   Abu Nu'aym, *Hilya*, 7:107; Hindi, *Kanz al-'Ummal*, 1:199.
[117]   *Muslim*, "Ashriba," 140.
[118]   *Bukhari*, "Fada'il al-Sahaba," 9.
[119]   *Nasa'i*, "Zinat," 39.
[120]   *Bukhari*, "Fada'il al-Sahaba," 5; Ibn Hanbal, 2:205.
[121]   Qadi Iyad, *Shifa'*, 1:67.
[122]   Ibn Hanbal, 3:425; Ibn Hisham, *Sira*, 1:209.
[123]   Ibn Hajar, *Al-Isaba*, 1:337.
[124]   'Ajluni, *Kashf al-Khafa'*, 1:147.
[125]   *Ibn Hanbal*, 4:65; 5:64.
[126]   *Bukhari*, "Manaqib al-Ansar," 1:2; *Muslim*, "Zakat," 132-41.
[127]   Hindi, *Kanz al-'Ummal*, 11:412.
[128]   *Ibid.*, 11:425.
[129]   *Tirmidhi*, "Qiyama," 59.
[130]   *Tirmidhi*, "Zuhd," 25.
[131]   *Bukhari*, "Adab," 69; *Muslim*, "Birr," 105; *Abu Dawud*, "Adab," 80.
[132]   *Bukhari*, "Adab," 96; *Muslim*, "Birr," 165.
[133]   *Bukhari*, "Hudud," 4:5.
[134]   *Tirmidhi*, "Birr," 55; Ibn Hanbal, 5:153.
[135]   Hindi, *Kanz al-'Ummal*, 6:89.
[136]   *Bukhari*, "Bad'u al-Wahy," 1; *Muslim*, "'Imara," 155; *Abu Dawud*, "Talaq," 11.
[137]   Dahabi, *Majma' al-Zawa'id*, 1:61, 109.
[138]   *Bukhari*, "Iman," 4.
[139]   *Tirmidhi*, "Zuhd," 11; *Ibn Maja*, "Fitan," 12.
[140]   *Bukhari*, "Iman," 37; *Muslim*, "Iman," 1.
[141]   *Bukhari*, "Jana'iz," 43; *Muslim*, "Jana'iz," 14, 15.
[142]   *Bukhari*, "Wasaya," 9; "Zakat," 18; *Muslim*, "Zakat," 94; Ibn Hanbal, 2:4.
[143]   *Muslim*, "Iman," 171-4; Suyuti, *Al-Fath al-Kabir*, 2:57.
[144]   *Tirmidhi*, "Birr," 40.
[145]   *Bukhari*, "Riqaq," 23.
[146]   *Muslim*, "Tahara," 41; *Tirmidhi*, "Tahara," 39.
[147]   *Bukhari*, "Tawhid," 35.
[148]   *Bukhari*, "Riqaq," 28; *Muslim*, "Janna," 1.

[149] *Tirmidhi*, "'Ilm," 16; for different versions, see, *Ibn Maja*, "Muqad-dima," 6.

[150] *Bukhari*, "Adab," 83; *Muslim*, "Zuhd," 63.

[151] *Bukhari*, "Manaqib," 1; *Muslim*, "Birr," 160; Ibn Hanbal, 2:539.

[152] *Bukhari*, "Tafsir," 5; *Muslim*, "Birr," 61.

[153] Women who resist men are certainly included in the meaning of this *hadith*. The reason why men are mentioned is that they often are attracted to women and follow their desire. Men are at greater risk than women and more liable to fall. So, the *hadith* warns men to protect themselves against illicit relationships. Men exploit the charm and beauty of women for their benefit, and unfortunately women are used to spread immorality and obscenity. It is rare in human history that women command and use men in such ways.

[154] *Bukhari*, "Adhan," 36; *Muslim*, "Zakat," 91; *Tirmidhi*, "Zuhd," 53.

[155] *Bukhari*, "Tayammum," 1; "Salat," 56.

[156] *Muslim*, "Iman," 326.

[157] Ibn Kathir, *Al-Bidaya*, 2:350-51.

[158] *Bukhari*, "Hajj," 42; *Ibn Kathir*, "Al-Bidaya," 2:350.

[159] *Tirmidhi*, "Qiyama," 49; *Ibn Maja*, "Zuhd," 30.

[160] *Ibn Kathir*, "Tafsir" 3:539.

[161] A Prophetic saying whose meaning is directly from God.

[162] *Bukhari*, "Riqaq," 38; Ibn Hanbal, 6:256.

[163] Judah is not mentioned in the Qur'an as a Prophet. However, the Qur'an mentions the sons of Jacob as grandchildren worthy of following. Although they wronged Joseph out of jealousy, they must have corrected their ways later. According to the Bible, not to the Qur'an, some of the Israelite Prophets were descended from Judah.

[164] See note 214 above.

[165] Ibn Kathir, *Al-Bidaya*, 2:313-14.

[166] *Bukhari*, "Anbiya'," 48; Muslim, "Fada'il," 144.

[167] *Bukhari*, "Tahajjud," 7, "Sawm," 59; *Muslim*, "Siyam," 182.

[168] For different versions of the *hadith*, see, *Bukhari*, "Hudud," 22; *Abu Dawud*, "Hudud," 17; *Tirmidhi*, "Hudud," 1; *Ibn Maja*, "Talaq," 15,16.

[169] *Bukhari*, "Tafsir," 3; *Tirmidhi*, "Qadar," 2; Ibn Hanbal, 2:287, 314.

[170] *Muslim*, "Iman," 271.

[171] Mulla Jami', *Nafahat al-Uns*, 521.

[172] *Bukhari*, "Anbiya'," 11.

[173] Ibn Kathir, *Shama'il*, 84-85.

[174] *Bukhari*, "Anbiya'," 8; *Muslim*, "Fada'il," 154.

[175] *Bukhari*, "Anbiya'," 21:19; Ibn Hanbal, 2:96, 332.

[176] *Qurtubi*, "Tafsir," 8:31; Ibn Hanbal, 1:383.

[177] He could not make them reveal their real reasons. This is why hypocrites, who are outwardly Muslims but inwardly unbelievers, are treated as Muslims in a Muslim society. There were many such people in Madina during the Prophet's time. The Prophet never disclosed their identities.

[178] Qurtubi, 8:98-99; Fakhr al-Razi, *Mafatih al-Ghayb*, 16:73-74.

[179] Said Nursi, *Eptiomes of Light* (Mathnawi al-Nuriya) (Izmir, Kaynak: 1999), II.

[180] *Abu Dawud*, "Diyat," 70; *Tirmidhi*, "Diyat," 17.

[181] *Ibn Hanbal*, 411.

[182] Suyuti, *Al-Khasa'is al-Kubra*, 1:123; Hindi, *Kanz al-'Ummal*, 7:168.

[183] Nursi, *The Letters*, 2:84-85.

CHAPTER 5
PROPHET MUHAMMAD AS HUSBAND AND FATHER

[1] The reason was not specified in sources. However, there were rare debates among his wives because of jealousy, which might have caused them to speak to him improperly. Another reason may be that it was rare for them to ask the Prophet for something that he could not procure. There was not the least record that something happened between the Prophet and his wives because of sexual reasons. Visiting was not restricted to sexual relations. He may have been offended at her behavior in her room.

[2] *Muslim*, "Rada'," 47.

[3] *Bukhari*, "Salat," 80.

[4] *Tirmidhi*, "Nikah," 41:4; *Bukhari*, "Adab," 68.

[5] *Bukhari*, "Adab," 68.

[6] *Bukhari*, "Shurut," 15.

[7] *Abu Dawud*, "Sunna," 15; *Tirmidhi*, "Rada'," 11.

[8] *Muslim*, "Talaq," 34, 35.

[9] Abu Nu'aym, *Hilyat al-Awliya'*, 8:100.

[10] *Muslim*, "Talaq," 35.

[11] *Tirmidhi*, "Manaqib," 64.

[12] *Muslim*, "Fada'il," 63.

[13] *Ibid.*, 62.

[14] *Bukhari*, "Jana'iz," 44; *Muslim*, "Fada'il," 62; *Ibn Maja*, "Jana'iz," 53.

[15] Hindi, *Kanz al-'Ummal*, 13:650.

[16] *Ibn Hanbal*, 2:279; *Muslim*, "Zakat," 161.

[17] *Bukhari*, "Adab," 18; Ibn Sa'd, *Tabaqat*, 8:39.

[18] *Muslim*, "Fada'il," 98, 99; *Bukhari*, "Manaqib," 25.

[19] *Nasa'i*, "Zinat," 39.

[20] *Bukhari*, "Fada'il al-Ashab," 9; *Muslim*, "Dhikr," 80, 81.

[21] Bediüzzaman Said Nursi, *Lemalar*, 4. "Lema."

[22] According to I Kings 11:3, Solomon had *700 wives, princesses, and 300 concubines.*

[23] *Bukhari*, "Tawhid," 22.

[24] *Bukhari* and *Muslim*.

[25] Ibn Hanbal, *Musnad*, 6:277.

CHAPTER 6
PROPHET MUHAMMAD AS EDUCATOR

[1] *Bukhari*, "Manaqib," 18; *Muslim*, "Fada'il," 20-23.

[2]   Isaac Taylor, who spoke at the Church Congress of England, relates how Islam changes the people who accept it:

The virtues which Islam inculcates are temperance, cleanliness, chastity, justice, fortitude, courage, benevolence, hospitality, veracity, and resignation... Islam preaches a practical brotherhood, the social equality of all Muslims. Slavery is not part of the creed of Islam. Polygamy is a more difficult question. Moses did not prohibit it. It was practiced by David, and is not directly forbidden in the New Testament. Muhammad limited the unbounded license of polygamy. It is the exception rather than the rule... (Abu'l-Fazl Ezzati, *An Introduction to the History of the Spread of Islam*, London) (Tr.)

[3]   To give just one example, Lamartine asks:

Philosopher, orator, apostle, legislator, warrior, conqueror of ideas, restorer of rational dogmas, of a cult without images; the founder of twenty terrestrial states and of one spiritual state, that is Muhammad. As regards all standards by which human greatness may be measured, we may well ask: Is there any man greater than he? (*Historie de la Turquie*, 2:276-77.) (Tr.)

[4]   *Nasa'i*, "Sahw," 18.

[5]   Ibid., "Ishrat al-Nisa'," 4.

[6]   Those who became apostates after the Prophet's death were not Companions. (Tr.)

[7]   There is a rule in logic: Exceptions do not invalidate the rule. We do not know of any heretics among his descendants. But this does not mean that there will not be, because it is possible. Considering this possibility, we speak with caution.

[8]   *Bukhari*, "Nikah," 36; *Abu Dawud*, "Talaq," 33.

[9]   A nineteenth-century Western writer notes his impressions of the influence of Islamic moral values on Africans:

As to the effects of Islam when first embraced by a Negro tribe, can there, when viewed as a whole, be any reasonable doubt? Polytheism disappears almost instantaneously; sorcery, with its attendant evils, gradually dies away; human sacrifice becomes a thing of the past. The general moral elevation is most marked; the natives begin for the first time in their history to dress, and that neatly. Squalid filth is replaced by some approach to personal cleanliness; hospitality becomes a religious duty; drunkenness, instead of the rule, becomes a comparatively rare exception. Chastity is looked upon as one of the highest, and becomes, in fact, one of the commoner virtues. It is idleness that henceforward degrades, and industry that elevates, instead of the reverse. Offenses are henceforward measured by a written code instead of the arbitrary caprice of a chieftain—a step, as everyone will admit—of vast importance in the progress of a tribe. The mosque gives an idea of architecture at all events higher than any the Negro has yet had. A thirst for literature is created and that for works of science and philosophy as well as for commentaries on the Qur'an. (Waitz quoted by B. Smith, Muhammad and Muhammadanism, 42-3.) (Tr.)

[10] Al-Ezzati, *An Introduction to the History of the Spread of Islam*.

[11] Ibn al-Athir, *Al-Kamil fi al-Tarikh*, 4:106.

[12] Kufa, a famous city in the early history of Islam, is located on the west branch of the river Euphrates, south of the ruins of Babel (Iraq). (Tr.)

[13] Ibn al-Athir, *Usd al-Ghaba*, 7:88-90; Ibn Hajar, *Al-Isaba*, 4:287.

[14] Tabari, *Tarikh*, 5:195; Ibn Sa'd, *Tabaqat*, 3:305; Abu Nu'aym, *Hilya*, 1:53.

[15] Munawi, *Fayd al-Qadir*, 2:290.
[16] Muttaqi al-Hindi, *Kanz al-'Ummal*, 3:907.
[17] *Abu Dawud*, "Buyu'," 54; Ibn Hanbal, *Musnad*, 2:84.
[18] 'Ajluni, *Kashf al-Khafa'*, 1:370.
[19] *Muslim*, "Qadar," 34; *Ibn Maja*, "Muqaddima," 10; Ibn Hanbal, 3:366.
[20] *Bukhari*, "Wasaya," 9.
[21] *Nasa'i*, "Nikah," 36.
[22] *Muslim*, "Zakat," 108; *Ibn Maja*, "Jihad," 41.
[23] *Muslim*, "Hudud," 22-23.
[24] *Bukhari*, "Tafsir," 6; *Muslim*, "Ashriba," 172.

CHAPTER 7
THE MILITARY DIMENSION

[1] 'Ajluni, *Kashf al-Khafa'*, 1:424.
[2] Imam Rabbani, Ahmad Faruq al-Sarhandi, *Maktubat*, 1:157.
[3] Ibn Hanbal, *Musnad*, 3:344; 359.
[4] As is known, night vigils are times when impression is more keen and recitation more penetrating.
[5] The Muslim envoy to the Persian commander during the war of Qadisiya. This took place in 637 CE, during 'Umar's caliphate.
[6] *Abu Dawud*, "Malahim," 5; Ibn Hanbal, 5:278.
[7] *Muslim*, "Fada'il al-Sahaba," 63; Ibn Kathir, *Al-Bidaya*, 6:336.
[8] *Muslim*, "'Imara," 39; *Ibn Maja*, "Jihad," 40.
[9] This battle took place during Abu Bakr's caliphate. (Tr.)
[10] *Abu Dawud*, "Jihad," 96; *Tirmidhi*, "Jihad," 36; Ibn Hanbal, 2:70, 86.
[11] Such modern historians as Muhammad Hamidullah tend to regard as the first constitution in Islamic history.
[12] *Bukhari*, "Manaqib," 25.
[13] Ibn Hisham, *Sira*, 2:241; Ibn Sa'd, *Tabaqat*, 2:7.
[14] Ibn Hisham, 2:241, 248.
[15] Ibn Hisham, 2:252.
[16] Ibn Hisham, 4:39-42; Ibn Kathir, *Al-Bidaya*, 4:332-335.
[17] Hakim. Mustadrak, 3:188; Ibn Kathir, 3:334.
[18] Ibn Hajar, *Al-Isaba*, 1:286-287.
[19] He had been on the verge of becoming king of Madina when the Emigration began. Seeing that many people had accepted the Prophet as the new leader of Madina, he eventually converted to Islam. However, his lost kingship continued to gall him inside and caused him to become a leading Hypocrite and thorn in the side of the Muslim community.
[20] *God promised you that one of the two hosts would be yours, and you wished that the one with no power should be yours. But God willed to establish the truth through His words and to annihilate the unbelievers to the last remnant, that He might prove the truth to be true and falsify falsehood, even if the sinful are averse* (8:7-8).

21 Ibn Saʿd, 3:162.
22 *Muslim*, "Kitab al-Jihad wa al-Siyar," 30; Waqidi, *Maghazi*, 1:48-49.
23 Tabari, *Tarikh al-Umam wa al-Muluk*, 2:430.
24 *Ibn Hanbal*, 1:411, 418.
25 Ibn Saʿd, 3:120.
26 *Ibn Hanbal*, 1:159.
27 Ibn Hisham, 2:127.
28 *Ibid.*, 1:621.
29 *Ibid.*, 1:668; *Ibn Hanbal*, 1:368.
30 Ibn Hisham, 2:277.
31 *Ibid.*, 2:280-287; Ibn Kathir, 3:350.
32 *Abu Dawud*, 2:53; *Muslim*, 5:170.
33 Ibn Hisham, 3:58.
34 An advisory system of government is an indispensable article of the Islamic constitution. Those who are learned, pious, and have sound judgment and expert knowledge, and who enjoy the people's confidence, are to be sought. In turn, they are
   expected to express their opinions, according to the dictates of their conscience,
   with precision and integrity. This advisory system is so important that God praises
   the first, exemplary Muslim community as one whose affair is by counsel among
   them (42:8).

   This importance becomes more explicit when the Prophet's leadership is considered. He never spoke out of caprice and on his own authority, but only spoke
   what God revealed (53:3-4). Thus, he preferred the majority opinion to his own.
   But since he had to execute their decision in full submission to and confidence in
   God, he could not change his decision for several reasons: First, this would cause
   some to pressure others to accept their opinions; second, leaders who change their
   decisions according to individual feelings and fancies can lose their authority and
   reliability; third, any resulting hesitation passes fear, anxiety, and confusion to the
   followers; fourth if the Messenger had changed his decision and defended the
   Muslims from within Madina, a defeat would have caused his opponents to criticize him and the leading Companions.

   In his every word and deed, the Messenger set an example to be followed. All
   the above reflections refer to his behavior prior to Uhud and his words: "It does
   not befit a Prophet to take off his coat of mail after he has put it on."

35 Ibn Hisham, 3:664/667.
36 *Bukhari*, "Iʿtisam," 28; Ibn Hisham, *Sira*, 3:68.
37 Ibn Hisham, 3:68.
38 *Bukhari*, "Jihad," 164; *Abu Dawud*, "Jihad," 6.
39 *Muslim*, "Fadaʾil al-Sahaba," 128; Ibn Hanbal, 3:123.
40 Haythami, *Majmaʿ al-Zawaʾid*, 6:109.
41 Ibn Saʿd, *Tabaqat*, 3:12; Waqidi, *Maghazi*, 221.
42 Qadi ʿIyad, *Shifaʾ*, 1:78-9; Hindi, *Kanz al-ʿUmmal*, 4:93.
43 Ibn Hisham, 3:99.
44 Ibn Saʿd, *Tabaqat*, 8:413-15.
45 Ibn Hanbal, 3:201; Bayhaqi, *Sunan*, 9:44.

[46]	Ibn Kathir, *Al-Bidaya*, 4:35-6.

[47]	Tabari, *Tarikh*, 3:17; Ibn Athir, *Al-Kamil*, 2:74; Ibn Hisham, *Sira*, 3:100.

[48]	Said Nursi, *Lemalar* (Istanbul: 28).

[49]	Ibn Hisham, 3:120-1; Ibn Kathir, *Al-Bidaya*, 4:43.

[50]	Ibn Hisham, 3:101.

[51]	Ibn Hisham, 3:94; Ibn Sa'd, 2:59.

[52]	Ibn Hisham, 3:213.

[53]	Ibn Kathir, 4:178-79.

[54]	Ibn Hisham, 3:225-26; Waqidi, 441-43.

[55]	*Bukhari*, "Manaqib al-Ansar," 9; "Maghazi," 29; *Muslim*, "Jihad," 123-25.

[56]	*Bukhari*, "Manaqib," 9; *Muslim*, "Jihad," 127.

[57]	Ibn Hisham, 3:230; Ibn Kathir, *Al-Bidaya*, 4:116.

[58]	Ibn Hisham, 3:239.

[59]	Ibid., 3:240-42.

[60]	Ibid., 3:235-36.

[61]	Ibn Kathir, 4:123.

[62]	Ibn Hisham, 3:243.

[63]	*Bukhari*, "Maghazi," 29; *Ibn Hanbal*, 4:262.

[64]	*Bukhari*, "Maghazi," 30.

[65]	Ibn Hisham, 3:249-51.

[66]	Ibn Hisham, 3:238, 262; Ibn Sa'd, 3:423-24; Tabari, *Tarikh*, 3:49.

[67]	Ibn Hisham, 3:226; Diyarbakri, *Khamis*, 1:540.

[68]	*Bukhari*, "Maghazi," 38.

[69]	*Bukhari*, 5:77; *Muslim*, 4:1872.

[70]	*Bukhari*, "Maghazi," 44.

[71]	*Ibn Hanbal*, 5:299; Tabari, 3:110.

[72]	Ibn Hisham, 4:31.

[73]	Ibid., 4:39.

[74]	Ibid., 4:41.

[75]	Ibn Kathir, *Al-Bidaya*, 4:330; Ibn Hisham, 6:41-45.

[76]	Ibn Kathir, 4:331-32.

[77]	Ibn Sa'd, 2:142; Ibn Hisham, 4:55; Tabari, 3:120; Baladhuri, *Futuh al-Buldan*, 1:47.

[78]	Bukhari, 5:93; Muslim, 3:1408; Ibn Hisham, 4:59; Ibn Sa'd, 2:136.

[79]	*Bukhari*, "Jihad," 52; *Muslim*, "Jihad," 78.

[80]	Ibn Kathir, 4:373.

[81]	*Bukhari*, "Tafsir," 18; Ibn Hisham, 4:161; Tabari, *Tarikh*, 3:143; "Tafsir," 10:161.

[82]	Ibn Sa'd, 2:165-68; Tabari, *Tarikh*, 3:100-11.

[83]	Ibn Kathir, *Al-Bidaya*, 5:13.

[84]	Andrew Miller, *Church History*, 285; Bukhari, "Manaqib," 9.

[85]	Ibn Hisham, 2:269.

[86]	Bukhari, "Tayammum," 1, "Salat," 56.

[87]	Nasa'i, *Sunan*, 5:212; Ibn Hisham, 4:13; Ibn Sa'd, 2:121.

CHAPTER 8
A UNIVERSAL LEADER

1.   Ibn Kathir, *Al-Bidaya*, 3:40-1, 102-3; Ibn Hisham, *Sira*, 1:234.
2.   *Muslim*, "'Imara," 16-17.
3.   Muttaqi al-Hindi, *Kanz al-'Ummal*, 11:563, 13:15.
4.   *Bukhari*, "Fada'il al-Ashab," 5:7; *Muslim*, "Fada'il al-Sahaba," 29.
5.   *Muslim*, "Musafirin," 294; Ibn Hanbal, *Musnad*, 4:112.
6.   His story, which appears in Volume 1, is as follows: One day, Julaybib asked the Messenger for permission to fornicate, since he could not restrain himself. Those who were present reacted in various ways. Some scoffed at him, others pulled his robe, and still others readied themselves to hit him. But the compassionate Prophet drew him near and began talking with him: "Would you let someone do this with your mother?" to which the young man replied: "My mother and father be your ransom, O Messenger, I don't agree with that." The Prophet said: "Naturally, no one agrees that his mother should be a party in such a disgraceful act."

   He then continued asking Julaybib the same question, substituting *daughter, wife, sister,* and *aunt* for *mother.* Every time Julaybib replied that he would not agree to such an act. By the end of this conversation, Julaybib had lost all desire to fornicate. The Messenger concluded this "spiritual operation" by placing his hand on Julaybib's chest and praying: "O God, forgive him, purify his heart, and maintain his chastity."
7.   *Muslim*, "Fada'il al-Sahaba," 131.
8.   *Bukhari*, "Fada'il al-Ashab," 9; *Muslim*, "Fada'il al-Sahaba," 34.
9.   *Bukhari*, "Fada'il al-Ashab," 25.
10.   Each clan claimed the honor of reinserting the sacred Black Stone in its place. Requested by the tribe to solve this problem, the future Prophet of Islam spread his mantle on a piece of cloth on the ground and, putting the Black Stone on it, invited the chiefs of the four major clans entrusted with repairing the Ka'ba to each take one corner of the cloth. When they raised the Black Stone to the spot where it was to be inserted, he took it and inserted it firmly in itsposition.
11.   Some Ansar were not happy with the way the Prophet divided the spoils after this battle, which occurred soon after Makka was conquered. The Prophet gave large shares to the new Makkan Muslims to strengthen their faith. To avoid a communal split, he called the Ansar together and reminded them of what he had bought them, how they had received him, and that he would always be with them. When he asked them if they still wanted the booty, they answered in unison that all they wanted was for him to stay with them.
12.   *Bukhari*, "Manaqib al-Ansar," 3; Ibn Kathir, 3:279.
13.   *Bukhari*, "Hiba," 35; *Muslim*, "Jihad," 70.
14.   Ibn Hisham, 2:147.
15.   *Bukhari*, "Maghazi," 25; Ibn Sa'd, 2:42-49; Ibn Hisham, 3:99-111, 128.
16.   Halabi, *Insan al-'Uyun*, 2:613.
17.   Haythami, *Majma' al-Zawa'id*, 2:280.
18.   Ibn Sa'd, *Tabaqat*, 3:162; Muslim, "Jihad," 83 ; Ibn Hisham, 2:266-67.
19.   Ibn Hisham, 2:272.

20   Ibid., 3:235; Ibn Sa'd, 2:66.
21   *Bukhari*, "Shurut," 15.
22   Muslim, Hadith No.1834; Bukhari, 4:256.
23   Bukhari, 3:180; Ibn Hanbal, 4:324; Tabari, 3:75.
24   Ibn Hisham, 3:330.
25   Ibn Hisham, 3:321-33; Ibn Kathir, 4:188-93.
26   Ibn Hisham, 3:337-38.
27   Ibn Hanbal, 5:441.
28   Muslim, "'Imara," 37.
29   Ibn Hajar, *Al-Isaba*, 1:165.
30   Muslim, "Fada'il al-Sahaba," 63.
31   Ibn Sa'd, *Tabaqat*, 4:70; Ibn Hajar, 1:564.
32   *Bukhari*, "Tafsir," 1; *Muslim*, "Iman," 355.
33   Bukhari, "Manaqib," 25.

CHAPTER 9
OTHER DIMENSIONS OF HIS PROPHETHOOD

1   *Bukhari*, "Da'awat," 6; *Muslim*, "Dhikr," 56.
2   *Bukhari*, "Adhan," 89; *Muslim*, "Masajid," 147.
3   Ibn Hanbal, *Musnad*, 6:147.
4   *Bukhari*, "Adhan," 155; *Muslim*, "Salat," 205; *Abu Dawud*, "Salat," 139.
5   Ibn Hanbal, *Musnad*, 5:191.
6   Nasa'i, "Sahw," 62; Ibn Hanbal, 5:191.
7   *Ibn Hanbal*, 5:191.
8   Haythami, *Majma' al-Zawa'id*, 10:117.
9   *Muslim*, "Dhikr," 73; *Abu Dawud*, "Witr," 32.
10   *Tirmidhi*, "Da'awat," 23; *Nasa'i*, "Sahw," 61.
11   *Tirmidhi*, "Tafsir al-Qur'an," 39; Imam Malik, *Muwatta'*, "Qur'an," 73.
12   Hakim, *Mustadrak*, 1:520.
13   Ibid., 1:499.
14   *Ibn Maja*, "Du'a," 2; *Muslim*, "Dhikr," 72; *Tirmidhi*, "Da'awat," 73.
15   Ibn Hanbal, 4:181; Hakim, 3:591.
16   *Tirmidhi*, "Da'awat," 89.
17   *Bukhari*, "Anbiya'," 54; *Muslim*, "Jihad," 104.
18   Ibn Hisham, *Sira*, 4:55; Ibn Kathir, *Al-Bidaya*, 4:344.
19   *Muslim*, "Fara'iz,' 14; *Bukhari*, "Istiqraz," 11.
20   *Muslim*, "Birr," 87.
21   *Ibn Hanbal*, 4:395; *Muslim*, "Fada'il," 126.
22   Qadi 'Iyad, *Al-Shifa'*, 1:17.
23   *Muslim*, "Hudud," 17-23; *Bukhari*, "Hudud," 28.
24   *Bukhari*, "Adhan," 65; *Muslim*, "Salat," 192.
25   *Bukhari*, "Adab," 18.
26   *Bukhari*, "Adab," 18; *Muslim*, "Fada'il," 64; *Ibn Maja*, "Adab," 3.

27 *Tirmidhi*, "Birr," 16.
28 *Bukhari*, "Jana'iz," 45; *Muslim*, "Jana'iz," 12.
29 Bukhari, "Jana'iz," 3.
30 Muslim, "Ayman," 31, 33; Ibn Hanbal, 3:447.
31 Ibn Sa'd, *Tabaqat*, 1:195.
32 *Bukhari*, "Anbiya'," 54; "Musaqat," 9; *Muslim*, "Salam," 153; Ibn Hanbal, 2:507.
33 *Abu Dawud*, "Adab," 164; "Jihad," 112; Ibn Hanbal, 1:404.
34 *Bukhari*, "Jihad," 153; *Muslim*, "Salam," 147.
35 *Nasa'i*, "Hajj," 114; *Ibn Hanbal*, 1:385.
36 Hakim, *Mustadrak*, 4:231, 233.
37 Suyuti, *Al-Khasa'is al-Kubra'*, 2:95; Haythami, *Majma'*, 9:9.
38 *Muslim*, "Zakat," 142, 148; *Bukhari*, "Adab," 95; "Manaqib," 25.
39 *Bukhari*, "Adab," 95; *Muslim*, "Zakat," 142.
40 *Bukhari*, "Hiba," 28; *Abu Dawud*, "Diyat," 6.
41 *Abu Dawud*, "Adab," 1; *Nasa'i*, "Qasama," 24.
42 Suyuti, *Al-Khasa'is*, 1:26; Ibn Hajar, *Al-Isaba*, 1:566.
43 *Bukhari*, "'Ilm," 28; "Adhan," 61.
44 *Muslim*, "Salat," 179; *Nasa'i*, "Iftitah," 71; *Bukhari*, "Adab," 74.
45 Hakim, *Mustadrak*, 3:242.
46 Said Nursi, *Sözler* (Istanbul: 1986), 459.
47 *Muslim*, "Iman," 158; *Ibn Maja*, "Fitan," 1.
48 *Bukhari*, "Iman," 22.
49 Ibn Kathir, *Al-Bidaya*, 3:158-9.
50 Ibn Hisham, 4:135; Ibn Hajar, *Al-Isaba*, 2:187; *Muslim*, "Fada'il," 57.
51 *Bukhari*, "Riqaq," 3.
52 *Bukhari*, "Tafsir," 2; *Muslim*, "Talaq," 31.
53 *Muslim*, "Ashriba," 140; *Abu Nu'aym*, "Hilya," 1:30.
54 *Tabari*, "Tarikh," 4:252.
55 *Muslim*, "Fada'il," 48; *Bukhari*, "Manaqib," 23.
56 Suyuti, *Al-Khasa'is*, 1:123; Hindi, *Kanz al-'Ummal*, 7:168.
57 Ibn Kathir, 6:63.
58 *Tirmidhi*, "Birr," 40.
59 Hindi, 6:571.
60 Said Nursi, *Letters*, 2:315.
61 Haythami, *Majma'*, 9:21.
62 Ibn Hisham, 2:137.
63 Bukhari, 1:111; Muslim, 2:65; Semhudi, *Wafa'*, 1:237; Ibn Sa'd, 1: 240.
64 Tirmidhi, "Zuhd," 39.
65 Ibn Maja, "At'ima," 30; Haythami, 9:20.
66 Qadi 'Iyad, *Al-Shifa'*, 1:131, 133.
67 Tirmidhi, *Shama'il*, 78; Ibn Hanbal, 6:256.
68 *Bukhari*, "Riqaq," 18.
69 *Ibn Maja*, "Manasik," 5; *Tirmidhi*, "Da'awat," 109; *Abu Dawud*, "Witr," 23.
70 Ibn Hanbal, 2:231; Haythami, 9:18.

[71] Hindi, *Kanz al-'Ummal*, 3:113; Haythami, 10:325.

[72] Tirmidhi, Hadith No. 3880.

[73] George Sarton, in his monumental *Introduction to the History of Science*, divided his work into chronological chapters, naming each chapter after the most eminent scientist of that period. From the middle of the second century AH (eight century CE) to the middle of the fifth century AH (eleventh century CE), each 50-year period carries the name of a Muslim scientist. Thus we have the "Time of al-Kharizmi," the "Time of al-Biruni," and so on. These chapters also contain the names of many other important Islamic scientists and their main works. (Tr.)

CHAPTER 10
THE SUNNA AND ITS PLACE IN ISLAMIC LEGISLATION

[1] *Muslim*, "Zakat," 69; *Ibn Maja*, "Muqaddima," 203.

[2] *Ibn Maja*, "Muqaddima," 7.

[3] *Ibn Maja*, "Wasaya," 6; *Tirmidhi*, "Wasaya," 5.

[4] *Ibn Hanbal, Musnad*, 1:313.

[5] *Tirmidhi*, "Zakat," 14; *Bukhari*, "Zakat," 55.

[6] *Abu Dawud*, "Tahara," 41; *Tirmidhi*, "Tahara," 52; *Nasa'i*, "Tahara," 47. Generally, the Qur'an forbids eating animals that were not slaughtered according to Islamic rules. The Sunna, however restricts this general rule (commandment) by allowing the consumption of sea animals that die in water.

[7] Bukhari, "Adhan," 18; Ibn Hanbal, 5:53.

[8] Bukhari, "Salat," 70; Muslim, "Nikah," 5.

[9] *Darimi*, "Tahara," 65; *Abu Dawud*, "Tahara," 126.

[10] *Darimi*, "Maghazi," 30; "Khawf," 5.

[11] *Abu Dawud*, "Sunna," 5.

[12] This covers such cosmetic surgery procedures as changing the shape of the nose or lips, inserting breast implants, or somehow altering other bodily features through cosmetic surgery to look more beautiful. Such operations are allowed only when medically necessary, as in the case of severe burns or deformity.

[13] *Muslim*, "Libas," 120.

[14] *Bukhari*, "Ahkam," 1; *Ibn Maja*, "Muqaddima," 1.

[15] *Bukhari*, "I'tisam," 2; *Ibn Hanbal*, 2:361.

[16] *Abu Dawud*, "Sunna," 5; *Tirmidhi*, "'Ilm," 16; *Ibn Maja*, "Muqaddima," 6.

[17] Abu Nu'aym, *Hilya'*, 8:200; Daylami, *Musnad al-Firdaws*, 4:198.

[18] *Tirmidhi*, "Tafsir al-Qur'an," 2; *Tabari*, "Tafsir," 1:61, 64.

[19] *Bukhari*, "Tafsir," 31/1.

[20] *Tirmidhi*, "Tafsir al-Qur'an," 3.

[21] *Abu Dawud*, "Salat," 2; *Tirmidhi*, "Mawaqit," 1.

[22] *Nasa'i*, "Manasik," 220; *Ibn Hanbal*, 3:366.

[23] *Bukhari*, "I'tisam," 5; "Khums," 1; *Muslim*, "Jihad," 51; Ibn Hanbal, 2:463.

[24] *Tirmidhi*, "Fara'id," 17.

[25] *Bukhari*, "Buyu'," 82; *Muslim*, "Buyu'," 51.

[26] *Muslim*, "Buyu'," 5:14-17.

CHAPTER 11
ESTABLISHING THE SUNNA

1 *Tirmidhi,* "'Ilm," 7.
2 *Ibn Maja,* "Muqaddima," 18.
3 *Bukhari,* "Tafsir," 2:1; *Muslim,* "Iman," 322.
4 *Bukhari,* "Manaqib," 23; *Muslim,* "Fada'il al-Sahaba," 160.
5 *Muslim,* "Salat," 61; *Abu Dawud,* "Salat," 178.
6 *Tirmidhi,* "'Ilm," 3; *Ibn Maja,* "Muqaddima," 24.
7 *Muslim,* "Dhikr," 38; *Ibn Maja,* "Muqaddima," 17.
8 *Ibn Athir,* "Usd al-Ghaba," 3:600.
9 *Muslim,* "Iman," 178; *Bukhari,* "Iman," 178.
10 *Muslim,* "Iman," 182.
11 *Muslim,* "Fada'il al-Sahaba," 161.
12 *Bukhari,* "Tafsir," 98:1-3; *Muslim,* "Fada'il al-Sahaba," 122.
13 *Ibn Maja,* "Muqaddima," 17.
14 Muhammad 'Ajjaj al-Khatib, *Al-Sunna Qabl al-Tadwin,* 160.
15 *Bukhari,* "'Ilm," 9; *Ibn Hanbal,* 5:41.
16 Ibn Sa'd, *Tabaqat,* 2:190.
17 Suyuti, *Tarikh al-Khulafa',* 74.
18 *Bukhari,* "Fara'id," 3.
19 *Bukhari,* "Khums," 1; *Muslim,* "Jihad," 52.
20 *Ibn Hanbal,* 4:403; Hindi, *Kanz al-'Ummal,* 15:118.
21 *Muslim,* "Adab," 7:33; Ibn Hanbal, 3:19.
22 *Bukhari,* "Ahkam," 51.
23 Ibn Hajar, *Fath al-Bari',* 3:83.
24 *Bukhari,* "Mawaqit," 33.
25 Ibn Hanbal, 1:134.
26 It should be as strong as one can walk it for 3 miles, and both itself and whatever is worn with it (e.g., socks or shoes) should be clean. It is usually worn over socks.
27 *Abu Dawud,* "Tahara," 63.
28 *Abu Dawud,* "Fara'id," 18; *Tirmidhi,* "Fara'id," 18.
29 *Bukhari,* "Tib," 30; Ibn Athir, *Usd al-Ghaba,* 3:48.
30 *Muslim,* "Jumu'a," 43; *Nasa'i,* "Idayn," 22; *Abu Dawud,* "Sunna," 5.
31 *Bukhari,* "I'tisam," 2.
32 *Muslim,* "Fada'il," 17,18; *Bukhari,* "Riqaq," 26.
33 *Abu Dawud,* "Sunna," 5; *Ibn Maja,* "Muqaddima," 2; *Tirmidhi,* "'Ilm," 10.
34 *Abu Dawud,* "Sunna," 5.
35 *Tirmidhi,* "'Ilm," 16; *Abu Dawud,* "Sunna," 5, *Ibn Maja,* "Muqad-dima," 6.
36 Imam Malik, *Muwatta',* "Qadar," 3.
37 Those people who are the first two or three narrators cited in a Tradition's chain of authority.
38 *Bukhari,* "'Ilm," 38; *Muslim,* "Zuhd," 72; *Abu Dawud,* "'Ilm," 4; Tirmidhi, "Fitan," 70.

39 *Muslim,* "Muqaddima," 1.

40 *Bukhari,* "Istitaba," 6; Abu Dawud, "Sunna," 28.

41 *Ibn Maja,* "Muqaddima," 3.

42 *Bukhari,* "'Ilm," 38; Muslim, "Zuhd," 72.

43 *Darimi,* "Muqaddima," 25.

44 Dhahabi, *Siyar A'lam al-Nubala',* 4:263.

45 *Ibn Maja,* "Muqaddima," 3.

46 Abu Dawud al-Tayalisi, *Musnad,* 248.

47 Khatib al-Baghdadi, *Al-Kifaya fi 'Ilm al-Riwaya,* 178.

48 *Bukhari,* "Da'awat," 6.

49 A Prophet is one who receives revelation but is not given a Book, and so follows the way of a previous Messenger. A Messenger is one who usually receives a Book or Pages and sets a way to follow. (Tr.)

50 *Darimi,* "Muqaddima," 51.

51 *Tirmidhi,* "Fara'id," 10.

52 *Bukhari,* "'Ilm," 35; *Muslim,* "Janna," 79.

53 *Bukhari,* "Khusuma," 4; *Muslim,* "Musafirin," 270; *Abu Dawud,* "Witr," 22. Some words of the Qur'an can be pronounced with slight differences. For example, in *Surat al-Fatiha,* the word *Málik* also can be pronounced as *Melik* with no significant difference in meaning. As another example, the word *heyte* in 12:23 also can be pronounced as *hîte* with no difference in meaning. This is a difference of accent only. (Tr.)

54 *Bukhari,* "Maghazi," 3; *Muslim,* "Birr," 58.

55 Khatib al-Baghdadi, "Al-Rihla fi Talab al-Hadith," 118-24.

56 Ibn Sa'd, *Tabaqat,* 3:178; Bukhari, *Al-Adab al-Mufrad,* 337.

57 Al-Baghdadi, "Al-Rihla fi Talab al-Hadith," 78; Ibn Maja, "Muqad-dima," 17.

58 Khatib al-Baghdadi, *Al-Kifaya fi 'Ilm al-Riwaya,* 178.

59 The Ahl al-Sunna wa al-Jama'a (the People of Sunna and Community) are the great majority of Muslims who follow the way of the Prophet and Companions. Various factions differ from them in matters of belief (such as the Mu'tazila and Jabriya) or the role of the Companions in religion (such as the Kharijites and Shi'a), partly because of political inclinations and partly because they were influenced by ancient philosophies. (Tr.)

60 *Muslim,* "Muqaddima," 5.

61 M. 'Ajjaj al-Khatib, *Al-Sunna Qabl al-Tadwin,* 178.

62 *Muslim,* "Muqaddima," 5.

63 M. 'Ajjaj al-Khatib, *Al-Sunna Qabl al-Tadwin,* 222.

64 *Ibid.,* 229.

65 *Muslim,* "Muqaddima," 5.

66 Ibn Hajar, *Tahdhib al-Tahdhib,* 5:176; Dhahabi, *Mizan al-I'tidal,* 2:401.

67 Ibn Hajar, *Tahdhib al-Tahdhib,* 6:84.

68 M. 'Ajjaj al-Khatib, *Al-Sunna Qabl al-Tadwin,* 229.

69 Ibid., 234.

70 Ibn Salah, *'Ulum al-Hadith,* 389.

71 'Ajluni, *Kashf al-Khafa',* 1:132; 'Ali al-Qari, "Al-Asrar al-Marfu'a," 269.

72   Ibn Hajar, *Tahdhib al-Tahdhib*, 9:49.

73   'Ajluni, *Kashf al-Khafa'*, 1:33.

74   *Ibid.*, 1:36.

75   *Ibid.*, 1:43.

76   *Ibid.*, 2:340.

77   *Muslim*, "Tahara," 1; *Tirmidhi*, "Da'awat," 86.

78   'Ajluni, *Kashf al-Khafa'*, 1:299; Daylami, *Musnad al-Firdaws*, 56.

79   *Abu Dawud*, "'Ilm," 1; *Tirmidhi*, "'Ilm," 19.

80   *Bukhari*, "Tafsir," 48/3; "Buyu'," 50; *Darimi*, "Muqaddima," 2.

81   *Bukhari*, "Istithqa'," 3; "Fada'il al-Ashab," 11.

82   *Bukhari*, "Istithqa'," 14; *Abu Dawud*, "Istithqa'," 2; *Ibn Maja*, "Iqama," 154.

83   *Ibn Maja*, "Iqama," 189; *Tirmidhi*, "Da'awat," 118.

84   *Muslim*, "Tahara," 91; *Bukhari*, "Wudu'," 33; *Abu Dawud*, "Tahara," 37.

85   *Bukhari*, "Tib," 58; *Abu Dawud*, "At'ima," 48; *Ibn Maja*, "Tib," 31; *Darimi*, "At'ima," 12.

86   *Bukhari*, "Al-Salat fi Masjid Makka," 1; *Muslim*, "Hajj," 511; *Tirmidhi*, "Salat," 126.

87   *Muslim*, "Hajj," 510; *Bukhari*, "Masjid Makka," 1; *Nasa'i*, "Manasik," 124.

88   *Muslim*, "'Imara," 170; *Bukhari*, "I'tisam," 10; *Abu Dawud*, "Fitan," 1.

89   *Abu Dawud*, "Tahara," 50; *Bukhari*, "Wudu'," 26; *Muslim*, "Tahara," 87-88.

90   *Muslim*, "Fitan," 119; *Abu Dawud*, "Malahim," 15; *Ibn Maja*, "Fitan," 33.

91   *Bukhari*, "Salat," 1; *Nasa'i*, "Salat," 1; *Muslim*, "Iman," 263; *Ibn Maja*, "Iqama," 194.

92   *Muslim*, "Fitan," 25.

93   *Ibn Hanbal*, 1:210.

94   Sarakhsi, *Muqaddima li-Usul al-Sarakhsi*, 5.

95   M. 'Ajjaj al-Khatib, *Al-Sunna qabl al-Tadwin*, 150-51.

96   Ibn Athir, *Usd al-Ghaba*, 7:90. This blessed woman found eight linguistic or poetic mistakes in a stanza of Hassan ibn Thabit, a famous Companion and poet. After the Revelation, she gave up poetry and focused on the Qur'an and the Hadith.

97   *Ibn Hanbal*, 5:186.

98   Ibn Hajar, *Hadiy al-Sari'*, 487.

99   Dhahabi, *Tadhkirat al-Huffaz*, 2:556.

100   Ibn Hajar, *Tahdhib al-Tahdhib*, 9:52.

101   Ibn Sa'd, *Tabaqat*, 2:22.

102   *Muslim*, "Zuhd," 72; *Darimi*, "Muqaddima," 42.

103   Khatib al-Baghdadi, *Taqyid al-'Ilm*, 34.

104   *Bukhari*, "'Ilm," 39.

105   *Abu Dawud*, "'Ilm," 3; Ibn Hanbal, 2:162; *Darimi*, "Muqaddima," 43.

106   *Tirmidhi*, "'Ilm," 12.

107   Hindi, *Kanz al-'Ummal*, 10:232.

108   *Darimi*, "Muqaddima," 43.

109   *Abu Dawud*, "'Ilm," 3; *Tirmidhi*, "'Ilm," 12.

110   *Bukhari*, "'Ilm," 39; Ibn Hanbal, 1:100.

111   M. 'Ajjaj al-Khatib, *Al-Sunna qabl al-Tadwin*, 352.

112   *Darimi*, "Diyat," 12.

[113] Khatib al-Baghdadi, "Al-Kifaya," 330.

[114] Ibn Sa'd, 7:2; Khatib al-Baghdadi, "Al-Kifaya," 354.

[115] *Bukhari*, "'Ilm," 34.

CHAPTER 12
THE COMPANIONS AND THE TABI'UN

[1] Ibn Hajar, *Al-Isaba*, 1:7.

[2] Ibn Athir, *Usd al-Ghaba*, 4:132.

[3] *Bukhari*, "Tafsir," 7:3.

[4] Hakim, *Ma'rifat 'Ulum al-Hadith*, 22-24.

[5] The Messenger declares: "My Companions are like stars; whomever of them you follow, you will be guided to the True Path." This *hadith* is explicitly corroborated by the verse: *Remember you said to him whom God favored...* (33:37) By *him whom God favored*, the verse refers to Zayd ibn Haritha, the Messenger's emancipated slave who is not included among the greatest Companions. God orders all Muslims to follow the way of those whom He favors: *Guide us to the Straight Path, the path of those whom You favored* (1:5). This means that the Companions, especially the greatest among them, are guides by whom one can find the True or Straight Path. (Tr.)

[6] Haythami, *Majma' al-Zawa'id*, 1:57; Hindi, *Kanz al-'Ummal*, 13:353.

[7] *Ibn Hajar*, 1:10.

[8] *Bukhari*, "Tafsir," 59/6.

[9] *Bukhari*, "Fada'il al-Ashab," 5; *Muslim*, "Fada'il al-Sahaba," 221.

[10] *Tirmidhi*, "Manaqib," 58; *Ibn Hibban*, 9:189; Ibn Hanbal, 5:57. *Hurt* is used figuratively, in the sense of displeasing, offending, or attracting the wrath of God to yourself.

[11] *Muslim*, "Fada'il al-Sahaba," 207. That is, Heaven is maintained by the stars' delicate order. When this order collapses, it means the final destruc-tion of the universe. The Prophet was a means of security for his Companions. Twenty years after his death, people began slandering the Companions. Their existence, particularly of the leading ones, was a means of security for the Muslim nation. After their deaths, misfortune began to visit the Muslims. (Tr.)

[12] *Muslim*, "Fada'il al-Sahaba," 212; *Bukhari*, "Fada'il al-Ashab," 1.

[13] Abu Nu'aym, *Hilya*, 1:305.

[14] Ibid., 1:375.

[15] Ibid., 1:135.

[16] *Ibn Hajar*, 4:202.

[17] *Muslim*, "Fada'il al-Sahaba," 158; Ibn Sa'd, 4:328.

[18] Hakim, *Mustadrak*, 3:508.

[19] *Muslim*, "Fada'il al-Sahaba," 159; Ibn Sa'd, 4:329, 330.

[20] *Bukhari*, "At'ima," 1.

[21] *Bukhari*, "Fada'il al-Ashab," 10.

[22] *Bukhari*, "'Ilm," 42; *Muslim*, "Fada'il al-Sahaba," 159; Ibn Sa'd, 4:332.

[23] Ibn Sa'd, 4:330-1.

[24] *Hakim*, 3:512; Ibn Kathir, *Al-Bidaya*, 8:109.

25 Ibn Hajar, 4:205.

26 Ibn Sa'd, 4:335-6; Ibn Athir, 6:321; Ibn Hajar, 4:210.

27 *Bukhari*, "Fitan," 9; *Muslim*, "Fitan," 10.

28 *Bukhari*, "Fitan," 3; Ibn Hanbal, 2:288.

29 Ibn Kathir, 8:122.

30 *Muslim*, "Fada'il al-Sahaba," 160.

31 *Hakim*, "Mustadrak," 3:509-10.

32 *Bukhari*, "Wudu'," 10; *Muslim*, "Fada'il al-Sahaba," 138.

33 Ibn Athir, 3:291.

34 *Bukhari*, "Tafsir," 110/3.

35 Ibn Hajar, 2:332.

36 Ibn Kathir, *Tafsir: Surat al-Fajr,* verses 27-30; Haythami, *Majma',* 9:285.

37 Ibn Hanbal, *Musnad*, 2:131.

38 Ibn Hisham, *Sira*, 1:374.

39 *Bukhari*, "Maghazi," 6; Ibn Sa'd, 4:143.

40 Ibn Khalliqan, *Wafayat al-A'yan*, 2:30.

41 Ibn Sa'd, 4:185-87.

42 *Bukhari*, "Fada'il al-Ashab," 27; Ibn Sa'd, 3:153.

43 *Ibn Maja*, "Muqaddima," 11; Hakim, *Mustadrak*, 2:318; Ibn Hajar, *Al-Isaba*, 2:369.

44 *Tirmidhi*, "Tafsir al-Qur'an," 5.

45 Ibn Sa'd, 3:155.

46 Ibid., 157.

47 Ibn Kathir, 7:183.

48 Ibn Hajar, 1:213.

49 Hakim, *Mustadrak*, 4:86; Haythami, *Majma',* 10:20; Hindi, *Kanz al-'Ummal*, 11:530.

50 *Bukhari*, "Tafsir," 31/2; *Abu Dawud,* "Sunna," 16; *Muslim*, "Iman," 5-7.

51 Muslim, "Fada'il al-Sahaba," 223-24.

52 Ibid.

53 Abu Nu'aym, *Hilya*, 3:146.

54 Ibn al-Jawzi, *Sifat al-Safwa*, 3:15.

55 Abu Nu'aym, *Hilya*, 4:291-5; Ibn Kathir, *Al-Bidaya*, 9:117.

56 M. 'Ajjaj al-Khatib, *Al-Sunna qabl al-Tadwin*, 485.

57 Abu Nu'aym, *Hilya*, 1:163.

58 Ibid., 2:172.

59 Ibn Sa'd, *Tabaqat*, 5:126.

60 Ibid., 5:138; Dhahabi, *Siyar A'lam al-Nubala'*, 4:234.

61 Ibn Sa'd, 6:86; Abu Nu'aym, 2:98.

62 Ibn Sa'd, 6:90-91.

63 Ibid., 6:86; Abu Nu'aym, 2:100.

64 Abu Nu'aym, 2:179.

65 Ibid., 3:364; Dhahabi, *Tadhkirat al-Huffaz*, 1:109.

66 Ibn Kathir, 9:375.

67 M. 'Ajjaj al-Khatib, *Al-Sunna qabl al-Tadwin*, 509-10.

INDEX

A

'Abd Allah ibn 'Abbas, 350, 381, 383
'Abd Allah ibn 'Amr, 11, 314, 350, 364, 388
'Abd Allah ibn al-Mubarak, 365
'Abd Allah ibn Hudafa al-Sahmi, 50, 255, 297
'Abd Allah ibn Jahsh, 44, 219, 222, 230, 232, 234, 373
'Abd Allah ibn Jubayr, 230, 231
'Abd Allah ibn Jud'an, 8
'Abd Allah ibn Mas'ud, 100, 192, 227, 319, 378, 386, 392, 393
'Abd Allah ibn Rawaha, 88, 245, 253
'Abd Allah ibn Salam, 12, 15, 16, 88
'Abd Allah ibn Ubayy ibn Salul, 218, 222, 230, 263, 395
'Abd Allah ibn 'Umar, 314, 339, 378, 381, 384, 385, 391
'Abd Allah ibn Zubayr, 385, 395, 396
'Abd al-Malik ibn 'Abd al-'Aziz ibn Jurayj, 365
'Abd al-Malik ibn Marwan, 385
'Abd al-Muttalib, 6, 8, 14, 248, 291, 331
'Abd al-Qadir al-Jilani, 204, 283
'Abd al-Rahman ibn Abi Layla, 338, 339, 343
'Abd al-Rahman ibn al-'Awf, 249, 336
'Abd al-Razzaq ibn Hammam, 365
'Ad, 19
'Amr ibn al-'As, 29, 83, 84, 235, 246, 270, 292, 314, 350, 363
'Amr ibn Rabi'a, 14, 15, 383

'Aqaba, 83
'Aqabah, 27, 44, 46
'Arafat, 26, 28, 68, 332, 385
'As ibn Sa'id, 227
'As ibn Wa'il, 8
'Aynayn, 44, 289
A'la al-Khadrami, 301
Aaron, 126, 156, 165
abdal, 25
Abraha, 6
Abraham, vi, xxi, 9, 10, 15, 17, 43, 72, 119, 122, 126, 127, 128, 133, 134, 135, 136, 137, 138, 139, 140, 144, 290
Abu 'Ubayda ibn al-Jarrah, 29, 370
Abu al-'Aliya, 342
Abu al-Darda', 314
Abu Ayyub al-Ansari, 57, 341, 343, 381, 383, 394
Abu Bakr ibn Muhammad, 364, 365
Abu Basir, 270
Abu Dawud al-Tayalisi, 365, 418
Abu Dharr, 4, 9, 259, 260, 294
Abu Dharr al-Ghifari, 4
Abu Dujana, 230, 232, 254
Abu Hanifa, 186, 192, 302, 303, 315, 339, 344, 348, 359, 382, 393
Abu Hasan al-Shadhili, 283
Abu Hurayra, 37, 65, 90, 196, 197, 350, 353, 362, 363, 364, 375, 379, 380, 381, 382, 383, 392, 395
Abu Jahl, 18, 19, 26, 50, 73, 79, 192, 227, 268, 292, 386